Also in the Variorum Collected Studies Series:

MICHEL HUGLO
La théorie de la musique antique et médiévale

STANLEY BOORMAN
Studies in the Printing, Publishing and Performance of Music in the 16th Century

MICHEL HUGLO
Chant grégorien et musique médiévale

MICHEL HUGLO
Les anciens répertoires de plain-chant

MICHEL HUGLO
Les sources du plain-chant et de la musique médiévale

STEPHEN BONTA
Studies in Italian Sacred and Instrumental Music in the 17th Century

H. COLIN SLIM
Painting Music in the Sixteenth Century
Essays in Iconography

TIM CARTER
Monteverdi and his Contemporaries

BONNIE J. BLACKBURN
Composition, Printing and Performance
Studies in Renaissance Music

TIM CARTER
Music, Patronage and Printing in Late Renaissance Florence

MICHAEL TALBOT
Venetian Music in the Age of Vivaldi

RUTH STEINER
Studies in Gregorian Chant

RICHARD SHERR
Music and Musicians in Renaissance Rome and Other Courts

VARIORUM COLLECTED STUDIES SERIES

Music in Renaissance Florence:
Studies and Documents

To the memory of
Howard Mayer Brown

Frank A. D'Accone

Music in Renaissance Florence: Studies and Documents

ASHGATE
VARIORUM

This edition © 2006 by Frank A. D'Accone

Frank A. D'Accone has asserted his moral right under the Copyright, Designs and Patents Act, 1988, to be identified as the author of this work.

Published in the Variorum Collected Studies Series by

Ashgate Publishing Limited
Gower House, Croft Road,
Aldershot, Hampshire
GU11 3HR
Great Britain

Ashgate Publishing Company
Suite 420
101 Cherry Street
Burlington, VT 05401–4405
USA

Ashgate website: http://www.ashgate.com

ISBN–10: 0–7546–5900–3
ISBN–13: 978–0–7546–5900–6

British Library Cataloguing in Publication Data
D'Accone, Frank A.
 Music in Renaissance Florence : studies and documents. –
 (Variorum collected studies series)
 1. Music – Italy – Florence – History and criticism
 2. Musicians – Italy – Florence – History – To 1500
 3. Musicians – Italy – Florence – History – 16th century
 4. Musicians – Italy – Florence – Sources
 I.Title
 780.9'4551'0902

Library of Congress Cataloging-in-Publication Data
D'Accone, Frank A.
 Music in Renaissance Florence : studies and documents / Frank A. D'Accone.
  p. cm. – (Variorum collected studies series ; CS856)
 Papers originally published 1961–2001.
 Includes bibliographical references and index.
 ISBN 0–7546–5900–3 (alk paper)
 1. Music – Italy – Florence – History and criticism.
 I. Title. II. Collected studies ; CS856.

ML290.8F6D33 2006
780.945'5109031–dc22   2006042741

The paper used in this publication meets the minimum requirements of the American National Standard for Information Sciences – Permanence of Paper for Printed Library Materials, ANSI Z39.48–1984. ∞ ™

Printed and bound in Great Britain by TJ International Ltd, Padstow, Cornwall

VARIORUM COLLECTED STUDIES SERIES CS856

CONTENTS

Introduction   vii–xiii

Acknowledgements   xiv

I   Music and musicians at the Florentine monastery of Santa Trinita, 1360–1363   131–151
Memorie e contributi alla musica dal medioevo all'età moderna offerti a Federico Ghisi nel settantesimo compleanno (1901–1971) (= Quadrivium 12). Bologna: A.M.I.S., 1971

II   Una nuova fonte dell'Ars Nova Italiana: il codice di San Lorenzo, 2211   3–31
Studi Musicali 13. Florence, 1984

III   Music and musicians at Santa Maria del Fiore in the early Quattrocento   99–126
Scritti in onore di Luigi Ronga. Milan: Riccardo Ricciardi, 1973

IV   The singers of San Giovanni in Florence during the 15th Century   307–358
Journal of the American Musicological Society 14. Philadelphia, 1961

V   Lorenzo the Magnificent and music   259–290
Lorenzo il Magnifico e il suo mondo, ed. Gian Carlo Garfagnini. Florence: Leo S. Olschki, 1994

VI   Sacred music in Florence in Savonarola's time   311–354
Una città e il suo profeta, Firenze di fronte al Savonarola, ed. Gian Carlo Garfagnini. Florence: SISMEL, Edizioni del Galluzzo, 2001

VII   Heinrich Isaac in Florence: new and unpublished documents   464–483
The Musical Quarterly 49. New York, 1963

VIII	Some neglected composers in the Florentine chapels, ca, 1475–1525 *Viator 1. Berkeley/Los Angeles/London, 1970*	263–288
IX	Alessandro Coppini and Bartolomeo degli Organi: two Florentine composers of the Renaissance *Analecta Musicologica 4, Studien zur italienisch-deutschen Musikgeschichte 4. Cologne/Graz, 1967*	38–76
Addenda and Corrigenda		1–5
Index		1–13

This volume contains xiv + 330 pages

INTRODUCTION

In this volume I have brought together a number of my essays that have appeared in journals, congress reports and *Festschriften* over a period of some forty years. All of them reflect aspects of my continuing interest in Florentine music and musicians of the Renaissance, and all will leave little doubt that I am an unabashed archivist: a *topo d'archivio*, as the Italians would say. After almost a half century of digging in archives, I am as fascinated now as I was when I first discovered their secret allure. I have never forgotten my excitement upon reading the first document I found relating to musicians. It was in an account book that listed the monthly salaries earned by Heinrich Isaac and his colleagues in the Florentine Cathedral's chapel of singers. At the time, knowledge of Isaac's Florentine years was based on a few vague references to his service at the court of Lorenzo the Magnificent and on a few of his surviving works with Italian texts in Florentine sources that were presumably composed for his Medici patrons. In other words, except for the aforementioned, there was little tangible evidence of when and how long Isaac had actually been in Florence and what role, if any, he played in Florentine musical life, subjects to which I later returned in essay VII of the present volume.

That early moment of discovery was just the beginning. Suddenly, I realized – despite well-intentioned warnings from a veteran Italian scholar that there were no documents in Florentine archives and libraries relating to music in Renaissance times – that some kind of written record of the musicians who had been there did exist. As a result of speaking to scholars in other fields, I also saw that I would do well to look into the mundane sources that could possibly lead me to a better understanding of the quotidian lives of musicians in those times. These included, as I learned, tax collector's records, legal materials relating to acquisition and sales of properties, marriage contracts and other business transactions, wills, baptismal records, judicial documents and even records of investments in the state dowry fund. And it was heartening to know that I could do this research while continuing to work with what, I now understood, might be more immediate sources of information such as the Cathedral's account books and the minutes of its administrators' meetings.

The decision to investigate both kinds of sources led me, first, to search systematically through all the extant volumes in Cathedral archives from the time of Lorenzo the Magnificent, and then, over the course of many years, to expand the search chronologically and to extend it to materials from other churches. At the same time, I began delving into the *terra incognita* of the Florentine State Archives. I concentrated particularly on institutions – churches, monasteries and religious companies – because almost from the start these yielded names of the musicians, both local and foreign, and information about their employment that was indispensable in establishing the necessary chronological parameters of my research. A good deal of that research subsequently furnished the background for a study of music in Florence during Savonarola's time, included here as essay VI.

In my quest to learn more about musicians' activities and about whatever supplemental means, if any, they might have had to earn their livings, I also consulted other 15th-century sources such as financial records and household accounts of leading private citizens. These were less fruitful, though in a few instances similar records from early in the following century proved to be more rewarding, as I and others subsequently would learn.[1] Medici household documents, in which the de facto ruling family's ties to performers and composers would assuredly have been mentioned, were unfortunately lacking for this period. However, some information about Medici relations with musicians is found in the remarkably well preserved records of their correspondence, as has been demonstrated over the years by a number of scholars. Some of my findings from that source appear here in essays IV, V and VIII. In a few cases the records of the corporate guilds that built, administered and supported the Cathedral and the venerable Baptistry of San Giovanni provided valuable information. Both churches, along with the convent church of the Santissima Annunziata, were the principal venues for public musical performance in the city, but it was from San Giovanni that the Florentine chapel singers took their name. All of these avenues of inquiry yielded the documents that formed the background for my account, in essay IV, of the singing chapels in those places and of the many musicians, local and foreign, who turned Florence into a vibrant center of Renaissance musical culture. A glance at the Index of this volume will reveal just how many of those musicians there were.

---

[1] For example, a search among the papers of the Strozzi family in the Florentine State Archives, which other musicologists have since turned to, yielded a good deal of evidence about the musical interests of the poet Lorenzo di Filippo Strozzi and his relations with the composer Bartolomeo degli Organi. Lorenzo's library included, besides musical manuscripts, printed collections of Masses by Josquin Desprez and the *Musica* of his Florentine contemporary Bernardo Pisano as well as treatises by Franchinus Gaffurius and Pietro Aaron. See my "Transitional Text Forms and Settings in an Early 16th-Century Florentine Manuscript," *Words and Music: The Scholar's View. A Medley of Problems and Solutions Compiled in Honor of A. Tillman Merritt by Sundry Hands*, ed., Laurence Berman (Cambridge, MA, 1972): 29–58.

INTRODUCTION

Notwithstanding the absence of primary private sources and a dearth of information in extant guild records, there was more than enough information to lead to me to suggest, as I did in essays IV and V of the present volume, that the political climate of republican Florence obscured most Medici forays into musical patronage within a system that was at once public, private and corporate. Although the performing groups at the Cathedral and the Baptistry were administered independently, the two churches, perhaps in an agreement brokered by the Medici, hired many of the same musicians, who were sometimes also employed at the church of the Santissima Annunziata. It seems that Medici approval, particularly in Lorenzo's time, as noted in essay V, was a necessary prerequisite to a post in the Florentine chapel. All told, the available sources allowed me to prepare a continuous account of performance in Florence's leading churches throughout the Renaissance, as illustrated in essays IV and VI. Subsequently, in essays I, II and III here, I was able to provide information about musical activities in late medieval times, notably, about singers and organists at the Cathedral and other churches, and about the venerable companies of laudesi, whose singers and instrumentalists performed at the Cathedral and elsewhere.[2] Knowledge of this rich musical culture furnished some necessary background against which newer currents in the 15th century could eventually be juxtaposed and evaluated.

Some of my research into late medieval sources was motivated by my fascination with the apparent lack of musical creativity in Florence during the 15th century. This was much commented upon by musicologists, who could only suggest a sudden eclipse that was all the more surprising in view of the brilliant outburst of the previous century. An initial breakthrough occurred when I was able to establish the identity of the composer called "Magister Jouannes horganista de Florentia" in the Squarcialupi Codex.[3] The compilation of this comprehensive and most lavishly decorated anthology of Trecento music occurred during or shortly after his lifetime. The projected inclusion of his music in it, alongside the works of great masters of previous generations, offered tangible evidence of his accomplishments in the eyes of his contemporaries. Documents I uncovered call him Giovanni degli Organi, in deference to his profession, or

---

[2] The singers and instrumentalists employed by the principal Florentine companies of laudesi over a period of some two hundred years are discussed in "Le compagnie dei Laudesi in Firenze durante l'Ars nova," *L'Ars nova italiana del Trecento* 3 (Certaldo, 1969): 253–280; and in "Alcune note sulle Compagnie fiorentine dei Laudesi durante il Quattocento," *Rivista italiana di musicologia* 10, *in onore di Nino Pirrotta* (Florence, 1975): 86–114. Blake Wilson subsequently studied the laudesi in his *Music and Merchants. The Laudesi Companies of Republican Florence* (Oxford, 1992).

[3] See my "Giovanni Mazzuoli: a late representative of the Italian ars nova," *L'Ars nova italiana del Trecento* 2 (Certaldo, 1968): 23–38. Additional information about Giovanni appears in my study of the San Lorenzo manuscript, reprinted as essay II in this volume.

Giovanni Mazzuoli, his family name. New information about his professional life – his decades-long career led him to the Cathedral, where he was organist until his death in 1426 – gave good reason for supposing that the city's musical life had not gone into an abrupt and complete decline after the turn of the 15th century. The discovery of a new source of polyphony, the MS San Lorenzo 2211, with works by Giovanni and by his son, the completely unknown Piero, provided further evidence of the continuity of the Florentine tradition. In essay II, where I presented a preliminary description of the manuscript and its contents, I furnished information about Piero's activities as an organist at San Lorenzo in the early 15th century and his parallel career as a notary and judge in the city of Florence. Piero (d. 1430) also served as Cathedral organist during the last months of his father's illness, the post then passing within a few years to the young Antonio Squarcialupi.

Previously, I was able to document Squarcialupi's birth date, family and early career prior to his appointment at sixteen as organist at the Cathedral in 1432.[4] Squarcialupi, friend of the great Du Fay, composer and proponent of the new polyphonic music of the North, was the leading Florentine musician of his time, his fame enshrined for posterity in the portrait bust of him that Lorenzo the Magnificent had placed in the Cathedral after the organist's death in 1480. With the triumph of Franco-Flemish musicians in Florence during Squarcialupi's lifetime the foundations of a new school were laid down. Most of the northerners were itinerant, but a few, like Isaac, married there and made the city their home. In his last years Isaac presided as honorary head of the Florentine chapel, thanks to a pension arranged for him by his former Medici patrons. In my study of Isaac among the Florentines (essay VII of this volume), I suggested that in his later years he spent more time in the city than had previously been acknowledged and that the major portion of his celebrated *Choralis Constantinus* may have well been composed in Florence, where he lived from 1509 until his death in 1517. Among the young clerks who were familiars – and probably pupils – of Isaac was Giovan Piero Masacone, who in later life was a sometime composer as well as the most productive of Florentine music copyists.[5] He served in the chapel under Francesco Corteccia, a good many of whose works survive only in copies made by Masacone. A continuous line of development within the

---

[4] "Antonio Squarcialupi alla luce di documenti inediti," *Chigiana* 23, n. s., 3, ed., Mario Fabbri (Florence, 1966): 3–24.

[5] On Masacone, see Iain Fenlon and James Haar, *The Italian Madrigal in the Early Sixteenth Century. Sources and Interpretation* (Cambridge, 1988): 32–34, 123–126, 130, 133, 138, 153. Recent discoveries about hitherto unrecognized manuscripts copied by Masacone and new information about him and his important place in Florentine musical life of the Cinquecento is given by Philippe Canguilhem in "Lorenzo Corsini's Libri di Canzone and the madrigal in mid-sixteenth century Florence," *Early Music History* 25 (2006): 1–58.

works of the city's newly rediscovered composers, manifest in the works of other Florentines mentioned below, was now apparent. The mysterious forces that lay behind the *segreto del Quattrocento*, as that period in Italian musical history was so provocatively called by an older generation of scholars, seemed not so mysterious after all, at least in the case of Florence.

A word about the intended scope of my essays. Although best described as "documentary studies," they are by no means confined to lists of musicians employed at various places in Florence or to biographical vignettes of one or the other of them, though, of course, employment lists, conditions deriving from them and biographical facts often illustrate issues under consideration. Other avenues of inquiry led me to research liturgical usages, political and social conditions, the financial status of musicians and musical pedagogy. These, as well as musical analysis, inform no small part of several of these essays, which nevertheless stem from information gleaned directly from the documents. In some instances the documents provided first-hand data about the formation and maintenance of musical choirs, the role of local agents in recruiting singers and instrumentalists, the numbers and kinds of voices that were employed within the choirs, the use of instruments if any, the roles of the organist, the days and services at which the choirs performed, possible and documented repertories.[6] All of these topics found resonance in later studies of Renaissance courts and churches by Lewis Lockwood, Allan Atlas, Anthony Cummings, Richard Sherr, Pamela Starr and others.[7] International conferences featuring papers that examined Florentine achievements in the arts, the Cathedral's dedication, Medici anniversaries and the city in Savonarola's time resulted in the publication of volumes containing articles that have contributed enormously to our knowledge of Florentine Renaissance music.[8] The same is true of several studies under-

---

[6] Inquiries such as mine also helped bring to the fore issues regarding performing practices of sacred music, a subject barely touched upon when I first turned to it. Later it was of some interest to scholars and performers of early music. It also proved to be of relevance in the debate regarding approaches to historical performance that subsequently enlivened the pages of several journals.

[7] Lewis Lockwood, *Music in Renaissance Ferrara 1400–1505* (Cambridge, MA, 1984); Allan Atlas, *Music at the Aragonese Court of Naples* (Cambridge, 1985); Anthony M. Cummings, *The Politicized Muse. Music for Medici Festivals, 1512–1537* (Princeton, 1992); Richard Sherr's many articles can be found in his *Music and Musicians in Renaissance Rome and Other Courts* (Aldershot, 1999); Pamela Starr, *Music and Music Patronage at the Papal Court*, Ph.D. dissertation, Yale University, 1987 (UMI, 8810283).

[8] To cite but a few of these: *Musica e spettacolo, Scienze dell'uomo e della natura*, Firenze e la Toscana dei Medici nell'Europa del '500 2, ed., Gian Carlo Garfagnini (Florence, 1983); *La musica a Firenze al tempo di Lorenzo il Magnifico*, ed., Piero Gargiulo (Florence, 1993); *Lorenzo de' Medici: New Perspectives*, ed., Bernard Toscani, Studies in Italian Culture, Literature in History 13 (New York, 1993); *Cantate Domino; Musica nei secoli per il Duomo di Firenze*, Atti del VII Centenario del Duomo di Firenze 3, eds., Piero Gargiulo, Gabriele Giacomelli, Carolyn

taken independently of such conferences, which, to name only a few, include those by Patrick Macey, who thoroughly documented Savonarola's musical legacy; by Gabriele Giacomelli who brought new light to bear on Antonio Squarcialupi's contributions to organ building in the city; by Blake Wilson, who added further to our knowledge of the *laudesi* companies and who will soon be publishing newly discovered documents regarding some of Isaac's Florentine works – commissioned and non-commissioned – and the presence in the city of a discriminating audience among the non-elites as well as the ruling classes; by Richard Agee, who revealed unknown aspects of Strozzi patronage; and by William F. Prizer, who brought much needed clarification to issues regarding the composition and performance of Florentine Carnival music and to the role and participation of its patrons.[9]

Another aspect of my research traced recruitment and hiring practices and tracked the travels and movements of musicians who had stayed in Florence, a necessary first step in any discussion of the diffusion of musical genres and styles and of manuscript production. My research also led to the identification and chronological placement of three generations of Florentine composers of the late 15th- and early 16th centuries. The careers and works of some of the more obscure ones, along with a few equally lesser known Northern composers with ties to Florence, were considered in essay VIII. The few surviving sacred works by one of the oldest of the Florentines, Alessandro Coppini, a prominent cleric, organist and papal singer, reveal the influence of the northern composers who dominated Florentine musical life during his formative years. His younger contemporary, Bartolomeo degli Organi, a former boy singer of laudi and later Cathedral organist, counted Medici and Strozzi among his patrons and was a prominent teacher of aspiring professional musicians and amateurs alike. Alessandro's and Bartolomeo's secular songs and carnival music, dating for the most part from the early years of the 16th century, heralded the beginnings of what I have called the new Florentine school of composition in my study of their lives and works in essay IX. Further research helped clear away some of the confusion

---

Gianturco (Florence, 2001*)*; *Papal Music and Musicians in Late Medieval and Renaissance Rome*, ed., Richard Sherr (Oxford, 1998).

[9] Patrick Macey, *Bonfire Songs. Savonarola's Musical Legacy* (Oxford, 1998); Gabriele Giacomelli and Enzo Settesoldi, *Gli organi di S. Maria del Fiore di Firenze. Sette secoli di storia dal '300 al '900* (Florence, 1992); Gabriele Giacomelli, *Antonio Squarcialupi e la tradizione organaria in Toscana* (Rome, 1992); Richard Agee, "Ruberto Strozzi and the Early Madrigal," *Journal of the American Musicological Society* 31 (1983): 1–17; Richard Agee, "Filippo Strozzi and the Early Madrigal," *Journal of the American Musicological Society* 38 (1985): 227–237; William F. Prizer, "Wives and Courtesans: the Frottola in Florence," *Music Observed. Studies in Memory of William C. Holmes*, eds., Colleen Reardon and Susan Parisi (Warren, MI, 2004): 401–415; William F. Prizer, "Reading Carnival: The Creation of a Florentine Carnival song," *Early Music History* 23 (2004): 185–252.

regarding the lives and works of a younger generation of Florentine composers, notably, of Bernardo Pisano, Cathedral chapelmaster, papal singer and a pioneer of the early madrigal, and of the Florentine exile in Lyons, Francesco de Layolle, whose madrigals were published only in 1540, the year of his death.[10] Both were contemporaries of Francesco Corteccia, later chapelmaster at the Cathedral and Baptistry, whose entire published oeuvre was dedicated to his principal patron, Duke (later Grand Duke) Cosimo de' Medici. Early on, archival research and analysis of sources containing music by these men and those of other Florentines led to my editions of the complete works of Alessandro Coppini, Bartolomeo degli Organi, Bernardo Pisano, Giovanni Serragli, Francesco de Layolle, Mattia Rampollini and Francesco Corteccia (in progress), all of whose names figure in the essays included in this volume.[11]

FRANK A. D'ACCONE

Laguna Beach, California
December 2005

---

[10] See my "Bernardo Pisano: An Introduction to His Life and Works," *Musica Disciplina* 17 (1963): 115–135 ; "Bernardo Pisano and the Early Madrigal," *Report of the Tenth Congress of the International Musicological Society, Ljubljana 1967*, ed., Dragotin Cvetko (Kassel, 1970): 96–107; for Layolle, see the Introduction to his Collected Secular Works for 2, 3, 4 and 5 Voices, Vol. 3 (1969) of the series cited in the following note.

[11] Music of the Florentine Renaissance, 12 vols., Corpus Mensurabilis Musicae 32 (American Institute of Musicology, 1966–1996).

ACKNOWLEDGEMENTS

For permission to reprint these essays I am grateful to *Quadrivium*, University of Bologna (for essay I); *Studi Musicali*, Rome (for essay II); Riccardo Ricciardi Editore (for essay III); The American Musicological Society (for essay IV); Casa Editrice Leo S. Olschki (for essay V); SISMEL-Edizioni del Galluzzo e Fondazione Ezio Franceschini (for essay VI); Oxford University Press (for essay VII); The Center for Medieval and Renaissance Studies, University of California, Los Angeles (for essay VIII); Laaber-Verlag (for essay IX).

I

MUSIC AND MUSICIANS AT THE FLORENTINE MONASTERY OF SANTA TRINITA, 1360-1363

Records concerning musicians who were employed by the principal churches in Florence during the fourteenth century have not survived in any great quantity or in any systematic order. Because of this, any new source of information is bound to be of considerable interest to students of the period. Thus it is with a great deal of pleasure that I take this opportunity, on the occasion of Federico Ghisi's seventieth birthday, to make known hitherto unpublished documents relating to the Florentine Trecento, a subject which has always been of particular interest to him.

A few years ago, while searching through the contents of the library of the Vallombrosan monastery of Santa Trinita, I was fortunate enough to uncover a volume of accounts which not only provides a continuous record of musical activities at Santa Trinita for a period of three years, but also mentions a number of well-known musicians of the time who had connections with the monastery. My purpose in this study is to present the information found in the volume, along with pertinent data drawn from other contemporary sources, with a view towards adding to our biographical knowledge of these musicians. In addition, I shall also draw together what references there are to musical practices at the monastery during the period under discussion.

Santa Trinita's volume, listed as *Ricordanze, 1359-1362* in the catalogue of the *Corporazioni Religiose Soppresse* in Florentine State Archives, actually contains accounts from the years 1360-1363 (1).

---

(1) Archivio di Stato, Florence, Corporazioni Religiose Soppresse N. 89, Santa Trinita di Firenze, Vol. 45. The volume is hereafter referred to as ST.

I

The discrepancy in dates arises from the fact that the Florentine new year began on March 25 and that as a result documents recorded before that day carry the date of the preceding year (In the course of the text such dates have been changed to conform to our modern system). A brief note on folio 2 explains the reason why the volume was compiled and gives as well the name of the clerk who kept the records:

> Thursday, the 8th of January 1360
> Here and on the following pages I, don Lorenzo di Guidotto Martini, monk of the Vallombrosan monastery of Santa Trinita of Florence, shall make note of all of the money I spend on behalf of the said monastery, both for the convent's living expenses and for whatever else must be spent for the monastery's needs (2).

The first item of musical interest was entered into the volume only a week later:

> Thursday, the 16th [sic, 15th] of January 1360
> This evening the abbots of [the monasteries of] Poppi and San Pancrazio, maestro Biagio, ser Giovanni degl'Organi, ser Lando, ser Franciesco, brother of the abbot of [the monastery of] Fontana (3), and another youth dined with us (4).

---

(2) ST, fol. 2:
MCCCLVIIII [1360] giovedì, dì VIII di gennaio
Qui apresso e per inanzi io don Lorenzo di Guidotto
Martini, monacho del monistero di Sancta Trinita di
Firenze dell'ordine di Valembrosa, scriverò tutti i
danari i quali io spenderò per lo detto monistero,
si' per la vita del convento e si' per qualunque altra
cosa sarà bisogno di spendere per lo detto monistero.
(Here, as in the documents that follow, original spellings have been retained, punctuation added.)

(3) The three monasteries mentioned here belonged to the Vallombrosan Order. San Pancrazio, located within the city walls, was originally in the possession of the Benedictines and passed to the Vallombrosans ca. 1234-1240. (See W. PAATZ, *Die Kirchen von Florenz*, Frankfurt am Main 1940, Vol. 4, p. 565). The monastery at Poppi, in the Val d'Arno Casentinese, was also under the Benedictine rule originally, the Vallombrosan reform being introduced there sometime around the end of the eleventh century. (See E. REPETTI, *Dizionario fisico storico geografico della Toscana*, Florence 1841, Vol. I, p. 188). The abbey of Fontana (Fonte Taona), in the Apennines outside Pistoia, was under the Vallombrosan rule from 1090 until the end of the fourteenth century. (*Ibid.*, p. 12).

As is the case with some of the other musicians who were frequent guests at the monastery, there is no evidence to suggest that ser Giovanni degl'Organi was regularly employed at Santa Trinita, so it is probable that he was there that evening for purely social reasons. There are, however, several accounts which show that from time to time organists were brought in to perform at services on principal feast days. This may have been true also in ser Giovanni's case, though he is not mentioned in this connection in any of the surviving documents. His name appears once again in the following year, when, in a list of the expenses incurred for the feast of the Blessed Trinity on Sunday, 23 May 1361, it is reported that ten *soldi* were spent « for fetching and carrying the organs back to ser Giovanni's » (5). Evidently, two organs were used for the occasion because another entry, dated Wednesday, 26 May 1361, records the sum of one *soldo* and eight *denari* spent « in having the organs carried back to the house of Francescho ciecho [Landini] » (6).

Knowledge that an organist named Giovanni was associated with Santa Trinita at this time (during the same period in which, as will be shown below, several other Florentine musicians of repute are reported to have been there) raises an intriguing question: is it possible that this Giovanni can be identified as one of the oldest and foremost composers of Trecento polyphony, Giovanni da Cascia (Johannes de Florentia)? Such an identification is certainly within the realm of possibility, though extraordinarily difficult to prove, based as it must be on a large amount of conjecture. The composer, who was active from about the mid-1330's on, is reported to have been in Verona as late as 1351 (7). His whereabouts in the following

---

(4) ST, fol. 2:
  MCCCLVIIII [1360] gennaio, a dì XVI giovedì...
  Questa sera ci cenarono l'abate di Poppi e quel di San Branchazio e 'l maestro Biagio e ser Giovanni degl' Organi e ser Lando e ser Franciesco, fratello dell' abate di Fontana, e un altro giovane.
(5) See note 35 below.
(6) ST, fol. 32:
  MCCCLXI maggio, a dì XXVI mercholedi...
  Pagai per fare rechare gl'organi da casa di Francescho ciecho, s. I, d. VIII.
(7) The most recent summary of the composer's life and works is that given by N. Pirotta in « Die Musik in Geschichte und Gegenwart » 7, cols. 90-92.

I

years remain unknown, as do the place and date of his death. Perhaps he returned to Florence, and if indeed he did, he might well be the same person as Santa Trinita's musician. Giovanni degl'Organi is not mentioned there after 1361, possibly because he left the city at that time or died. Either possibility, in turn, would not be inconsistent with our current knowledge of the composer, since he appears to have been in and out of Florence a good deal during his lifetime and also must have been well along in years by 1361.

Ser Giovanni degl'Organi's name itself, on the other hand, might seem to preclude the possibility of identifying him with the composer. The title « ser » implies that he was a cleric, and the composer apparently was not. But « ser » was also used to designate notaries and other people of professional standing, and in this same account book it appears before the name of the organist Matteo da Siena, who was not a priest. Santa Trinita's musician, therefore, cannot be rejected on this count. Another objection stems from the fact that ser Giovanni was an organist, whereas, reports to the contrary notwithstanding, there is apparently no evidence in contemporary sources to indicate that the composer was (8). There the matter must rest, for until further documents are uncovered, the grounds for identifying the two Giovannis as one and the same musician are inconclusive.

Four other organists are recorded at Santa Trinita between 1361-1363. The first mentioned is Nuccio Landini, brother of the composer, who performed at services on 25 July 1361, the feast of St. James Apostle (9). Francesco Landini himself was present on two other feast days in the following months:

[1] Tuesday, the 10th of August 1361
This morning the abbots of [the monasteries of] Monte Schalari and Marradi (10), Francescho ciecho, who played the

---

(8) See E. Li Gotti, *Il più antico polifonista italiano del sec. XIV*, in « Italica », XXIV, 1947, pp. 197-200.

(9) ST, fol. 38:
MCCCLXI luglio a dì XXV domenica
Questo dì facemmo la festa di Sancto Jachopo Apostolo
e furonci l'abate di Monte Piano e'l priore di San
Fabiano e Nuccio che sonò gl'organi.

(10) The abbey of Monte Scalari, in the Apennines, was given to the Vallombrosans around the middle of the eleventh century. They retained

organ, and his brother Nuccio, who worked the bellows, dined with us because today we celebrated the feast of St. Lawrence, precious martyr of Christ (11).

[2] Sunday, the 10th of October 1361
Today we celebrated the feast of St. John Gualberto [founder of the Vallombrosan Order] and messer the abbot preached. The abbots of [the monasteries of] Monte Schalari, Razuolo and Coneo (12), Francescho ciecho, who played the organ, and his brother Nuccio, who worked the bellows, dined with us (13).

Although Nuccio Landini is recorded as having assisted at services in Santa Trinita on a few other occasions during the next two years, Francesco is not mentioned again in the monastery's account book (14). The reason for this can perhaps be attributed

---

possession of it until 1775. (See E. REPETTI, *Op. cit.*, p. 19). The monastery of Marradi, situated in the Valle del Lamone in Romagna, adopted the Vallombrosan reform in 1112. (*Ibid.*, p. 24).
(11) ST, fol. 40:
    MCCCLXI, martedì a dì X d'agosto
    Questa mattina ci desinarono l'abate di Monte Schalari
    e l'abate di Marradi e Francescho ciecho, che sonò gl'
    organi, e Nuccio suo fratello, che menò i mantici, po'
    che facemmo hoggi la festa di San Lorenzo, pretioso
    martire di Xpo.
(12) The monastery of San Paulo in Razzuolo, in the Val di Sieve, was the third built by the founder of the Vallombrosan Order. (See E. REPETTI, *Op. cit.*, p. 190). In 1592 the administration and revenues of the monastery of Santa Maria di Coneo in the Val d'Elsa, which had previously been in the possession of the Vallombrosans, were transferred to the cathedral of Colle. (*Ibid.*, p. 791).
(13) ST, fol. 45v:
    MCCCLXI, domenicha a dì X d'octobre, il dì di San Giovanni
    Gualberto...
    Questo dì facemo la festa di San Giovanni Gualberto e
    predicò messer l'abate e furonci a desinare l'abate
    di Monte Schalari e quel di Razuolo e quel di Coneo
    e Francescho ciecho, che sonò gl'organi, e Nuccio suo
    fratello, che menò i mantici.
(14) ST, fol. 65v:
[1] MCCCLXII, sabato a dì XXIII di luglio
    Questo dì cantò la messa novella dom Symone de'
    Gianfigliazzi e furonci a la messa e a desinare l'abate
    di Razuolo e quel di Coneo e due monaci di Ripole e
    due da San Branchazio e Nuccio, che sonò gl'organi...
[2] ST, fol. 79:

I

to a new turn in the composer's career: documents in a series of account books in San Lorenzo's archives suggest that he became organist at that church just around this time. His name, for example, does not appear in lists of San Lorenzo's personnel found in volumes dating from 1358 and 1359 (15). But the next extant volume, dated 1369, makes it clear that he was regularly employed there by then (16). Thus his initial appointment could have occurred several years earlier.

Landini's long association with San Lorenzo is amply documented in this series of account books, which contain hitherto unpublished records both of salary payments and of other emoluments that he received as a member of San Lorenzo's establishment. Although Landini is often mentioned along with the church's chaplains, the marked absence of any ecclesiastical titles before his name serves to confirm our knowledge that he was not a cleric. Various other titles, however, do appear in conjunction with his name over the course of a quarter of a century. Documents from 1370, 1375, and 1376 refer to him simply as Francischo organista (17). In 1378 he is called Francischus de Organis for the first time, while the more familiar form, Francesco degli Organi, occurs in many documents from the following years (18).

    MCCCLXII [1363] gennaio a dì XVII...
    Questo dì facemmo la festa di Sancto Antonio e fucci
    Nuccio e 'l fanciullo suo che sonarono gl'organi e
    desinaronci...
  (15) Archivio Capitolare di San Lorenzo, Florence, Vol. 7, *Entrata & Uscita*, 1358; Vol. 8, *Entrata & Uscita* 1359.
  (16) *Ibid.*, Vol. 9, *Entrata & Uscita, 1369[-1370]*, fol. 22v:
    Exitus. Die 1 Novembris... Francischus organista, s. 10.
  (17) *Ibid.*, Vol. 9, *Entrata & Uscita, 1369[-1370]*, fol. 25v:
    Exitus. Aprilis [1370]... Francischo organista... s. 10
    Ibid., Vol. 10, *Entrata & Uscita*, 1375 [-1376], fol. 18v: Exitus. Novembris... a Francischo organista...
    Ibid., fol. 20:
    Exitus. Februarius [1376]... a Francischo organista, s. 12.
  (18) *Ibid.*, Vol. 11, *Entrata & Uscita, 1378[-1379]*, fol. 61:
    Francischus de organis hic venit die XXXI mensis iulii
    per parte sui salari, L. X.
    Item... die VI mensis octobris, L. XIII, s. X.
    Item... die XXII mensis decembri, L. X, s. X.
    Item... die XXVIIII mensis februari [1379], L. X.
    Item... die XV mensis maii pro residuo dicti anni, L. XV.
    Ibid., Vol. 13, *Entrata & Uscita, 1380*, fol. 6v:

Entries from 1379 refer to him both as Francesco ciecho and Francesco maestro (19).

Beginning in 1384 the title maestro (or magister) is used more frequently (20), doubtless to distinguish him from a younger colleague, ser Francesco di Bartolomeo, who apparently began serving as assistant organist at San Lorenzo in that year (21). Though the latter musician was to be associated with San Lorenzo for many years afterwards — eventually succeeding Landini (22), the accounts make it clear that Landini continued as principal organist until at least a year before his death (23). Earlier entries in Landini's name generally record isolated monthly payments to him without giving any indication of his yearly salary. It seems,

> Novembre. La vigilia d'Ongni issanti... Item dì decto diedi a Francesco degli Organi, s. 10...

(19) *Ibid.*, Vol. 12, *Entrata & Uscita, 1379*, fols. 19v, 24.
(20) *Ibid., Entrata & Uscita, 1384*, fol. 26:

> Uscita. Novembre... Item a' chappellani e al altra famiglia... al maestro Franciesco che suona... a ser Franciescho che suona... Fl. uno.

(21) This musician is mentioned at San Lorenzo for the first time in a document from several years earlier. *Ibid.*, Vol. 14, *Entrata & Uscita, 1381*, fol. 38v:

> Exitus mensis novembris 1381.
> Die secundo predicti mensis novembris pro festivitate...
> preposito Fesulani
> ser Arduino
> ser Laurentio
> ser Lolo   cappellani ecclesie
> ser Domenico   Sancti Laurenti
> prelebano Nastasio cuilibet s. decem
> ser Francischus
> domino Bartolo
> Francesco de Organis

(22) Ser Francesco is recorded at San Lorenzo as late as 1436. *Ibid.*, Vol. 38, *Entrata & Uscita, 1436-1437*, fol. 127v:

> Ser Francesco di Bartolomeo, nostro capellano e sonatore degl'organi, de' avere per suo salario l'anno L. 100, a uscita, c. 132.

A few years earlier, on 1 February 1433, ser Francesco di Bartolomeo was appointed to succeed Antonio Squarcialupi as organist of Orsanmichele. (See my *Antonio Squarcialupi alla luce di documenti inediti*, in « Chigiana » XXIII, Nuova Serie 3, 1966, p. 12).

(23) Archivio Capitolare di San Lorenzo, Florence, Vol. 21, *Entrata & Uscita, 1395-1396*, fol. 30:

> Uscita, Aprile 1396
> Item... a dì 28... a Francesco degli organi... s. 10.

however, that he was earning sixty *lire* per annum by 1375, a figure which is corroborated by a complete account from 1394 (24). The last mention of Landini in this series of volumes dates from over a decade after his death, when it is recorded that four *lire* « which were left by maestro Francesco degli Organi » were distributed to San Lorenzo's chapter for the feast of St. Francis, on 4 October 1408 (25).

Other organists mentioned at Santa Trinita around the same time as the Landinis include ser Matteo da Siena and the Florentine Niccolò Mazzuoli. The Sienese musician is recorded as having performed at services on the feast of St. Benedict, 21 March 1362 (26), while the Florentine's name occurs in an entry dated 15 July 1363, which lists expenses for the previous 28 May, the feast of the Blessed Trinity (27). Maestro Matteo di Martino da Siena, as he is called in documents from the cathedral of Lucca, was organist at that church from 1374-1401, though he apparently was residing in Lucca from as early as 1357 (28). His presence at Santa Trinita is a good indication of the close musical connections that must have existed among the major cities of north-central Italy at this time and also may perhaps help to explain the diffusion in other

---

(24) *Ibid.*, Vol. 20, *Entrata & Uscita, 1394-1395*, fol. 72:
Francesco degl'Organi debba avere l'anno per suo salario lire sexanta. L. 60
Ricevette Francesco predetto a dì XI di settembre
per parte di pagamento di suo salario lire venti. L. 20
Item a dì XXII di dicembre ricevette Franciesco lire
venti sopra il suo salario. L. 20
Item a dì XVIII d'aprile [1395] ricevette Francescho
per intero pagamento di suo salario lire venti. L. 20
(25) *Ibid.*, Vol. 23, *Entrata & Uscita, 1408*, fol. 29v:
Uscita d'ottobre 1408
Item a dì 4 decto mese per la festa di Sancto Francescho che lasciò maestro Francescho degli Organi che si distribuisse lire quattro a tutto il capitolo...
(26) ST, fol. 55:
MCCCLXI [1362], lunedi a dì XXI di marzo
Questo dì facemmo la festa di San Benedetto: predicò messer l'abate, la messa disse l'abate di Coneo co' ministri. Ser Matheo da Siena sonò gl'organi e fucci l'abate di Razuolo e tutti ci desinarono.
(27) See note 38 below.
(28) See L. NERICI, *Storia della Musica in Lucca*, Lucca 1879, pp. 149-150.

parts of Tuscany of the Florentine Trecento repertory (29). Niccolò Mazzuoli, also called degli Organi, is recorded between 1370-1376 as serving among the « singers and players of laudi » in the church of Orsanmichele (30). He was the father of Giovanni degli Organi, one of the leading Florentine musicians from around the turn of the 15th century.

Giovanni Mazzuoli degli Organi succeeded his father as organist and accompanist to the *laudesi* at Orsanmichele and later became organist at the Florentine cathedral (31). He also had close ties with the church of San Lorenzo. Elsewhere I have suggested that this was probably so because of his long-standing association with Francesco Landini, first as pupil and later as colleague and friend (32). There is good reason to believe that this Giovanni is the same person as the « Magister Jouannes Horganista de Florentia, » whose works were to have been included in the Squarcialupi Codex (33). Whether the suggestion is tenable needs not detain us here, for the important point to be made is that Giovanni's father Niccolò was associated with Santa Trinita at the same time as several other well-known musicians and composers and this in itself offers ample testimony to the continuity of Florentine musical traditions during the Trecento.

It is clear from a group of entries in Santa Trinita's account book that the monastery made a regular practice of engaging singers and other instrumentalists, as well as organists, to help celebrate its

---

(29) The Lucca Codex furnishes one such example of this diffusion. For descriptions and inventories of this manuscript see F. GHISI, *Bruchstücke einer neuen Musikhandschrift der italienischen Ars Nova*, in « Archiv für Musikforschung », VIII, 1942, pp. 17-39 and *Italian Ars Nova Music, The Perugia and Pistoia Fragments of the Lucca Codex and Other Unpublished Early Fifteenth Century Sources*, in « Musica Disciplina » I (« Journal of Renaissance and Baroque Music», 1946), pp. 173-191 (with a musical supplement); see also N.PIRROTTA,and E. LI GOTTI, *Il Codice di Lucca*, in « Musica Disciplina », III, 1949, pp. 119-138; IV, 1950, pp. 111-152; V, 1951, pp. 115-142.

(30) See my *Le compagnie dei laudesi in Firenze durante l'Ars Nova*, in « L'Ars Nova Italiana del Trecento », III, Certaldo 1970, pp. 271-272. Further information about this musician is given in my *Giovanni Mazzuoli, A Late Representative of the Italian Ars Nova*, in « L'Ars Nova Italiana del Trecento », II, Certaldo 1968, pp. 25-28.

(31) *Ibid.*, pp. 36-37.

(32) *Ibid.*, p. 30.

(33) It is possible that two works of his have been preserved. (*Ibid.*, p. 24).

I

dated 17 June 1360, enumerates expenses for the feast which occurred on the previous 31 May and lists, among other things,

> 15 *soldi,* for having the platform for the singers constructed
> 9 *soldi,* 2 *denari,* for 2½ pounds of nails for the said platform
> 2 *lire,* 10 *soldi,* for 10 pounds of fish from the Arno and eels in the morning, and for a pie in the evening for the singers
> 1 *soldo,* 4 *denari,* for salad for the singers in the evening
> 2 *lire,* for the trumpeters (34).

An account from the following year once again records the cost of having the platform constructed, of food for the singers and of the trumpeters' salaries and also lists the previously mentioned expenses for moving ser Giovanni's organ (35). No mention is made of the platform in 1362, but it appears that the singers performed at the ceremonies that year, for it is reported that they

---

(34) ST, fols. 10v-11:
   MCCCLX, mercholedì dì XVII di giugno
   Qui saranno scripte tutte le spese che si feciano per
   la festa nostra di Sancta Trinita, la quale fu domenicha
   a dì XXXI di maggio 1360; erano scripte in su un fogl[i]o...
   per far fare il palchetto pe' cantori, s. XV
   per lib. II ½ d'aguti pel detto palchetto, s. VIIII, d. II...
   per lib. X di pesci d'arno et d'anguille per la mattina
   et per una crostata pe' la sera pe' cantori, L. II, s. X
   la sera per insalata pe' cantori, s. I, d. IIII
   a' trombadori, L. II
Lighter forms of entertainment were also provided to help celebrate the feast day. Appended to the above list is the following:
   A un Catalano, il quale era chiamato Bartolotto, che
   fece molto begli acti et forti et torné schiavineschi
   et altre cose maravigliose assai, L. I, s. X
(35) ST, fols. 35v-36:
   MCCCLXI
   Qui saranno scripte tutte le spese che si feciano per
   la festa nostra di Sancta Trinita, la quale fu domenicha
   a dì XXIII di maggio 1361; erano scripte in su un foglio.
   In prima per lib. III d'aguti pel palchetto pe' cantori, s. X
   a Andrea maestro per fare il detto palchetto, s. XV...
   per insalata pe' cantori, s. I, d. VI
   per rechatura e riportatura gl'organi da ser Giovanni, s. X...
   a' trombadori, L. II
As in the previous year, other forms of entertainment are also recorded:
   a uno giochatore che fece molto begli acti di leggerezza
   e scherma co' la donna sua, L. I

were the monastery's guests at dinner on the evening before the feast day (36). Also assisting at services in 1362 were three local musicians, Maso and Bonaiuto, *trombadori,* and Bartholo, *nacherino,* as well as « two French players, one of the *cornamusa,* the other of the *sveglone* and other instruments » (37). In 1363 expenses for food « for the singers and the others » are again listed, as are the gratuities given to the three Florentine instrumentalists and to Niccolò, « who played the organ » (38). Unfortunately, no indication is given in the accounts of the kind of music sung on these occasions. It is logical to assume, however, that the singers in question were performers of polyphony simply because there is no reason to believe that Santa Trinita's monks were incapable of performing the chant without assistance from professional singers. Thus if extra singers were engaged, it must have been because they were to perform some special kind of music, in this case polyphony. Furthermore, Santa Trinita's volume shows that composers and singers of polyphonic music were frequent guests there, and it is

(36) ST, fols. 63v-64:
MCCCLXII
Qui saranno scripte tutte le spese che si feciano pe' la
nostra festa di Sancta Trinita, la quale fu domenicha
a dì XII di giugno 1362...
a Baldese pesciauolo per lib. VI d'anguille per fare una
crosta pel sabato sera pe' cantori e pe' gli altri, L. I, s. XIII
(37) A payment to the instrumentalists is recorded in the list cited in the previous note, on fol. 64v:
a Maso e a Bonaiuto trombadori, a Bartholo nacherino, L. II
a due Franceschi sonatori, l'uno la cornamusa e l'altro
lo sveglone e altri stormenti, L. IIII
The foreign musicians apparently remained in Florence for some time, since they are recorded at the monastery again in the following month. ST, fol. 13:
MCCCLXII, giovedì a dì III di luglio
Questo dì ci desinarono l'abate di Razuolo e quel di
Coneo e due monaci da Vaiano e due sonatori di più
stormenti franceschi che ci furono pe' la festa.
(38) ST, fols. 90v-91:
MCCCLXIII
Qui saranno scripte tutte le spese che si feciono pe' la
festa nostra di Sancta Trinita, la quale fu domenicha
a dì XXVIII di maggio MCCCLXIII...
per insalata con cipolle fresche pel sabato sera pe'
cantori e pe' gli altri, s. I...
a Nicholò che sonò gli organi, L. I
a Maso e a Bonaiuto trombadori e a Bartholo nacherino, L. II

I

not unlikely that some of them were the same singers who were also called upon to help celebrate the monastery's principal feast day.

The first well-known musician to be mentioned in the account book is the Florentine composer ser Gherardello. An entry from 30 April 1360 states that eight *soldi* were spent that evening

> for roast pork bought from the innkeeper because ser Gherardello, prior of San Romeo, and another priest who was with him dined with us (39).

It is clear from entries such as the following that ser Gherardello was a frequent guest at the monastery during the next few months:

> [1] Thursday, the 21st of May 1360
> 1 *soldo*, 4 *denari*, for 4 loaves of white bread because the abbot of [the monastery of] Monte Piano (40), ser Gherardello and ser Jachopo, singers, dined with messer the abbot [of Santa Trinita] (41).
> [2] Tuesday, the 2nd of June 1360
> 15 *soldi*, 3 *denari*, for 8 pounds, 2 ounces of lamb because the abbot of [the monastery of] Monte Piano was here and ser Gherardello and ser Jachopo, singers, came to dine [with us] (42).

---

(39) ST, fol. 7:
    MCCCLX, aprile a dì XXX giovedì
    la sera per arista che si comprò da l'oste chè ci cenarono
    ser Gherardello, priore di San Romeo, e un altro prete
    ch'era con lui, s. VIII

(40) The Vallombrosans were established at the monastery of Monte Piano, located outside Prato in the Apennines between Tuscany and Romagna, by the middle of the twelfth century. (See E. REPETTI, *Op. cit.*, p. 186) Another document from ST (fol. 10) suggests that the abbot of Monte Piano was himself a musician:
    MCCCLX, venerdì a dì V di giugno
    Pagai per far riportare a Prato un paio di organetti
    dell'abate di Monte Piano, contanti L. I

(41) ST, fol. 8v:
    MCCCLX, maggio a dì XXI giovedì
    per IIII pani bianchi chè cenarono con messer l'abate
    l'abate di Monte Piano e ser Gherardello e ser
    Jachopo cantori, s. I, d. IIII·

(42) ST, fol. 9v:
    MCCCLX, giugno a dì II martedì
    per lib. VIII oncie II di castrone chè c'era l'abate di
    Monte Piano et vennonci a desinare ser Gherardello et

[3] Thursday, the 4th of June 1360
9 *soldi*, 6 *denari*, for a pair of large pigeons [because] the abbot of [the monastery of] Monte Piano, ser Gherardello and another priest dined with us (43).

[4] Tuesday, the 30th of June 1360
This evening the abbot of [the monastery of] Spugna (44), and ser Gherardello, [who was] with another priest dined with us (45).

[5] Wednesday, the 8th of July 1360
This evening the abbots of [the monasteries of] Razuolo, Alfiano and Spugna, ser Gherardello, his brother and another priest who was with the abbot of [the monastery of] Alfiano dined with us; don Francesco, who had departed from Forcole (46), was also here (47).

[6] Sunday, the 12th of July 1360, the feast of St. John Gualberto.

---

ser Jachopo cantori, s. XV, d. III
(43) ST, fol. 9v:
   MCCCLX, giugno a dì IIII giovedì
   la sera per un paio di pippioni grossi: cenaronci l'abate
   di Monte Piano et ser Gherardello et un altro
   prete, s. VIIII, d. VI
(44) The abbey of Spugna in the Val d'Elsa was founded in the eleventh century and given to the Vallombrosans by Pope Boniface VIII in 1301. (See E. REPETTI, *Op. cit.*, pp. 28-29).
(45) ST, fol. 12:
   MCCCLX, martedì dì XXX di giugno
   Questa sera ci cenarono l'abate di Spugna et ser
   Gherardello con un altro prete.
(46) The abbey of Sant'Ellero in Alfiano, situated on the Arno below the Order's first monastery at Vallombrosa, was assigned to the followers of St. John Gualberto in the middle of the thirteenth century. (See E. REPETTI, *Op. cit.*, p. 67).This action was the cause of protracted controversy between the Papacy and the city of Florence. (See R. DAVIDSOHN, *Storia di Firenze*, Florence 1956, Vol. II, pp. 632-635). The abbey of San Michele in Forcole in the city of Pistoia was also in the possession of the Vallombrosans. (See E. REPETTI, *Dizionario fisico storico geografico della Toscana*, Florence 1841, Vol. II, p. 324).
(47) ST, fol. 13:
   MCCCLX, mercholedì dì VIII di luglio
   Questa sera ci cenarono l'abate di Razuolo et quel
   d'Alfiano et quel di Spugna et ser Gherardello e 'l
   fratello et un altro prete ch'era con l'abate d'Alfiano
   predetto et anche c'era don Francescho che s'era
   partito da Forcole.

I

This morning the abbot of [the monastery of] Spugna and ser Gherardello [who was] with two others dined with us (48).

After a lapse of almost a year it is reported that on

[1] Thursday, the 17th of June 1361
6 *denari* [were spent] for plums for the abbot of [the monastery of] Monte Schalari, ser Gherardello, his brother, ser Jachopo, and ser Ardovino who drank Trebbiano [with us] (49).

[2] Saturday, the 19th of June 1361
4 *denari* [were spent] for plums for ser Gherardello and for another priest who was with him; they came to drink Trebbiano [with us] (50).

The composer is recorded as having been at the monastery three times in the following year:

[1] Sunday, the 20th of March 1362
5 soldi [were spent] for greens, fritters [and] lupines because today ser Gherardello with other friends [of his] came to drink with us (51).

[2] Sunday, the 1st of May 1362
This evening dom Lucha bought a kid; ser Gherardello and a friend [of his] stopped by and dined with us. Also present

---

(48) ST, fol. 13:
MCCCLX, luglio a dì XII domenicha, il dì di San Giovanni Gualberto
Questa mattina ci desinarono l'abate di Spugna et ser Gherardello co' due altri.

(49) ST, fol. 34:
MCCCLXI, giugno a dì XVII giovedì
per susine per l'abate di Monte Schalari e per ser Gherardello e per ser Jacopo suo fratello e per ser Ardovino che bevvono del Trebbiano, d. VI

(50) ST, fol. 34:
MCCCLXI, giugno a dì XVIIII sabato
per susine per ser Gherardello e per un altro prete che era con lui che vennono a bere del Trebbiano, d. IIII

(51) ST, fol. 54:
MCCCLXI [1362], marzo a dì XX domenicha
per herbe, per frittelle, per lupini chè ci venne hoggi ser Gherardello a bere con altri compagni, s. V

were the abbots of [the monasteries of] Razuolo, Spugna and Coneo (52).

[3] Sunday, the 15th of May 1362

This evening messer the abbot gave a dinner party; present were the prior of San Romeo [ser Gherardello] with a priest, ser Ardovino, ser Nicholò del Proposto with a youth of the Adimari family, his pupil, ser Filippo the singer, two Friars Minor and the abbots of [the monasteries of] Razuolo and Coneo (53).

In addition to providing some positive data towards a biography of ser Gherardello, to whom we shall return presently, the last document also furnishes an important bit of information about another well-known Trecento composer, ser Niccolò del Proposto of Perugia. Hitherto it has been assumed that this musician resided in Florence for several years (ca. 1360-1365) because of the numerous settings he made of texts by the Florentine poet Franco Sacchetti (54). To my knowledge, however, this is the earliest document that records ser Niccolò's presence in the city at a given time. The document also shows that he must have been on friendly terms with ser Gherardello and other Florentine musicians of the day. Ser Ardovino, who is identified as a singer in a later account in this volume, was a chaplain at San Lorenzo, where he is mentioned

---

(52) ST, fol. 57v:
   MCCCLXII, domenicha dì I di maggio
   Questa sera comprò dom Lucha un cauretto; capitòci ser
   Gherardello e un compagno e cenaronci. Eranci l'abate
   di Razuolo e quel di Spugna e quel di Coneo.

(53) ST, fol. 58:
   MCCCLXII, domenicha a dì XV di maggio
   Questa sera fece messer l'abate una cena e furonci il
   priore di San Romeo con un prete, ser Ardovino, ser
   Nicholò del Proposto con un garzone degl'Adimari, suo
   discepolo, ser Filippo cantore, due frati minori,
   l'abate di Razuolo e eraci l'abate di Coneo.

(54) An account of this composer's life and works is given by K. von Fischer in «*Die Musik in Geschichte und Gegenwart*» 9, cols. 1456-1457. Detailed information about settings of Sacchetti's poetry is found in E. Li Gotti and N. Pirrotta, *Il Sacchetti e la tecnica musicale del trecento italiano*, Florence 1935.

(55) ST, fol. 72:
   MCCCLXII, octobre a dì XX giovedì
   Questo dì ci desinò ser Ardovino cantore.

For the record of ser Ardovino at San Lorenzo in 1381 see note 21 above.

in records dating from 1381-1386 (55). Obviously, he was well acquainted with Francesco Landini, who in turn must have known ser Niccolò. Although ser Gherardello's brother Jacopo, who was also a singer and composer, is not mentioned in this document, he too visited the monastery frequently and must have had occasion to meet ser Niccolò (56). Ser Filippo the singer is probably the same person as the Florentine cathedral chaplain who is mentioned as early as the mid-1330's among the members of the *Compagnia di San Zanobi detto de' laudesi,* a society to which ser Gherardello and the organist Niccolò Mazzuoli also belonged (57). Thus far it has not been possible to identify ser Niccolò's pupil, the « youth of the Adimari family, » though his surname suggests that the composer also had close ties with one of the most influential Florentine families of the time. All in all, together with the settings of Sacchetti's poetry, Santa Trinita's document makes it clear that during his Florentine sojourn ser Niccolò del Proposto entered fully into the city's artistic and social life.

As a result of the information furnished by Santa Trinita's volume, it has been possible to trace ser Gherardello further in other

---

He is recorded there again in a similar list dating from 1 March 1386. (Archivio Capitolare di San Lorenzo, Florence, Vol. 16, *Entrata & Uscita, 1385[-1386]*, fol. 36v).

(56) None of the settings of Sacchetti's poetry that ser Jacopo is known to have made seem to have survived. This musician is recorded at Santa Trinita on two other occasions:
    [1] ST, fol. 9v:
    MCCCLX, lunedì dì 1 di giugno
    per savor biancho che ci desinarono l'abate di Monte
    Piano et quel di Marradi et ser Jachopo, fratello di
    ser Gherardello... s. II
    [2] ST, fol. 32:
    MCCCLXI, giovedì a dì XX di giugno
    Questa sera cenarono l'abate di Razuolo e due monaci
    di Poppi e ser Jachopo, fratello di ser Gherardello.
(57) Archivio di Stato, Florence, Compagnie Religiose Soppresse Z. I, San Zanobi di Firenze, Vol. 2176, fasc. 12. *Libro di tasse di fratelli e note d'effetti posseduti dalla compagnia* 1333-1357, fol. 16:
    MCCCXXXVI
    ser Filippo prete di Santa Liperata, rechò Borghese
    paghò soldi due, s. II
    Ibid., fol. 91:
    MCCCLXVIII
    [d]a Nicholò di Lapo, popolo Sancta Reparata, rechò
    Boldrone, s. III

contemporary Florentine documents. In the monastery's records he is called « the prior of San Romeo, » which was the medieval name of the present-day Florentine church of San Remigio (58). Named in honor of St. Remy, bishop of Reims, the church served during the middle ages as a hostel for French pilgrims bound for Rome (59). In 1060 it was given to the monastery of St. Peter Major, and a few years later became a parish church (60). In 1265 patronage of San Remigio passed to the Bagnesi family, under whose jurisdiction it remained until ca. 1363, when authority to appoint its rectors was assumed by the bishop of Florence (61). According to the eighteenth-century historian Giuseppe Richa, who furnishes most of this information, a list of San Remigio's rectors from 1363-1428 was at one time to be found in the Archiepiscopal Archives of Florence (62). It was not possible for me to consult that list, but during the course of a recent visit to Florence I was able to call at the home of the parish priest of San Remigio, which was then still undergoing restoration of damages caused by the 1967 flood. There I was most graciously received and after explaining the purpose of my visit, I was led across the hallway to the parish records room where a volume entitled *Libro di ricordi della chiesa di San Remigio, C* was placed at my disposal. On folio 1 was the information I had been seeking, a list of « the rectors and priors of San Remigio. » The first three names and dates given are as follows:

    1336 Pr[ete] Bruno
    1361 Pr[ete] Gherardello, so called but his real name was Niccolò di [the son of] Francesco
    1363 Banchino di Sandro (63)

---

(58) See W. Paatz, *Die Kirchen von Florenz,* Frankfurt am Main 1953, Vol. 5, p. 5.
(59) *Loc. cit.*
(60) G. Richa, *Notizie istoriche delle chiese fiorentine,* Florence 1754, Vol. I, p. 256.
(61) *Loc. cit.*
(62) *Loc. cit.*
(63) *Libro di ricordi della chiesa di San Remigio, C,* fol. 1:
    1336 Pr. Bruno
    1361 Pr. Gherardello così detto ma per suo vero nome Niccolò figliuolo di Francesco
    1363 Banchino di Sandro

I

Though the list does indeed confirm the statement in Santa Trinita's volume that ser Gherardello was prior of San Remigio, the date given here must be read as an approximate one because Santa Trinita's records also show that he was already holding that position on 30 April 1360 (64). There is, on the other hand, every reason to believe that 1363 was in fact the year in which his successor took office. Like ser Niccolò del Proposto, ser Gherardello is mentioned as having set to music several of the poems by Franco Sacchetti which are contained in an autograph copy of the poet's oeuvre (65). From the chronological position of two other poems in this volume, both of which mourn ser Gherardello's death, it has been conjectured that he died sometime between 1362-1364 (66). It now appears that the date of his death can be even more closely approximated. As we have seen, he is not mentioned at Santa Trinita after 15 May 1362, even though other musicians such as ser Ardovino are recorded there in the following months. The inference, of course, is that ser Gherardello either died or left the city around that time. In San Remigio's volume it is reported that his successor at that church was already holding the post in 1363. Ser Gherardello, therefore, must have died either in the latter part of 1362 or early in 1363.

Knowledge that ser Gherardello's real name was Niccolò di Francesco implies that he assumed the new name either when he was ordained to the priesthood or even later in his career, if he were then to have become a member of a religious order. That the second possibility was perhaps the case is suggested by some documents found in a volume from the archives of the previously mentioned Company of San Zanobi, which contains records of dues paid by the society's members. The composer's name first appears in an entry dated 27 April 1343, where he is referred to as « Nicholò di Francesco, a clerk in Santa Reparata, » as the cathedral of Florence was then called (67). Another entry, from 12 June 1345,

---

(64) Perhaps the earliest documents that the compiler of the list had access to dated only from 1361.

(65) For a modern edition of the poetry see F. SACCHETTI, *Il libro delle rime*, ed. A. Chiari, Bari 1936.

(66) The poems are printed *Ibid.*, p. 93.

(67) On fol. 77v of the volume cited previously in note 57:
   27 aprile 1343

refers to him as « ser Niccholaio, a chaplain in Santa Reparata, » so we can be sure that he had meanwhile been ordained a priest and appointed to a chaplaincy at the cathedral (68). An entry from 1347 also calls him by his first name only (69), while one dating from 24 October 1349 gives him his full name, « ser Nicholò di Francesco, a chaplain in Santa Reparata » (70). That the chaplain in question is indeed the same person as the composer is shown by a final entry, dating from 10 May 1351, which reads:

[from] ser Gher [crossed out] Nicholò, called ser Gherardello, a chaplain in Santa Reparata [gap] (71)

The information contained in the volumes mentioned above makes it possible to give a brief sketch of ser Gherardello's career. He was still a clerk in 1343, but an ordained priest by 1345. Thus we may assume that he was born between 1320-1325, since it was customary in that period for priests to be ordained at around the age of twenty-one. He was a chaplain at the cathedral of Florence from 1348 until at least 1351. During those years he may have had an opportunity to become acquainted with the Florentine composer Bartolo, who is said to have introduced his polyphonic « Credo » into the cathedral's liturgy sometime around the middle of the century (72). Significantly, ser Gherardello also set portions

---

   [d]a Nicholò di Francescho cherico di Sancta Reparata,
   rechò Bartolo Paganegli, s. I
(68) *Ibid.*, fol. 86v:
   MCCCXLV, a dì XII di giugno
   [d]a ser Niccholaio chapellano di Sancta Reparata, rechò
   elgli istesso [gap]
(69) *Ibid.*, fol. 86v:
   MCCCXLVII
   [d]a ser Nicholaio [gap] chapellano di Sancta Reparata,
   rechò Tendi barbiere a dì VIIII di setenbre
(70) *Ibid.*, fol. 105v:
   MCCCXLVIIII, dì 24 d'otobre
   [d]a ser Nicholò di Francescho chapelano di Sancta Reparata,
   rechò ser Nicholò prete, s. [illegible]
(71) *Ibid.*, fol. 115v:
   MCCCLI
   [d]a ser Gher [crossed out] Nicholò, vochato ser
   Gherardello, chapelano di Sancta Liperata, a dì X di
   magio [gap]
(72) See PIRROTTA, *The Music of Fourteenth Century Italy*, Amsterdam 1954, Vol. I, p. 1.

of the ordinary of the Mass in polyphony (73). By 1351 ser Niccolò had assumed the name ser Gherardello, probably because he entered a religious order in that year. His friendship with the monks of Santa Trinita would make it appear that it was the Vallombrosan Order. In this respect it is interesting to note that his idealized portrait in the Squarcialupi Codex shows him in a monk's habit, though the color of the cloth — of a brown and pink hue — offers little assistance in determining the order to which he belonged (74). In any case ser Gherardello's membership in a religious order did not stand in the way of an appointment to the priorate of San Remigio, a post which he apparently held until the time of his death, ca. 1362-1363.

Unfortunately, it has not proved possible to trace musical events at Santa Trinita during the later decades of the fourteenth century because of an apparent gap in the monastery's records until 1405 (75). Nevertheless, the information contained in this one volume which covers the comparatively short period of three years is more than sufficient to give us an idea of Santa Trinita's important position in the history of Florentine Trecento music. In addition to testifying to the rich musical life of the monastery, the presence there of the Landinis, ser Gherardello, ser Jacopo, ser Giovanni degl'Organi, ser Ardovino, ser Filippo and Niccolò Mazzuoli also furnishes concrete evidence of the close artistic relationships that must have existed among Florentine musicians as well as of the continuity of Florentine musical traditions during the period. Knowledge that non-Florentines such as Niccolò del Proposto of Perugia, ser Matteo da Siena and the abbots of various Vallombrosan monasteries were associated with Santa Trinita at this time suggests an avenue by which the Florentine repertory was disseminated and that it was not necessarily confined to large urban centers but made

---

(73) Ser Gherardello apparently composed a « Credo » and a « Hosanna » (now lost) as well as a « Gloria » and an « Agnus Dei ». (*Ibid.*, p. ii; pp. 53-56).

(74) The color of the Vallombrosan habit was evidently grey.

(75) The next surviving volume containing information about musicians is an *Entrata & Uscita* from 1405-1416, which preserves payments to the monastery's organists. Another volume from 1416-1423 shows that the monastery was still engaging extra musicians to help celebrate its principal feast days, in this case Giovanni Mazzuoli « and his company ». (See the first of my studies mentioned in note 30 above, p. 278).

its way to the very outposts of Tuscany. Finally, the volume's significance may also be measured in terms of the new light it casts on the Vallombrosan Order's hitherto unsuspected connections with Trecento music. Surely, there could be no more fitting tribute to Santa Trinita's enlightened patronage and encouragement of musicians during Florence's golden age of music.

II

UNA NUOVA FONTE DELL'ARS NOVA ITALIANA: IL CODICE DI SAN LORENZO, 2211 *

Alla memoria di Bianca Becherini

Sono meno di dieci anni da quando la collezione di pergamene, manoscritti, documenti archivistici e libri di musica dell'Archivio Capitolare di San Lorenzo di Firenze è diventata più facilmente accessibile agli studiosi. Pertinente quasi esclusivamente all'amministrazione e alle funzioni religiose della famosa chiesa dei Medici, la collezione era da tempo conosciuta e consultata, benché l'uso ne fosse severamente ristretto dopo la seconda guerra mondiale per mancanza di personale e di un inventario moderno. L'Archivio è situato al piano terreno del chiostro di San Lorenzo, proprio sotto le stanze occupate dalla Biblioteca Medicea Laurenziana che raccoglie l'incomparabile collezione di manoscritti della famiglia dei Medici. Dato lo stretto rapporto fisico e culturale che le due istituzioni hanno avuto nei secoli, apparve più che naturale che, su iniziativa della Biblioteca Laurenziana e d'accordo con il Capitolo di San Lorenzo e col Cardinale Arcivescovo di Firenze, il compito di riordinare e catalogare l'Archivio fosse affidato a persona indicata dalla direzione della Biblioteca. L'ordinamento fu terminato nel 1975 e così, in base a quanto concordato, è possibile ora consultare, dandone il preavviso di un giorno, il materiale dell'Archivio Capitolare.

Negli ultimi anni, in connessione con i miei studi sulla musica fiorentina medievale e rinascimentale, ho esaminato sistematicamente moltissimi volumi dell'Archivio di San Lorenzo. Naturalmente, nelle mie ricerche, non avrei consultato quello al quale mi riferisco, se esso non mi fosse stato segnalato dal signor Ronald Forsyth Millen di Firenze, che qui sentitamente ringrazio per la sua cortese premura. Nel catalogo disponibile presso la Biblioteca Laurenziana il volume è segnato come « Archivio San Lorenzo, San Lorenzo MS 2211 », ed è descritto breve-

---

* Mi fa piacere ricordare che questo articolo fu da me presentato il 17 luglio 1982 quale conferenza al Centro di Studi per l'Ars Nova Italiana di Certaldo, la cui fondazione tanto si deve alla volontà ed alle fatiche della musicologa fiorentina Bianca Becherini. Nel dedicare questo mio scritto alla Sua Memoria voglio renderLe testimonianza della riconoscenza che Le debbo. Fu proprio nel lontano 1957 che Bianca Becherini m'incoraggiò ad intraprendere le mie ricerche negli archivi di Firenze, tanto ricche di documentazione come Lei giustamente riteneva. Mi sembra inoltre doveroso ringraziare la direzione e il personale della Biblioteca Medicea Laurenziana per l'assistenza e le facilitazioni che mi hanno accordato durante il corso delle mie ricerche. Particolarmente debbo ringraziare l'amico Mario Tesi per avermi aiutato a tradurre il mio testo in italiano.

mente come « Campione dei beni, 1504 »; esso è infatti relativo ai beni immobili della chiesa nel 1504. Benché esistano nell'Archivio altri volumi di tale tenore per i periodi precedenti e successivi, il MS 2211 risulta essere il più completo fra essi. Descrive con minuti dettagli ogni casa, edificio e negozio sia in città che fuori, e tutti i poderi, sia in Toscana che altrove, appartenenti alla chiesa di San Lorenzo; fornisce informazioni preziose sul loro acquisto, sulla loro affittanza e sulla loro rendita e vi si fa menzione anche di edifici e poderi acquistati dopo il 1504. Su alcune pagine son aggiunti anche vari aggiornamenti, come per esempio sul foglio 28v che porta in margine date che vanno dal 1590 al 1634. Nel suo insieme il volume contiene un tesoro di dati legali e finanziari ed una raccolta esattissima di informazioni sull'amministrazione e sui beni immobili della chiesa. Si capisce perciò come esso sia stato gelosamente custodito attraverso i secoli.

Quando il signor Millen studiava il volume, si accorse che molte pagine contenevano tracce di notazione musicale e mi segnalò con un biglietto questo fatto. Come si sa, non è cosa insolita trovare volumi di contenuto più vario che conservino come fogli di guardia, o come vere e proprie rilegature, fogli provenienti da manoscritti o da libri a stampa. È meno comune che tali fogli contengano musica polifonica, per quanto in questi ultimi anni ne siano stati scoperti alcuni, la maggior parte dei quali, salvo quelli ultimissimi, sono o saranno segnalati nei vari volumi del RISM.[1]

Pensavo che il MS 2211 avesse conservato esempi di canto gregoriano, ma ciò nonostante mi precipitai a consultarlo. La mia curiosità fu premiata perché nel manoscritto non erano conservati casualmente brani di canto gregoriano. Si trattava invece di un intero volume, o la maggior parte di un volume di composizioni polifoniche tutte scritte su fogli di pergamena che successivamente erano state raschiate per servire per il « campione dei beni » di San Lorenzo. Va detto, parenteticamente, che il caso di codici riscritti era piuttosto frequente a causa dell'alto costo della pergamena e della carta. Il volume, in breve, rappresenta un classico caso di palinsesto. In più, esso presenta trenta facciate, quasi tutte alla fine del volume, raschiate e preparate per la scrittura ma poi non riscritte. Quando avvertii il signor Millen dell'importanza della sco-

---

[1] Vedi i vari volumi finora usciti del « Répertoire International des Sources Musicales »: *Manuscripts of Polyphonic Music, 11th-Early 14th Century* (B IV 1, 2), a cura di Gilbert Reaney; e *Handschriften mit mehrstimmiger Musik des 14., 15. und 16. Jahrhunderts* (B IV 3, 4), a cura di Kurt von Fischer e Max Lütolf, München-Duisburg, Henle 1966-1972. Per una scoperta recentissima di polifonia sia strumentale che vocale, vedi G. CATTIN, *Ricerche sulla musica a S. Giustina di Padova all'inizio del Quattrocento, I*, « Annales Musicologiques », VII, 1964-1977, pp. 17-41.

perta, egli generosamente rinunciò al privilegio di comunicarla ufficialmente per primo e mi lasciò la libertà di decifrare e identificare il testo. È un compito che io non ho ancora completato. Posso però anticipare alcune notizie sul contenuto del manoscritto e sulla sua struttura e far così conoscere preliminarmente il suo significato e la sua importanza nella storia della musica fiorentina.

Il MS 2211 è composto da centoundici fogli di pergamena, di cm. 21,5 per 28,5. Aggiunto ad essi alla fine del volume è un fascicolo cartaceo del secolo sedicesimo di sei carte, ed in più quattro carte di guardia, sempre cartacee e del sedicesimo secolo, stanno due all'inizio, due alla fine. (C'è anche un bifolio volante). I primi due fogli membranacei non sono numerati e furono usati nel 1504 come carte di guardia e per l'indice del « Campione ». La numerazione araba che va dal foglio 1 all'85 è del sedicesimo secolo, forse della stessa mano del copista cui si deve la maggior parte delle registrazioni amministrative riscritte sopra le rasure. I ff. 86-87 e 88 sono stati numerati rispettivamente da una seconda e da una terza mano e contengono notizie relative alle entrate della fine del secolo sedicesimo. (Una di queste ultime, del 1598, fu scritta da Michele Federighi, allora priore di San Lorenzo, allievo di Francesco Corteccia e principale copista delle opere del maestro.[2] Fra le opere copiate da lui posso citare il manoscritto « C » della basilica di San Lorenzo, con tutti i responsori per la Settimana Santa di Corteccia, ed il MS Mediceo Palatino 7 della Biblioteca Laurenziana, che presenta il celebrato « Innario » dello stesso compositore). La numerazione dei fogli 89-109 è stata fatta recentemente a lapis e si trova in basso sul lato sinistro del foglio. Tutte le carte da 1-89v, ad eccezione di undici pagine (cc. 8r, 8v, 24r, 24v, 33v, 79r, 79v, 80r, 80v, 83r, 86r, 86v), sono state nuovamente riscritte, mentre le carte 90-109, anche se raschiate, sono rimaste bianche.

La rilegatura, del sedicesimo secolo, è in assi coperte di pelle impressa a freddo. Su ogni piatto vi sono quattro angoli metallici sbalzati ed una placchetta sbalzata d'ottone al centro. Due lacci e due fermagli coevi completano la legatura, il cui dorso fu rilegato con un frammento di legatura antica alla fine del secolo sedicesimo e fu restaurato forse durante il diciottesimo secolo. All'interno del piatto anteriore è incollato un cartiglio sagomato del secolo diciottesimo con l'indicazione del con-

---

[2] Federighi diventò priore di San Lorenzo nel 1574 e morì il 31 maggio 1602. (D. MORENI, *Continuazione delle memorie istoriche dell'ambrosiana imperial basilica di San Lorenzo di Firenze*, vol. I, Firenze 1816, p. 330, p. 354). Fu menzionato dal Corteccia nel suo ultimo testamento, dove è ricordato come « mio creato ». (La parte pertinente del testamento è riportato da M. FABBRI, *La vita e l'ignota opera-prima di Francesco Corteccia, musicista italiano del Rinascimento*, « Chigiana », XXII, n.s., 2, 1965, p. 202).

tenuto, « Campione dei beni del 1504 ». Un foglio staccato e scritto, forse nel secolo diciottesimo, contiene una breve descrizione del volume colla notizia che esso fu fatto compilare per il Capitolo di San Lorenzo nel 1504 dal priore messer Castoro de' Bozzolini di Fiesole e da messer Gregorio Epifani, « eccellente filosofo e dotto uomo, amicissimo di Marsilio Ficino ».[3] Sulle pergamene erano stati originariamente segnati sette righi, ciascuno di sei linee, ad inchiostro rosso, come in rosso erano stati indicati i nomi dei compositori (al centro della pagina, in alto). Anche la foliazione (in numerali romani, in alto, sul lato destro del foglio) era in rosso. Il testo e le note sono in inchiostro nero, le maiuscole sono di colore giallo. La raschiatura avvenuta nel sedicesimo secolo fu assai decisa; tuttavia sotto la scrittura cinquecentesca di colore assai più intenso, molti fogli conservano tracce della foliazione antica, della notazione e del testo originali. Il testo originale è, naturalmente, molto più leggibile nei fogli che non sono stati riscritti.

Quando si destinò il manoscritto a nuovo uso, non si rispettò la sua originaria composizione. Ciò appare evidente da alcuni fogli contenenti una stessa composizione che si trovano separati anche a una certa distanza: vedi per esempio i fogli 84v e 93r, attinenti allo stesso pezzo, ed anche i fogli 86r e 96v, e i fogli 102v e 104r. Il confronto della foliazione originale (quella romana) con quella più recente araba dimostra che il manoscritto subì gravi mutilazioni quando fu destinato a divenire un registro amministrativo. Così l'attuale 90r (numero arabo) porta il numerale romano CXXXXI, mentre il foglio 94r è numerato CLII. La numerazione dei fogli 91r, 92r, e 93r non si legge facilmente. Cifre non progressive si vedono chiaramente anche sui ff. 95r (CLVIIII), 96r (CLXVI), 97r (CLXVIII), 98r (CLXX), 100r (CII), 101r (CXXVII), 105r (CXXXVI) e 107r (CXXXVII). È possibile che un'analisi accurata dei punti d'allineamento a secco (ma quelli visibili sembrano tutti del sedicesimo secolo), della rigatura e dei caratteri della scrittura possano fornirci informazioni più esatte sulla composizione e la foliazione originale del volume.

Considerando che la numerazione romana arriva almeno fino al centosettanta e quella araba soltanto al centoundici, appare evidente che il volume era composto da molte più carte di ora. Non è possibile deter-

---

[3] La deliberazione per la compilazione del volume ci è tramandata dalla seguente registrazione, cavata da un libro di Partiti di San Lorenzo, vol. 2366, *Partiti A 2, 1482-1501*, f. 2v:
 [in margine: Commessione del Campione]
 Addì 22 di novembre 1482 si vinse un partito che si dovesse fare un libro overo campione nel quale si scrivino tutti e bene della chiesa [casa, cancellata] di Sancto Lorenzo di qualunche rag[i]one con loro fitti, misure e confini. Dettesi la commissione di detto libro a messer Chastorio e a messer Gregorio.

minare però quanti fogli siano andati perduti oltre i cinquantanove che sono certamente mancanti. Senza dubbio il MS 2211 comprendeva una raccolta abbastanza consistente, e quanto resta è sufficiente a dimostrare che esso era diviso in sezioni, anche se a volte in alcune si trovano mescolate composizioni di uno o più autori. Resta da determinare se tali pezzi siano stati aggiunti casualmente dallo scriba per riempire carte rimaste bianche (rimangono ancora carte rigate che non hanno ricevuto scrittura né in un primo, né in un secondo tempo), o se invece la confusione sia dovuta al nuovo ordinamento degli inizi del Cinquecento, o se essa sia attribuibile all'una e all'altra causa.

Ciò che è possibile leggere sarà indicato nell'inventario che accompagna questo saggio. Per ora sarà utile un breve elenco sommario di ciò che ho potuto ricavare sul contenuto del manoscritto. Non dubito che studi e ricerche seguenti serviranno ad identificare molti altri brani e a farci recuperare in modo più esatto quelle composizioni che appaiono alla fine del volume e che sembrano essere uniche.

Contrariamente al resto del manoscritto, i primi due fogli membranacei non numerati, cioè il primo foglio di guardia e quello contenente l'indice degli atti amministrativi, segnati da me come foglio A e B, risultano ora capovolti rispetto alla disposizione originale. Sul recto del foglio A si può, con molta difficoltà, leggere qualche frammento di un testo italiano che non sono riuscito finora ad identificare. Sul verso dello stesso foglio, come può ricavarsi da qualche parola leggibile, appare la parte del contratenore della ballata di Francesco Landini, *Quanto più caro fai*. In fondo al foglio, sui tre righi più bassi, c'è un altro testo italiano, come risulta dalla parola « innamora » sul quinto rigo. Il settimo rigo porta la *Prima Pars* e la *Secunda Pars* di una voce di tenore, ma senza testo. Le composizioni sul recto e sul verso del foglio B sembrano di autore italiano, ma non son riuscito ad identificarle.

Si può affermare ad ogni modo che questi fogli siano appartenuti originariamente a un fascicolo o ad un gruppo di fascicoli dedicati al più vecchio maestro dell'Ars Nova toscana e cioè a Giovanni da Cascia, o Johannes de Florentia, come a volte è chiamato. Il suo nome, abbreviato o per intero, appare più volte, e si legge chiaramente sui ff. 19*v* e 20*r*. Inoltre, frammenti di parole e musica di due suoi madrigali, *La bella stella* e *Nascoso 'l viso*, si possono leggere sui ff. 17*v*-18*r* e 19*v*-20*r* rispettivamente. Quattro composizioni di altri autori sono interposte in questa sezione. Si tratta dei madrigali di Bartolino da Padova, *La douce cere* (f. 8*r*) e *La fiera testa* (f. 8*v*), e di *Uselletto selvaggio* di Jacopo da Bologna, presente sia in forma di caccia che in forma di madrigale (ff. 11*v*-12*r* e 15*v*).

II

8

Sebbene il nome di don Donato da Firenze appaia sul f. 22*r*, e sul f. 21*r* e 21*v* si possano leggere alcuni frammenti del suo *I' fu' già bianc'uccel* e del suo *Dal cielo scese per iscala d'oro*, la sezione che segue, che va dal f. 22*v* al 29*v*, riporta composizioni di un altro Giovanni che penso, almeno finora, sia l'ultimo rappresentante dell'Ars Nova in Toscana, Magister Johannes Florentinus Organista. Questi è il poco conosciuto organista della cattedrale di Firenze, Giovanni Mazzuoli degli Organi, morto nel 1429.[4] Come tutti sanno, un posto era stato riservato per le sue musiche nel codice Squarcialupi, ma ne è rimasto privo. Si conoscono solo due composizioni che gli sono state attribuite, ma queste non appaiono neppure nel nostro manoscritto, a quanto sembra. Frammenti di parole e musica si possono leggere su alcune pagine e se eventualmente se ne potranno trarre porzioni consistenti dell'una o dell'altra, saremo in grado di poter meglio giudicare il significato e l'importanza di questo compositore. Altre musiche di Magister Johannes Florentinus Organista si trovano anche in alcuni fogli seguenti e, come avrò occasione di dire in seguito, sembra che l'inclusione delle sue opere in questo manoscritto possa essere in relazione con i suoi rapporti personali colla chiesa di San Lorenzo.

La terza sezione, dal f. 31*v* al 39*r*, comprende composizioni di Bartolino da Padova, le cui iniziali, « f. b. », sono visibili in alcuni luoghi. Si leggono anche frammenti di due suoi madrigali: *Se premio di virtù* (ff. 33*v*-34*r*) e *Quando la terra* (f. 39*v*), e forse altri. Sul foglio 41*r* e 41*v*, fra questa sezione e la seguente, si trovano opere ascritte a un certo « Idem f » che, come si può accertare da alcuni fogli che si ritrovano in fondo al volume, è Francesco Landini. Tali frammenti son seguiti, sui ff. 44*r*-49*r*, da un gruppo di composizioni di Jacopo da Bologna (« Magister Jacobus »), del quale è stato possibile identificare alcuni madrigali: *I' me son un* (f. 44*v*), *Sotto l'imperio* (ff. 45*v*-46*r*), *O in Italia felice Liguria* (f. 47*r*), e il madrigale triplo, *Aquila altera / Creatura gentil / Uccello di Dio* (ff. 48*v*-49*r*). Ci sono ancora due altre composizioni con testi italiani ascritte a Jacopo sui ff. 47*v* e 48*r* che non sono riuscito a leggere chiaramente.

Una quinta sezione, sui ff. 51*v*-59*r*, presenta le musiche di don Donato da Firenze. Il nome si legge in alcuni luoghi, dove si vedono anche frammenti di suoi madrigali: *Un cane, una oca e una vecchia pazza* (f. 52*r*); *Un bel girfalco* (ff. 52*v*-53*r*); *S'i', monocordo gentil* (f. 58*v*), che contiene parti del testo finora creduto perduto; e *I' fu' già ussignol*

---

[4] Vedi il mio *Giovanni Mazzuoli, A Late Representative of the Italian Ars Nova*, in *L'Ars Nova italiana del Trecento*, vol. II, Certaldo 1968, pp. 23-38.

(f. 59*v*). Seguono poi un certo numero di pagine che non hanno nessuna relazione apparente con la sezione che precede e quella che segue. Sono i ff. 60*r* e 60*v*, che portano opere di « Abbas Paulus », cioè don Paolo Tenorista da Firenze, 61*r*, dove si possono leggere frammenti di *Diligite iustitiam*, la parte del contratenore del mottetto *Lux purpurata* di Jacopo da Bologna, 62*r*, che conserva il nome del poco conosciuto compositore oltremontano Hubertus (Ymbertus) de Salinis, e 62*v*, sul quale, grazie al collega Gilbert Reaney, è stato possibile identificare il *triplum* del mottetto *Flos ortum / Celsa cedrus / Quam magnus pontifex*, dedicato a San Lodovico di Tolosa, figlio di Carlo II di Napoli e pronipote di San Luigi di Francia, morto nel 1297 e canonizzato nel 1317. Questo mottetto si conserva nei manoscritti di Ivrea, di Parigi e di Cambrai. Frank Lloyd Harrison informa che il culto di San Lodovico era vivo principalmente a Marsiglia e a Napoli e che gli Spagnoli lo portarono nel Nuovo Mondo, dando il suo nome ad una città, San Luis Obispo, della California.[5] Harrison inoltre osserva che questo Santo fu dipinto da Giotto nella « Morte di San Francesco » in Santa Croce e da Simone Martini nell'arcata della basilica di Assisi. In ambedue i casi è conosciuto come San Luigi, re di Francia. Inoltre posso aggiungere che una scultura di San Lodovico di Tolosa, ora nel refettorio di Santa Croce, fu commissionata a Donatello dalla Parte Guelfa per la chiesa di Orsanmichele nel 1423. Questo fatto e l'inclusione del mottetto in suo onore nel nostro manoscritto che, come dirò più tardi, è stato probabilmente compilato in questo periodo, fanno pensare che il culto di San Lodovico fosse diffuso anche a Firenze.

Coll'eccezione del f. 72*v*, che porta il nome di Hubertus de Salinis, i ff. 63*v*-73*v* contengono per la maggior parte opere di « Vgolinvs de Vrbeveteri », o Ugolino da Orvieto, il cui nome si legge su almeno dodici dei venti fogli di questo gruppo. Da una parola qua e là e da frammenti delle frasi che è stato possibile decifrare, appare chiaro che le composizioni sono in italiano (ff. 63*v*, 64*v*, 71*v*) e in francese (ff. 66*v*, 67*r*). Ugolino era cantore della cattedrale di Santa Maria del Fiore nel 1415 e l'inclusione di alcune delle sue musiche in una collezione fiorentina compilata in questa stessa epoca non sorprende.[6] Sorprende invece

---

[5] Vedi la sua prefazione a *Motets of French Provenance*, Monaco, L'Oiseau-Lyre 1969 (« Polyphonic Music of the Fourteenth Century », V), p. XIV; le pp. 42-45 dello stesso volume contengono la sua edizione del mottetto.

[6] Per Ugolino a Firenze, vedi il mio *Music and Musicians at Santa Maria del Fiore in the Early Quattrocento*, in *Scritti in onore di Luigi Ronga*, Milano-Napoli, Ricciardi 1973, p. 106. La più recente biografia del musicista orvietano si trova in *The New Grove Dictionary of Music and Musicians*, Londra 1980, che contiene voci su quasi tutti i musicisti menzionati in questo studio.

il numero delle sue composizioni in questo manoscritto: un'indicazione che Ugolino era un compositore molto più prolifico di quanto si sospettasse. Una composizione con testo latino sul f. 69r, sfortunatamente priva del nome dell'autore, è di grandissimo interesse locale e mi porta a chiedere se essa sia stata commissionata a Ugolino durante la sua permanenza a Firenze. Incomincia con una preghiera al Padre di Misericordia: « Parce, pater pietatis, tolle donum caritatis quod Florentia ». Un'altra composizione con testo latino (f. 70v), invece, conserva il *triplum* di un mottetto politico che, a quanto sembra, è stato uno dei pezzi più conosciuti del quattordicesimo secolo, *Rex Karole, Johannes genite / Leticie, pacis concordie*. Si tratta di un mottetto, attribuito a Philippus Royllart nel perduto manoscritto di Strasburgo ma pervenutoci nei codici di Chantilly e di Washington, che esalta Carlo V, figlio di Giovanni II di Francia. Ursula Günther ha messo molto bene in evidenza che il pezzo fu scritto nel 1375, in occasione di una tregua fra francesi e inglesi nella guerra dei cento anni.[7] La composizione è anche citata da due teorici (Anonimo V e nel *Tractatus de diversis figuris*), ed è chiaramente documentato che essa fu copiata nel 1423 o 1424 per l'*Illustre Lieve Vrouwe Broederschap* in 's Hertogenbosch. Va anche fatta menzione di una composizione in questa sezione, sul f. 68r, che è scritta per intero in notazione bianca, indicazione che qui si tratta di musica molto più tarda del mottetto in onore di Carlo V.

La maggior parte dei fogli della sezione che segue (75r-99r) contengono composizioni di Magister Petrus Johannis Organista, compositore finora completamente sconosciuto nella storia dell'Ars Nova Italiana. Poiché molti dei fogli hanno avuto un ordinamento diverso da quello originale, è difficile stabilire se tanto spazio fosse tutto destinato alle sue opere. Comunque le testimonianze attuali sono sufficienti per stabilire che egli era qualcosa di più di un compositore occasionale e che molte delle sue musiche si trovavano disponibili per il compilatore del manoscritto. La presenza delle sue opere, collocate originariamente con ogni probabilità alla fine del volume, può fornire un elemento sicuro per determinare la data del manoscritto stesso e il luogo della sua compilazione. Ma di ciò riparleremo in seguito. Tutte le poesie musicate da maestro Piero di Giovanni, per dare al suo nome la forma italiana, sono in italiano, e alcune sembrano essere in forma di ballata. Eccole qui elencate:

---

[7] Quest'informazione è ripresa dall'Introduzione a *The Motets of the Manuscripts Chantilly, Musée Condé, 564 (olim 1047) and Modena, Biblioteca Estense, α. M. 5, 24 (olim 568)*, American Institute of Musicology 1965, pp. XXIX-XXXII (« Corpus Mensurabilis Musicae », 39). Il volume contiene vari mottetti di questo periodo, incluso a pp. 17-22 quello qui ricordato.

Donna, non fu già mai, a due voci (le parti si trovano rispettivamente sui ff. 86*r* e 96*v*); *Lasso dolente o mea gentil figura*, a tre voci (sui ff. 84*v* e 93*r*); *Donna, s'io ò errato*, a due voci (sui ff. 93*v* e 96*r*); e *A Febo Damne amante*. Quest'ultimo testo appare in una versione a tre voci sui ff. 91*v*-92*r*, e in una versione a due voci su ff. 97*v*-98*r*.

Ci sono alcune altre composizioni italiane in questa sezione ma senza il nome del compositore. Fra queste ce n'è una che incomincia *Chi non può quel che vuole* (f. 81*v*); una che ha solo queste parole: *Così comincia la nostra caccia* e *Qui finì la nostra caccia* (f. 94*r*); un'altra con un testo che sembra una caccia, della quale alcune parole si possono leggere così: « compagno d'amore ... O Chaleffo, vellane, vellane, pigliala, pigliala » (f. 82*v*); e una composizione a due voci che comincia *Quando [si] può, si de' sempre fuggire* (f. 95*r*). Nella prima composizione si legge, in cima al foglio, la parola « organista », che potrebbe indicare maestro Piero, ma la presenza di due pezzi assegnati ad un altro organista, Magister Johannes Florentinus sul foglio 85*r* e 85*v* invita ad esser cauti nelle attribuzioni.

In questa sezione composizioni sono ascritte anche a Landini (« Idem f »): una che non si legge sul f. 89*r*, ed un'altra, la ballata *Nè 'n ciascun mie pensier* sul foglio 89*v*. Inoltre io ho potuto identificare frammenti di testi di cacce assai conosciute: quella di ser Gherardello, *Tosto che l'alba* (f. 83*v*) e quella di Vincenzo da Rimini, *Nell'acqua chiara* (f. 94*v*). Ci sono anche tre composizioni con testo francese, due sui ff. 80*r* e 90*v* rispettivamente con qualche parola leggibile, ed una sul f. 95*r* che riporta soltanto l'incipit *Qui fault voyr* [?]. Infine dovrei ricordare due composizioni con testo latino. La prima, sul f. 70*r*, evidentemente fa riferimento ad un papa (« plene largiatur ... laudatur pontificem »). Ma è la seconda (f. 79*v*) che è di grande interesse perché ci dimostra come fosse diffuso a Firenze il repertorio più antico dell'Ars Nova francese. Si tratta di un mottetto a tre voci attribuito a Filippo de Vitry, di cui c'è qui il *triplum, Impudenter circumivi*. Per quanto io so esso rappresenta il solo esempio di una composizione di Vitry in un manoscritto di origine italiana di questo periodo.[8]

La parte finale del manoscritto presenta musiche, coi nomi sufficientemente leggibili, di Francesco Landini (qui indicate sempre come « Idem

---

[8] Il mottetto ci è giunto senza attribuzione nel manoscritto di Ivrea, che oggi si pensa sia stato redatto nella Francia meridionale. L'attribuzione del mottetto a Filippo de Vitry nel perduto manoscritto di Strasburgo è stata respinta da H. BESSELER, *Falsche Autornamen in den Handschriften Strassburg (Vitry) und Montecassino (Dufay)*, « Acta Musicologica », XL, 1968, pp. 201-202. Comunque il mottetto è ancora citato fra le opere del de Vitry da Ernest Sanders nella voce per *The New Grove Dictionary of Music and Musicians*, XX, p. 27.

II

f ») e di don Paolo Tenorista (qui chiamato o « Abbas paulus » o « Paulus abbas »). Come ho detto prima, quest'ultima parte del volume conferma il fatto che i fogli subirono nel secolo quindicesimo, oltre alla raschiatura, anche un ordinamento diverso da quello primitivo. È più che probabile che originariamente le composizioni dei due musicisti non fossero frammischiate come appaiono nell'ordinamento attuale, ma fossero disposte in sezioni distinte, una dopo l'altra. Due ballate di Landini, *Vita non è più miser* (f. 100r) e *S'andray sanza mercè* (f. 100v), appaiono all'inizio di questo gruppo, e cinque altre sono sparse in tutto il resto del manoscritto: *Va pure amore* (f. 103r), *Se pronto non sarà* (f. 103v), *Po' che partir convienme* (f. 106r), *Gl'ochi che in prima* (f. 106v), e *S'i' ti so' stato* (f. 109v).

Tutte le opere di Landini sono conosciute per altre testimonianze, come lo sono quasi tutte quelle ascritte qui a don Paolo Tenorista. Fra quest'ultime, però, ce ne sono alcune che appaiono anonime in altre fonti ed una che sembra sconosciuta. Le opere di Paolo che si trovano qui e conosciute come sue anche altrove sono il madrigale *Corse per l'onde* (la sola parte del tenore, f. 101r) e le ballate *Or sie che può* (f. 105r), *Poc'anno di mirar* (f. 105v), *Amor de' dimmi* (f. 107r) e *Una cosa di veder* (f. 108v). Sono confermate qui le attribuzioni a Paolo fatte da Nino Pirrotta e Kurt von Fischer e da Ursula Günther di due ballate già anonime: *Amor mi stringe assai* (f. 107v) e *Sie mille volte benedetta* (f. 108v).[9] Già anonimi ma ora assegnati a Paolo sono il madrigale *Girando un bel falcon* (ff. 101v-102r) e la ballata *Astio non morì mai* (f. 104v).[10] Inoltre, nel MS 2211 c'è una composizione la cui testimonianza potrebbe essere unica. Si trova sui ff. 102v e 104r, su entrambi i quali si legge il nome di Paolo. Ha un incipit che è illeggibile. Per di più, frammenti del testo, anch'essi molto difficili da leggere (« caccia'l mio

---

[9] Per il primo, che si trova qui a tre voci, vedi K. VON FISCHER, *Studien zur italienischen Musik des Trecento und frühen Quattrocento*, Bern, P. Haupt 1956, pp. 40-41 e N. PIRROTTA, *Paolo Tenorista in a New Fragment of the Italian Ars Nova*, Palm Springs, E. E. Gottlieb 1961, p. 54. Per l'altro vedi U. GÜNTHER, *Die anonymen Kompositionen des Manuskripts Paris, B. N., fonds italiens 568 (Pit)*, « Archiv für Musikwissenschaft », XXIII, 1966, p. 83, p. 89.

[10] *Girando un bel falcon* è dato come anonimo da W. T. MARROCCO, *Italian Secular Music*, Monaco, L'Oiseau-Lyre 1972 (« Polyphonic Music of the Fourteenth Century », 8), pp. 32-34. Ursula Günther, esaminando il manoscritto di Parigi citato nella nota precedente, crede di legger nel nome cancellato del compositore « fra Andrea », cioè fra Andrea de' Servi di Firenze. Essa tuttavia lo presenta con un punto interrogativo, non essendo sicura della lettura. Vedi p. 84, p. 90 del suo studio sopracitato. *Astio non morì mai*, che è dato anonimo nel manoscritto di Parigi, è pubblicato in edizione moderna da N. PIRROTTA, *The Music of Fourteenth Century Italy*, V, American Institute of Musicology, 1964 (« Corpus Mensurabilis Musicae », 11), p. 43 e da W. T. MARROCCO, *Italian Secular Music*, Monaco, L'Oiseau-Lyre 1978 (« Polyphonic Music of the Fourteenth Century », 11), pp. 11-12.

gentil amore ... ne ch'io vechio [?] arrabiato [?] strega [?] »), non si trovano in nessuna altra composizione attualmente conosciuta come sua.

Due altri pezzi, scritti in fondo alle pagine che riportano il nome di Paolo, richiamano la nostra attenzione. La prima, *C'estoit mon*, a due voci, si trova sul f. 102r, proprio sotto la parte del tenore di *Girando un bel falcon*. Benché vi appaia solamente l'incipit del testo, le musiche per la *Prima* e *Secunda Pars* sono complete, e si tratta di due voci, il *cantus* ed il tenore, di un *virelai* a tre voci finora conosciuto soltanto nella versione conservata nel Codice Reina, *C'estoit ma douce nourtuire*. La sezione del Codice Reina in cui si trova questo pezzo è stata copiata verso il 1400, e sembra sicuro che il manoscritto stesso sia della regione Padova-Venezia.[11] Sul f. 108r, sotto la ballata *Sie mille volte benedetta*, si trova un'altra breve composizione a due voci, della quale non sono riuscito neppure a leggere l'incipit del testo, e sarà da vedere se si tratti ancora di una nuova composizione di Paolo. Ma anche se non lo è, Paolo è qui rappresentato da dieci pezzi, che insieme a quelli ascritti a lui nell'altra sezione, danno buon motivo di ritenere che il MS 2211, prima dello smembramento, fosse una delle maggiori testimonianze delle sue opere.

Questa descrizione del codice, anche nel suo stato attuale, dimostra chiaramente che, come per le altre fonti fiorentine di questo periodo, il suo contenuto era suddiviso per autori, tenendo conto dell'ordine cronologico e del genere delle composizioni stesse. Nino Pirrotta ha osservato che quando i fiorentini procedevano alla compilazione di questo genere di raccolte – con i madrigali e cacce dei maestri più vecchi preposti generalmente alle composizioni dei musicisti della generazione successiva per i quali la ballata stava assumendo un'importanza maggiore, e con alla fine compositori più giovani che coltivavano quasi esclusivamente la ballata – cercavano di dare una veduta retrospettiva della musica e poesia per musica nel periodo 1340-1415.[12] Pirrotta, inoltre, ha anche osservato che « for the sake of completeness » (per dare maggior completezza alle loro raccolte) i fiorentini includevano in esse opere di compositori del nord Italia, ciò in netto contrasto con i compilatori dell'Italia settentrionale che generalmente includevano opere fiorentine nelle

---

[11] Per particolari sulle origini del manoscritto vedi pp. 485-486 del primo volume dell'opera di von Fischer e Lütolf, sopra citato nella nota 1. *L'estoit mon* è pubblicato in edizione moderna da N. E. WILKINS, *A Fourteenth-Century Repertory from the Codex Reina*, American Institute of Musicology 1966, (« Corpus Mensurabilis Musicae », 36), pp. 43-44.

[12] Vedi il suo *Novelty and Renewal in Italy: 1300-1600*, in *Studien zur Tradition in der Musik: Kurt von Fischer zum 60. Geburtstag*, a cura di H. H. Eggebrecht e M. Lütolf, München, E. Katzbichler 1973, p. 50.

loro raccolte solo « for pragmatic reasons of immediate relevance » (per ragioni pragmatiche di rilevanza immediata).[13] In parole povere, il criterio dei fiorentini rispondeva a un senso storico, mentre ciò non accadeva per gli altri.

Le opinioni del Pirrotta trovano per la maggior parte conferma nel nostro manoscritto. Di sicuro la scomposizione dei fogli avvenuta prima del 1504 ha annullato il piano originale e rende la ricostruzione dell'ordine delle sezioni completamente ipotetica. Ovviamente sarebbe stato più logico, dal punto di vista del contenuto e della cronologia, che alle opere di Giovanni da Cascia (anche ora sezione uno) seguissero quelle di Jacopo di Bologna (ora sezione quattro), e che le opere di Magister Johannes Florentinus Organista (ora sezione due) trovassero posto verso la fine del volume, dove infatti ora se ne trova qualcuna. Sarebbe stato anche logico che le sezioni tre e cinque, dedicate a Bartolino da Padova e a don Donato da Firenze (che, come i più vecchi compositori, sono rappresentati per la maggior parte da madrigali), dovessero normalmente susseguirsi l'una dopo l'altra, o che vi fosse anche una sezione interposta ad esse con le composizioni di un musicista loro contemporaneo.

La cosa che sorprende nel MS 2211 è l'assenza di un corpo di musiche di Gherardello e di Niccolò del Proposto, che erano attivi in Firenze subito dopo la metà del secolo quattordicesimo.[14] È certo che le opere di Gherardello erano conosciute al compilatore del manoscritto perché vi ha incluso una sua famosa caccia. A questo riguardo è interessante notare che *Tosto che l'alba* (f. 83v) si trova molto vicina ad un pezzo che sembra una caccia (f. 82v) e che la caccia di Vincenzo da Rimini, *Nell'acqua chiara*, è sul verso di un foglio (94r) che conserva un'altra caccia sconosciuta. Forse esse rappresentano ciò che rimane di una piccola sezione di cacce, un'indicazione che anche le divisioni per generi sono state tenute presenti nella redazione del manoscritto. È difficile stabilire se ci fossero sezioni con testi francesi e latini, generalmente non molto abbondanti nelle fonti fiorentine, poiché finora non ne sono stati identificati molti. Ma non sarebbe sorprendente se così fosse.

Allo stato attuale, le restanti sezioni del MS 2211 ci conservano musiche dei più giovani autori dell'Ars Nova italiana. Visto ciò, sorprende come manchino le opere di Andrea de' Servi che cronologicamente ap-

---

[13] *Loc. cit.*

[14] La documentazione della presenza di Gherardello e di Niccolò del Proposto nella città in questo periodo si trova nel mio *Music and Musicians at the Florentine Monastery of Santa Trinita, 1360-1363*, in *Memorie e contributi alla musica dal medioevo all'età moderna offerti a F. Ghisi nel settantesimo compleanno (1901-1971)*, vol. I (« Quadrivium », XII, 1971), pp. 142-149.

partiene a questo gruppo. Forse è da attribuire questo fatto alla sparizione di alcuni fogli. In ogni modo, in queste ultime sezioni la ballata è la forma che si riscontra più frequentemente. E anche se non possiamo essere sicuri dell'ordine assegnato originariamente alle musiche del Landini e di Paolo Tenorista, è assai evidente che a ciascuno di essi fosse assegnata una sezione separata. È molto probabile anche che tali sezioni fossero seguite, e non precedute come al presente, dalle opere di Piero di Giovanni. Qui basti ricordare che alcune pagine contenenti opere di Piero hanno la foliazione in cifre romane da CXXXXI a CLXX. Il che indica che se esse non erano alla fine del volume, dovevano esserle molto vicine. La considerazione che le opere di Piero fossero poste alla fine del volume trae conferma dalle informazioni biografiche che io ho potuto recentemente reperire su di lui.

Il nome di Piero, come appare nel MS 2211, offre la chiave migliore per la sua identificazione. Egli era figlio di un Giovanni, ed era organista. Il suo nome di famiglia era Mazzuoli. Suo padre era proprio quel Johannes Florentinus Organista di cui abbiamo parlato prima. Alcuni anni or sono ho potuto stabilire che Johannes Florentinus, o Giovanni Mazzuoli, era figlio a sua volta di un altro organista chiamato Niccolò a cui egli era succeduto come organista nella chiesa di Orsanmichele. Più tardi, Giovanni divenne organista in Santa Felicita, e finì la sua carriera come organista della cattedrale fiorentina. Aveva stretti legami anche con la chiesa di San Lorenzo, il cui capitolo inviò una delegazione ai suoi funerali il 14 maggio 1426. Nel mio studio precedente ho potuto citare un passo della denuncia fatta al catasto nel 1427 da parte del figlio Piero. In quel tempo Piero, che era notaro e aveva quasi quarantun anni, dichiarò fra i suoi averi cinquanta lire che i canonici di Santa Maria del Fiore gli dovevano « dare di salario servì mio padre e in parte io ser Piero ».[15] Notai allora che Piero, oltre che notaro, doveva essere un eccellente musicista se dopo la morte del padre prese il suo posto come organista della cattedrale fino a quando non si fosse trovato un altro organista stabile.

Documenti dell'Archivio di San Lorenzo, recentemente scoperti, non solo confermano questa supposizione ma fanno anche vedere che Piero aveva esercitato la professione di organista già molti anni prima. Sebbene essi non siano completi come si vorrebbe (ci sono lacune per gli anni 1405-1409 e per di più mancano a volte in alcuni volumi i nomi dei musicisti impiegati dalla chiesa), i restanti registri contengono nondimeno informazioni sufficienti della presenza di Piero di Giovanni Mazzuoli come organista in San Lorenzo dall'agosto 1403 al settembre 1415 e

---

[15] Vedi p. 37 del mio studio sopra citato nella nota 4.

dimostrano come egli fosse uno degli immediati successori di Francesco Landini. Sono ricordati alcuni pagamenti fatti a lui in questi anni; il più notevole riguarda il periodo aprile 1414-aprile 1415, dove ricorre ampiamente il suo nome: « ser Piero del maestro Giovanni che ssuona gli orghani ».[16] L'ultimo pagamento per salario di sei mesi, datato 30 settembre 1415, contiene una nota che dice che egli « non volea sonare più gli organi nostri e però nonn à avere altro da nnoi ».[17] Questa notizia è confermata da ricordi posteriori nei quali appare che un mese dopo gli successe il monaco don Piero del Marrone che fu organista in San Lorenzo fino al giugno 1426.[18] Non si sa se Piero di Giovanni prestò il suo servizio in un'altra chiesa dopo aver lasciato San Lorenzo, ma è certo che in quest'epoca egli esercitò appieno la carriera giuridica. Riassunti di tre processi legali da lui curati nel 1420 dimostrano come egli fosse notaro pubblico e giudice del Comune di Firenze.[19] Era una posizione di

---

[16] Il più antico pagamento fatto a lui che ho trovato è in un volume di *Entrata & Uscita, 1403*, dell'Archivio di San Lorenzo, vol. 2450, f. 37r:
Uscita d'aghosto [1403]
Item a Piero che sona gl'orchani soldi quaranta, L. II.
Un pagamento posteriore si trova nel vol. 1918[4], *Entrata & Uscita, 1414*, a f. 29v:
MCCCCXIIII
Uscita delgli orghani
Ser Piero del maestro Giovanni che ssuona gli orghani de' avere l'anno per suo salario lire novanta inchomingiò l'anno dì 4 d'aprile 1414, L. LXXXX.
Ànne auto a dì XXVI di settembre lire quarantacinque, e detti gli decto Giovanni d'Antonio linaiuolo in fiorini nuovi, L. XLV.
Ànne auto a dì XVII d'aprile 1415 lire quarantacinque e è pagato per tutto dì 4 d'aprile 1415, L. XLV.
[17] Vol. 1919[1], *Entrata & Uscita, 1415*, f. 31r:
Ser Piero di Giovanni che ssuona gli orghani debba avere l'anno lire novanta per sonare gli orghani nostri, inchominciò l'anno suo a dì 4 d'aprile 1415; quello gli darò porrò qui di sotto, L. LXXXX.
Ànne auto a dì 30 di settembre lire quarantacinque piccioli furono per resto di suo salario, portò Antonio chiericho, disse non volea sonare più gli organi nostri e però nonn à avere altro da nnoi, L. XLV.
[18] Il primo documento riguardante don Piero del Marrone segue subito dopo quello a ser Piero di Giovanni nella nota sopra citata. Riporto integralmente il documento perché le condizioni sono probabilmente simili a quelle, attualmente irreperibili, offerte a ser Piero di Giovanni quando fu assunto,
Don Piero del Marrone tolse messer lo priore e 'l capitolo per sonare gli orghani nostri e deba avere uno anno lire cinquanta inchominciando dì primo di novembre 1415 e finisce il detto anno dì ultimo d'ottobre 1416, e poi debba sonare i detti orghani anni 4 prossimi che venghano e debba avere ongni anno i detti 4 anni lire sessanta per anno, e debba essere pagato i detti 5 anni in chapo dell'anno, e questo patto fece chol priore e chol chapitolo [...] in presenza del detto priore e chapitolo.
[19] I tre documenti che si trovano in vari fondi dell'Archivio di Stato, Firenze, sono:
(1) Archivio Generale, tomo 2, parte II, datato *1405, 28 novembre, Ind. XIV*: « Donna Piera [...] moglie di Tommaso del fu Franco di Giovenco de Medici [...] nel 31 dicembre 1405 detta donna crea suo procuratore el detto Tommaso suo marito [...] Copia Piero di Giovanni Mazzuoli, giudice e notaio pubblico ».
(2) Archivio Generale, tomo 2, parte II, datato *1420, 20 giugno, Ind. XIII*: « Deliberazione dei regolatori dell'entrata ed uscita del Comune di Firenze per la quale

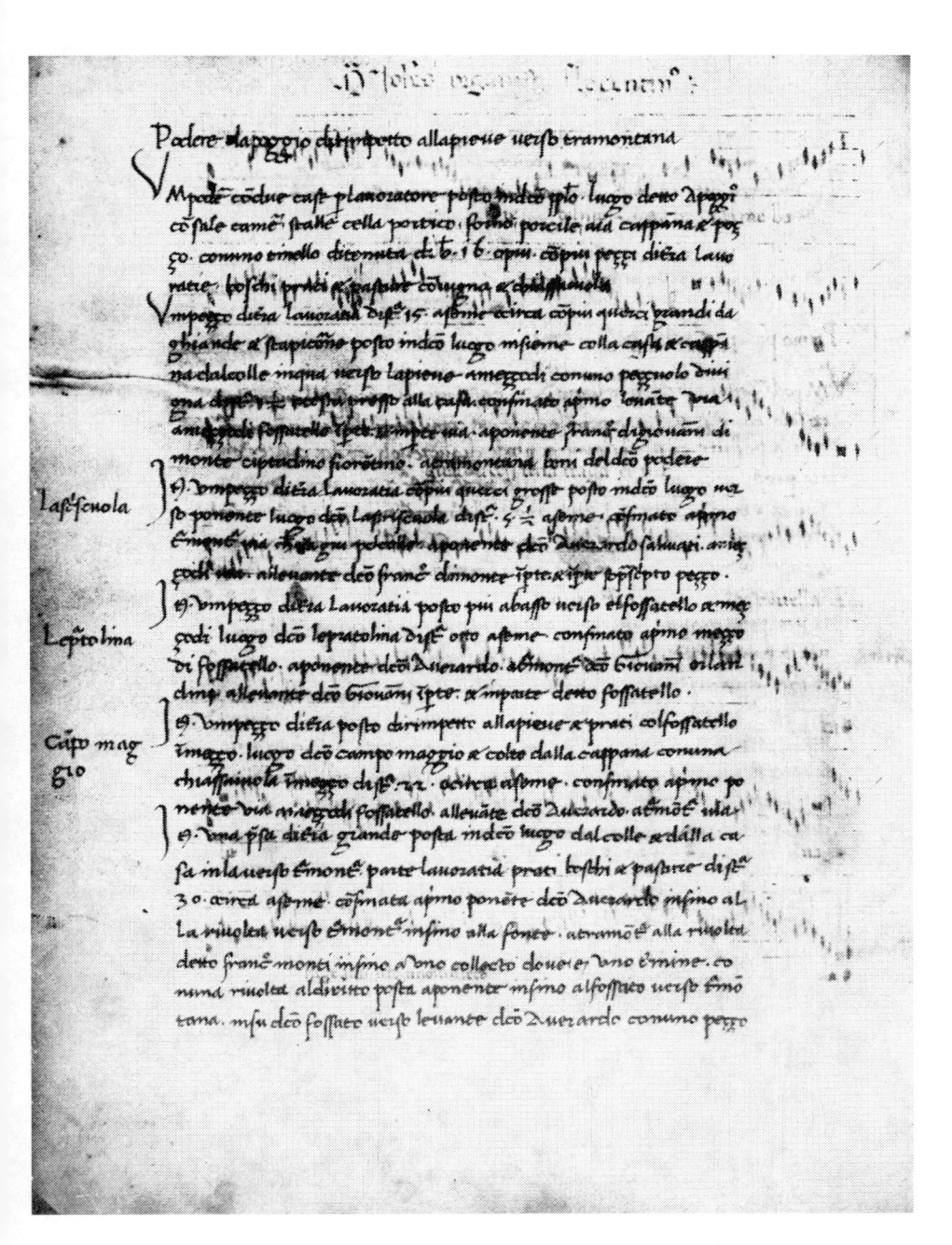

Plate 1. - Firenze, Biblioteca Laurenziana, Archivio San Lorenzo, MS 2211, fol. 22v.

Plate 2. - Firenze, Biblioteca Laurenziana, Archivio San Lorenzo, MS 2211, fol. 104v.

qualche rilievo sociale e politico, discretamente lucrativa, a giudicare dalla dichiarazione fatta al catasto nel 1427, dalla quale, inoltre, si ricava che egli aveva un numero considerevole di proprietà, la maggior parte delle quali, senza dubbio, aveva avuto in eredità dal padre.[20] Finora non ho trovato altri documenti su ser Piero di Giovanni ad eccezione di una notizia sulla sua morte, avvenuta domenica, 10 settembre 1430, e della sua sepoltura nella chiesa di Santa Maria Maggiore.[21]

Piero di Giovanni emerge come una delle ultimissime figure dell'Ars Nova fiorentina e lo si può considerare come tratto di unione fra gli epigoni quale Paolo Tenorista e la nuova generazione di musicisti fiorentini, come Antonio Squarcialupi, che accoglievano con entusiasmo le innovazioni stilistiche dei franco-fiamminghi che da allora cominciavano ad inondare la penisola con le loro soavi composizioni ed il loro canto splendido. Benché sia ragionevole supporre che Piero studiasse musica con suo padre, i suoi legami professionali con San Lorenzo indicano anche che egli aveva rapporti con Francesco Landini, il quale morì quando Piero aveva circa tredici anni. Quel poco che io ho potuto ricavare sul suo stile dalla lettura di lezioni incomplete in un piccolo numero di pezzi, mi fa supporre che la sua musica tenda verso la semplicità tipica dell'epoca, ma conservi reminiscenze della tradizione dei predecessori fiorentini. La notazione, quando si può leggere, è quella consueta dell'inizio del Quattrocento e non presenta molte difficoltà. I ritmi non sono molto complessi, le sincopazioni non sono pronunciate. Inoltre

---

tassano in L. 15 da pagarsi nel termine di 6 mesi il debito con la Gabella di Iacopo di Giunta di Prato. Rogò Pietro di Giovanni Mazzuoli, notaio di detti regolatori ».

(3) Spoglio delle Cartapecore dello Spedale di S. Giovanbattista detto di Bonifazio di Firenze, tomo 14, f. 434v, N. 1875: « Deliberazione dei regolatori dell'entrata ed uscita del Comune di Firenze con le quale confermavano [...] che donna Bartolommea, moglie di Antonio delli Alterati, sia esente dalle prestanze per quei beni assegnati alla medesima in dote [...] Rogato da Piero di Giovanni Manzuoli [sic], giudice ordinario e notaio e cop[iato] da Tommaso del fu altro Tommaso Viviani, cittadino fiorentino, giudice ordinario e notaio ».

[20] I suoi beni immobili, elencati nella sua denuncia di quell'anno, comprendevano: Una casa dove habitiamo, posta alla forca di Canpo Corbolini [...] una casa posta nella via dell'Alloro [...] òne di pigione da Piero dal Banbo barbierei [...] un podere posto nel popolo di San Miniato [...] uno poderetto con casa da lavoratore posto nel popolo di S. Martino la Palma luogo detto Vigliano [...] uno poderetto con casa da lavoratore [...] uno poderuzzo posto in decto popolo con casolare, terre lavorative, arborate, vignate, sode e bosco, loco detto Bricoli [...].

Un'altra parte del documento (Archivio di Stato, Firenze, Catasto, vol. 55, *San Giovanni, Drago, 1427,* cc. 592r-597r) è riportata a p. 37, nota 41 del mio studio sopra citato nella nota 4.

[21] La notizia della sua morte si trova in Archivio di Stato, Firenze, Grascia, *Morti*, vol. 3, f. 173r:
[1430]
Domenicha a dì X di Settembre
Ser Piero di Giovanni degli Organi, popolo S. Maria Maggiore presso alla chiesa, riposto in detta chiesa.

II

sono molto preminenti una melodia più ornata nella parte più alta, con i soliti melismi sulla prima sillaba della prima parola o sulla penultima sillaba di parole che vengono alla fine di sezioni separate, e vi sono anche passaggi che adoperano la così detta cadenza Landini. Comunque, tutte le parti portano il testo e a volte esse si muovono tutte insieme.

Ritorno al MS 2211. Questo sommario sul suo contenuto visibile è sufficiente a far vedere come il manoscritto era, ed è ancora, una raccolta di una certa consistenza e di una certa ampiezza, tale da richiamare l'immagine di un arco che abbracci cronologicamente uno spazio notevole. È, per dirla in altri termini, un'antologia che conserva alcuni dei pezzi più antichi del repertorio italiano del Trecento, quali *O in Italia felice Liguria* del 1346 e *Sotto l'imperio* del 1354, ambedue di Jacopo di Bologna, e anche composizioni che rappresentano le ultime fasi dell'Ars Nova fiorentina.[22] Inoltre, vi sono contenuti mottetti di provenienza francese che si riferiscono all'intero periodo dell'Ars Nova francese, dalle sue prime manifestazioni nelle opere di Filippo de Vitry ai mottetti della seconda metà del quattordicesimo secolo fino al *virelai* della fine del secolo. Questo repertorio è ampliato da composizioni con testi latini dell'oltremontano Hubertus de Salinis, attivo nel nord Italia nel primo Quattrocento. A questi si possono aggiungere un notevole numero di composizioni di Magister Johannes Florentinus Organista e di Ugolino da Orvieto, che operarono in Firenze nella prima e nella seconda decade del secolo quindicesimo. L'inclusione di questi ultimi, secondo me, indica chiaramente l'origine fiorentina del codice. Per di più, la presenza delle opere di Piero di Giovanni non solo conferma la teoria dell'origine fiorentina ma suggerisce ancora che il volume sia stato redatto verso il 1420 se non più tardi.

Per molte ovvie ragioni io non posso dire ora quando le prime sezioni del manoscritto fossero copiate e se il codice sia opera di uno o più scribi. In ogni modo, data la presenza di molte opere di Giovanni e di Piero Mazzuoli, sembra che l'antologia, e credo che così si possa definire il manoscritto, anche se non compilata nella loro cerchia, sia pervenuta nelle mani di qualcuno che conosceva la loro produzione e che l'abbia inclusa nelle ultime sezioni del codice in parola.

Ma il codice apparteneva originariamente a San Lorenzo? e se non, come vi era pervenuto? Come prima impressione viene fatto di pensare

---

[22] K. VON FISCHER, *Jacopo da Bologna*, in *The New Grove Dictionary of Music and Musicians*, vol. IX, pp. 449-450, ha riassunto le varie teorie riguardanti le datazioni delle opere di Jacopo, qualcuna delle quali fu per la prima volta presentata da G. THIBAULT, *Emblèmes et devises des Visconti dans les oeuvres du Trecento*, in *L'Ars Nova italiana del Trecento*, vol. III, Certaldo, 1969, pp. 131-160.

che il volume fosse in possesso della Chiesa da lungo tempo quando nel 1504 si decise di trasformarlo in un campione di beni. Certamente è possibile che si fosse allora comprato di seconda mano un vecchio volume di pergamene, ma sembra più logico che le costose ma durevoli membrane fossero destinate a nuovo uso proprio perché esse si trovavano già nell'archivio di San Lorenzo. Ma quando e come il volume sia giunto a San Lorenzo è una questione che forse non potremo mai risolvere a meno che una ricerca accurata nei restanti inventari ci offra la scoperta giusta.

Volumi di musiche polifoniche dovevano essere presenti in San Lorenzo fin dai tempi di Francesco Landini, ma nel primo inventario esistente del 1393 e quello seguente del 1399 non se ne fa menzione. Quello del 1399, per esempio, non parla di altro che di messaletti, messali, quadernucci di processioni ed altre cose, fra le quali « uno antifonario di dì overo graduale in tre volumi per tutto l'anno di nota franciescha, bellissimo » ed « un libro mezzano parte di note francissche e parte di note all'antica colla messa di Sancto Lorenzo et altre cose sscritti suvvi ».[23] Le « note francissche » si riferiscono alla notazione quadrata che, nata in Francia, aveva preso piede anche in Italia.[24] Forse il nostro manoscritto non figura negli inventari del tardo Trecento per la semplice ragione che non era stato ancora compilato. Il più antico inventario del sedicesimo secolo che io conosco è sfortunatamente posteriore di tre anni. È del 1507 e offre testimonianze di volumi di polifonia in San Lorenzo quando elenca « tre libretti notati, due da processione, l'altro per lo orghanista ».[25] Questi volumi son anche ricordati in un inventario del 1477 ed anche in uno del 1457, che descrive il libro dell'organista come « un libriciuolo di canto per gl'orghani ».[26] Per quanto posso determinare nessuno degli inventari del Quattrocento fa menzione del nostro manoscritto. È un'indicazione che esso non faceva parte della biblioteca di San Lorenzo? Forse, ma forse ciò sta ad indicare che esso si trovava in mani private e che giunse più tardi in San Lorenzo. Non possiamo dare la parola definitiva su questo argomento poiché gli inventari sono spesso incompleti, come è stato rilevato dal Baldasseroni e D'Ancona che si

---

[23] Tutti e due gli inventari, che per la maggior parte elencano le stesse cose, sono stati pubblicati da F. BALDASSERONI e P. D'ANCONA, *La biblioteca della basilica fiorentina di San Lorenzo nei secoli XIV e XV*, Prato-Firenze 1906, pp. 12-13. Cito da quello del 1399 perché le sue descrizioni sono più complete.
[24] La notazione quadrata (« francigena nota ») era conosciuta nell'Italia centrale almeno dalla terza decade del Duegento. Vedi S. J. P. VAN DIJK, *Sources of the Modern Roman Liturgy*, Leiden 1963 (« Studia et Documenta Franciscana », I), pp. 113-115.
[25] Archivio di San Lorenzo, vol. 2634, *Inventario di sagrestia, 1507*, f. 14v.
[26] Vedi l'opera di Baldasseroni e D'Ancona, sopra citata nella nota 23, pp. 18-19.

sono accorti di registrazioni solo saltuarie: « fra le uscite della sagrestia ritroviamo di quando in quando, per tutta la metà del secolo XV, il ricordo di codici che gli inventari non registrano ».[27] Date le circostanze, sembra ragionevole supporre che il volume sia appartenuto a persona vicina all'ambiente laurenziano che lo abbia poi lasciato alla Basilica alla fine del quindicesimo secolo.

Ma anche se il volume non appartenne originariamente a San Lorenzo, si può forse supporre che la sua presenza servisse per gli usi pratici, cioè che fu forse adoperato per le esercitazioni quotidiane? Al presente la domanda non trova risposta. Comunque esiste una lunga tradizione relativa alle esecuzioni di musica polifonica in San Lorenzo che lascia credito a questa ipotesi. Francesco Landini era organista là almeno dal 1369.[28] Documenti recentemente portati alla luce ci dicono che egli era stato preceduto nel 1347 e 1348 da un certo Filippo degli Organi,[29] e che cantori erano ingaggiati in giorni speciali per dare alle festività una solennità particolare. Questo fu il caso nell'agosto del 1352, quando sono ricordate le spese « a dì 9, la vigilia di Sancto Lorenzo per lo palchetto de' cantori ».[30] Ugualmente voglio ricordare che nel 1360 son registrate spese simili « per fare un palchetto pe' cantori » nella chiesa di Santa Trinita per una loro festività speciale.[31]

Più vicino al tempo della compilazione del nostro volume, c'è un ricordo da San Lorenzo in data 28 maggio 1405 che dice: « fu ricevuto per cantore maestro Giovanni con tre fanciugli cantori, debbano avere il mese di salario fiorini d'oro sei e lluso della cucina e lle distri-

---

[27] *Ivi*, p. 11.
[28] La carriera del Landini a San Lorenzo è documentata nel mio studio citato alla nota 14, pp. 136-138 e nello studio di F. Alberto Gallo, citato più avanti in nota 33.
[29] Pagamenti a questo musicista si trovano nel vol. 1915³, *Entrata & Uscita, 1347-1348*, dell'Archivio di San Lorenzo, a cc. 11v, 13r, 13v, 18v e 35r.
[30] Il documento si trova nell'Archivio di San Lorenzo, vol. 1915⁵, *Entrata & Uscita, 1352-1357*, alla c. 18r che contiene un altro interessante pagamento:
Item per a[g]uti per lo palchetto de' chantori, s. 1, d. VIIII.
Un documento appena anteriore, a c. 9r dello stesso volume, menziona fra le spese per la festa di San Lorenzo nel 1347 pagamenti « pro fructibus pro cantoribus [...] tubatoribus domini capitanei [...] aliis tubatoribus ». A San Lorenzo la festa del santo patrono era certamente celebrata ogni anno con solennità anche se non è sempre possibile documentare le spese e la preparazione della festa per la mancanza di molti libri di sagrestia. Che si continuasse ancora così durante l'epoca in cui Piero di Giovanni era organista a San Lorenzo è provato dal documento seguente in cui si mostra che perfino i cantori del Papa venivano invitati ad assistere alla festa.
Uscita d'agosto 1413
Item decto dì [10] diedi a' cantori del Papa che gli feci venire a honorare la festa [di San Lorenzo], lire dieci, L. 10
(Archivio di San Lorenzo, vol. 1918³, *Entrata & Uscita, 1413*, f. 26v).
[31] Vedi p. 140 del mio studio sopra citato alla nota 14.

butioni per uno cappellano».³² Dato l'alto salario, non sembra dubbio che si trattasse di cantori di polifonia, impiegati proprio durante gli anni in cui si trova menzionato Piero di Giovanni come organista, e che i cantori fossero ingaggiati per cantare più di frequente che nei soli giorni festivi. Malgrado ciò è molto difficile sostenere che il manoscritto servisse per esercitazioni pratiche in San Lorenzo. Il suo contenuto può far pensare che esso servisse per riunioni conviviali nella canonica piuttosto che per le funzioni religiose in chiesa. Che tali riunioni conviviali potessero avvenire anche qui non è improbabile, vista la presenza di luminari musicali come Lorenzo Masini,³³ Landini, e più tardi i Mazzuoli, ed anche perché esse sono attestate agli inizi del 1360 nel convento di Santa Trinita.³⁴

La possibilità che il volume sia stato composto come un'antologia storica piuttosto che per uso pratico mi sembra molto più ragionevole. Consideriamo ancora una volta il fatto che esso conserva composizioni che abbracciano tutta l'Ars Nova, dal punto di vista cronologico e tipologico, sia francesi che italiane, e che una buona parte del suo contenuto è dedicato alle opere di musici fiorentini dell'ultima generazione, Paolo Tenorista, Giovanni e Piero Mazzuoli, e di altri loro contemporanei come Ugolino da Orvieto e Hubertus de Salinis. Ma per confermare questa supposizione bisognerà attendere più fortunate ricerche. Per il momento basti sapere che il MS 2211, anche se il suo contenuto è in larga parte cancellato, è di considerevole importanza per la storia dell'Ars Nova Italiana, non solo perché esso può presentare eventuali lezioni alternative di brani musicali o testuali o nuove lezioni di brani testuali ora considerati perduti, ma anche perché apporta nuovi dati sulla produzione di Magister Johannes Florentinus Organista e di Ugolino da Orvieto ed infine di un compositore finora completamente sconosciuto alla storia della musica. In conclusione io direi che il nuovo codice di San Lorenzo costituisce una viva testimonianza della potenza dello spirito del nascente umanesimo fiorentino che nella ricerca del nuovo traeva la sua ispirazione dall'eredità del passato.

---

³² Il documento si trova nell'Archivio di San Lorenzo, vol. 1918¹ *Entrata & Uscita*, *1404*, f. 47*v*. Di maestro Giovanni cantore si fa menzione anche nell'Uscita di Maggio dello stesso anno a cc. 37*r* e 37*v*. Senza dubbio c'era a San Lorenzo molta più attività polifonica di quella che sembra risultare dalla documentazione frammentaria, o verosimilmente frammentaria. Per quanto ho potuto accertare finora, credo di poter affermare che San Lorenzo ebbe una notevole vita musicale durante la seconda metà del Trecento, tale da richiedere la presenza non solo di Francesco Landini e di Lorenzo Masini ma forse anche quella di ser Niccolò del Proposto e di ser Gherardello. Sembra anche che San Lorenzo fosse proprio in prima linea nelle attività musicali nella Firenze di quest'epoca.

³³ Per la presenza di Lorenzo Masini a San Lorenzo vedi F. A. GALLO, *Lorenzo Masini e Francesco degli Organi in S. Lorenzo*, «Studi Musicali», IV, 1975, pp. 57-63.

³⁴ Vedi il mio studio su Santa Trinita, citato in nota 14, passim.

INVENTARIO

Nell'inventario i nomi degli autori sono dati in parentesi quadre quando non risultano da attribuzioni presenti nel MS ma sono desunti sulla base di altri criteri indicati nei commenti. Seguono gli incipit, quando sono leggibili o ricostruibili (in tal caso sono dati in parentesi quadre). Nella colonna dei commenti sono indicate parole o note leggibili, o altri elementi degni di rilievo.

Foglio		Incipit	Commenti
A*r*	—	—	frammenti al 7º rigo: « nel ... sco », indicano un testo italiano
A*v*	[Idem f: Landini]	[Q]uanto più caro fay	la sola parte del contratenor; al 5º rigo incomincia un altro pezzo (a 2?) con testo italiano: 5º rigo: « innamora »; 7º rigo: « [T]enor, prima, s[e]c[un]da pars »
B*r*	—	—	—
B*v*	—	—	frammenti al 1º rigo: « di bel », indicano un testo italiano
1*r*	—	—	—
1*v*	—	—	—
2*r*	M Jo	—	—
2*v*	I[dem] f [Landini]	—	—
3*r*	M [Jo de Ca]scia	—	—
3*v*	M Jo	—	—
4*r*	—	—	—
4*v*	—	—	—
5*r*	—	—	—
5*v*	—	—	—
6*r*	—	—	—
6*v*	—	—	—
7*r*	—	—	—
7*v*	—	—	—
8*r*	[frater bartolinus]	[La] douce cere	le parti del tenor (col testo intero) e contratenor
8*v*	[frater bartolinus]	[L]a fiera testa	la sola parte del cantus
9*r*	—	—	—

Foglio		Incipit	Commenti
9v	—	—	—
10r	—	—	—
10v	—	—	—
11r	—	—	qualche nota di una parte superiore visibile; notazione italiana
11v	[Mr Jacobus de Bononia]	[U]selletto selvagio	cantus completo del madrigale a 2
12r	[Mr Jacobus de Bononia]	u[sel]letto selvagio	tenor completo del madrigale a 2; al 5º, 6º, 7º rigo, una parte di un altro pezzo
12v	—	—	—
13r	M Jac[obus de Bononia]	—	—
13v	—	—	da qualche parola, « servi ... stringer la », il testo risulta italiano
14r	—	—	—
14v	—	—	—
15r	—	—	—
15v	[Mr Jacobus de Bononia]	[Uselletto selvaggio]	da quanto risulta dal testo (1º rigo: « per stagion »; 3º rigo: « si fa bel canto »), è una delle parti superiori della caccia a 3
16r	—	—	—
16v	—	—	—
17r	M [Jo de] Cascia	—	—
17v	[M Jo de Cascia]	[La] bella stella	cantus completo
18r	[M Jo de Cascia]	[La] bella stella	tenor completo
18v	Mr J[o de Cascia]	—	—
19r	Mr J[o de Cascia]	—	—
19v	Mr Jo de Cascia	[Na]sco[so 'l viso]	qualche parola visibile
20r	M Jo de Cascia	[N]a[s]coso 'l viso	qualche parola visibile
20v	—	—	—
21r	[Don Donatus]	Io fu' già bianco uccel	tenor completo
21v	[Don Donatus]	[D]a[l] cielo scese per iscala	qualche parola visibile
22r	Do[n] Donatus	—	—
22v	Mr Joh[ann]es organista florentin[us]	—	poche note e parole visibili
23r	—	—	4º rigo: « allor la grata »; numerale romano LXXVII?

II

24

Foglio		Incipit	Commenti
23v	Mr Jo org[anista]	—	—
24r	M^r [J]o	—	2º rigo: « per »; numerale romano LXXVIII?
24v	M^r Jo	[N]o[n] me servia signor?	un'altra parte comincia al 7º rigo con le stesse parole
25r	—	—	—
25v	M Jo organista	—	—
26r	—	—	—
26v	M Jo organ[ista]	—	1º rigo: « da llei vaga fioretta li fa più di »
27r	M^r [Jo] organ[ista]	—	due parti, come risulta dalle stesse parole, « sia gli », al 4º rigo e al 7º; numerale romano LXXV?
27v	M^r [J]o organista	—	—
28r	M^r [J]o organ[ista]	—	numerale romano LXIX
28v	M^r Jo organ[ista]	—	—
29r	M^r Jo organista	—	numerale romano LXXXVIII
29v	M^r Jo organista	—	—
30r	—	—	—
30v	—	—	—
31r	—	—	—
31v	f[rater bartolinus]	[Le aurate chiome?]	la sola parte del cantus?
32r	—	—	—
32v	—	—	—
33r	f[rater] b[artolinus]	—	—
33v	f[rater] b[artolinus]	[Se] premio di virtù	cantus completo
34r	[frater bartolinus]	[Se premio di virtù]	tenor completo
34v	—	—	—
35r	f[rater] b[artolinus]	—	—
35v	—	—	—
36r	f[rater] b[artolinus]	—	—
36v	f[rater] b[artolinus]	—	—
37r	f[rater] b[artolinus]	—	—
37v	f[rater] b[artolinus]	[Donna liçadra?]	due parti; l'incipit di quella superiore suggerisce questo madrigale
38r	f[rater] b[artolinus]	—	—
38v	f[rater] b[artolinus]	—	—
39r	—	—	—
39v	[frater bartolinus]	[Q]uando la terra	visibile qualche nota e parola delle due parti
40r	—	—	—
40v	—	—	—
41r	Idem f [Landini]	—	5º rigo: « volge gli ochi »?

UNA NUOVA FONTE DELL' « ARS NOVA »

Foglio		Incipit	Commenti
41v	Idem f [Landini]	—	—
42r	Mr Jacobus [de Bononia]	—	—
42v	M	—	—
43r	M	—	—
43v	—	—	—
44r	Mr Jacobus [de Bononia]	—	—
44v	[Mr Jacobus de Bononia]	[I]o [me] son un	qualche parola visibile
45r	Mr Jacob[us de Bononia]	—	—
45v	Mr Jacobus	[S]otto [l'imper]io	visibile qualche nota e parola del cantus
46r	Mr Jacobus	[S]otto l'imperio	una, forse due, delle parti inferiori
46v	Mr Jacobus	—	—
47r	Mr Jacobus	[O in Italia felice Liguria]	visibile l'incipit del cantus; al 5° rigo si legge l'incipit: « o in Italia » del tenor
47v	Mr Jacob[us de Bononia]	—	—
48r	Mr Jacobus	—	—
48v	Mr Jacobus	[Aquil' al]tera	visibile qualche nota e parola del cantus
49r	[M^r] Jacobus	[C]reatura gentil [U]ccel de dio	visibile qualche nota e parola del contratenor; il tenor incomincia al 5° rigo
49v	—	—	—
50r	[I]dem f[?]	—	7° rigo: « Aperto, Clo »
50v	—	—	—
51r	—	—	—
51v	D[?]	—	—
52r	[Don donatus]	[Un cane, un'oca] e una vecchia [pazza]	frammenti di testo al 1° e 2° rigo
52v	Do[n] donat[us]	[Un bel girfalco]	frammenti di testo al 1°, 3°, 5° rigo indicano il cantus completo
53r	[Don donatus]	[Un bel girfalco]	visibili le prime note del tenor e qualche parola
53v	Do[n] donat[us]	—	—
54r	Do[n] donat[us]	—	—
54v	Do[n] donatus	[Lucida pecorella]	frammenti di testo al 1° e 3° rigo
55r	[Don donatus]	[Lucida pecorella]	visibile le prime note del tenor e qualche parola

II

Foglio		Incipit	Commenti
55v	Do[n] donat[us]	—	—
56r	D[on donatus]	—	—
56v	D[on donatus]	—	—
57r	Do[n donatus]	—	—
57v	Do[n] donat[us]	—	—
58r	Do[n] donat[us]	[Faccia chi de' se 'l po]	le poche parole visibili suggeriscono questa caccia
58v	Do[n] donat[us]	[S'i'] monacordo gentil	buona parte del testo visibile
59r	D[on donatus]	—	—
59v	Do[n] donatus	[Io] fu' già usignolo	cantus completo
60r	A[bbas paulus]	—	—
60v	Abbas paulus	—	—
61r	[Jacobus de Bononia]	[Di]ligite iustitiam	la sola parte del contratenor
61v	—	—	l'incipit musicale visibile
62r	Hubert[us] de Salinis	—	l'incipit musicale visibile
62v	—	[F]los ortum inter lilia	triplum incompleto: mancano 4 versi, come risulta dalla fine del 7º rigo: « miraculorum bravia »
63r	Vg[olinvs]	—	numerale romano CLXXIII?
63v	Vg[olinvs]	—	testo italiano, rigo 2: « tu ascolti »
64r	Vgo[linvs]	—	—
64v	Vgo[linvs]	—	rigo 2: « pellegrina gentil »; rigo 3: « fra l'altre »; rigo 5: « guardai dentro la perfida »
65r	Vgolinus	—	—
65v	Vgolinus	—	testo francese? rigo 1: « adieu »; rigo 2: « plus a »
66r	V[golinvs]	—	—
66v	—	—	—
67r	Vgolinvs	—	notazione bianca e nera; testo francese? al 2º rigo: « est elle paradys »; al 3º « visage »; al 7º: « Sda pars »
67v	—	—	—
68r	J?	—	notazione bianca
68v	—	—	—
69r	—	Parce pater pietatis	notazione nera; 10 righi; una parte finisce al 9º rigo

Foglio		Incipit	Commenti
69v	—	—	notazione nera; 10 righi; una parte finisce al 6º rigo
70r	—	—	notazione nera; 10 righi
70v	—	[R]ex Karole, Iohannis genite	triplum incompleto; mancano 6 versi, come risulta dalla fine del 10º rigo: « principatui »
71r	—	—	
71v	Vgolinvs de Vrbe[veteri]	—	notazione nera; testo italiano: al 3º rigo: « O li giorni »
72r	Hubert[us] de Salinis	—	notazione nera, ma qualche nota bianca al 7º rigo; testo latino come risulta dal 2º rigo: « cui pius appareas ... pietatis opera »; numerale romano CLXXX?
72v	—	—	—
73r	Vgolinus	—	notazione nera; testo italiano? rigo 2: « ogne »
73v	[Vgo]linvs	—	notazione bianca?
74r	—	—	visibile l'incipit della parte superiore
74v	—	—	notazione nera
75r	M [petrus] ioh[ann]is	—	testo italiano, come risulta dai versi alla fine: « da tua »
75v	Mr pet[rus] ioh[ann]is organista	—	notazione nera
76r	Mr [petrus] iohannis [o]rga[nista]	—	notazione nera
76v	M pet[rus] ioh[ann]is	—	notazione nera
77r	—	—	—
77v	—	—	—
78r	—	—	notazione bianca, in parte mista
78v	—	—	visibile l'incipit, notazione bianca, in parte mista
79r	—	—	testo latino; 2º rigo: « plene largiatur »; 5º rigo: « laudatur pontificem »; 9 righi
79v	[Philippus de Vitriaco]	Impudenter circumivi	triplum incompleto; 9 righi

II

28

Foglio		Incipit	Commenti
80r	—	—	3 righi con note; al 1º, « Contratenor »; al 2º: « Scda pars »; alla fine del 3º altri versi che indicano un testo francese: « Se non pour quant? ... en que je »
80v	originariamente bianco		
81r	—	—	—
81v	[?] [or]ganista	Chi chi non può quel che vuol	visibili poche note e parole
82r	—	—	al 6º rigo: « Contratenor, Prima [pars] »; al 7º rigo: « Scda pars »
82v	—	—	sembra una caccia; al 3º rigo: « forte te te te »; al 5º: « compagno d'amore sete ... che non scapi »; al 6º: « O Chaleffo vellane vellane pigliala pigliala vellane »; al 7º: « quel che »
83r	—	—	visibile l'incipit di una parte ai primi tre righi; ai righi 4-7, un'altra parte; al 5º rigo: « Prima pars, Scda pars »
83v	[Ser gherardellus]	Tosto che l'alba	cantus incompleto, mancano gli ultimi brani
84r	M pet[rus] ioh[ann]is	—	
84v	M [petrus iohannis] organ[ista]	Lasso dolente	forse la parte superiore di un pezzo a 2; vedi fol. 93r
85r	M g? organista	—	l'incipit visibile; al 7º rigo: « poco venir ... gratiosa amore »
85v	M g organista	—	
86r	M pet[rus] ioh[ann]is	[D]onna non fu già mai	parte inferiore di un pezzo a 2; vedi fol. 96v
86v	M pet[rus] ioh[ann]is	—	testo italiano; rigo 5: « questa bella »
87r	—	—	—
87v	—	—	notazione nera
88r	—	—	notazione nera
88v	—	—	—
89r	Idem f [Landini]	—	—
89v	Idem f [Landini]	[Nè 'n ciascun mie pensiero]	frammenti di testo visibili ai primi 5 righi

UNA NUOVA FONTE DELL' « ARS NOVA »

Foglio		Incipit	Commenti
90r	—	—	notazione nera; numerale romano CXXXXI
90v	—	—	testo francese; al 3° rigo: « par bel plusieurs »; al 5° rigo: « Tenor »; al 6° rigo: « Secunda ps, vert, clous »
91r	originariamente bianco		
91v	M pet[rus] ioh[ann]is organista	A Febo Damne	due parti di un pezzo a 3
92r	M pet[rus] ioh[ann]is organista	A Febo Damne	l'altra parte di un pezzo a 3
92v	M pet[rus] ioh[ann]is [or]ganista	—	testo italiano; al 2° rigo: « che mi fu »
93r	M pet[rus] ioh[ann]is	Lasso dolente	forse la parte inferiore di un pezzo a 2; vedi fol. 84v
93v	M pet[rus iohannis] organista	Donna s'io ò errato	parte superiore di un pezzo a 2; vedi fol. 96r
94r	—	—	l'incipit visibile; note su 5 righi; al 1°: « così comincia la nostra chaccia »; al 5°: « così finì la nostra caccia »; numerale romano CLII
94v	[Vincentius de Arimino]	[Nel]l'acqua chiara	cantus incompleto; manca l'ultimo terzo
95r	—	Qui fault voyr?	notazione nera; al 5° rigo incomincia un altro pezzo: « Amor »; al 7° rigo: « Tenor »; numerale romano CLVIIII
95v	—	Quando [si] può si de' sempre fuggire	al 2° rigo: « Scda pars »; al 4° rigo: « Tenor Quando si può »
96r	[M petrus iohannis]	Donna s'io ò errato	parte inferiore di un pezzo a 2; vedi fol. 93v numerale romano CLXVI
96v	M pet[rus] ioh[ann]is	[Donna non fu già mai	parte superiore di un pezzo a 2; vedi fol. 86r
97r	M pet[rus] ioh[ann]is	—	testo italiano; al 1° rigo: « perch'io »; al 2° rigo: « per l'amor »; numerale romano CLXVIII
97v	M pet[rus] ioh[ann]is organista	A Febo Damne	una parte di un pezzo a 2

II

30

Foglio		Incipit	Commenti
98r	M pet[rus] ioh[ann]is organista	A Febo Damne	l'altra parte di un pezzo a 2; numerale romano CLXX
98v	—	—	notazione nera
99r	—	—	notazione nera; al 1° rigo: « Contratenor, prima pars »; al 2° rigo: « Scda pars »; al 4° rigo incomincia un altro pezzo a 3; al 5° rigo: « Tenor, Contra- »; al 6° rigo: « tenor, prima pars, scda pars »
99v	—	—	notazione nera; a 3; al 4° rigo: « Tenor »; al 5° rigo: « Contratenor »
100r	[Idem f Landini]	[Vita non] è più misera	cantus e tenor completi; numerale romano CII
100v	[Idem f Landini]	[S'andray sança merçe]	cantus e tenor completi
101r	[Paulus abbas]	[Corse per l'onde]	tenor completo; al 6° rigo incomincia un altro pezzo; numerale romano CXXVII
101v	P[aulus] abbas	Girand'un bel falcon	cantus completo
102r	P[aulus] abbas	Girand'un bel falcon	tenor completo; al 5° rigo: « C'estoit mon »; al 7° rigo: « Tenor, prima pars, Scda, v[er]te, Clo »; numerale romano CXXXIIII?
102v	P[aulus] abbas	—	le parole visibili dimostrano che appartiene insieme al fol. 104r.
103r	Idem f [Landini]	[V]a pure amore	cantus e tenor completi
103v	Idem f [Landini]	[Se pronto non sarà]	cantus e tenor completi
104r	P[aulus] abbas	—	le parole visibili dimostrano che appartiene insieme al fol. 102v
104v	Abbas paulus	Astio non morì mai	cantus e tenor completi
105r	P[aulus] abbas	[O]r sie che può	cantus e tenor completi; numerale romano CXXVI
105v	Abbas paul[us]	[Poc'anno di mirar]	cantus e tenor completi
106r	Idem f [Landini]	[P]o' che partir convien	cantus e contratenor completi della ballata a 3

Foglio		Incipit	Commenti
106v	Idem f [Landini]	[G]li ochi che in prima	cantus e tenor completi
107r	Abbas paulus	[Amor de' dimmi]	cantus e tenor completi della ballata a 3; al 6º e 7º rigo, la continuazione, forse, di un altro pezzo a 2; numerale romano CXXVII
107v	Abbas paulus	Amor mi stringe assai	cantus, tenor e contratenore completi
108r	[Abba]s pa[ulus]	[Sie] mille volte benedetta	cantus e tenor completi; al 6º e 7º rigo, due parti di un altro pezzo
108v	Abba[s] pau[lus]	[Una cosa di veder]	cantus, tenor e contratenor completi
109r	—	—	notazione nera; testo italiano: al 2º rigo « mercede »; al 4º rigo: « da tal donna »
109v	Idem f [Landini]	[S']i' ti so' stato	cantus e tenor completi

III

MUSIC AND MUSICIANS AT SANTA MARIA DEL FIORE IN THE EARLY QUATTROCENTO*

In 1375 work on the new cathedral of Florence had progressed sufficiently to allow demolition of the walls of the ancient church of Santa Reparata around which the newer structure was rising.[1] At that time the celebration of religious services in the new cathedral was also made possible by the erection of provisory altars in the already finished sections of the nave. Thereafter, though major construction was not to be completed for well over half a century, celebration of the Mass and the Divine Offices continued without interruption in Santa Maria del Fiore, as the new cathedral came to be called, and the church quickly assumed its position as a focal point of both civic ceremony and popular devotion in the city's life.[2]

Surviving documents in the cathedral's archives are strangely silent not only about the place of music in worship at Santa Maria del Fiore during the latter half of the fourteenth century, but also about the musicians who must have assisted in the services there.[3] It is possible, of course, that this information appears in volumes that are either now lost or preserved elsewhere and have yet to be examined. Nevertheless, miscellaneous documents, such as one from 1357 recording the inauguration of new construction work « with a great exultation of songs and of the sound of the bells, the organ and trumpets » and another from 1387 reporting the decision to have a new pair of organs built, indicate that music other than the chant was being performed during that period.[4]

---

* Abbreviations:
ASF   Archivio di Stato, Florence
SMDF Archivio dell'Opera di Santa Maria del Fiore, Florence
Delib.   Deliberazioni
QC   Quaderno Cassa
Stanz. Stanziamenti

The Florentine new year began on March 25, and as a result documents recorded before that day usually carry the date of the preceding year. In the course of the text such dates have been changed to conform to our modern system.

1. C. GUASTI, *Santa Maria del Fiore, la costruzione della chiesa e del campanile*, Florence 1887, p. CIII; doc. 237, p. 226.
2. The official decree changing the church's name is printed *ibid.*, doc. 465, p. 311.
3. Other sources, for example, show that the composer ser Gherardello was employed at the cathedral as a chaplain around the middle of the century. See my *Le compagnie dei laudesi in Firenze durante l'Ars Nova*, in *L'Ars Nova italiana del Trecento*, III, Certaldo 1970, p. 280.
4. The first document is printed by C. GUASTI, op. cit., pp. 97-8; the second, by

III

Fortunately, documents concerning musicians at Santa Maria del Fiore in the early decades of the fifteenth century are somewhat more plentiful, for several volumes containing a few records of their appointments, salary-appropriations and housing arrangements are still preserved in the cathedral's archives. Though these documents by no means furnish a complete or continuous account of the musicians' activities, they do give some idea of musical practices at the cathedral in those years. My object in the following pages, therefore, is twofold: to present, insofar as is possible, a chronological report of the musicians who were associated with Santa Maria del Fiore, as well as to set down whatever information, implicit in the documents, is relative to the music performed there during the early decades of the Quattrocento.

Throughout the fifteenth century, as in subsequent centuries, the plainchant choir at Santa Maria del Fiore was comprised of canons, chaplains and clerk-choristers. The two principal positions in the choir were those of the proposto and the corista. The propositura was one of the five ancient «Dignities» of the Florentine Cathedral Chapter, and was held by a canon, who was responsible for selecting the chant sung at various services.[1] The proposto's position is recorded as early as 1050, when certain legal documents were signed by the priest Rozo, cantorum prepositus.[2] Later, when management of the cathedral's Opera was entrusted to the Arte della Lana, authority for making appointments to the position became the privilege of the consuls of that guild, or of their surrogates, the overseers of the Opera.[3] The corista was also appointed by the consuls or the overseers. He was usually a chaplain who, in addition to his singing duties, was charged with directing and keeping order in the choir. Sometime during the early decades of the fifteenth century his duties were expanded to include those of the appuntatore, who noted down misconduct, tardiness and absences from the required services.[4] The corista was not empowered to excuse absences or grant leaves, but his disciplinary authority in the choir during services was unquestionable. He was also responsible for distributing the monthly stipends to chaplains who sang at the various services.[5]

G. Poggi, in *Il Duomo di Firenze, documenti sulla decorazione della chiesa e del campanile*, Berlin 1909, doc. 1321, p. 263.

1. F. Del Migliore, *Firenze città nobilissima illustrata*, Florence 1684, p. 52.
2. See R. Piattoli (ed.), *Le carte della canonica della cattedrale di Firenze*, Rome 1938, p. 102.
3. F. Del Migliore, op. cit., p. 53.
4. See Docs. 44, 45 in the Appendix to this study.
5. See Docs. 46 and 49 in the Appendix. The second document, though dating from

The number of canons and chaplains in Santa Maria del Fiore's plainchant choir varied throughout the fifteenth century. Extant lists from 1429 and 1439 name eleven canons,[1] a figure more or less corroborated by Ferdinando Del Migliore who, writing in 1684, states that «anticamente» there were twelve of them.[2] Del Migliore also reports that the number of canons was increased several times after the first quarter of the fifteenth century and that funds for support of the new positions were furnished largely by the Arte della Lana.[3] Del Migliore's information is confirmed by Salvino Salvini who reports that twenty-four canons were associated with the cathedral between 1445-1455 and that there were twenty-two of them during the period 1467-1480.[4] A similar fluctuation is evident in the number of chaplains. A document from 1407 states that there were twenty of them, but a list from 1429 names only fourteen.[5] Another list from 1439 names ten, while documents from 1450 and 1459 give nineteen.[6] In the following decades the number of chaplains was steadily increased so that in 1475 there were twenty-eight and in 1481, thirty-three.[7] No records seem to have survived indicating the number of clerk-choristers at the cathedral before 1436. With the establishment of the Scuola Eugeniana in that year, their number was fixed at thirty-three.[8] Whether all of them actually sang in the choir is open to question, but it seems likely that they did, since the master of the school was required to be present at all services.

The prebend received by each canon apparently included remuneration for his participation in the choir. There are no records which show that the clerk-choristers were paid for their assistance. The chaplains, on the other hand, received, in addition to their regular benefices, a monthly stipend

---

a later period, is interesting because it combines both titles, corista-appuntatore, in one and the same payment.

1. The first list is given in the Appendix, Doc. 27. The second is found in SMDF, QC, VIII. 1. 4, fols. 36v, 72v, 78v-79r.
2. F. DEL MIGLIORE, op. cit., p. 50.
3. Loc. cit.
4. S. SALVINI, *Catalogo cronologico de' canonici della chiesa metropolitana fiorentina compilato l'anno 1751*, Florence 1782, pp. 43-56.
5. See Docs. 1 and 27 in the Appendix.
6. These lists are found in SMDF, *Stanz.*, II. 2. 14, fols. 72r-72v; QC, VIII. 1. 15, fols. 11r, 21r, 28r, 29r, 32r, 33r, 57r, 58r, 59r, 63r; QC, VIII. 1. 29, fols. 50r, 51r, 52r, 54r, 55r, 85r.
7. SMDF, QC, VIII. 1. 61, fols. 4r, 9r, 15r, 20r, 21r, 26r, 29r, 31r, 36r, 37r, 41v; QC, VIII. 1. 69, fols. 27r, 38r, 40r, 43r, 54r, 70r, 72r, 84r, 89r, 91v.
8. The Papal Bull which established the school is published by A. SEAY, *The 15th-Century Cappella at Santa Maria del Fiore in Florence*, in «Journal of the American Musicological Society», XI (1958), pp. 46-9.

known as the distribuzione for singing at the various services.[1] Surviving documents make it clear that the cathedral's chaplains were admitted to the plain-chant choir, and consequently made eligible to receive the distribuzione, only upon recommendation of the consuls of the Arte della Lana or of the overseers, who had first consulted with the archbishop of Florence or with the Cathedral Chapter.[2]

As is apparent from the above discussion, records regarding the plainchant choir are by no means abundant for the early decades of the fifteenth century. Exact figures from 1429 and 1439, however, show that there were twenty-five and twenty-two adults respectively who participated at services in those years. Though their numbers were to increase greatly later in the century, it is clear that even at this earlier time the cathedral choir was respectably staffed and able to fulfill its functions effectively.

It appears to have been the practice at Santa Maria del Fiore in the early Quattrocento to have two cantores among the chaplains who sang in the plain-chant choir. This practice is, in fact, recorded in the first extant document regarding musicians, a deliberation of the overseers dating from 20 June 1407 (Doc. 1). On that day it was decided that «the two cantores, namely presbiter Paulus de Aquila and presbiter Lucas de Urbeveteri [Orvieto], newly elected by the canons and Chapter of the said church», were to have a salary of thirty-five gold florins per annum, with the understanding that «the two said chaplains, together with the other eighteen, will bring the number [of chaplains] to twenty». The overseers also decided that were the number of chaplains to be diminished in any way, then half of the benefice accruing from the vacant chapel would be assigned to the canons and Chapter «as a subsidy and salary for the said cantores and their successors, of which number of twenty chaplains there are always two cantores».

Subsequent documents show that Paulus of Aquila and Lucas of Orvieto were associated with the cathedral for several months after the date of this deliberation, and that they were paid jointly in quarterly installments for three-month periods of service which began on the twentieth day of every fourth month[3] (Docs. 2, 3). Two records of appropriation for the trimester

1. See Doc. 46 in the Appendix.
2. SMDF, *Delib.*, II. 2. 5, fol. 53v.
3. Knowledge that these cantores were paid for three-month periods makes it possible to ascertain that the record of an earlier appropriation, which would have included the month of June 1407, is now lost. And since the document of 20 June 1407 states that they were «newly elected», it is probable that they began serving a month before that time.

26 March - 25 June 1408 indicate, however, that some new arrangement was later made with these musicians (Docs. 4, 5). In the first of these Lucas of Orvieto is described as «one of the cantores», but a sum equivalent to his salary only is mentioned. In the second the usual three-months' salary for two musicians is appropriated in his name alone. It is clear, therefore, that some one else was serving with him at the time, even though Paulus of Aquila is not mentioned. Equally clear is the fact that the date on which the previous quarterly installments began has been changed: payments now begin on the twenty-sixth day of every fourth month, thereby creating a gap between this newly established date (26 March) and the last day included under the previous appropriation (19 February) for which no record of payment exists.

The absence of any appropriations for Lucas of Orvieto and his associate in those five weeks can perhaps be explained by the appearance during that time of two other musicians, whose presence at the cathedral is first mentioned in a deliberation of 13 March 1408 (Doc. 6). On that day the overseers assigned living quarters in the upper floor of a house owned by the Opera to «dopnus Paulus and ser Marchus, priests and cantores in the said church of Santa Reparata». These accomodations were changed the very next day, when it is reported that the overseers decided that «dopnus Paulus monachus and ser Marchus presbiter, cantores of the said church of Santa Reparata», were to live instead on the ground floor of the same house (Doc. 7).

Although it would seem that dopnus Paulus and ser Marchus had been engaged to remain for some time, there are no salary-appropriations recorded in their names in any of the surviving account books. Thus we can only speculate about the terms of their appointment and the length of their service. It may be that they were hired because of some temporary difficulty with the other musicians and that they were later discharged when the problem was resolved. It may also be that their appointment was originally intended to last only for a short while, or that they themselves were forced to leave because of other commitments. Whatever the circumstances, it is impossible to know precisely what happened, since they are not mentioned again in the Opera's volumes.

Another intriguing question remains to be considered with regard to the musician called dopnus Paulus monachus. Is it possible that he is the same person as the composer don Paolo tenorista da Firenze, whose name is given as «Magister Dominus Paulus Abbas de Florentia» in the Squarcialupi Codex? I believe that such an identification is possible because the sudden appearance at – and perhaps equally sudden departure from – the Florentine cathedral of dopnus Paulus monachus fits in well with the information currently available about this seemingly peripatetic composer.

Several years ago Nino Pirrotta discovered a document which disclosed that a «Dominus Paulus de Florentia abbas Pozzoli Aretine diocesis» was in Rome in 1404, perhaps in the entourage of the Florentine bishop Angelo Acciaiuolo.[1] Pirrotta identified this abbot with the composer and conjectured that Paolo was a Camaldolite monk who held an abbacy *in commendam.* Later Pirrotta also suggested that Paolo was a member of the Capponi family and that he may have been in Lucca in 1407-1408 and at the Council of Pisa in 1409.[2] Bianca Becherini subsequently adduced evidence to suggest that Paolo was a member of the Florentine family of the Leoni.[3] In a recent study Ursula Günther agreed with Becherini's findings and showed that Paolo's madrigal, *Godi, Firenze*, celebrating the definitive acquisition of Pisa by the Florentines must have been written sometime after 9 October 1406, though not necessarily in Florence.[4] More recently, however, Kurt von Fischer has not only presented evidence to support Pirrotta's hypotheses about Paolo's family and Camaldolite connections, but also new documents which show that a «don Paolo da Firençe», who was evidently a musician as well as an abbot, died in Arezzo in 1419.[5]

The conflicting opinions about Paolo's family notwithstanding, knowledge that a singer named dopnus Paulus monachus was in Florence for a brief period during June 1408 does not raise any contradictions with what is currently known or conjectured about the composer's whereabouts during the first decade of the fifteenth century. It is, of course, quite possible that there were other musicians called Paolo, also monks, who were associated with Florence in one way or another during the same period. But the coincidence of names and dates is striking, and I am inclined to think that until evidence can be summoned to the contrary there is every reason to believe that the cathedral singer dopnus Paulus monachus is the same person as the composer of *Godi, Firenze.*

1. N. PIRROTTA, *Paolo tenorista, fiorentino «extra moenia»*, in *Estudios dedicados a Menendez Pidal*, III, Madrid 1952, p. 580.
2. N. PIRROTTA, *Paolo Tenorista in a New Fragment of the Italian Ars Nova*, Palm Springs 1961, p. 25.
3. B. BECHERINI, *Antonio Squarcialupi e il codice Mediceo Palatino 87*, in *L'Ars Nova italiana del Trecento*, I, Certaldo 1962, pp. 161-5.
4. U. GÜNTHER, *Zur Datierung des Madrigals «Godi, Firenze» und der Handschrift Paris, B. N. fonds it. 568 (pit)*, in «Archiv für Musikwissenschaft», XXIV (1967), pp. 103-5.
5. K. VON FISCHER, *Paolo da Firenze und der Squarcialupi-Kodex*, in «Quadrivium», IX (1967), pp. 5-19.

MUSIC AND MUSICIANS AT SANTA MARIA DEL FIORE 105

Ser Lucas of Orvieto is the only musician mentioned in salary-appropriations for the period ending June 1408, so it is not clear whether two *cantores* continued to be employed at the cathedral up to that time. And since he is not mentioned in any records after June 1410 (Docs. 8-13), it is impossible to know whether he was still in the church's service on 10 December of the same year when the overseers appointed «ser Curradus ser Gualandi de Bracciolinis de Pistorio [Pistoia] as a *cantore*» for the period of one year at a salary of seventeen and a half gold florins per annum (Doc. 14).

The musician in question is doubtless to be identified with the composer «fr. Corradus de pistoria, ordinis heremitarum», two of whose works have been preserved in the Modena manuscript *Estense Lat. 568*.[1] On the basis of musical style and the text of one of these works, Pirrotta conjectured that Curradus was active as a composer during the second decade of the fifteenth century and was probably connected with the musicians employed by one of the contending popes during the great schism, sometime before 1417.[2] As far as I can ascertain, however, the Florentine record of appointment furnishes us with the first concrete documentary evidence regarding the activities of this otherwise obscure musician.

As in the case of ser Lucas of Orvieto, salary-appropriations for ser Curradus of Pistoia are lacking, and there is no way of knowing how long his association with the cathedral continued. Likewise, no documents recording either appointments or appropriations of salaries for other musicians have survived from the years immediately following ser Curradus's appointment. Thus it is impossible to determine how many *cantores* were at the cathedral in those years – there may have been two, there may have been only one, or perhaps even none at all. This final possibility seems more than reasonable in view of the fact that three singers, whose names unfortunately are not given in the accounts, were especially brought in to perform at services on 25 March 1414, the feast of the Annunciation of the Blessed Virgin Mary (Doc. 15).

The next surviving record of appointment shows that on 25 January 1417 the overseers engaged the *cantore* Pasquale to assist «at the celebration of the Divine Offices in the church of Santa Maria del Fiore for the period of one year, beginning today» (Doc. 16). The lack of a title, such as ser or presbiter, before this musician's name may indicate that he was not an

1. I am grateful to Ursula Günther for help in identifying this musician. For an inventory of the contents of the Modena manuscript see N. Pirrotta, *Il codice Estense Lat. 568 e la musica francese in Italia al principio del '400*, in «Atti della Reale Accademia di Scienze Lettere e Arti di Palermo», Serie II, vol. V; offprint (Palermo 1946).

2. *Ibid.*, pp. 42-3.

ecclesiastic, and it was probably for this reason that his salary, which was fixed at three florins per month, was to be twice as much as that previously given other musicians. But apparently Pasquale did not consider even this amount sufficient: appended to the record of his appointment is a «note that he did not accept and did not serve and nothing can be paid him».

The cathedral was undoubtedly without cantores at the time of this rejected appointment, for only a few weeks later, on 17 February 1417, the overseers «elected the two priests ... dominus Ugolinus Francisci de Urbeveteri [Orvieto] and ser Jacobus Masii de Frullivio [Forlì] as cantores» for the period of one year, at a salary of two gold florins each per month (Doc. 17). The document is of some significance because it not only shows that the overseers were attempting to maintain the practice of having two cantores, but also reveals that one of the newly engaged musicians was the theorist-composer Ugolino of Orvieto. Prior to this time Ugolino was a canon at the cathedral of Forlì, where he was to return in the 1420's after apparently having attended the Council of Constance.[1] Knowledge of his presence in Florence, as well as of his activities as a performing musician, is thus a welcome addition to the scanty biographical information regarding this period in his life.

That Ugolino and his associate were dissatisfied with the salaries originally offered them is apparent from a note appended to the record of their appointment two days later. There it is stated that each musician was to receive an additional half gold florin per month. A deliberation from the same day, 19 February 1417, confirms this increase in salary (Doc. 18). Whether Ugolino and Jacobus of Forlì actually fulfilled more than the first four months of their contract, however, is difficult to assess (Docs. 19-22). Salary-appropriations for them are no longer recorded after 22 June 1417, even though the series of volumes in which these accounts were entered continues without interruption for several years.

There is another gap in the records of appointment and salary-appropriations from this time until 1437. Some information about the cantores employed during this twenty-year period, however, is found among the overseers' deliberations regarding housing accomodations for the various chaplains who were associated with the cathedral. From one such record, dated 7 February 1420, we learn that the overseers granted living quarters in a house owned by the Opera to ser Niccolaus Zaccherie, «a cantore and chaplain of the church of Santa Maria del Fiore» (Doc. 23).

---

1. The most recent summary of Ugolino's life and works is that of A. SEAY, in *Die Musik in Geschichte und Gegenwart*, 13, cols. 1022-3.

As with Curradus of Pistoia and Ugolino of Orvieto, it is possible once again to identify one of the cantores as a composer as well. Although no documents have come down to us indicating when Niccolaus Zaccherie first joined the cathedral's establishment, others reveal that he did not remain there long after the date of the deliberation just mentioned. The records of the Papal chapel, then resident in Florence, show that he was engaged as a singer to Pope Martin V on 1 June of the same year.[1] Consequently, he must have left Florence in the Pope's train the following September. Niccolaus Zaccherie was associated with the Papal chapel until the end of June 1424. After a ten-year absence he rejoined the group for the period April-November 1434.[2] His whereabouts during the previous decade, however, are as yet unknown. Could it be that he returned to Florence in those years? A list of the cathedral's chaplains, dating from 2 December 1429, does, in fact, mention a ser Niccola, tenorista, but since the singer's full name is not given, it is impossible to make a positive identification (Doc. 27).

The presence at Santa Maria del Fiore of another cantore, ser Jacobus of Arezzo, is indicated in a document of 19 May 1424, which states that «fifteen soldi» were spent for «repairs to the wardrobe and the sink of the house» in which he was living (Doc. 24). This musician was in the cathedral's employ for several years. Another document, dated 31 August 1428, shows that on that day the overseers granted new living quarters to «ser Jacobus de Aretio, a cantore and chaplain of the Major Florentine Church» on condition that their provision «be approved by the consuls of the Arte della Lana, otherwise the said concession will be null and void» (Doc. 25).

The practice of having two cantores among the cathedral's chaplains was apparently upheld during the years of ser Jacobus of Arezzo's service. A deliberation from 30 October 1427 records housing arrangements made on behalf of a certain ser Bartholomeus, cantore (Doc. 26). Although this musician is not mentioned again in the surviving documents, ser Jacobus's name does appear in the previously mentioned list of chaplains of 2 December 1429 (Doc. 27). He may have relinquished his duties as a cantore by that time, however, for the two musicians named in the document are ser Johannes, cantore and ser Niccola, tenorista.

Only a few other documents have survived which record the presence

1. F. X. HABERL, *Wilhelm du Fay. Monographische Studie über dessen Leben und Werke*, in «Vierteljahrsschrift für Musikwissenschaft», 1 (1885), p. 453. According to the documents published by Haberl, Niccolaus Zaccherie was from Brindisi.

2. *Ibid.*, pp. 454, 463. Further information about this musician is given by G. REANEY, in *Die Musik in Geschichte und Gegenwart*, 14, cols. 960-3.

of cantores at the cathedral in the following years. One of these shows that ser Johannes Herrigi of Rieti was appointed as «a cantore and chaplain of the Major Florentine Church» on 22 May 1437 (Doc. 28). A salary-appropriation for this musician from the same year (without indication of day or month) reveals that his wages were fixed at five florins per month, an exceptionally high amount in view of what had previously been paid a musician as well known as Ugolino of Orvieto (Doc. 29). Perhaps ser Johannes Herrigi was a virtuoso singer or maybe the overseers had come to realize that it was impossible to retain outstanding musicians unless higher salaries were offered. Whatever the case, subsequent documents indicate that this musician was employed at the cathedral until the end of December 1437 (Docs. 30-34).

At least two other cantores are mentioned in documents dating from the time of ser Johannes Herrigi's tenure. The duties of one of them, however, seem to have changed after the first few weeks of his employment. The first document concerning the musician in question, ser Johannes Aldobrandini of Perugia, names him «a chaplain and cantore of the Florentine cathedral», and records a payment of ten florins made to him at the time of his appointment on 24 July 1437 (Doc. 35). All subsequent salary-appropriations, however, merely refer to him as a chaplain, and even the record of his reappointment, dated 13 February 1438, gives no indication that singing was to form a part of his duties (Docs. 36, 37). Thus we may suppose that his services as a cantore were of a temporary nature.

There is evidence to suggest that the overseers attempted to replace ser Johannes Aldobrandini only six weeks after his appointment. A deliberation dating from 30 August 1437 states that a tenorista was to be engaged «for one month starting on the first of September» with the same salary given such singers «on other occasions» (Doc. 38). The absence of the musician's name in this document, as well as the record of yet another deliberation from the same day, is an almost certain indication that the appointment was not accepted. The second document records the overseers' decision to have their colleague Lorenzo Spinelli «appoint a tenorista for the Major Florentine Church for that length of time and with whatever salary seems most advantageous to him» (Doc. 39). Lorenzo Spinelli was evidently successful in fulfilling his commission, since two salary-appropriations for the cantore ser Giorgius Christofani de Durazo [Durazzo, Albania] reveal that this musician was engaged shortly after the date of the second document (Docs. 40, 41). A final salary-appropriation for ser Giorgius of Durazzo from 19 December 1437, in which he is described as a tenorista, shows without a doubt that he was the musician appointed by Lorenzo Spinelli (Doc. 42).

After this time there are no other documents that record the presence of singers at the cathedral until December 1438, when a chapel of polyphonic music, modelled on those of the North, was instituted. In this case the lack of information is not due to an absence of documents, for there are extant two series of account books covering this and the immediately following years. Rather it seems that for reasons unknown to us no cantores were employed at Santa Maria del Fiore during the year preceding the establishment of the new chapel.

From the records assembled here it is reasonable to suppose that the practice of having two cantores among the chaplains who served in the cathedral's plain-chant choir – as set forth in the first extant document of 1407 – prevailed throughout the first four decades of the fifteenth century. It appears, however, that this practice was not standard, for some of the documents indicate that at times there was only one of them and at others none at all. Evidently, having two cantores must have been considered an ideal practice, one which was observed only when circumstances permitted it.

Only a few of the documents make any mention of the specific duties of these cantores. One such statement is found in the deliberation of 20 June 1407, where it is reported that Paulus of Aquila and Lucas of Orvieto were engaged because the overseers were «desirous of honoring the church of Santa Reparata with regard to the Divine Offices» (Doc. 1). But a salary-appropriation for these two men from six months later, though couched in more general terms, implies broader duties: it states that they were being paid «for singing, celebrating and doing all those things which are required in the said church» (Doc. 2). The record of Pasquale's appointment, dated 17 January 1417, is again more exact, mentioning that his services were to be employed «in honoring the Divine Offices» (Doc. 16). Similar wording is given in the following month in a salary-appropriation for Ugolino of Orvieto and his associate. Here, their duties are described as «singing in the church of Santa Maria del Fiore in celebration of the Divine Offices» (Doc. 19).

It is clear from these scanty remarks that the cantores performed primarily at the Offices. But at which Offices and on what days? And what are the implications of the second document just mentioned? Are there any grounds for assuming that «doing all those things which are required in the said church» included performances at Matins on Christmas and the last three days of Holy Week as well as at Masses on major feast days – services that are known to have been celebrated with special solemnity at Santa Maria del Fiore later in the fifteenth century? I believe that some answers to these questions can be found by examining the duties of the chapel of polyphonic music, established only a year after the departure of the last of the cantores.

From the outset the chapel was employed at both the cathedral and the baptistry of San Giovanni, and its services were divided almost equally between the two churches.[1] The record of the singers' appointment, dating from 9 December 1438, states that they were to perform «only at Vespers» of the feasts celebrated by the cathedral.[2] Still another record, from 1479, indicates that these included Sundays as well as a number of other feast days, a specific list of which appears in a later document of 1502.[3]

According to the list, the chapel sang the fifth psalm at Vespers on all Sundays of the year and more than twenty other days.[4] On several major feasts – among them, Christmas, Easter, Corpus Christi, the Annunciation and the Assumption of the Blessed Virgin Mary – the singers performed instead the first psalm at Vespers. Presumably this arrangement allowed them, on those few occasions which were also celebrated with polyphonic music at the baptistry, to move across the piazza in time to perform at the services that were being conducted simultaneously in San Giovanni. A similar division of duties was apparently made for performing at Masses on nine special occasions – for example, Christmas, Easter and such traditionally Florentine holidays as the feasts of Sts. John the Baptist, Zenobius and Reparata – when the chapel sang first at the one church and then at the other. (The singers' regular duties included performing at Mass in San Giovanni on Sundays and all the feast days normally observed there).[5] The chapel was also required to sing Matins at both churches on Christmas and the last three days of Holy Week, and at times such as those the singers were customarily divided into two groups.

Although this information dates from a period considerably later than the one under consideration, there are good reasons for assuming that the

---

1. For an account of the chapel see my *The Singers of San Giovanni in Florence during the 15th Century*, in «Journal of the American Musicological Society», XIV (1961), pp. 307-58.

2. *Ibid.*, p. 310.

3. The document from 1479 is published by A. SEAY, *The 15th-Century Cappella*, p. 50.

4. The list is given in my *The Musical Chapels at the Florentine Cathedral and Baptistry during the First Half of the 16th Century*, in «Journal of the American Musicological Society», XXIV (1971), pp. 4-5.

5. See my *Singers of San Giovanni*, p. 311.

days when the chapel performed were more or less the same ones as those on which the cantores sang earlier in the century. The principal argument in favor of such an assumption is that of tradition. Liturgical practices change slowly, and it is highly unlikely that the feast days celebrated by the cathedral would have been significantly altered in the span of several decades, especially with regard to Sundays and major feasts.

Other evidence in favor of this assumption is furnished by the statutes of the Arte della Lana in the early fifteenth century. These contain a calendar of the feast days traditionally observed by the guild.[1] With one or two exceptions, all of the principal feasts listed in the calendar, that is, days when the guild-members' shops were to remain closed, correspond exactly to the days mentioned in the document of 1502. One would, of course, expect this to have been so, since the Arte della Lana was not only the cathedral's principal patron, but was also responsible for the church's secular administration. What is noteworthy, however, is the fact that the guild's principal feast days were also observed with special musical services at the cathedral. And since this was a documented practice from 1438 on – after the formation of the chapel – there is every reason to believe that the same days were celebrated with similar if not equal ceremony during the earlier decades of the century, when the cantores were employed.

The fact that the chapel performed regularly at Vespers and only occasionally at Masses and Matins helps to explain the few statements that have survived regarding the cantores' duties. Thus it is possible that the term «Divine Offices» was used in the early Quattrocento to refer primarily to Vespers. Vespers were, after all, the only Offices to be singled out for mention in the record of the chapel's appointment in 1438, barely a year after the last references to cantores. Furthermore, Vespers were the Offices that were generally most accessible to the public and the ones that were apt to have been celebrated with more elaborate musical ceremony, as they were later in the century. Similarly, the general description found in the salary-appropriation of 1407 – «doing all those things which are required in the said church» – may have been an allusion to the few days, specified in the document of 1502, when Masses and Matins were celebrated with greater pomp.

There are grounds, however, for believing that the cantores performed at services in the cathedral even more frequently than did the chapel later

---

1. ASF, Arte della Lana, *Statuti (1428, e successive aggiunte fino al 1589)*, vol. 7, fols. 55r-56r. In the calendar major feasts are designated by the rubric «cum apothecis clausis», while lesser feasts are indicated with the term «ad sportellam».

in the century. All the available evidence suggests that the cantores were associated only with Santa Maria del Fiore. This being the case, they were not obliged to divide their duties between the two churches, and might well have been called upon to assist at Masses as well as at Vespers on many of the major feast days.[1]

One final question remains to be considered with regard to the duties of the cantores: what kind of music did they sing – that is, were they performers of the chant or of polyphony, or of both? Evidence implicit in the documents already cited as well as information from other sources can aid us in answering this question, if not unequivocally, at least with a reasonable degree of certainty.

The problem, as I see it, revolves around the use of the word cantore to describe the office of these «special» singers who were engaged to assist in Santa Maria del Fiore's plain-chant choir. Since these men were also chaplains, it could be that their duties consisted merely of intoning and guiding the chant sung by the rest of the choir as well as singing the sections that were intended for soloists. This is a logical assumption, for contemporary records from several Italian cathedrals make it clear that a cantore was most often an ecclesiastic who performed and taught the chant.[2] In certain other Italian cathedrals, on the other hand, the cantore's position was more com-

---

[1]. Only two documents concerning San Giovanni's musicians in the early decades of the fifteenth century have survived (see Docs. 47, 48 in the Appendix). From the information contained in them it is clear that the baptistry, like the cathedral, maintained its own musicians. It is impossible, however, to determine how many cantores were normally employed there. Nevertheless, these documents offer additional grounds for assuming that it was only with the establishment of the chapel that the practice arose of engaging the same singers for service in both churches.

[2]. A frate Gaspare, cantore, is recorded at the cathedral of Fano as early as 1427. His successor, frate Biaxio de Antonio de Caglie (recorded from 1436-1464) was obliged «to sing, to direct the chant in the choir, to play the organ . . . and to obey the preposto» (see R. PAOLUCCI, *La cappella musicale del Duomo di Fano*, in «Note d'archivio per la storia musicale», III, 1926, pp. 83-4). The positions of a cantor (who directed the chant) and a magister scholarum are recorded at the cathedral of Padova in 1399. In 1402 it is reported that the two cantores, Antonio, magister scholarum, and Guglielmus, magister cantus, were also obliged to sing in the choir. It was only in 1419 that a tenorista was engaged (see R. CASIMIRI, *Musica e musicisti nella Cattedrale di Padova nei secoli XIV, XV, XVI*, in «Note d'archivio», XVIII, 1941, pp. 2-5). The office of the cantor existed at the cathedral of Brescia from as early as 1275. He was usually a canon who had full authority in all things pertaining to the divine cult, and he apparently also taught chant (see P. GUERRINI, *I canonici cantori della Cattedrale di Brescia*, in «Note d'archivio», I, 1924, pp. 82-3). At the cathedral of Vicenza the offices of the preposto and the cantor were included among the ancient «Dignities» of the Cathedral Chapter. The canonico-cantore was apparently responsible for teaching as well as singing and directing the chant (see G. MANTESE, *La cappella musicale del Duomo di Vicenza*, in «Note d'archivio», XIX, 1942, pp. 169-81).

prehensive in scope. For example, von Fischer has recently shown that from as early as the beginning of the thirteenth century the cantores of the cathedral of Siena were not only charged with leading the choir and intoning and singing the chant, but also with singing polyphony on a number of feast days.[1] Likewise, Claudio Sartori has brought to light documents exactly contemporary with the period under discussion which show that in 1402 Matteo da Perugia was engaged as a cantore by the cathedral of Milan to perform both polyphony and the chant.[2] It is my contention that a similar situation existed in Florence, as is implied by the documents presented in this study.

The documents indicate that as many as ten of the fifteen cantores who are known to have been employed at Santa Maria del Fiore during the early decades of the fifteenth century were non-Florentines. It seems strange that this should be so if their duties were merely those ordinarily associated with the plain-chant choir. Surely Florentine ecclesiastics could have been found for that purpose. Apparently, then, the cantores were expected to perform a special musical function, that of singing polyphony. If this were indeed the case, it also appears that singers of polyphony were not generally available in Florence at the time, since the overseers were continually obliged to seek them from outside the city. Interestingly, a similar situation existed when the chapel was established in 1438. At that time four singers, none of them Florentines, were brought from Ferrara to staff the new group.[3]

The documents also show that there was a constant change of personnel at the cathedral during the period under consideration. Only in a few instances is the presence of the same singer recorded for more than a year. A possible explanation for this state of affairs may be that the type of singer employed at the cathedral was very much in demand. And since performers of polyphony were apparently much sought after in Italy at this time, it is not unlikely that the singers left Florence because they were offered higher salaries elsewhere.

More direct evidence in favor of the cantores having performed polyphonic music is provided by the knowledge that composers such as Curradus of Pistoia, Ugolino of Orvieto and Niccolaus Zaccherie were employed in 1410, 1417 and 1421 respectively. And if dopnus Paulus monachus is to be identified with the composer don Paolo tenorista, then there is evidence

1. K. VON FISCHER, *Das Kantorenamt am Dome von Siena zu Beginn des 13. Jahrhunderts*, in *Festschrift Karl Gustav Fellerer*, Regensburg 1962, pp. 155-60.
2. C. SARTORI, *Matteo da Perugia e Bertrand Feragut, i due primi Maestri di Cappella del Duomo di Milano*, in «Acta Musicologica», XXVIII (1956), pp. 13-4.
3. See my *Singers of San Giovanni*, pp. 309-10.

that a composer was engaged by the cathedral as early as 1407. Furthermore, there is no question that polyphony was being performed at Santa Maria del Fiore in 1429 and 1437, for documents from those years specifically refer to some of the singers as tenoristae, that is, those who sang the tenor part in the execution of a polyphonic piece.

In addition to the documentary evidence, there is Filippo Villani's testimony that vocal polyphony was performed at «our major church» from the early part of the fourteenth century onwards.[1] Villani reports that it had been customary for the choir to sing the *Credo* in alternation with the organ during the celebration of the Mass. Later, probably around 1340, however, a vocal performance of Bartholus's two-part *Credo* was so successful that «having abandoned the customary alternation with the organ, it was sung from that time on by living voices, with a great crowd of people following the vocal harmony».[2] The successful reception of Bartholus's *Credo* evidently inspired other Florentine composers in the following years to complete, with the exception of the *Kyrie*, polyphonic settings of the Ordinary of the Mass. Doubtless, vocal performances of these pieces were also eventually given at the cathedral.

Knowledge that vocal polyphony was customarily sung at Santa Maria del Fiore from the middle of the fourteenth century on raises the question of when the practice of having two cantores originated. It was obviously well established by 1407, for at that time it was stated that «there are always two cantores» among the chaplains. How soon before 1407, however, is more difficult to assess. Perhaps the practice arose in conjunction with the introduction of vocal polyphony at the time of Bartholus's *Credo*: Villani states that «from that time on it was sung by living voices». And if this was indeed the case, it is easy to understand why the practice of having two cantores became a traditional one. The other surviving Florentine sacred works of the period, like Bartholus's *Credo*, are written for two parts.[3] Having two singers to perform these and similar works would have been in accordance with medieval practice in general, which usually called for one

---

1. F. Villani, *Liber de origine civitatis Florentiae et eiusdem famosis civibus*, ed. G. C. Galletti, Florence 1847, pp. 34-55. For corrections to the passage quoted here see E. Li Gotti, *Il più antico polifonista italiano del sec. XIV*, in «Italica», XXIV (1947), pp. 196-200.

2. This date has been suggested by N. Pirrotta, *The Music of Fourteenth Century Italy*, I, Amsterdam 1954, p. 1.

3. A newly discovered two-part introit, *Gaudeamus omnes in domino*, by Paolo tenorista may also be mentioned here. It is published in a modern edition by K. von Fischer in the supplement to *Paolo da Firenze*.

singer to a part in polyphonic performance. The documents cited above indicate that when polyphony was performed at the cathedral during the early decades of the fifteenth century it was with solo voices. There is, therefore, no reason to suppose that it was performed in any other way during the latter half of the fourteenth century, especially since the same documents make it clear that having two cantores was already considered a traditional or ideal practice by the turn of the fifteenth century.

That Trecento methods of performance continued to prevail at the cathedral throughout the first four decades of the fifteenth century is not surprising, for this adherence to traditional practice is consistent with the entire character of polyphonic music as it appears to have been cultivated in Florence during that period. It is undoubtedly another manifestation of what Pirrotta has called «the closed and absolutely peculiar character» of Florentine polyphony.[1] For a long time Florentine music remained faithful to its own stylistic traditions, admitting but reluctantly the influence of other regions. And it was probably because of this conservative attitude that the new «international» music of the North and Northern ideals of performance (such as chapels of polyphonic music staffed with greater numbers of singers) were so slow in gaining acceptance in Florence.

The newer concepts of Northern polyphony, however, were not completely unknown in Florence during the early Quattrocento. There must have been, for example, some opportunity to hear Northern music during the first week of Pentecost, 1410, when a group of «cantori tedeschi», that is, Northerners, were guests at the convent of the Santissima Annunziata (Doc. 43). Doubtless there were similar visits by itinerant Northern musicians in the ensuing years, the records of which have not survived. Northern musicians, such as a certain Christiano da Fiandra, whose death is reported in the Florentine Obituary of 1425, were also privately employed by the city's more influential citizens – in this case the archbishop of Florence.[2] One wonders how many other Northern musicians might have been retained in a similar manner, all traces of whom, unfortunately, have disappeared.

There was also frequent opportunity to hear the new music of the North during the extended visit of Pope Martin V, who resided in the city from February 1419 - September 1420. The Pope had brought his chapel

---

1. N. Pirrotta, *Il Codice di Lucca III*, in «Musica Disciplina», v (1951), p. 120.
2. ASF, Arte de' Medici e Speziali, *Registro di morti della città di Firenze, 1424-1430*, vol. 3, fol. 71r: «A dì 30 di luglio 1425 ... Christiano da Fiandra, cantore in Vescovado, popolo San Salvadore, riposa in Santo Niccolò, affogò».

with him, and the group apparently performed at the services in Santa Maria Novella at which he presided.[1] One payment has survived from this time which indicates that the Papal chapel also sang occasionally at the cathedral.[2] Similar performances by the Papal singers must have taken place between 1434-1436, when Pope Eugene IV was living in Florence.[3] Indeed, during the course of this sojourn the Papal chapel assisted at the most important event in the history of the cathedral, the consecration ceremony of 25 March 1436, at which Pope Eugene himself officiated. Dufay, who was then in the Pope's service, was commissioned to write the motet *Nuper Rosarum Flores* in honor of the occasion.[4] The impression created by the performance of this motet, and probably other similar works, was such that the humanist-statesman Gianozzo Manetti was moved to include a highly laudatory description of it in his account of the consecration ceremony.[5] Clearly, after experiences such as this the City on the Arno was well prepared to welcome the newer ideals of Northern polyphony, and it is small wonder that by the end of the following year the practice of having two cantores among the cathedral chaplains was discontinued, thus opening the way for the establishment of the chapel of polyphonic music and a new era in Florentine musical history.

    1. Before arriving in Florence the Papal chapel included nine singers. Their number was increased to fifteen during Martin V's sojourn in the city. See F. X. HABERL, op. cit., p. 461.

    2. The payment is found in a record of appropriations for the feast of the Purification of the Blessed Virgin Mary on 2 February 1420: «et idem solvit cantoribus... Fl. 4 pro canendo in vesperis dicte feste» (SMDF, *Delib.*, II. 1. 77, fol. 62r). One might assume that this payment was intended for the cantores regularly employed at the cathedral (at least one is mentioned in this year). But since there is good reason to believe that there were never more than two of them, and since at this time their salaries rarely exceeded two florins per month, it seems obvious that such a large sum would hardly have been paid them for their services on a single occasion. Apparently, then, it was the Papal chapel for whom the payment was intended. Another noteworthy feature of this document is the mention of Vespers as the services at which the singers performed.

    3. The Papal chapel numbered nine singers in October 1434. There were ten singers from February-April 1436, and these were apparently the musicians who sang at the consecration ceremony. See F. X. HABERL, op. cit., pp. 463-4.

    4. The most recent modern edition of this work may be found in GUILLELMI DUFAY, *Opera Omnia*, I, ed. H. BESSELER, Rome 1966, pp. 70-5.

    5. «Prefatio... de secularibus et pontificalibus ponpis ad dominum Angelum Acarolum», in the manuscript Rome, Biblioteca Apostolica Vaticana, Lat. 1603, fol. 4vff; published by G. DE VAN (ed.), GUILLELMI DUFAY, *Opera Omnia*, I[2] Rome 1948, p. XXVII. A partial English translation is given by D. GROUT, *A History of Western Music*, New York 1960, p. 148.

APPENDIX

Doc. 1   (SMDF, *Delib.*, II. 1. 52, fol. 18r)

20 giugno 1407

Advertentes etc. ad honorandam ecclesiam Sancte Reparate circa divina offitia providerunt, ordinaverunt, deliberaverunt quod duo captores, videlicet presbiter Paulus de Aquila et presbiter Luchas de Urbeveteri, noviter electi et deputati per canonicos et capitulum dicte ecclesie ... pro eorum salario et mercede ... habeant ... flor. auri triginta quinque ... cum hoc quod dicti duo cappellani veniant insi[m]ul ad numerum viginti cum aliis decem et otto, ita quod inter omnes sunt viginti. Et ad hoc ut dictus numerus non deficiat providerunt quod si aliquis ex dicto numero viginti deficeret propter vacationem alicuius XX cappellarum et propter dictam vacationem aliqui fructus dicte cappelle vacantis veniet ad dictum capitulum, medietas dictorum fruttorum cappelle vacantis deveniat capitulum et canonicos in sussidio et salario dictorum captorum et seu eorum successorum, de quo numero viginti cappellani semper sunt duo captores.

Doc. 2   (SMDF, *Delib.*, II. 1. 53, fol. 6v)

die XII decembris 1407

Item dicta die stantiaverunt presbitero Paulo de Aquila et presbitero Luce de Urbeveteri, cantoribus in dicta ecclesia S. Reparate de Florentia, pro ca[n]tando, celebrando et omnia alia faciendo quod requiritur in dicta ecclesia ut patet in eorum eletione et in libro signato pro duobus QQ, a c. 94, floren. auri otto, libras duas, sol. decemsettem floren. parvorum, pro eorum salario trium mensium initiatorum die vigesima augusti 1407 et finiendorum ut sequitur.

Doc. 3   (SMDF, *Delib.*, II. 1. 54, fol. 24v)

10 aprile 1408

Prefati operarii ... stantiaverunt religiosis viris ser Luche Dominici et ser Paulo Masi, presbiteribus cantoribus in ecclesia S. Reparate, pro eorum salario et paga sive mercede trium mensium initiatorum die vigesimo mensis novembris proxime preteriti finitorum ut sequitur, in totum flor. octo auri et s. quindecim ad aurum, Fl. 8 et s. 10 ad. aur.

Doc. 4   (SMDF, *Delib.*, II. 1. 54, fol. 28r)

die XXI junii 1408

Stantiamentum ... religioso viro ser Luche Dominici, uni ex cantoribus ecclesie S. Reparate, pro eius salario et mercede trium mensium initiatorum die 26 mensis martii proximi preteriti ad rationem florenorum septem [sic] auri s. 10 pro anno ...

III

118

Doc. 5 (SMDF, *Stanz.*, II. 4. 7, fol. 24v)

1408

A prete Lucha, cantore nella chiesa di Santa Liperata, per suo salario e paga di tre mesi di Fl. XVII e mezo l'anno, cominciati a dì 26 di marzo 1408 e finiti a dì 25 di giugno 1408, a lib. QQ. Fl. VIII d. 6.

Doc. 6 (SMDF, *Delib.*, II. 1. 54, fol. 3r)

13 marzo 1407 [1408]

Item servatis servandis providerunt quod ser Macteus de Monte Murlo, cappellanus in dicta ecclesia S. Reparate, possit et valeat inhabitare terrenum et a primo palcho infra cuiusdam domus dicte Opere que olim fuit ser Nicolai Pierozzi, posite in populo S. Petri Celorum. Et quod a dicto primo palcho dicte domus supra, dopnus Paulus et ser Marchus [gap] presbiteri et cantores in dicta ecclesia S. Reparate inhabitent... donec aliud pro eorum offitio non deliberetur.

Doc. 7 (SMDF, *Delib.*, II. 1. 54, fol. 3v)

14 marzo 1407 [1408]

Item servatis servandis providerunt quod dopnus Paulus monachus et ser Marchus presbiter, cantores dicte ecclesie Sancte Reparate, habeant usum et habitationem terreni et a primo palco infra domus dicte opere posite obvia ecclesie S. Petri Celorum heri assignate ser Johanni Tinghi...

Doc. 8 (SMDF, *Delib.*, II. 1. 55, fol. 7v)

4 gennaio 1408 [1409]

Item stantiaverunt... ser Luce Dominici, presbitero cantori in S. Reparata, flor. otto auri pro eius salaris sex mensium initiatorum die xxv iunii proxime preteriti et finitorum ut sequitur.

Doc. 9 (SMDF, *Delib.*, II. 1. 56, fol. 9r)

17 giugno 1409

Item stantiaverunt... presbitero Luce Dominici, cantori ecclesie S. Reparate de Florentia, pro suo salario sex mensium initiati die xxv decembris proxime preteriti, ad rationem Fl. decem septem et dimidii pro anno, in totum fl. octo et sold. quindecim auri. Fl. 8 s. 15 ad aurum.

Doc. 10 (SMDF, *Delib.*, II. 1. 58, fol. 18r)

7 agosto 1409

Item stantiaverunt quod dictus eorum camerarius... det et solvat ser Luce Dominici, cantori in S. Reparata, pro parte solutionis eius salarii quod habere

MUSIC AND MUSICIANS AT SANTA MARIA DEL FIORE 119

debet a dicta opera pro canendo in dicta ecclesia Sancte Reparate, florenos quinque auri.

Doc. 11 (SMDF, *Delib.*, II. 1. 57, fol. 2v)
1 ottobre 1409
Item ... stantiaverunt ... ser Luce Dominici, presbitero ecclesie Sancte Reparate pro eius salario 3 mensium proxime preteritorum initiatorum die xxv iunii proximi preteriti ... flor. auri 4 et s. 7.

Doc. 12 (SMDF, *Delib.*, II. 1. 57, fol. 14r)
28 febbraio 1409 [1410]
Item ... stantiaverunt quod dictus eorum camerarius det et solvat ser Luce Dominici, cappellano ecclesie Sancte Reparate, pro eius salario trium mensium proximi preteritorum initiatorum die xxv septembris proxime preteriti et finitorum ut sequitur, flor. auri quatuor s. VII d. 6 ad aurum.

Doc. 13 (SMDF, *Stanz.*, II. 4. 7, fol. 37v)
1410
A ser Lucha di Domenicho, prete e cantore in Santa Liperata, per suo salario e paga di VI mesi cominciati a dì xxv di dicembre prossimo passato e finiti a dì 24 di giugno 1410 a ragione di Fl. XVII s. XIV l'anno. Fl. VIII s. 14

Doc. 14 (SMDF, *Delib.*, II. 1. 59, fol. 7v)
10 dicembre 1410
Item predicti offitiales opere S. Reparate ... eligerunt in cantore[m] pro ecclesia Sancte Reparate de Florentia, ser Curradus ser Gualandi de Bracciolinis de Pistorio in cantorem dicte ecclesie Sancte Reparate, pro uno anno incipiendo hodie presenti die x mensis decembris 1410 cum salario florenorum decem septem cum dimidio auri pro anno, Fl. XVII ½.

Doc. 15 (SMDF, *Stanz.*, II. 4. 7, fol. 82v)
1414
A dì 25 di marzo 1414 prossimo passato, per l'infrascritte cose paghate per la festa di Santa Maria del Fiore ... a tre cantori vennono cantare in choro, L. I s. 13

Doc. 16 (SMDF, *Delib.*, II. 1. 70, fol. 5r)
25 gennaio 1416 [1417]
Item eligerunt Pasqualem [gap] in cantorem et ad divina officia colenda in ecclesia Sancte Marie del Fiore pro tempore et termino unius anni hodie initiati, cum salario Flor. trium auri per camerarium Operis et de denariis operis sibi

III

solvendis de mense in mensem pro quolibet mense quo in dicta ecclesia servi-
verit ad predicta etc.
Nota quod non acceptavit et non servivit et nihil sibi solvi potest etc.

Doc. 17   (SMDF, *Delib.*, II. 1. 70, fol. 7v)
17 febbraio 1416 [1417]
Item eligerunt infrascriptos duos presbiteros, quorum nomina sunt ista, videlicet
dominum Ugolinum Francisci de Urbeveteri et ser Jacobum Masii de Frullivio,
in cantores et pro cantoribus ad cantandum in ecclesia Sancte Marie del Fiore
pro termino et tempore unius anni proxime futuri, cum salario flor. duorum
auri pro quolibet eorum et quolibet mense dicti temporis quo serviverint ad
predicta etc. Additum dimidium florenum auri pro quolibet eorum quolibet
mense, die 19 dicti mensis, ut constat in facie proxime sequenti.

Doc. 18   (SMDF, *Delib.*, II. 70, fol. 8r)
die XVIIII dicti mensis februarii 1416 [1417]
Operarii ... deliberaverunt quod dominus Ugolinus Francisci de Urbeveteri et
ser Jacobus Masii de Frulivio, quos ipsi die XVII presentis mensis februarii eligerunt in cantores et pro cantoribus ad cantandum in ecclesia Sancte Marie del
Fiore pro uno anno proxime futuro, tamen initiato cum salario flor. duorum
auri pro quolibet eorum et quolibet mense dicti temporis quo servirent, habeant
et habere intelligantur et debeant flor. duos auri cum dimidio alterius floreni
auri, ita quod quolibet mense dicti temporis augeatur cuilibet eorum dimidium floreni auri etc.

Doc. 19   (SMDF, *Delib.*, II. 1. 70, fol. 13r)
24 marzo 1416 [1417]
Item stantiaverunt ... quod Donatus, camerarius ... det et solvat ... domino
Ugolino Francisci de Urbeveteri et ser Jacobo Masii de Frullivio, per dictos
operarios electis et deputatis in canpsoribus et ad canendum in ecclesia Sancte
Marie del Fiore in celebratione divinorum officiorum pro tempore et termine
unius anni initiati die XVII mensis februarii proxime preteriti ... pro eorum et
utriusque eorum salario et paga primi mensis dicti temporis initiati ut supra, in
totum inter ambos flor. quinque auri. Fl. 5

Doc. 20   (SMDF, *Delib.*, II. 1. 70, fol. 19r)
29 aprile 1417
Operarii ... stantiaverunt ... domino Ugolino Francisci de Urbeveteri et ser
Jacobo Masi de Frullivio, cantoribus in Sancta Maria del Fiore ... eorum salario et paga secondi mensis dicti temporis initiati die XVII mensis martii ...
flor. quinque auri. Fl. 5

Doc. 21   (SMDF, *Delib.*, II. 1. 70, fol. 22r)
21 maggio 1417
Item stantiaverunt quod Donatus . . . det et solvat . . . domino Ugolino Francisci d'Urbeveteri et ser Jacobo Masi de Frullivio, cantoribus in Sancta Maria del Fiore . . . eorum salario et paga terti mensis dicti temporis initiati die XVII aprilis 1417, flor. quinque auri. Fl. 5

Doc. 22   (SMDF, *Delib.*, II. 1. 70, fol. 25r)
22 giugno 1417
Operarii . . . stantiaverunt . . . domino Ugolino Francisci d'Urbeveteri et ser Jacobo Masi de Frullivio, cantoribus Sancte Marie del Fiore . . . eorum salario et paga quarti mensis initiati die XVII maii 1417, flor. quinque auri. Fl. 5

Doc. 23   (SMDF, *Delib.*, II. 1. 77, fol. 16r)
7 febbraio 1419 [1420]
Item quod ser Niccolao Zaccherie, cantori cappellano ecclesie Sancte Marie del Fiore, intelligatur concessa et concesserunt pro eius habitatione domus dicte opere in qua de proximo habitabat ser [gap], olim cappellanus dicte ecclesie, solvendo pro introytu dicte domus id quod propteres taxatum fuit si taxata reperietur.

Doc. 24   (SMDF, *Stanz.*, II. 4. 9, fol. 82r)
1424
E a dì 19 di maggio per achonciare ghuardaroba e aquaio della chasa tiene ser Jacopo chantore della chiesa; portò Biagio di Jacopo, s. 15.

Doc. 25   (SMDF, *Delib.*, II. 2. 1, fol. 90v)
die XXXI mensis augusti 1428
Prefati operarii servatis servandis . . . concesserunt atque consignaverunt ser Iacobo de Aretio, cantori et cappellano maioris ecclesie Florentine, medietatem domus in qua ad presens habitat dominus Bernardus, prior S. Petri Maioris de Florentia et canonicus Florentinus, si et in quantum approbetur per offitium consulum Artis Lane, alias dicta concessio sit nulla.

Doc. 26   (SMDF, *Delib.*, II. 2. 2, fol. 71r)
die xxx octobris MCCCCXXVII
Item prefati operarii . . . servatis servandis dederunt ac tribuerunt baliam ac auctoritatem Bernardo Amerigii de Donatis, provisori prefate opere, conducendi ad pensionem nomine dicte opere quandam domum cuiusdam de Amannatis, posita penes coquina presbiterorum, pro eo pretio quo eidem videbitur utilius fore pro dicta opera: qua conducta, eam concesserunt ser Bartholomeo

cantori qui stabat in domo in qua olim stetit dominus Johannes domini Masi de Albiziis que postea fuit et est concessa domino Filippo Pauli de Albiziis; et quicquid circa predicta fecerit, intelligatur per dictam operam et operarios fuisse factum.

Doc. 27   (SMDF, *Delib.*, II. 2. 1, fol. 176r)
Indictione VIII die secundo decembris 1429
Prefati domini consules Artis Lane civitate Florentia una cum operaris opere S. Marie del Fiore de Florentia existentes congregati in domo Artis Lane in superiori eorum solita audientia pro factis dicte opere per agendis deliberaverunt quod omnes et singuli canonici infrascripti teneantur et debeat quilibum ipsorum eligesse unum ex infrascripti cappellanis ad standum et habitandum contrarie in domibus eis assignatis et assignasse eidem cappellano locum ubi dictis tali cappellani, stare et habitare teneatur et debeat pro suo habitatione et mora pro totam die quinta decimam presentis mensis decembris; qui contrafecerit ipso facto intelligatur et sit privatus sua domo eidem pro dicta offitia seu pro quodlibus eorum assignatam.

Nomina et pronomina canonicorum de quibus...
dominus Bartolomeus de Freschobaldis
dominus Andreas Dominici Fiocchis
dominus Filippus de Albiziis
dominus Salutatis de Salutatis
dominus Johannes de Rondinellis
dominus Dinus de Pecoris
dominus Marinus de Guadagnis
dominus Thomas de Bordella
dominus Matteus de Bucellis
dominus Michus de Capponibus
dominus Andreas de Empulo et
ser   Antonius vocato ser Massey unus cappellanus de ecclesie. Nomina vero cappellanorum de quibus...
ser   Simoni Donati
ser   Johannes cantor, seu eius successor
ser   Johannes de valle sevis
ser   Niccola tenorista
ser   Lapus sacrista
plebanus Arlottus
ser   Pierus de Pistorio non velit stare ubi est ad pensis
ser   Jacobus de Aretio
ser   Santus
ser   Iacobus pignis alias ser Papi
ser   Niccolaus de Lanciano

ser   Niccolaus Pieri cappellanus chardinalis
ser   Thomaxius Blaxii

Doc. 28   (SMDF, *Delib.*, II. 2. 2, fol. 19r)

22 maggio 1437
Item eligerunt in cantorem et cappellanum ecclesie maioris Florentine ser Johannem Herrigi clericum, pro eo salario et modo et forma prout deliberabitur per Bartolomeum de Ridolfis et Andream Guidonis Iuntini, duas ex ... operariis.

Doc. 29   (SMDF, *Stanz.*, II. 4. 14, fol. 11v)

1437
A ser Giovanni d'Arrigho da Rieti, eletto chapelano e chantore della chiesa magiore di Firenze, L. quarantotto piccioli per parte di suo salario a ragione di Fl. 60 l'anno a lire 4 per fiorino.

Doc. 30   (SMDF, *Stanz.*, II. 4. 14, fol. 18v)

1437
A ser Giovanni d'Arricho da Rieti, prete e chantore dela chiesa magiore di Firenze, L. 1 s. 16.

Doc. 31   (SMDF, *Stanz.*, II. 4. 14, fol. 19r)

1437
A ser Giovanni d'Arricho da Rieti, chantore della chiesa magiore di Firenze, L. 40 piccioli: sono per suo salario di dua mesi ...

Doc. 32   (SMDF, *Stanz.*, II. 4. 16, fol. 8v)

30 aghosto 1437
Ser Johanni Arrigi de Reate, cantori ecclesie maioris Florentine, L. 1 s. 16 pro parte solutione sui salarii.

Doc. 33   (SMDF, *Stanz.*, II. 4. 16, fol. 9v)

25 settembre 1437
Ser Johanni Arrigi de Rieti, cantori ecclesie maioris Florentine, L. 40 pro parte solutionis sui salarii.

Doc. 34   (SMDF, *Stanz.*, II. 4. 16, fol. 22v)

10 gennaio 1437 [1438]
Ser Johanni Herrigi de Reate, olim cappellano et cantori ecclesie maioris Florentine, L. 50 s. 4 pro resto sui salarii serviti per totum mensem decembris 1437, ad rationem Fl. 60 pro anno. L. 50 s. 4

Doc. 35   (SMDF, *Stanz.*, II. 4. 15, fol. 6v)

24 luglio 1437

Prefati operarii... deliberaverunt atque stantiaverunt quod camerarius opere de pecunia opere solvere teneatur ser Johanni Aldobrandini de Perusio, cappellano et cantori cathedralis ecclesie florentine, florenos auri decem quos opera ei mutuat super eius electione.

Doc. 36   (SMDF, *Stanz.*, II. 4. 14, fol. 40r)

1438

A ser Giovanni d'Aldobrandino da Perugia, chappellano della chiesa maggiore di Firenze, Fl. 3 L. 1 s. 5 piccioli, e quali gli si danno per resto di suo salario è servito in chappellano in detta chiesa d'uno anno cominciato a dì xx di luglio 1437 e finito per tutto dì xvIIII di luglio 1438 a ragione di Fl. 28 l'anno.

Doc. 37   (SMDF, *Delib.*, II. 2. 2, fol. 32r)

13 febbraio 1437 [1438]

Item simili modo refirmaverunt ser Johannem de Perusio in cappellanum dicte ecclesie pro uno anno proxime futuro initiando die qua finit prima eius electio, cum salario et aliis in prima electione ordinatis.

Doc. 38   (SMDF, *Delib.*, II. 2. 2, fol. 28r)

30 agosto 1437

Item simili modo dicti operarii eligerunt in tenoristam maioris ecclesie florentine dominum [gap], pro uno mense proximo futuro initiato die primo settembris predicti, pro eo salario quod alias per eorum offitio deliberabitur.

Doc. 39   (SMDF, *Delib.*, II. 2. 2, fol. 28v)

30 agosto 1437

Item prefati operarii simili modo deliberaverunt quod Laurentius de Spinellis, unus ex eorum offitio, possit et teneatur conducere tenoristam ecclesie maioris florentine pro eo tempore et salario prout et sicut videbitur eidem fore utilius pro dicta opera...

Doc. 40   (SMDF, *Stanz.*, II. 4. 16, fol. 13r)

10 ottobre 1437

Ser Giorgio Christofani de Durazo, cantori, L. 13 s. 19 quas opera eidem mutuavit pro offitiando ecclesiam maiorem civitatis Florentie. L. 13 s. 19

Doc. 41   (SMDF, *Stanz.*, II. 4. 16, fol. 14r)

10 ottobre 1437

Ser Giorgio Christofani de Durazo, cantori in ecclesia maiori florentina, L. 8

quas opera eidem mutuavit pro canendo in dicta ecclesia et celebrando divinum officium. L. 8

Doc. 42 (SMDF, *Stanz.*, II. 4. 16, fol. 18r)
19 dicembre 1437
Ser Giorgio Christofani de Durazo, olim tenoriste dicte ecclesie, s. 11 quos sibi mutuavit opera. s. 11

Doc. 43 (ASF, Corp. Rel. Sopp. 119, Santissima Annunziata, *Entrata & Uscita*, vol. 685, fol. 140r)
Exitus mensis maii 1410
Item addì otto diedi per fare honore a' cantori tedeschi che stettono in casa in quegli dì di Paschua della Pentecosta: diedi in più volte in uova e in carne, Fl. 1 s. XVI.

Doc. 44 (SMDF, *Delib.*, II. 2. 2, fol. 93r)
1 aprile 1440
Prefati operarii ut supra congregati, nullo absente, audito et intellecto quam bene et prudenter circha honorem divini cultus et ecclesie Sancte Marie del Fiore infrascriptus dominus Guaspar ser Gilippi de Toschanella, corista dicte ecclesie, se gerit et intellecta eius laudabili fama et virtute ... deliberaverunt quod omnes et singuli capellani dicte ecclesie Sancte Marie del Fiore et ad cultum divinum in dicta ecclesia deputati teneantur et oblighati sint in quibuscunque rebus ad quas oblighati sunt pro honore dicte ecclesie honorare et reverentiam gerere et eius mandatis parere circha cultum divinum dicto domino Guasparri eo modo et forma quibus teneatur ...

Doc. 45 (SMDF, *Chiesa* etc., I. 5. 1, fol. 8r)
Ancora considerato all'importanza dell'officio del corista e come per l'esecutione de' suoi obblighi è necessario che personalmente intervengha a tutte l'hore debite in coro per appuntare chi non intervenissi alle divini offitii. Per tanto deliberano che decto corista la cura del quale è d'appuntare sia tenuto ogni giorno e la notte ancora alli mattutini ritrovarsi a tutte l'hore del coro e messe cantate personalmente per iseguire e fare l'offitio suo con quella diligenza e fede che si conviene e appuntare tutti quelli che mancassino e non osservassino quanto sono tenuti in virtù delle presenti ordini e tenere di tutti diligente conto a' suoi libri ...

Doc. 46 (SMDF, *Stanz.*, II. 4. 14, fol. 40r)
1438
A ser Angnolo di Jacopo, chappellano e apuntatore della chiesa maggiore di

III

Firenze, L. 29 s. 4 d. 6 piccioli, e quali dinari a llui si danno perché gli dia a' chappellani di detta chiesa per distribuzione degli ufici divini 'anno chantato in detta chiesa del mese di luglio 1438.
A llui detto L. 30 s. 13 d. 6 piccioli, e quali dinari gli si danno perché gli dia a' sopradetti chappellani per la sopradetta cagione e per lo mese d'aghosto 1438.

Doc. 47   (ASF, Arte di Calimala, *Petizioni e Stanziamenti*, vol. 17bis, fol. 84v)
die xx aprilis 14... [gap]
Suprascripti consules... elegerunt vigore provisionis ser Johannem [gap] de Bononie in cappellanum et canptorem cum salario quolibet mense florenorum trium auri pro tempore quo serviret.

Doc. 48   (ASF, Arte di Calimala, *Petizioni e Stanziamenti*, vol. 17bis, fol. 85r)
die 24 aprilis 14... [gap]
Item ditti consules... deliberaverunt quod depositarius opere mutuat et sibi mutuari possit ser Johanni de Bononie, cappelano et cantori ecclesie S. Johannis, flor. auri duodecim cum hoc quod ser Iulianus Feducii, rettor S. Romuli, satisdet et se obliget ad dictam quantitatem restituendam in casu quod ipse ser Johannes non serviret. Qui ser Iulianus predicta die 24 aprilis presentibus Papio et Maffio nuntiis, promixit et se obligavit ut supra. Et dittus ser Johannes fuit confessus etc. et voluit ipsos flor. xii dari dicto ser Iuliano.

Doc. 49   (SMDF, QC, viii. 1. 50, fol. 34v)
Ser Lapo di Martino, corista e appuntatore del choro di duomo, de' dare a dì 5 d'aghosto L. ottantacinque s. 3 d. 8, portò ser Giuliano d'Antonio per dare a' cappellani di duomo la distribuzione del mese di luglio passato... [1469].

IV

The Singers of San Giovanni in Florence during the 15th Century*

ALTHOUGH THE PRESENCE of singers of polyphony at the Florentine Cathedral Church of Santa Maria del Fiore can be documented from as early as 1407, the establishment there of a polyphonic chapel did not occur until over thirty years later.[1] The same situation holds true for the Florentine Baptistry of San Giovanni, the city's oldest and most revered Christian monument, dedicated to the patron saint of Florence, St. John the Baptist. From the outset, the singers who were engaged for the chapel of one church also served in that of the other, and later in the century their duties were increased to include weekly performances at a third leading church, that of the Santissima Annunziata.

Florentine documentary sources of the 15th century often refer to the musicians who served in the three churches as *i cantori di San Giovanni*, a title which implies that special significance was attached to their services at the Baptistry. Frequent mention of the singers of San Giovanni in

---

* The opportunity to do research in Florence was made possible through a John Knowles Paine Traveling Fellowship awarded by the Department of Music, Harvard University, for the academic years 1957-59. A good deal of the research done during those years was later incorporated into my dissertation, the third and fourth chapters of which form the basis of the present study. Special thanks are due Messrs. Gino Corti, Mario Tesi, and Enzo Settesoldi, all of Florence, for their help in deciphering some of the more difficult documents. I should also like to express my gratitude to Professor Nino Pirrotta of Harvard University for his untiring assistance and encouragement during the course of my work.

Abbreviations:

ASF	Archivio di Stato, Firenze
SSA	ASF, Corporazioni Religiose Soppresse No. 119, Santissima Annunziata
SMDF	Archivio dell'Opera di Santa Maria del Fiore, Firenze
DC	Debitori-Creditori (Debit-Credit Registers)
Delib.	Deliberazioni (Deliberations)
EU	Entrata e Uscita (Income and Expenditures)
QC	Quaderni Cassa (Debit-Credit Registers)
Ricord.	Ricordanze (Contracts, Obligations, etc.)
Stanz.	Stanziamenti (Appropriations)

The Florentine new year began on March 25, and as a result documents recorded before that day usually carry the date of the preceding year. In the course of the text such dates have been changed to conform to our modern system.

[1] On singers of polyphony at Santa Maria del Fiore during the early decades of the *quattrocento*, see my "A Documentary History of Music at the Florentine Cathedral and Baptistry during the Fifteenth Century" (Harvard University Dissertation, 1960), pp. 71ff.

Copyright 1961 The American Musicological Society, rights reserved. Reprinted by permission.

non-Florentine sources, furthermore, shows that the title was not merely confined to local usage. Yet the reason why the singers were so named is never given in any of the sources, and remains unknown to this day.[2]

Further references to the singers of San Giovanni are found in personal letters of the Medici family, the merchant-princes who first rose to prominence on the Florentine political scene in the early *quattrocento*. The letters are of great interest for several reasons, but principally because they indicate that the singers of San Giovanni were also in the private employ of the Medici. It is clear from our other sources, however, that at first the Medici sought to conceal this relationship from the general public, and that they acknowledged it only after having consolidated their position of absolute authority in the state. The Medici's policies regarding the singers of San Giovanni thus appear to have been governed by political considerations; accordingly, a principal aim of the present study will be to disclose the degree to which politics influenced the musical scene in *quattrocento* Florence. In fact, the very establishment of the chapels at the Cathedral and the Baptistry is to be associated with an important political event in the city's history, the transferral to Florence on January 10, 1439, of the Council for Union between the Greek and Latin Churches.[3]

The Council had previously been in session for over a year at Ferrara. Although the ostensible reason for the transferral was an outbreak of the plague in that city, it was generally well known that Pope Eugene IV had agreed to make the move because of the generous financial aid which the Florentine government had promised to provide in defraying his expenses for the Council. For the Florentines, in turn, the transferral was a diplomatic success of a very practical nature. In addition to the political prestige and economic advantages to be gained from having the Council at Florence, the presence there of so many distinguished Greek and Latin scholars would give further impetus to the city's humanistic aspirations.

Contemporary chronicles relate the elaborate preparations made for the coming of the Council. Motivated by civic pride, prominent individuals and members of the government vied with one another in their efforts to accommodate and entertain the host of clerics, statesmen, merchants, scholars, and travelers who repaired to the city from all parts of the Christian world. Similar efforts were made to impress the visitors with the material prosperity and cultural achievements of the Florentine State. The establishment of a polyphonic chapel in the city's two leading churches at just that time was in keeping, therefore, with the general movement to ensure the successful reception of the Council.

[2] At one time San Giovanni served as the Cathedral of Florence. It may well be that sacred vocal polyphony was first given in Florence at that church, and as a result the custom arose of calling singers of polyphony *i cantori di San Giovanni*, i.e., after the church with which the performance of vocal polyphony was originally associated.

[3] Information on the Council is derived from J. Gill, *The Council of Florence* (Cambridge, 1959).

THE SINGERS OF SAN GIOVANNI IN FLORENCE

The transferral of the Council was a triumph in personal diplomacy for Cosimo de'Medici, the principal "citizen" of Florence since the restoration of his family to the city four years previously. Cosimo had been in Ferrara during the course of the Council, and apparently had been instrumental in persuading Pope Eugene IV, a good friend of his, to make the move.[4] Cosimo was aided in his efforts by his brother Lorenzo, Florentine ambassador to the Papal See in Ferrara. It was Lorenzo who successfully completed, early in December of 1438, the negotiations that secured the removal of the Council to Florence.[5]

In this undertaking Cosimo's influence was not generally well known. This was in accordance with his political philosophy, however, for Cosimo was ever careful not to give the impression that he was personally directing the affairs of the Republic. His position in Florence rested on public approval, and nothing was more distasteful to the Florentines than the thought that someone should attempt to deprive them of their political liberties. Realizing this, Cosimo was all the more successful in ruling, because he exercised his authority through a skillful manipulation of the traditional democratic forms. A result, however, of Cosimo's behind-the-scenes policies is that even in our own day very little is known of the measures for which he was directly responsible.[6]

We encounter such a situation when we examine the manner in which Cosimo secured the establishment of the chapel at the Cathedral. His name is never once mentioned in the documents that record the event. Yet it is the very absence of his name in these documents that makes us suspect that he was behind the move, and that he was content to enact his program through the officials traditionally responsible for appointing musicians to the Cathedral's service, the overseers of Santa Maria del Fiore.[7] The first of these documents is a deliberation of the overseers dated December 6, 1438. It contains instruction to Cosimo's brother Lorenzo—who, as we have already learned, was in Ferrara at the time—to seek the appropriate personnel for the chapel:

Cognizant of the excellence and wisdom of the herewith inscribed Lorenzo de'Medici, who is at present ambassador of the Commune of Florence to the Holy See, and desirous of augmenting the divine cult as much as possible so that the church of Santa Maria del Fiore is embellished and excels all other

---

[4] C. S. Gutkind, *Cosimo de' Medici Pater Patriae, 1389-1464* (Oxford, 1938), pp. 33, 148f.
[5] Gill, p. 183.
[6] Gutkind, p. 124.
[7] In 1336 the management of the Cathedral's building works as well as its secular administration (the *Opera*) was entrusted by the government to the consuls of the *Arte della Lana*, one of the city's largest merchant guilds. The authority delegated at that time to the *Arte della Lana* was vested in a group of overseers (the *operai*), composed of members of the Guild, who were elected to quarterly terms of office. Thus empowered, the overseers were responsible only to their immediate superiors in the Guild. See C. Guasti, *Santa Maria del Fiore, la costruzione della chiesa e del campanile* (Florence, 1887), p. 29, where G. Villani's account of the transferral of this authority to the *Arte della Lana* is printed.

churches in honor, and [after] considering how noble and honorable it would be to have singers continually in the service of the said church, and thus [gap] desirous of increasing the honor of the said church, [the overseers] decided to write to the honorable Lorenzo di Giovanni di Bicci de'Medici, who is in Ferrara at present as ambassador of the Commune of Florence to the Holy See, that he seek as best he can to engage a *magister capelle* and three singers or more, as is deemed necessary for the chapel, and that he may have the authority to spend up to [the sum of] two hundred florins yearly for the said singers. (Doc. 1. The documents will be found in the Appendix to this article.)

One wonders what motivated the decision to seek singers in Ferrara rather than any other city. Although there is no way of knowing absolutely, it would seem that the suggestion had come from Cosimo himself. Cosimo had been there during the course of the Council and would have had ample opportunity to audition the musicians who were eventually engaged. What makes it appear that this was actually the case is the fact that the appointment of the singers was recorded only three days after the commission was sent to Lorenzo:

December 9, 1438
Item ... by authority of the commission granted him by the overseers of the *Opera* of Santa Maria del Fiore, the Florentine canon Dominus Ugholinus olim Filippi de Giugnis ... appointed [the following] to sing ... in the Major Florentine Church, only at Vespers on the feast days of the said church:
Magister Benottus of Ferrara, with a salary of five *lire piccioli* each month, L. 5.
Frater Beltramus of the Order of St. Augustine, with a salary of four *lire piccioli* each month, L. 4.
Iannes de Monte of Ferrara, with a salary of four *lire piccioli* each month, L. 4.
Francischus Bartoli, with a salary of three *lire* and six *soldi piccioli* each month, L. 3 s. 6.
The total sum between them all for each month [being] XVI *lire* and 6 *soldi piccioli*. These singers must remain [in the Cathedral's service] until such time as seems convenient to the overseers of the said *Opera* then in office, and to a majority of them; and [the singers must be present] especially on the said days such as are required. (Doc. 2)

It seems extremely unlikely that the commission could have been dispatched to Ferrara, fulfilled, and the results returned in such a brief time, unless arrangements had already been made beforehand by Lorenzo, acting on Cosimo's suggestions. Thus although the commission was a mere formality, it presented the appearance of a decision independently reached by the properly constituted authorities. This was undoubtedly the way Cosimo preferred it.

Whether Cosimo acted in a similar manner with regard to the establishment of the chapel at the Baptistry cannot be known, for the records of the overseers of San Giovanni from that time are no longer extant.[8] Indeed,

---

[8] Like the Cathedral, since very early times the secular administration of the Baptistry had been placed in the hands of one of the city's large merchant guilds, the *Arte di Calimala*. Although the precise year in which the *Calimala* assumed this

the only indication found in the surviving account books of San Giovanni that the same singers were engaged for that church is in a document (to be given below) that concerns Maestro Benotto, from almost a decade later. More closely related chronological evidence, however, is provided by an entry in one of the Cathedral's account books, dated April 29, 1439, which states that on that day the overseers appropriated

for Benotto di Giovanni, *master of the chapel of San Giovanni*, 3 *lire* [and] 6 *soldi piccioli* for his and his associates' work singing at Vespers in the Major Church the day on which the body of the blessed Zenobius was translated. L. 3 s. 6. [italics mine] (Doc. 3)

From later documents we learn that the singers performed the Mass at the Baptistry on major feast days.[9] Perhaps it was also in 1439 that the custom (recorded only in 1504) arose of having the singers perform

in the morning of each day on which the magnificent and most excellent lords, the lord priors of the free people of Florence, make their bimestrial entrance [into office], that is, on the first day of the months of January, March, May, July, September, and November, and while the said magnificent lords are in the said church of San Giovanni, *as is customary from antiquity*, assembled on the above-said days in the said church in order to hear solemn Mass and other Divine Offices. . . . [italics mine] (Doc. 4)

These documents also make it clear that the chapel at the Baptistry was administered by the overseers of that church, and that the singers received a separate salary for their services there. The report given by Giuseppe Baccini in his article on the singers of San Giovanni,[10] although based on documents which dated from several years after the establishment of the chapel, shows that for their services at the Baptistry the singers received salaries almost commensurate with those given them at the Cathedral. It is most probable that they had been receiving the same salaries from the outset.

Of the singers appointed to the chapel on December 9, 1438, two were natives of Ferrara, and another also appears to have been an Italian. The fourth singer, on the other hand, is undoubtedly the Avignonese composer Bertrand Feragut. Feragut is known to have been in northern Italy in the preceding decade.[11] It is not unlikely that he had repaired to Ferrara

---

responsibility is not known, its duties in regard to San Giovanni are elaborated in the earliest surviving statutes of the Guild, dating from 1301. See G. Filippi, *L'Arte dei Mercatanti di Calimala in Firenze* (Turin, 1889), p. 76.

[9] ASF, Arte di Calimala, *Delib.*, Vol. XXIII, fols. 78r-78v.

[10] G. Baccini, "L'antica cappella dei musici di San Giovanni," *La Cordelia* XIV (1894); offprint (Rocca San Casciano, 1895), pp. 12f. Baccini failed to realize that the documents to which he had access were by no means the first ones in which the singers would have been mentioned, and consequently he placed the establishment of the chapel in the early 1440's, when the chapel numbered six singers. But despite the fact that Baccini does not report thoroughly (he neglects to give volume number, year, etc.), what information he gives is extremely valuable, coming as it does from a volume of the *Arte di Calimala* that has now disappeared.

[11] Frate Beltramo de Feragut of Avignon, *tenorista*, was employed at the Cathedral of Milan from July 1, 1425, to May 30, 1430. See C. Sartori, "Matteo da Perugia e

during the course of the Council, where he would have been brought to the attention of Cosimo and Lorenzo de'Medici.[12] They would undoubtedly have been more than pleased to secure the services of such a well-known figure.

The salaries the singers received for their services at the Cathedral and Baptistry throw considerable light on their relationship to the Medici. Each singer's total wages from the two churches amounted to a little less than two florins a month, a sum hardly representative of the salaries demanded by singers of polyphony in those days. For example, when Bertrand Feragut was employed at the Cathedral of Milan, he received six florins a month;[13] and even that was not excessively high, for the records of the Papal Chapel show that the members of that elite group normally earned between five and eight florins monthly.[14] How was it, then, that Feragut and the other singers were induced to go to Florence for such a low salary? Undoubtedly because they were to receive an additional stipend from some other source; and what more logical source could there have been in Florence than the Medici? The Medici were, after all, one of the richest families in Europe at the time, and they could have well afforded to give the singers an extra allowance. The reason why the Medici might have done so, furthermore, is not difficult to deduce.

One can easily imagine that Cosimo would have wished to emulate the rulers of other European states by maintaining his own musicians. Yet it would have been politically inexpedient for him to do so in his nominal position as an ordinary citizen. Social conditions in Florence forbade any such outward display of prominence. Knowing this, Cosimo must have waited for a propitious moment, such as the transferral of the Council, to put his plan into action. The singers he privately employed would also be associated with the chapels of the two major churches, and his role in selecting the musicians and contributing to their support (if it had to be known to the general public at all) would appear to be for the benefit of the entire city. To be sure, there are no documents from this time that state that the singers were in the private employ of the Medici, or for that matter, that state that the Medici were responsible for the establishment of the chapels. But these are most logical assumptions, not only in view of the low salaries paid the singers and the circumstances under which the Cathedral chapel was established; but also because less than a decade after

---

Bertrand Feragut i due primi Maestri di Cappella del Duomo di Milano," *Acta musicologica* XXVIII (1956), pp. 23ff; F. Fano, *La cappella musicale del Duomo di Milano* (Milan, 1956), pp. 97f.

[12] There is a good possibility that Feragut was in Ferrara even before the Council. See Sartori, p. 27, and A. Pirro, *Histoire de la musique de la fin du XIV° siècle à la fin du XVI°* (Paris, 1940), pp. 65f.

[13] Sartori, p. 24; Fano, p. 97.

[14] F. X. Haberl, "Die Römische 'schola cantorum' und die päpstlichen Kapellsänger bis zur Mitte des 16. Jahrhunderts," *Vierteljahrsschrift für Musikwissenschaft* III (1887), pp. 224ff.

that time a letter to the Medici from the manager of their bank at Bruges testifies to their exclusive authority in selecting and engaging the singers of San Giovanni.[15]

The Cathedral's account books regularly list appropriations for the singers in the decade following the transferral of the Council.[16] Individual names, other than Maestro Benotto's, are rarely given. The documents make it clear, though, that while there were never less than four singers, their number was at times increased to six. An appropriation dated March 6, 1445,[17] names the musicians serving at that time: Maestro Benotto, Francesco Bartoli (the only remaining members of the original group), Ser Antonio di Matteo da Prato,[18] Ser Ghoro di Maso, *tenorista*, Egidio, and Guglielmo.[19] Further changes in the chapel's personnel are indicated in an appropriation dated February 28, 1447:

> for Magister Benottus and five associates, *singers newly appointed*, 27 gold florins [which] are for their salary and pay of four and one half months begun on the 15th day of October just past, *the day on which the office of the previous singers was finished*. [italics mine] (Doc. 5)

It is impossible to know who the new appointees were, since after this time no other appropriations for singers are recorded in the Cathedral's account books until 1479. Indeed, the absence of appropriations during that thirty-year interval would suggest that the singers of San Giovanni were disbanded some time after February, 1447. On the other hand, several of the Baptistry's account books from the late 1440's have survived, showing that Maestro Benotto was associated with that church until the end of January, 1448. These same volumes also show that other singers continued to be employed there even after his departure. In view of this, one might conclude that the singers were discharged from the Cathedral but retained at the Baptistry, were it not that a change of a different nature is indicated. It seems, instead, that in the spring of 1447 the overseers of the Cathedral and the Baptistry made new arrangements, which provided for a more centralized administration of the separate chapels. The singers of San Giovanni were henceforth to be paid a single salary for their services in the two churches, and the expenses as well as the administration of the chapel would be assumed by the Baptistry's overseers.

Evidence in favor of such an administrative change is provided by the Baptistry's account books mentioned above. These volumes show that

---

[15] See below, p. 315.
[16] SMDF: *Stanz.*, II, 4, 16, fols. 85ʳ, 99ᵛ, 125ʳ, 128ʳ, 143ʳ, 150ᵛ, 169ᵛ; *Stanz.*, II, 4, 17, fols. 19ʳ, 25ᵛ, 37ᵛ, 49ʳ, 58ʳ, 65ʳ.
[17] SMDF, *Stanz.*, II, 4, 17, fol. 75ᵛ.
[18] It is quite possible that he was the son of the famous Tuscan organ builder Matteo da Prato.
[19] These two musicians come too late chronologically to be identified with the composers Magister Frater Egidius and Guglielmus da Francia whose works are preserved in various collections of *trecento* polyphony. On the composers, see K. von Fischer, *Studien zur italienischen Musik des Trecento und frühen Quattrocento* (Bern, 1956), p. 8.

during 1448 the singers were each receiving three florins a month from the overseers of San Giovanni.[20] According to Baccini's report, the singers had previously been paid less than one florin a month each for their services there.[21] Setting aside the unlikely possibility that their salaries would have suddenly been more tripled, it seems that this new sum also includes payment for their services at the Cathedral.

Other evidence in favor of an administrative change during 1447 is found in the record of a deliberation made by the consuls of the *Arte della Lana* almost thirty years later (Doc. 6). On August 26, 1475, after reviewing their traditional prerogatives in the secular administration of the Cathedral, the consuls "entrusted and delegated" to the overseers of Santa Maria del Fiore the authority to elect and appoint singers to the Cathedral's service. This action would not have been necessary at the time if authority in such matters had not been transferred to the Baptistry's overseers some thirty years earlier.

From later events in the chapel's history it is not difficult to discern why this administrative change was made in 1447. The Medici, anxious to embark upon a more ambitious program for the chapel, had evidently decided to bring Northern musicians to Florence. By centralizing the administrative and financial affairs of the chapel, the Medici were merely simplifying matters for themselves. The appointments of new singers and other changes could be effected more readily with a smaller, more efficient administrative group; and the Medici, dealing with fewer people, could exercise their influence less obviously. Although Cosimo by this time had been in power for almost fourteen years, he still preferred to wield his authority as inconspicuously as possible.

We may now return to the singers. Maestro Benotto, as we have already learned, had retained his position when the new group of singers was appointed on October 15, 1446. But it seems that he was not happy with the changes in the chapel after that time, for on January 23, 1448, he appeared before the Baptistry's overseers and asked to be relieved of his post:

After hearing Benotto [gap], a singer in the church of San Giovanni, who said that he wished to withdraw from the said office of singing and no longer wished to sing in the said church, the above-said consuls provided and decided after due consideration that the said Benotto could and should withdraw and go when he wishes to, and that he should no longer take part in the services of the said church. And to be sure [of this] they discharged the same Benotto from this moment as useless for the said church, and they removed [him] from the said office of singing in the said church. And [they also decided] that he could and should be paid his salary up to and through all the present day. (Doc. 7)

The consuls were quick to take offense at Benotto's request, and their displeasure was made all the more apparent by the prompt and decisive

---

[20] ASF, Arte di Calimala, *Delib.*, Vol. 20, fols. 5ᵛ, 10ᵛ.
[21] *Op. cit.*, p. 13.

action with which they answered it. After all, they had previously given him evidence of their esteem by retaining him when they engaged the new group of singers. Benotto's position, on the other hand, must have become intolerable. At least until the end of February, 1447, he had continued as master of the chapel; but from the above document, in which he is simply called *cantore*, it is apparent that he had been demoted after that time. He had evidently had to stand by and watch his position of many years endangered and then finally usurped by a newcomer. Later documents suggest that the new singers were Northerners. Cosimo's sons, Piero and Giovanni, had by this time begun to take an active interest in the chapel, and their enthusiasm for contemporary music had undoubtedly led them to prefer Northern musicians. Thus Benotto may have decided that he no longer wished to remain in a chapel which was so Northern in its orientation that he had become an insignificant member. From the manner in which he was discharged, however, it is also evident that he had in some way incurred the displeasure of the Medici, for the Medici always did well by their favored retainers.

Appropriations for the singers are regularly recorded for several months after Benotto's departure.[22] Names, however, are never mentioned; nor is any indication given of the number of singers serving during that period. An appropriation for the month of June, 1448, on the other hand, shows that by that time their number had been reduced to three.[23]

From another source there is evidence that the Medici were meanwhile attempting to fill the vacant positions in the chapel, and had delegated one of their retainers, the singer Pitratto, to go to the Low Countries in search of musicians. On June 6, 1448, Angniolo Tani, the branch manager of the Medici bank at Bruges, wrote the following letter to Piero de'Medici informing him of the success which Pitratto had had in engaging two singers:

RESPECTED SIR AND WITH ALL HONOR TO MY SUPERIORS, ETC.

I wrote you a few lines from Antwerp through Pitratto the singer, telling you how we could not engage that Mattis, the *tenorista*, but that [Pitratto] had found another whom he says he didn't like less. And because he [also] came across a good soprano, of whom he says the chapel has need and [whom] you would be pleased to have, he agreed to bring him. And I, hoping to content you and give you pleasure, and also encouraged by Fruosino da Panzano, agreed to give him the money for [his] expenses; and as I told you, I paid him in all XIV *lire di grossi* which I charged to the account of our [main office] at Florence. At the rate of 51 and ½ *grossi*, these are 65 and ¼ Venetian ducats that you must make good to them. And Pitratto has taken the responsibility in case you should not be pleased with the soprano. And then only 10 or 12 ducats will be lost on the food and drink [consumed] en route of which Fruosino says he would be happy to pay half, and I have taken responsibility for the rest. The said [Pitratto] must render you all the horses there. You will make sure to get them. Pitratto left Antwerp on the 24th of last month and went to

[22] ASF, Arte di Calimala, *Delib.*, Vol. 20, fols. 11ʳ, 15ʳ, 18ᵛ, 23ᵛ.
[23] ASF, Arte di Calimala, *Delib.*, Vol. 20, fol. 27ʳ.

fetch his companions; at any rate he promised me to be there before [the feast of] San Giovanni, and thus I should be pleased to hear that he has done so and happy to know that you are well satisfied with the matter. . . .[24]

Subsequent appropriations show that the new singers were not immediately given a formal appointment to the chapel—probably because Piero de'Medici could not decide whether he wished to retain them. It was well over nine months after the time of their arrival when the two musicians were finally confirmed in their positions:

Being informed that at present there are only three regularly appointed singers in the church of San Giovanni and that the same are not sufficient for the honor of the said church, and that Petrus Petri and Guglelmus de Ver . . . [illegible] have already spent several months serving as singers in the said church without an appointment being made on their behalf [only] because they hoped that a provision would be made for their work . . . and wishing, at the same time, to provide for the honor of the said church and to maintain the promise made to the said singers, [the consuls] appointed . . . the said Petrus and Guglelmus as singers of the said church with that provision and those other usual things that the other singers have. . . . (Doc. 8)

On the same day the consuls also appropriated

for the singers newly elected above, their provision and salary owed them for the time past in which they served as singers, up to and for all the present month of March notwithstanding the fact that they were unappointed. (Doc. 9)

This matter had been settled but three months when another change was recorded:

July 5, 1449
Let it be known to all how Perettus [gap] and Florentinus [gap], singers in the church of San Giovanni, having appeared in the presence of the noble Bartholomeus Niccolai de Martellis, one of the present lord consuls of the said Guild, Iohannis Leopardi, and myself Franciscus, notary of the said Guild, *requested for themselves and their other associates* [who are also] *singers in the said church* permission from the said Bartholomeus to leave Florence and return to their own country, with the provision that they be paid the salary owed them for the month of June just past and that a gift be given them as a bonus. And they arrived at . . . this agreement with the said Bartholomeus, that is, that they should be paid for the one month finished on the last day of the said month of June and [that] three florins [should be given] each of them as a bonus. And the same promised the said Bartholomeus that they themselves or some of [their group] would return to the service of the said church of San Giovanni whenever they should be so requested by the future consuls of the said Guild, provided that the said consuls agree to pay the costs of the trip and other [expenses] incurred on the journey back, up to the sum of twenty florins for each of the same singers; and that the payment of the said provision and bonus having been made, a letter of recommendation should also be given them. And the said Bartholomeus had the 8 florins which were due the said Perettus paid him, and the said Florentinus . . . received 16 florins for himself and for his associate Cornelius. . . . [italics mine] (Doc. 10)

[24] Printed in A. Grunzweig, *Correspondance de la Filiale de Bruges des Medici* (Brussels, 1931), pp. 12f.

Although only three singers are mentioned by name, the wording of the document suggests that the request was made for all the members of the chapel. But it is impossible to know whether the entire group departed, for after that time no other documents regarding singers are found in the account books of San Giovanni until 1507.

Information about the singers of San Giovanni during the next few decades is drawn principally from published and unpublished letters found in the Medici archives. In these years there is little or no indication of the number of singers employed, how frequently the personnel changed, or what the salaries were; in only a few cases is it possible to identify individual musicians. Despite the many gaps in our information, however, it is discernible nevertheless that the Medici consistently pursued their policy, established in 1446, of employing Northern musicians.

From a letter published by Armand Grunzweig, there is an indication that other Northerners were immediately engaged to replace those who left Florence in July of 1449. The letter,[25] dated February 4, 1450, was written by Pierre de Langhe, master of the choirboys at the Cathedral of Tournai, to his friend and countryman Robijn Scufeleere who was then in Florence. From the tone of the letter, as well as from the frequent references in it to other singers, it can be inferred that Robijn himself was a singer then employed in Florence. For this reason Grunzweig has suggested that Robijn might be the soprano engaged by Pitratto in the spring of 1448.[26] But, as the record of appointment shows, the soprano was called either Petrus or Guglelmus. Robijn Scufeleere, therefore, must have joined the chapel after the departure of the other Northern singers.

An unpublished letter referred to by Baccini also provides some indirect evidence about the singers of San Giovanni in the following year.[27] The letter, written by Niccolò Strozzi to his brother Filippo, who was in Naples at the time, describes the visit to Florence in June, 1451, of the singers of the King of Naples, and states that they went to the Cathedral on Pentecost Sunday[28] to hear a solemn Vesper service with music. Even though Strozzi (or Baccini) does not say so, it is obvious that the Vesper service was performed by the singers of San Giovanni. This information is in accordance with our knowledge of the singers' duties, since it was stated at the time of the establishment of the chapel that they were to perform Vespers at the Cathedral on the major feast days. The letter also offers additional evidence that the singers of San Giovanni continued to perform at the Cathedral after February, 1447, *i.e.*, in those years when payments to them are no longer recorded in the Cathedral's account books.

[25] Printed in A. Grunzweig, "Notes sur la musique des Pays-Bas au XVe siècle," *Bulletin de L'Institut Historique Belge de Rome* XVIII (1937), pp. 87f.
[26] "Notes sur la musique," p. 81.
[27] *Op. cit.* (fn. 10), p. 20. Baccini states that the letter was among the Strozzi papers at the ASF. I was unable to locate it.
[28] June 13. See A. Cappelli, *Cronologia, cronografia e calendario perpetuo* (Milan, 1939), p. 104.

The visit of the singers of the King of Naples to Florence in 1451 furnishes an excellent example of the frequent cultural interchanges so characteristic of Renaissance Italy. It is doubtful in this case, however, that the invitation to the Neapolitans was extended for cultural reasons. At the time, Naples was leagued with Venice against Florence and Milan; war was imminent. By requesting the visit, the Florentines were apparently hoping to improve relations with King Alfonso of Naples and thus prepare the ground for a rapprochement between the two states. Indeed, the political motivation behind the invitation is well reflected in three successive communications from the Florentine government to its ambassador in Naples at the time, the humanist Giannozzo Manetti:

May 27, 1451
We here have nothing else to write except that here we are busy preparing a beautiful feast for the celebration of our protector, St. John. So if the royal singers come, it will be most pleasing to all our [people] and they will be seen most willingly by this Signory. . . . (Doc. 11)

June 5, 1451
Nor shall we add anything else but that with great desire the people await those royal singers, the adornment of the solemnity of the Baptist and the happiness of our city, who, *for many reasons and principally out of consideration for the prince whom they serve*, will be most happily received by us. And you must advise us of the day on which they are departing. . . . [italics mine] (Doc. 12)

June 11, 1451
And we are expecting the singers any moment now; *and they will be most willingly received out of consideration for that prince*. . . . [italics mine] (Doc. 13)

Although no record of the Neopolitan singers' visit has survived in the account books of either the Cathedral or the Baptistry, several documents are extant which record their visit to the Santissima Annunziata:

Saturday, the 19th of June, 1451
For food expenses, 15 *soldi* for 35 eggplants, and 54 *soldi* for 6 flasks of Trebbiano at 9 *soldi* the flask, and ten *soldi* for thirty [loaves of] white bread, and ten *soldi* for fruit, all of which were bought in order to entertain the singers of the King of Aragon. (Doc. 14)

Monday, the 21st of June, 1451
For extraordinary expenses, six *soldi* to the same Frate Biagio [organist of the Santissima Annunziata], [which] he said he had paid for having Antonio's [Squarcialupi] *organetto* brought [to the church] and carried back again. It was when the singers of the King of Aragon came to sing the Mass. (Doc. 15)

The singers of San Giovanni are next mentioned in the well-known letter of Dufay to Piero and Giovanni de'Medici:[29]

MAGNIFICENT AND NOBLE SIRS, ALL HUMBLE COMMENDATION BEFOREHAND!
Since I well know that you have always taken pleasure in song and since, I believe, you have not changed your preferences, I have felt encouraged to

[29] Printed in Grunzweig, "Notes sur la musique," p. 86; H. Kühner, "Ein unbekannter Brief von Guillaume Dufay," *Acta musicologica* XI (1939), p. 114; B. Becherini, "Relazioni di musici fiamminghi con la Corte dei Medici, nuovi documenti," *La Rinascita* IV (1941), p. 87.

THE SINGERS OF SAN GIOVANNI IN FLORENCE 319

send you some chansons which, at the request of some gentlemen of the King's court, I composed recently when I was in France with Monseigneur de Savoye. I also have some others which I shall send you at another time. In addition, in this past year I wrote four Lamentations for Constantinople which are rather good: three of them are for four voices and the texts were sent to me from Naples. I do not know whether you have them there. If you do not have them, be so kind as to let me know and I shall send them to you. Furthermore, I am very much pleased with Francesco Sachetti, your representative here, for during the past year I was in need of something at the court of Rome and he helped me most magnanimously and treated me most graciously for which I extend my unceasing thanks. I understand that you now have some good people in your chapel at San Giovanni and because of this, if it pleases you, I should like to send you some of my little things more often than I have done in the past. I do this also out of my regard for Antonio [Squarcialupi], your good friend and mine, to whom I beg you commend me cordially. Magnificent and noble sirs, if there is something which I can do here for your lordships, please let me know and I shall do it with all my heart through the aid of our Lord, who I hope will grant you a good and long life, and at the end paradise.

Written at Geneva, the 22nd of February [1454][30]

Your humble chaplain and unworthy servant,
GUILLAUME DUFAY, *Canon of Cambrai*

Dufay states that he had heard that there were some "good people" among the singers of San Giovanni. Indeed, during the 1450's the singers must truly have enjoyed wide fame, for their services were much in demand in Florence, and they are reported as having travelled extensively in those years. According to Baccini, in 1456 the singers of San Giovanni performed the Mass on St. Peter's day at the church of St. Peter Major in Florence at the request of Antonio di Maso degli Albizzi, a member of one of the city's most influential families.[31] Baccini, always citing the same lost account books of the Baptistry, also states that the singers made a small trip throughout Italy sometime during 1457, absenting themselves with the consuls' permission. They did not, however, receive any salary while they were away.[32] Elsewhere it is reported that on Easter Sunday, April 2, 1458, the "singers of Florence" performed at the Cathedral of Modena.[33] The singers also journeyed to Siena on the Feast of the Assumption, August 15, of the same year, to sing the Mass at the Cathedral.[34]

Without saying when, Baccini also reports that the singers of San Giovanni were disbanded for several years, and that as a result the Mass remained almost deserted at the Baptistry—an indication of the drawing

---

[30] The letter has no indication of the year in which it was written. Kühner (*op. cit.*, p. 115) states that it is more than probable that the Lamentations that Dufay says he wrote in the previous year were written under the direct impression of the fall of Constantinople (May, 1453), and for this reason assigns the date 1454 to the letter. I am inclined to agree with him rather than with Grunzweig (*op. cit.*, p. 75) who suggests 1456 as the earliest possible date.

[31] *Op. cit.*, p. 13.

[32] *Loc. cit.*

[33] L. F. Valdrighi, *Cappelle, concerti e musiche di Casa d'Este* (Modena, 1884), p. 4.

[34] Baccini, *op. cit.*, p. 13.

power of the chapel's performances. In an effort to recall the populace back to the Baptistry, especially on the major feast days, the consuls of the *Arte di Calimala* gave full faculty to Cosimo de'Medici to institute a chapel at his own expense, engaging as many singers as he pleased[35] (as though he had not done this from the very beginning). Since Cosimo died on August 1, 1464, and the last report of the singers is from August 15, 1458, it must be that musical services were suspended between those dates. A letter has survived, moreover, which shows that the singers were performing once again by June of 1464, so there is little doubt that the chapel was already re-established several months before Cosimo's death. Although Baccini gives no reason for the disbanding of the singers, it could very well be that Northern musicians were unavailable at the time. Another possibility which deserves consideration is that the Medici had purposely allowed the chapel to decline in order to acknowledge their policies publicly. Certainly after that time the Medici made no secret of the fact that they alone were responsible for the affairs of the chapel.

Evidence that for some years the Medici supported the re-established chapel with their own funds is provided by the letter mentioned above, written to Piero de'Medici:

MAGNIFICENT SIR ETC.

We cannot do anything but have confidence in your magnanimity, as we have always been accustomed to doing. And this is that having had out-of-town guests here in San Giovanni we were in honor bound to receive them according to custom. And this could not be done without some expense. For this reason all of us with great affection beg you to let us have our salary from the Annunziata as a loan [in advance]. If not all, at least a part of it. We would not be bothering you at the present time were it not for the great necessity which constrains us to do so. We shall say no more except that all of us commend ourselves to your magnanimity.
                    On the 19th day of June, 1464
                    All your servants,
                    The singers of San Giovanni in Florence[36]

The letter reveals that the singers had begun performing at the Santissima Annunziata some time before this date. Later documents show that their duties there comprised performing the Mass on Saturday mornings.[37] The letter also indicates that the singers' salaries were apportioned according to their services in each church. The account books of the Santissima Annunziata from these years are available and they record no payments to the singers of San Giovanni, as is the case fifteen years later. This offers additional evidence, therefore, that at the time the Medici were paying for the singers' services in three churches.

On the death of Cosimo, the leadership of the state passed to Piero, who was himself in feeble health. Noting Piero's infirmities and the ex-

---
[35] *Loc. cit.*
[36] Printed in Baccini, *op. cit.*, pp. 15f; Becherini, *op. cit.*, pp. 103f.
[37] See below Doc. 25.

treme youth of his eldest son, a dissident faction within the Medici's own party began to lay plans for deposing him. In August, 1466, the opposition, which had been growing for two years, erupted into an open revolt. But the hegemony of the Medici was by this time firmly established, and Piero was able to quell the conspirators within the month. That Piero had allowed the chapel to decline during those troubled times is evident from the following letter,[38] written, apparently, after the defeat of the Medici's opponents, by the singer Jachetto di Marvilla to the young Lorenzo de' Medici:

MY RESPECTED, MAGNIFICENT, AND MOST HONORED LORD!
After my unlimited and due commendations.

Maestro Lambino, singer of the Pope and retainer of the Magnificent Lord your father, has often spoken to me many times how you and the Magnificence of your father wanted to re-establish the chapel at San Giovanni. Therefore, when I came to Florence with the most reverend Lord Monsignor, Cardinal of Rieti, Legate of Bologna, I spoke of it to Messer Golino Martelli, he being your true friend and adherent. *Considering the situation at the time, he replied that the moment was not opportune to speak of such matters; that the Magnificent Lord your father, however, was of the intention that as soon as the affairs of the city of Florence were settled, then his Lordship would begin anew the chapel of singers.* Although I have been in the chapel of King Alfonso and then in that of King Ferrante (as the ambassador of King Ferrante, Messer Marino Pignatella, and the noble Messer Golino can inform you), and although I have been in the chapel of the Pope (so that seeing me your most honored Lordship would recognize me), I have always wanted to live in Florence rather than in Rome or Naples. This because I would be able to have news from home every day, and because I see and realize the great prosperity, victory, and eternal fame of the Lord your father, and of the wonderful condition, which may I say, it would be to place myself in your hands.... Nothing else, I commend myself, as always, to the Magnificent Lord your father and to your magnificence and greatness. May God make you both prosper and keep you from every illness; *and I say this because I know that you may fear that more than the men of this world.* [italics mine]
From Bologna, on the 15th day of September, 1566 [1466][39]

The humble servant of your Magnificent Lordship,
JACHETTO DI MARVILLA, the singer

Jachetto's request was not granted, for Piero had already made other plans to revitalize the chapel. Just around that time he had once again delegated one of his retainers, the singer Simone, to recruit new musicians. Simone went first to Lyon, where he was advised by the manager of the Medici bank in that city, Giuliano del Zacheria, to go to the Low Coun-

---

[38] Printed in Becherini, *op. cit.*, pp. 96ff.

[39] The references that Jachetto makes to the political situation in Florence clearly indicate that he was in the city immediately after the attempted coup d'état, and that he was writing but a few weeks after he had left Florence, *i.e.*, in September, 1466. The letter, however, is mistakenly dated 1566. Since the letter appears to be an original, it cannot be that a scribe erroneously copied a 5 for a 4. It must have been a slip of the pen on Jachetto's part, or it could also be that his 4 looks like our 5. Becherini also assigns the letter to 1466, without, however, giving any reason for doing so.

tries. Giuliano del Zacheria also furnished him with a letter of introduction to Tommaso Portinari, the Medici representative at Bruges. In the course of a letter[40] to Piero, dated February 13, 1467, Portinari communicated the following information:

And in the past days Simone the singer arrived here, whom you had sent from there [Florence] to Lyon to find and appoint some singers there for the chapel of San Giovanni, according to what G[i]uliano del Zacheria has written me. He [Simone] and I with him have done so much that this tenor of whom you wrote me one other time has agreed to come, and with him another associate. And I have sent Simone to Cambrai and Douai where there are many singers, and I have directed him to our friends [there] in order to help him find the others. And I await his return here every day, and I shall be sure to send them there [to Florence] as soon as possible, giving them the necessary [money] for the trip. And I shall keep you informed of everything through another [letter]. . . .

Evidently one of the "friends" in Cambrai to whom Portinari directed Simone was Dufay; and from the well-known letter[41] written to him by Antonio Squarcialupi on the following May 1, we learn that Dufay himself had had a hand in selecting singers for the chapel:

MY VENERABLE FATHER, RIGHTLY TO BE HONORED ABOVE ALL OTHERS!

With the greatest joy to my soul, I have read and often reread your most humane letter; and I embraced with all my heart the fellow-singers whom you sent, the best of your church, just as you wrote, and having heard them, I am easily induced to believe it. They are, indeed, absolutely excellent, both in sweetness of voice and in the knowledge and the art of singing, and worthy of you, their teacher. It is not possible to tell you how much this has pleased our Magnificent Piero de'Medici, who loves you very much, dear father, and always speaks of you with great respect. And he asserts what I can freely agree to, that you are the greatest ornament of our age. Also Lorenzo de'Medici, the son of Piero, regards you with admiration. Because of the excellence of his divine talent, [Lorenzo] enjoys quality in all the arts, and thus he delights exceedingly in the greater refinement of your music. And for that reason he admires your art and respects you as a father. . . .

It is interesting to note that somewhat later in the year one of the new singers got himself into some sort of difficulty with Piero. A report from the records of the *Stinche*, the Florentine prison, reveals that on November 1, 1467,

Johannes Franciosus, alias "the Abbot," a singer in San Giovanni, was brought to the said wardens in captivity by Ser Marianus de Pistorio, Captain of the Signory's constabulary, at the request of Pierus Cosimi de Medicis [one] of the Council of Ten [with the stipulation] that he should not be released without a letter or a note from him [Pierus]. (Doc. 16)

It was two weeks before Piero was content to see the singer released from prison:

---

[40] Printed in Grunzweig, "Notes sur la musique," p. 78, fn. 2.
[41] Printed in G. Gaye, ed., *Carteggio inedito di artisti* (Florence, 1839), Vol. I, pp. 208f; O. Kade, "Biographisches zu Antonio Squarcialupi, dem Florentiner Organist im XV. Jahrhunderte," *Monatshefte für Musik-Geschichte* XVII (1885), pp. 13ff.

On the 15th day of November, he was released as a result of the permission conceded him by the said Pierus, which was ascertained by Ser Marianus de Pistorio on the said day. (Doc. 16)

A report of the singers' activities in the following year comes from Baccini, who states that in 1468 they were ordered to accompany the lord priors of the Republic "first to Mantua and then to Milan and to remain in their constant service and according to their pleasure."[42] The document, dated May 31, 1468, which Baccini saw, recorded a payment to the singers for the expenses of their trip and for the time they remained at Milan. Baccini says that the document from which he drew this information did not reveal the reason for the trip. He conjectures, however, that the singers accompanied the priors to Milan on the occasion of the peace treaty signed in that city on April 25, 1468, between the Florentines and the Venetians.[43]

From another letter[44] written by Jachetto di Marvilla to Lorenzo de'Medici it is possible to discern that a crisis occurred in the chapel during the summer months of 1468. The letter informs us of the clandestine departure of all the singers of San Giovanni, among whom, evidently, were those sent by Dufay. As mentioned above, Piero had previously had some difficulties with one of the singers, and it could very well be that the instigator of this defection, the cleric Johannes Cordier of Tournai,[45] was himself the musician who had been imprisoned. Jachetto, however,

---

[42] *Op. cit.*, p. 17.
[43] *Op. cit.*, p. 18.
[44] Printed in Becherini, *op. cit.*, pp. 98ff. The letter is dated Rome, March 21, without indication of year. But from the reference that Jachetto makes to Lorenzo's forthcoming nuptials, at the close of the letter, it is clear that Jachetto was writing in 1469: "Dio vi conserva e faccia grazia che la prima notte che voi dormireti con la nobile e illustra vostra moglie possiate fare un figliolo masculo." Lorenzo had been affianced to Clarice Orsini during the month of December, 1468, and was married on June 4, 1469.
[45] Jo. Cordier, "cappellanus ad altare S. Danielis, situm in ecclesia collegiata S. Donatiani Brugen., Tornacen. dioc.," is recorded among the Papal singers for the first time on January 2, 1469, and was associated with that group until the end of July, 1471. See Haberl, *op. cit.*, p. 230. After that time Cordier joined the chapel of the King of Naples. See E. Motta, "Musici alla Corte degli Sforza," *Archivio storico lombardo*, Serie II, Vol. IV (1887), pp. 312f. Cordier was engaged as a singer to the Duke of Milan on October 12, 1474, and remained in that city until 1477. During the 1480's he is reported to have been in the chapel of the Archduke Maximilian of Austria, but later he re-entered the service of the Milanese court, where his singing was much admired by the Duchess of Milan, Beatrice d'Este. See Motta, *op. cit.*, pp. 536f., and G. Cesari, "Musica e musicisti alla corte sforzesca," *Rivista musicale italiana* XXIX (1922), p. 45. However, Cesari (p. 16) is mistaken when he states that Cordier fled Florence in the company of Guglielmus de Steynsel and Francesco Milletti, for, as will be noted below, those two musicians did not even arrive in Florence until the early 1480's. Cesari's erroneous assertion was reprinted by F. Ghisi in *I canti carnascialeschi nelle fonti musicali del XV e XVI secolo* (Florence, 1937), p. 57, and later, not only accepted, but further embellished by A. Einstein: "as a rule the liberal Lodovico [Sforza, Duke of Milan] was able to attract the miserly Medici's best musicians; in 1485, for example, Cordier, Wilhelm de Steynsel, and François Millet . . ." (*The Italian Madrigal* [Princeton, N. J., 1949], Vol. I, p. 277).

only discreetly alludes to what must have been an embarrassing situation for the Medici; he is more interested in communicating his own news:

MAGNIFICENT AND GENEROUS LORD, MY MOST SINGULAR LORD, AFTER MY CONTINUED COMMENDATIONS!

You know that when Cordiero and all his associates departed and left your chapel of San Giovanni I immediately went from Siena to Your Magnificence, to Golino Martelli, to his son Niccolò, and to Maestro Antonio degli Organi [Squarcialupi] in order that I might see, hear, and understand the intentions of each of you with regard to re-establishing your chapel. Then Your Magnificence as well as all the above named replied to me that at the moment the Magnificence of your mighty and generous father was exceedingly annoyed with the shortcomings and instability of the other singers who had left, as mentioned. But also that were there to come along a chapel with, first of all, a good tenor, and with three good treble voices of good habits, and with their contratenor, they would always be welcome. Then, since I had advised Vincinet before he came to Florence that he ought to consider the commission I had had from your generous father and from Golino Martelli—that is, to find some fellows for your chapel—I was patient about my place as I had it promised me by your father. So because of my great desire to live in Florence, I have been continually zealous and have worked hard to find such singers who were suitable and able and who had good voices and ability in order to re-establish your chapel. Thus I departed from Siena, having heard in the month of November of your intention of not wanting to remain without singers; I arrived in Rome on the 26th January with the purpose of learning and observing whether there were any singers there who would be worthy of your chapel. There, having found what you need, I spoke to them secretly and told them how good and fine it is for singers to stay in Florence when they are good.... And I swear to you and promise to bring you a good tenor who has a large voice, high and low, sweet and sufficient; and three very high treble singers with good, full, and suave voices; and myself for contra[tenor]. And meanwhile, when we wish to sing *a quattro voce*, Bartholomeo could be the bass. And when we have arrived in Florence, we shall send to France for a contra[tenor] who is a good bass as well. I inform Your Magnificence that none of these singers has ever been in Florence....

It appears that Jachetto's efforts were to no avail and that he never succeeded in achieving his wish to live in Florence. Documents in the archives of St. Peter's in Rome show that he was associated with that church from 1469 to 1471.[46] Later, in 1473, he is recorded at the court of the Este in Ferrara,[47] whence he passed to the service of the Duke of Milan in 1474.[48]

Since after this time all documentation ceases for several years, it is impossible to know whether Piero took any immediate steps to replace the musicians. The lack of documentation may signify that musical services were discontinued for a while and that the chapel was reorganized only under the patronage of the young Lorenzo, who succeeded to the rule of Florence on the death of Piero in December, 1469. From this

---

[46] Haberl, p. 237.   [47] Valdrighi, *op. cit.*, p. 7.
[48] Motta, *op. cit.*, pp. 323, 525; see also C. Sartori, "Josquin des Prés cantore del Duomo di Milano (1459-1472)," *Annales musicologiques* IV (1956), p. 64, fn. 1.

THE SINGERS OF SAN GIOVANNI IN FLORENCE

hitherto unpublished letter written to Lorenzo three years after the departure of Cordier and his associates it would certainly seem that the chapel was functioning normally again and that it had been doing so for some time. The writer of the letter, Filipotto de Dortenche, requests a position in the chapel. He does so not because he has heard that there was a position open at the time, but because of personal circumstances which constrain him to return to Florence. Indeed, from the many references to Florence, as well as from the familiar manner in which he addresses Lorenzo, it appears that Filipotto had formerly been a singer of San Giovanni:

IN THE NAME OF GOD, on the 27th day of May, 1471
DEAREST AND WISE MAN, TO BE HONORED AS A FATHER, AFTER DUE COMMENDATIONS ETC.

Dearest *Chompare*,[49] I have not written to you in the past because there was no occasion to do so; and these few lines are to let you know that this year His Majesty the King sent me to France in order to bring some singers back here. In doing so I passed by your city but having been ordered not to speak a word of it to you and not wanting to disobey, I passed [instead] outside [the walls] and went thus to fulfill the King's wishes. Later I returned but I was little rewarded for my services. This King nevertheless granted me X gold ducats a month, 5 lengths of fine material for clothing, and thirdly XX ducats . . . [illegible] a year, besides which he gave me a captaincy in Calabria for one year from which I draw 50 ducats, and [he did] all [this] most graciously. But since my wife is desirous of returning to her native city and nags me [about it] every hour of the day, I would for this reason be happy to return there. I would see to it that you would always have a good, superior chapel; with the condition that I would like you to provide me with a suitable house (*spedale*) for the rest of my life and in addition, 6 gold ducats a month. So, dear *Chompare*, see if you can recall me there since you know that you will always have a [faithful] servant; and answer me and give me your reply through the person who gives you this letter; and please keep it a secret and be cautious, for were this to be known here I should be undone. I have nothing else to say except that as always I commend myself to you. May Christ keep you happy.

Your servant,
FILIPOTTO DE DORTENCHE
singer of His Majesty, King Ferrante, at Naples (Doc. 17)

The only other information concerning the singers of San Giovanni before the early 1480's is contained in another letter, also previously unpublished, written to Lorenzo on September 3, 1473, by Braccio Martelli, one of his dearest friends and principal adherents. At the time, Lorenzo was staying at the Medici villa in Caffagiuolo, some distance from Florence. New singers had arrived from the North, and Braccio's purpose in writing was to present a certain Arnolfo, the leader of the group. Braccio, however, did not neglect to give other news about the state of affairs prevailing at the Baptistry during Lorenzo's absence:

---

[49] By addressing Lorenzo with this term, Filipotto lets us know that Lorenzo had stood as godfather to one of his children.

Arnolfo is coming there in order to be appointed as a singer in San Giovanni. And I, out of consideration for him as well as for the needs of the Guild, am writing you this letter recommending him to you and begging you to write a letter for him to Bernardo di Nichola Capponi to the effect that he should appoint [Arnolfo] and his companions. It would probably be better to go even further when you write, that is, you should mention [the necessity of] correcting [at least a] part of the inconveniences which, as you partially know, exist there less through the fault of the singers than through that of the chaplains, who because of somebody's ill-will are turning that church upside down. And now that I am there as treasurer I see it proved every day. That Bernardo, master of the chapel, gets a total sum for the singers and for those whom he hires on a monthly basis, and God only knows and understands the harm which the chapel receives from this arrangement. I think that he will eventually put even the poor who come begging to singing there so that he can make more [money]. You're wise; since you have to stay there [at Caffagiuolo] for a while yet, it might be a good idea to write a word about this to the said Bernardo Capponi. And in any case, recommend Arnolfo, the bearer of this letter, and I shall attend to the rest here.

        Farewell,
        Your BRACCIO MARTELLI (Doc. 18)

  The letter indicates that an important change had taken place in the administration of the chapel since the time of its re-establishment under the acknowledged direction of Cosimo. The singers were no longer being supported exclusively by Medici funds. Braccio's reference to "the Guild" shows that the *Arte di Calimala* had once again assumed financial responsibility for the singers' services at the Baptistry; and since no payments to the singers are yet recorded in the account books of the Cathedral and the Santissima Annunziata, this was undoubtedly true for those churches as well. Lorenzo, on the other hand, must have continued to supplement the salaries of those singers who were in his private employ. The plan for maintaining the singers had thus reverted to the arrangement inaugurated in 1447—but with one notable difference: Lorenzo was openly directing the affairs of the chapel. The Medici supremacy in artistic as well as in political affairs, cloaked in secrecy by Cosimo and only cautiously asserted by Piero, was now fully acknowledged by Lorenzo. Through a rare combination of personal charm and political genius he was able to exercise absolute authority in the State and yet maintain the existing constitution with its appearance of republican freedom.

  Freed from the rigors of internal politics, especially after the abortive conspiracy of the Pazzi in 1478, Lorenzo was able to turn his talents to the conduct of diplomacy abroad and to the arts of peace at home. Thus during his reign the Florentine chapel became one of the most outstanding institutions of its kind in Europe. His unceasing endeavors succeeded in attracting to Florence many of the most renowned musicians of the day. Some of them remained but briefly; others found a new home in the congenial atmosphere of a city where literature, art, philosophy, and music were patronized and encouraged by a "private citizen" whose liberality has rarely been equalled by princes or even kings. Indeed, Lorenzo's love of music was so well known that musicians whom he had never met felt encouraged to address him in such terms as the following:[50]

MY MOST HONORED LORD!
I commend myself most humbly to your good grace. There has come into my hands a newly composed motet [and] it seems to me that it will be found excellent [when] performed by those in your chapel. And because I have been advised that Your Lordship takes pleasure in such things, I am sending it to you; and it is my intention that, should anything else come to me which seems worthy of sending you, Your Lordship will be notified of it. I implore you, my most honored Lord, that it please you always to hold me in the ranks of your faithful servants [and] I pray to God, my most honored Lord, that He give you a good and long life.
Written at Lyon on the 26th day of June.

Your most humble servant,
LE PETIT, m° at Lyon

It was not, however, solely Lorenzo's reputation as a magnanimous and enlightened patron of music that raised the chapel to its pre-eminent position. From the records of his correspondence it is evident that he pursued with even greater vigor the policies inaugurated by his father and his uncle. Letters were written to Ferrara, to Naples, and to Flanders,[51] all with the same purpose—to secure the best musicians for the Florentine chapel:

in emulation [of King Ferrante of Naples] Lorenzo de'Medici, with the purpose that nothing should be superior to the dignity and adornment of his country, and in order not to appear that he was receiving any favor from that King (whom he himself had exhorted to form a private library), embellished the temple of San Giovanni most beautifully with the very sweetest concert of voices. . . .[52]

At first only the Baptistry and the Santissima Annunziata profited from Lorenzo's efforts on behalf of the singers of San Giovanni, for on February 1, 1478, an independent chapel was established at the Cathedral. Although the reasons that prompted the Cathedral's overseers to take such a step are not given in any of the surviving documents, it would seem that the decision came about as a result of the many irregularities in the administration of the singers of San Giovanni, as mentioned in Braccio Martelli's letter. The overseers' first move was to regain authority to appoint singers to the Cathedral's service. As previously noted, this authority was secured by a vote of the consuls of the *Arte della Lana* on August 26, 1475 (Doc. 6). The overseers were apparently content with

[50] The letter is printed in Becherini, *op. cit.*, p. 94.
[51] Records of these letters are printed in M. del Piazzo, ed., *Protocolli del carteggio di Lorenzo il Magnifico per gli anni 1473-74, 1477-92* (Deputazione di storia patria per la Toscana, Documenti di storia italiana, Serie II, Vol. II [Florence, 1956]), pp. 48, 218, 222, 377. Apparently none of these letters has survived.
[52] *Raphaelis Brandolini Lippi lunioris de musica et poetica opusculum*, quoted in A. de la Fage, *Essais de diphthérographie musicale* (Paris, 1864), Vol. I, p. 63.

that much in the beginning, since it was not until over two years later that the singers of San Giovanni were relieved of their duties at the Cathedral and a new group of singers appointed. Seven years were to pass before the singers of San Giovanni were readmitted to the Cathedral's service. Before recounting further developments at the Baptistry during those years we may consider the Cathedral's independent chapel.[53]

That chapel, established by a decree of the overseers dated February 1, 1478, was composed of five adult singers and four soprano choristers, the latter students in the Cathedral's school of chant and grammar.[54] Four of the five adults were regularly employed as chaplains in the Church, and served as well in the plainchant choir.[55] It was a very practical arrangement. Since the majority of the singers had permanent appointments at the Cathedral, it was doubtless expected that the frequent changes of personnel, so characteristic among the singers of San Giovanni, would no longer present a problem. For the same reason absences and other details of the chapel's administration could be dealt with more directly. It would not be necessary, moreover, to pay the chaplains the high salaries customarily given to itinerant Northern musicians. The expenses of the chapel, thus reduced, could easily be met with the Cathedral's own funds.

The appointment of the singers was confirmed in a deliberation of April 17, 1478,[56] and on the following June 26 salaries for the preceding five months were appropriated for Ser Francesco Boscherini, tenor; Ser Domenico Panichini, tenor; Ser Arnolfo da Francia, contratenor; Ser Felice di Giovanni, contratenor; Ser Antonio da Montughi, master of the chapel; and the four soprano choristers.[57] By December of the same year, however, the deaths of two singers and the departure of a third had sharply reduced the number of adults in the chapel.[58] On February 5, 1479, in an

---

[53] Most of the documents concerning the Cathedral's independent chapel have been collected and published in an excellent article by Albert Seay, this JOURNAL XI (1958), pp. 45ff. Seay, however, was unaware that the singers of San Giovanni had previously performed at the Cathedral, and that they subsequently returned there. Consequently his study draws the conclusion that musical services at the Cathedral were initiated with the independent chapel. I have included here only a few documents not given by Seay that are essential to the present study.

[54] Seay, p. 49.

[55] SMDF: QC, VIII, 1, 49, fol. 4ʳ; QC, VIII, 1, 50, fol. 34ʳ; QC, VIII, 1, 53, fol. 53ʳ. Ser Arnolfo, the fifth singer, as we have already learned, arrived in Florence in September of 1473. He is undoubtedly to be identified with the composer Arnolfo Schard (last name doubtful), two of whose works are preserved in a Florentine MS. See B. Becherini, "Autori minori nel codice fiorentino Magl. XIX, 176," *Revue belge de musicologie* IV (1950), pp. 24ff. Another piece in the MS Rome, Biblioteca Apostolica Vaticana, Cappella Giulia, XIII, 27, fols. 65ᵛ-66ʳ, may also be his.

[56] SMDF, *Delib.*, II, 2, 5, fol. 36ʳ.

[57] Seay, p. 49.

[58] *Ibid.*, pp. 49f. Although Arnolfo left the Cathedral chapel at that time, he remained in Florence for several months afterwards. A document, dated March 26, 1479, states that on that day the Cathedral's overseers ordered that one florin be paid to Ser Arnolfo, "a singer and chaplain in San Lorenzo [the family church of the Medici] for his work in having composed *canti*" (SMDF, QC, VIII, 1, 65, fol. 55ᵛ). Arnolfo left Florence a few months after the payment was made. The record of a letter

THE SINGERS OF SAN GIOVANNI IN FLORENCE

effort to increase the number of personnel, the overseers drew up another provision in favor of the chapel, granting special privileges to its two original members and formally appointing four other singers who had been serving since the previous January 1.[59] As a result the personnel now consisted of two contraltos, Ser Francesco di Lorenzo and Ser Matteo di Paolo; two basses, Ser Antonio di Bianciardi and Ser Niccolò di Lore; one tenor, Ser Francesco Boscherini; and the master of the chapel, Ser Antonio da Montughi.

It is of importance to note that no mention was made of the choristers on that occasion.[60] Their names, furthermore, are never again recorded in any subsequent appropriations for the singers. That they continued to assist in the chapel, however, is proved by the following documents, which also reveal that the choristers were now given instruction in polyphonic music. Doubtless it was felt that this instruction was sufficient remuneration for their services. It would, after all, eventually qualify them for higher paid positions as adult members of the chapel:

June 12, 1479
For Ser Antonio di Marco da Montughi, teacher of the boys who sing, twelve *lire* and eleven *soldi* for six months finished as above. . . . (Doc. 19)

January 11, 1480
The overseers . . . decided that the paymaster . . . should give and pay two *lire*, two *soldi*, and four *danari* to Ser Antonius de Montughio, a chaplain of the said church and teacher of figural music, for his work in instructing the choristers who sing figural music in the said chapel. . . . (Doc. 20)

The choristers were nevertheless given little gifts from time to time. On April 6, 1483, it is recorded that two *lire* each were paid to eight choristers "for their recompense" in performing polyphonic music. The overseers wished it to be clearly understood, however, that this monetary reward was "only for this time and never again in any way" (Doc. 21). It is interesting to note that by this time the number of choristers serving in the chapel had been increased from four to eight.

Some difficulty apparently arose during the summer months of 1479, for the singers were temporarily relieved of their positions and did not begin performing again until the following November 1. By that time one of the contraltos had left. He was replaced by the Spaniard Frate Piero di Giovanni who sang *tenore alto*.[61] The chapel numbered six adult singers until the end of 1480 when Frate Piero di Giovanni and the bass Ser Niccolò di Lore both left the Cathedral's service. The four remaining singers are recorded through the end of June, 1481, when the other bass,

---

written on August 2, 1480, reveals that Lorenzo de'Medici requested him "to defer sending the singers here [to Florence] for another time." See Del Piazzo, *op. cit.*, p. 113. As will be noted below, Arnolfo returned to Florence during the 1480's.
[59] Seay, p. 50.
[60] Seay, p. 49, reports that the four choristers were replaced by one adult at the end of June, 1479. The documents that I give apparently escaped his notice.
[61] Seay, p. 51.

Ser Antonio di Bianciardi, also departed. He was immediately replaced by Don Benedetto di Bartolomeo of the Camaldolese Order.[62] An attempt was also made at that time to re-engage Ser Niccolò di Lore. He must have refused the appointment, however, because no payments are recorded to him in the following months.[63]

The chapel numbered four adult singers during the last six months of 1481: Ser Antonio da Montughi, master; Ser Matteo di Paolo, contralto; Ser Francesco Boscherini, tenor; and Don Benedetto di Bartolomeo, bass.[64] After that time the overseers made no other attempts to enlarge the group. Salaries for these four singers are regularly recorded from January 1, 1482, through December 31, 1484. The only change during those years was the temporary replacement during the period September 1, 1482-February 1, 1483, of Ser Matteo di Paolo by Frate Francesco di Giovanni of the Order of St. Anthony of Florence.[65]

On January 19, 1485, the following decree was recorded among the deliberations of the Cathedral's overseers:

> Item having seen that the better and more learned singers of figural music in their chapel of Santa Maria del Fiore were absenting themselves from the said office of singing so that without them the said chapel remains incomplete and without its parts, and knowing also that the expenses made for that purpose are in vain, of no use, and add no honor to the said church, because of the above-said reasons, [the overseers] suppressed the chapel itself in the most complete way that they could, and they [also] abolished [it] in all its parts; and for the said reasons, they decided that the singers who sing there, or who used to sing there, cannot be paid for the said office by the paymaster, on penalty that the said paymaster pay them out of his own [funds]; and [they decided] that the aforesaid singers must stay and remain in that position which they held before the said election was made to that office. And if any of them for that reason enjoyed any exemption or [special] benefit, he should be understood to be deprived [of it], and from this moment they removed and took away the same [benefits] from everybody and in every way. [This decree] was drawn up by a notary public. (Doc. 22)

It was inconceivable, however, that services at the Cathedral should remain without some form of polyphonic embellishment, and thus only a few months later another plan was drawn up for maintaining an independent chapel.[66] The position of teacher of figural music was permanently established, and Ser Antonio da Montughi, apparently back in the good graces of the overseers, was called upon to be its first occupant. The choristers who received instruction from him were obliged to sing at various services, always under his direction. The only expense was the

---

[62] Seay, p. 52.

[63] As will be noted below, Ser Niccolò later returned to the Cathedral's service during the 1480's. Evidently Niccolò di Lore was one of the most famous singers of his time, for he was still remembered as late as 1567: "and here in Florence there was at one time a M. Nicolò di lore ... who used to sing with marvelous grace ..." (C. Bartoli, *Ragionamenti accademici sopra alcuni luoghi difficili di Dante* [Venice, 1567], p. 37).

[64] Seay, p. 52.   [65] *Loc. cit.*   [66] Seay, pp. 52f.

THE SINGERS OF SAN GIOVANNI IN FLORENCE

teacher's salary, for, as in the past, it was felt that the instruction given the choristers was sufficient remuneration for their services. From the decree confirming Ser Antonio's appointment, it appears that in addition to singing at the Saturday morning Mass, the choristers were to perform also at Vespers and other offices.[67] But since the establishment of this boys' choir was followed a few months later by the reinstatement of the singers of San Giovanni, it must be that the choristers sang only on Saturday mornings. Indeed, all the later documents concerning the boys' choir and the teacher of figural music speak only of their performances at the Saturday morning Mass and at no other time. The boys' choir continued to serve at the Cathedral until November 29, 1494, when the teacher's position was abolished by decree of the overseers, themselves apparently acting at the suggestion of Girolamo Savonarola.[68]

We may now return to the singers of San Giovanni. Although none of the Baptistry's records from this period has survived, it is possible to trace developments there through the account books of the Santissima Annunziata, for that Church continued to employ the singers of San Giovanni, even though it too established an independent chapel in the early 1480's.

The Annunziata's account books show that during that time the number of musicians appointed to serve as singers of San Giovanni was enlarged on a more permanent basis. It seems that this expansion of musical forces was brought about by the many abuses of the previous system of engaging singers. As described in Braccio Martelli's letter, that system had provided for a small number of permanent appointees, with additional singers being recruited from the ranks of local musicians who were hired on a monthly basis. While it can only be surmised that Lorenzo was responsible for the new policy, the records of his correspondence show that he himself took the initiative in searching for musicians worthy of the new positions.[69] Just how successful he was will be revealed by the names of the singers of San Giovanni who served at the Annunziata during the early 1480's.

The Annunziata's account books do not regularly list payments for musicians during the years 1481-83. For example, Ser Niccolò di Lore, "a singer and *tenorista* who is staying at the Convent," is mentioned as early as September 1, 1481.[70] He is not recorded again until June, 1483, although the payment at that time covers his salary for the two previous years.[71] Ser Niccolò was first named as a singer of San Giovanni in a document dated January 29, 1484.[72] He was given that title many times in the following years.

Don Angelo da Firenze, "a singer who is staying at the Convent," is first mentioned on September 16, 1481.[73] On December 18 of the same

---

[67] Seay, p. 52.
[68] Seay, p. 54.
[69] Del Piazzo, *op. cit.*, pp. 48, 218, 22, 377.
[70] SSA, DC, Vol. 197, fol. 238ᵛ.
[71] SSA, DC, Vol. 197, fol. 408ʳ.
[72] See Doc. 25 below.
[73] SSA, DC, Vol. 197, fol. 253ᵛ.

year he signed a contract to sing at the Annunziata for one year.[74] Although no payments to him are recorded in the following months, his signature in one of the Convent's Receipt Registers, dated December, 1482, suggests that he fulfilled the terms of his contract.[75]

Ghottifredo di Thilman de Liegio also signed a one year's contract with the Annunziata on December 18, 1481.[76] During the following week, on December 26, the Convent bought him a pair of shoes.[77] Three days later, however, he was given three *lire* and six *soldi* as a "farewell gift" from the Annunziata.[78]

Meanwhile, on November 26, 1481, another Northerner, Michele di Guglielmo da Ludicha di Brabante, had been engaged to sing in the Convent's chapel.[79] The terms of his contract state that he was to receive room and board only. But on May 15, 1482, he was given eight *lire* "as the rest of his salary for having sung at the Annunziata."[80] Presumably he, too, did not complete the year of service called for in his contract.

The Cathedral singers Ser Matteo di Paolo and Don Benedetto di Bartolomeo are both recorded at the Annunziata during January, 1482.[81] Although Don Benedetto is mentioned only once, Ser Matteo was associated with the Convent's chapel until September 25 of the same year.[82]

A payment of three months' salary is recorded to Don Francesco da Bologna, *cantore*, on January 4, 1482.[83] He is not mentioned again after that time.

On January 12, 1482, the soprano Johannes Hurtault entered into the following agreement with the Annunziata:

A record that on this day, the twelfth of January, 1482, a Saturday, in the morning, around the sixteenth hour, the herewith inscribed Ianesi Francioso obliges himself to stay in the Convent of the Annunziata for one year, at the expense of the Convent, and to sing in Church, in the Chapel, and in the Convent just like the other singers.
With the [understanding] that the prior and the Convent must keep and maintain him in clothing and shoes and give him half a gold ducat each month; and they must give good and honest company to the said Ianes, and also when he is ill, treat him as though he were a regular monk of the Convent. And in case the said Ianes the singer should lose his voice and should not be able to sing soprano, he is not be dismissed before [the end of] the said year. . . .
I Johannes Hurtault promise and swear to observe all that is said and written above; [signed] with my own hand. (Doc. 23)

Notwithstanding the terms of the contract, payments to Johannes Hurtault are recorded only until May 26, 1482.[84]

Rubinetto Francioso, *cantore*, is first mentioned on February 7, 1482. Payments to him are recorded until May 10 of the same year.[85]

---

[74] SSA, *Ricord.*, Vol. 49, fol. 26ʳ.
[75] SSA, *Ricevute*, Vol. 1049, fol. 31ʳ.
[76] SSA, *Ricord.*, Vol. 49, fol. 26ʳ.
[77] SSA, *DC*, Vol. 197, fol. 257ᵛ.
[78] SSA, *EU*, Vol. 246, fol. 228ᵛ.
[79] SSA, *Ricord.*, Vol. 49, fol. 25ʳ.
[80] SSA, *DC*, Vol. 197, fol. 261ᵛ.
[81] SSA, *EU*, Vol. 246, fols. 230ʳ, 231ʳ.
[82] SSA, *EU*, Vol. 246, fol. 274ʳ.
[83] SSA, *EU*, Vol. 246, fol. 230ᵛ.
[84] SSA, *EU*, Vol. 246, fol. 252ʳ.
[85] SSA, *EU*, Vol. 246, fols. 236ʳ, 250ʳ.

The soprano Iannes Piccardo, otherwise known as Johannes Comitus, is also mentioned for the first time on February 8, 1482.[86] On May 1 of the same year he and two other musicians signed the following contract with the Annunziata:

IN THE NAME OF CHRIST, AMEN.

Let it be known to those who examine this document how on this day, the first day of May, 1482, the herewith inscribed singers agreed . . . to sing in the Church of the Annunziata and in the Chapel of the Annunziata according to the custom already established [and] under the terms and conditions inscribed herein. First and above all the herewith inscribed singers and every one of them must observe the rules of good behavior when singing in the said Church and Chapel so that they do not make a scandal or noise either by speaking or by laughing, under the penalty of two *soldi* for each of them, and for every time.

Item in a similar manner they must behave honorably in the refectory and comport themselves well with the other brothers at table.

Item the herewith inscribed singers, together with the other singers of the Convent, are obliged to rehearse those things they themselves sing in the Church, whether it be a Mass, a motet, or a Magnificat, etc., and that is for every occasion on which they must sing in the Church, not only on feast days, but also on ferial days. And if one of them absents himself, he should be noted down and fined two *soldi*, etc.

Item each time one of the above said or herewith inscribed singers is absent, whether at Mass, at Vespers, or at Lauds, he incurs a fine of one *carlino* for each time (if on a ferial day), and of two *carlini* for each time (if on a feast day). And in case some or all of the same singers are absent from singing either in the Church or in the Chapel because they wish to sing in another church or in another place at that hour, then each one of them will incur a fine of one gold ducat. And having observed all these things the same singers may sing and teach and do what they please in whatever suitable place and in whatever church they so please.

Item . . . the Convent obliges itself to give each one of the same [singers] one and one-half gold ducats each month. . . . And besides the said salary they should have [their] living expenses just as the other monks have, and in addition, if one of them becomes ill, the Convent must provide medicine and a doctor. And in faith of all the above said things, I, Frater Antonius de Bononia, unworthy prior of the Convent of the Annunziata of the city of Florence, wrote all the above said things with my own hand, with [each] of the same singers signing below with his own hand.

I Bartolomeo de Castris am content with what is written above.
I Johannes Comitus am content with what is written above.
I Johannes Vitine [?][87] am content with what is written above.
Let it be known to all how beyond the above said pact . . . the said prior especially promised the singer Bartolomeo (who sings contralto) six ducats for a robe. . . . (Doc. 24)

After this time payments to Johannes Piccardo continue until September 30, 1482.[88] The other two musicians are recorded until August 22,

[86] SSA, *EU*, Vol. 246, fol. 236ʳ.

[87] The transcription of this name is doubtful. In some documents it appears to be Vitine, in others, Ubitine or Vitnich.

[88] SSA, *DC*, Vol. 197, fol. 286ᵛ.

1482, when it is stated that they were given two florins as their last payment for having sung at the Annunziata.[89] Johannes Vitine is mentioned once again after that time. A document, dated June 3, 1483, states that he was given two *lire* "for two Masses which he brought from Rome and for several *canti* which he composed here in the Convent."[90] Bartolomeo de Castris resumed his duties at the Annunziata on November 15, 1482.[91] He was named as a singer of San Giovanni for the first time on January 29, 1484, when he signed another contract with the Convent.[92]

During 1482 three of the Convent's monks, all of them foreigners, began serving in the chapel. Frate Andrea di Giovanni da Fiandra (also known as Frate Andrea Francioso) is first recorded on May 28, and was associated with the Annunziata for many years after that time.[93] The others, Frate Chimenti Tedesco (first mentioned on June 20)[94] and Frate Filippo Pichardo (first mentioned on September 14)[95] are recorded only until the end of the same year.

A certain Domenico Francioso is recorded on December 2, 1482, as having sung at the convent for one month.[96] Payments to Don Rinaldo Francioso, *maestro di canto e cantore*, begin on November 22, 1482, and continue until March 21, 1483, after which he is no longer mentioned.[97]

Cornelio di Lorenzo, "a soprano who is staying at the Convent," is first mentioned on July 5, 1483, and was associated with the Annunziata for several years after that time.[98] He is named as a singer of San Giovanni in a payment dated September 5, 1484.[99]

Payment for one month's service is recorded on February 12, 1483, to Don Thomaso da Venegia, *cantore*.[100] The same is true for Jacopo di Bartolomeo Francioso, *cantore*, who is mentioned only once, on September 13, 1483.[101] From a document dated October 8 of the same year, we learn that a certain Maestro Stefano da Napoli had been sent from Rome to assist in the Annunziata's chapel by the General of the Servite Order. But Maestro Stefano "was neither pleasing to the prior nor to the monks of the Convent," so he was given three florins and sent on his way.[102]

On January 29, 1484, the following contract was entered into a volume of the Convent's *Ricordanze:*

> A record that the herewith inscribed singers and men of good faith, singers in [the Church of] San Giovanni of Florence, oblige themselves to sing the Mass of figural music in the Chapel of the Annunziata on Saturday morning, throughout the year, serving the ceremonies of the Chapel honestly. And the Convent obliges itself to give them . . . the herewith inscribed things:

[89] SSA, *EU*, Vol. 246, fol. 266ʳ.
[90] SSA, *EU*, Vol. 247, fol. 83ʳ.
[91] SSA, *EU*, Vol. 247, fol. 55ᵛ.
[92] See Doc. 25.
[93] SSA: *EU*, Vol. 246, fol. 252ʳ; *EU*, Vol. 699, fols. 50ʳ, 127ᵛ.
[94] SSA, *EU*, Vol. 246, fol. 254ᵛ.
[95] SSA, *EU*, Vol. 246, fol. 269 bisʳ.
[96] SSA, *EU*, Vol. 247, fol. 55ʳ.
[97] SSA, *EU*, Vol. 247, fols. 53ᵛ, 60ʳ, 71ᵛ.
[98] SSA, *EU*, Vol. 247, fols. 88ᵛ, 215ʳ.
[99] SSA, *EU*, Vol. 247, fol. 165ᵛ.
[100] SSA, *EU*, Vol. 247, fol. 65ʳ.
[101] SSA, *DC*, Vol. 197, fol. 379ᵛ.
[102] SSA, *DC*, Vol. 197, fol. 375ᵛ.

THE SINGERS OF SAN GIOVANNI IN FLORENCE 335

First, a bed with sheets, a mattress, a spring, a pillow, and a blanket.
Item the laundering of all their clothes.
Item the barber who will shave them once a week, well and honorably, to their contentment and pleasure.
Item eight pairs of shoes and four pairs of slippers, according to their need, from time to time.
Item at Easter, material for a vest.
Item for [the feast of] St. John, a beret for each of them.
Item in the month of September, good cloth for a pair of trousers.
Item for Christmas, ten lengths of good cloth for a jacket.
And in faith of the above said, I, Frate Antonio da Bologna, have written this record with my own hand, as prior of the Convent, with the consent and approval of our magnificent overseers. And to this same record, Piovano Girolamo, Ser Arnolfo, Nicolò di Zovani of Florence, and Bartholomeo de Castris have signed below.
[space left vacant for Piovano Girolamo's signature]
I Ser Arnolfo d'Arnolfo am content with all these things said above, and for this reason I have subscribed with my own hand.
And I Nicholaus Ihoannis on this day confirm the above and am content etc.
I Bartholomeus de Castris am content with the aforesaid writings. (Doc. 25)

The latter two singers had been associated with the Annunziata for several years before signing the contract. Payments to Ser Arnolfo are regularly recorded from the following February 26 until July 2, 1485.[103] Although Piovano Girolamo did not sign the contract, monthly payments are recorded under his name for several years after this time.[104]

During 1484 four of the Convent's monks, all of them natives of Florence, also began serving in the chapel: Frate Marco di Domenico,[105] Frate Christofano di Niccolò,[106] Frate Stefano di Niccolò,[107] and Frate Battista di Biagio.[108] In addition, two German members of the Servite Order, Frate Currado Tedescho *Grande* and Frate Currado Tedescho *Piccolo*, are recorded as having joined the chapel during the same year.[109]

Antonio di Antonio Gabassoli, *contrabasso*, and Francesco di Martino Migliotti both joined the Convent's chapel on February 1, 1484.[110] Both are named as singers of San Giovanni for the first time in a payment dated September 2, 1484.[111] Antonio Gabassoli was associated with the Annunziata until November 2, 1485.[112] Francesco Migliotti left Florence rather abruptly, on August 1, 1485, in the company of another singer of San Giovanni, Guglielmo d'Arnoldo de Steynsel. The latter musician had been serving at the Annunziata since August 1, 1484.[113] The record of a letter written by Lorenzo de'Medici, dated August 10, 1485, informs us that Guglielmo "had most rudely departed from the church of San

---

[103] SSA, *DC*, Vol. 198, fol. 166ᵛ.
[104] SSA, *DC*, Vol. 198, fol. 165ᵛ.
[105] SSA, *DC*, Vol. 197, fol. 426ᵛ.
[106] SSA, *EU*, Vol. 247, fol. 142ᵛ.
[107] SSA, *EU*, Vol. 247, fol. 160ʳ.
[108] SSA, *EU*, Vol. 247, fol. 150ʳ.
[109] SSA, *EU*, Vol. 247, fols. 122ʳ, 122ᵛ.
[110] SSA, *DC*, Vol. 197, fol. 408ᵛ.
[111] SSA, *DC*, Vol. 198, fols. 165ᵛ, 166ᵛ.
[112] SSA, *EU*, Vol. 247, fol. 236ʳ.
[113] SSA, *EU*, Vol. 247, fol. 160ʳ.

Giovanni."[114] He was apparently forgiven by Lorenzo, however, for, as will be noted below, he returned to Florence a few years later.

The contralto Giovanni di Giovanni Pintelli, *cantore in San Giovanni*, began serving at the Annunziata on October 10, 1484.[115] He was associated with the Convent for several years after that time.

Payments to another singer of San Giovanni, Alberto d'Alesso, are recorded from December 6, 1484, to April 23, 1485, after which he is no longer mentioned.[116]

Gabriello Gabassoli, *cantore in San Giovanni*, is first mentioned in the Convent's account books on February 12, 1485. Monthly payments are recorded to him for several years after that time.[117]

A certain Martino, *cantore in San Giovanni*, is recorded only once at the Annunziata, on April 6, 1485.[118]

After this time the singers of San Giovanni began performing once again at the Cathedral, and thus we may turn to the documents preserved at that Church in continuing our account of the group. Before doing so, however, it will be of some interest to compare the chapels which the three churches maintained during the early 1480's.

Unfortunately, the Annunziata's records for the period 1481-83 are not very precise, and it is impossible to know which musicians serving there at the time were also employed at the Baptistry. Some of the musicians recorded in these years, on the other hand, are identified as singers of San Giovanni in later payments. Ser Niccolò di Lore is a typical example. He had been associated with the Annunziata for over two years when, on January 29, 1484, he signed a contract with the Convent in which he was named as a singer of San Giovanni. He was not given that title in the Convent's account books, however, until September, 1484. The same is true of Bartolomeo de Castris who had been employed at the Annunziata since February, 1482. In view of this it would seem that a good many of the musicians recorded at the Annunziata from 1481 to 1483 also served as singers of San Giovanni, even though they are not so identified in the Convent's account books.

The records for the latter months of 1484, however, are more precise.

---

[114] Del Piazzo, *op. cit.*, p. 334. After leaving Florence, Guglielmo and Francesco Migliotti were immediately engaged by Ludovico il Moro of Milan. Cesari (*op. cit.*, p. 16) reports that Lorenzo de'Medici was so incensed at the departure of the two musicians that he wrote the Florentine ambassador in Milan instructing him to request Ludovico not to engage them. Ludovico, however, did not comply, and the two fugitives remained in Milan for some time. Cesari (*loc. cit.*) also states that after a year Guglielmo responded to Lorenzo's repeated invitations and returned to Florence. Guglielmo, as will be noted below, is not recorded again in Florence until 1489.

[115] SSA, *DC*, Vol. 198, fol. 148^v. As will be noted below, Giovanni's brother, Thomaso, was also a singer of San Giovanni. It is not certain which of the two is the composer "Pintello," whose *Questo mostrarsi adirata di fore* is preserved in the MS *Banco Rari 230* (fols. 50^v-51^r) of the National Library in Florence.

[116] SSA, *EU*, Vol. 247, fols. 175^r, 199^r.

[117] SSA, *EU*, Vol. 247, fols. 187^v, 252^v.

[118] SSA, *EU*, Vol. 247, fol. 197^r.

THE SINGERS OF SAN GIOVANNI IN FLORENCE

They show that the following were singers of San Giovanni at that time:

Ser Arnolfo d'Arnolfo, contratenor
Ser Niccolò di Lore, bass
Bartolomeo de Castris, contralto
Piovano Girolamo di Ser Antonio
Antonio Gabassoli, bass
Cornelio di Lorenzo, soprano
Francesco di Martino Migliotti
Guglielmo d'Arnoldo de Steynsel
Giovanni Pintelli, contralto
Alberto d'Alesso
Gabriello Gabassoli.

This list, to be sure, represents the names of only those singers of San Giovanni who served at the Annunziata. How many others there were during those months who were never called upon to assist at that Church cannot be known.

We can, however, be more certain of the number of singers employed at the Annunziata in the same period. In addition to the eleven musicians named above, seven of the Convent's monks are also recorded, bringing the total number of singers in the Annunziata's chapel to eighteen. By comparison, the Cathedral's chapel at that time numbered four adults and eight boys.

During the last half of the 15th century it had become fashionable at the more important Italian courts to maintain large musical forces, in emulation of the Papal and Burgundian chapels. In those two chapels at least twenty singers were normally employed.[119] Similar numbers are found in the chapel of King Alfonso I of Naples (twenty-one singers and an organist in 1451),[120] in the chapel of Duke Amadeus IX of Savoy (fourteen singers and an organist in 1465),[121] and in the chapel of Duke Galeazzo Maria Sforza of Milan (twenty-two singers in 1474).[122] Even the

---

[119] For the records of the Papal chapel, see Haberl, *op. cit.*, pp. 228-247. The chapel of Duke Philip the Good numbered twenty-one singers in 1439, and this number was maintained until the time of his death in 1467. See J. Marix, *Histoire de la musique et des musiciens de la cour de Bourgogne sous le règne de Philippe le Bon* (Collection d'études musicologiques, Vol. XXVIII; Strasbourg, 1939), pp. 243-258. Under Philip's successor, Charles, the Burgundian chapel in 1477 numbered twenty-seven singers. Under Charles's daughter, Mary, and her husband, Maximilian, the Archduke of Austria, the chapel in 1481 numbered twenty-one singers. See G. Van Doorslaer, "La chapelle musicale de Philippe le Beau," *Revue belge d'archéologie et d'histoire de l'art* IV (1934), pp. 26ff.

[120] C. M. Riccio, "Alcuni fatti di Alfonso I di Aragona," *Archivio storico per le provincie napoletane* VI (1881), pp. 411f.

[121] A. Dufour and F. Rabut, "Les musiciens, la musique et les instruments de musique en Savoie du XIII° aux XIX° siècle," *Mémoires et documents publiés par la Société Savoisienne d'Histoire et d'Archéologie* XVII (1878), p. 51.

[122] In addition to twenty-two *cantori de cappelle*, the Duke also maintained eighteen *cantori de camera*. See Motta, *op. cit.*, p. 322. See also Sartori, "Josquin des Prés," p. 64, fn. 1, in which are reproduced all the known lists of the Milanese Ducal singers from the years 1474-75.

chapel of a small court like Ferrara in 1475 numbered eleven singers.[123] The chapels at the Baptistry and the Santissima Annunziata were thus keeping abreast of the most modern standards of performance practice while the Cathedral chapel was not.

Superiority in numbers, however, was not the only noteworthy feature of the chapels at the Baptistry and the Santissima Annunziata during the early 1480's. A far more significant advantage was that these chapels were, for the most part, staffed with Northern singers. It stands to reason that the Cathedral chaplains and choristers could not compare in skill with the foreigners. The latter, after all, were raised and trained in the culture in which the music of the late 15th century had its roots. The fact that the Cathedral's chapel compared so unfavorably in every respect with the chapels of the other two churches may well have had something to do with the decision to disband it.

On June 21, 1485, the decision was taken to reinstate the singers of San Giovanni at the Cathedral. The administration of the Cathedral chapel, however, was to remain in the overseers' hands:

Let it be known to all how the illustrious consuls of the *Arte della Lana* of the city of Florence, after due consideration, decided that the singers of San Giovanni and others can be appointed to the said church, with the terms, salaries, conditions, and other [stipulations] ordered on other occasions; [and they also decided] that up to the sum of two hundred florins can be spent on them each year.... (Doc. 26)

The Cathedral's Debit-Credit Register[124] for the last six months of 1485 shows that the following began serving there on July 1, 1485:

Antonio di Ghabascoli[125]
Arrigo [Isaac] da Fiandra
Bartolomeo d'Arricho [de Castris] da Fiandra
Francesco di Migliotti
Ghabriello di Ghabascoli
Ghuglielmo d'Arnoldo [de Steynsel]
Giannes d'Angio
Giovanni Pichardi
Frate Girolamo [di Ser Antonio da Firenze]
Nicholò di Giovanni [di Lore].

The account books of the Annunziata show that seven of the ten musicians named above were singers of San Giovanni at the time. In the same sources, somewhat later, both Arrigo Isaac[126] and Giannes d'Angio[127]

---

[123] Valdrighi, *op. cit.*, p. 7.
[124] SMDF, QC, VIII, 1, 77, fols. 31ʳ, 32ʳ, 33ʳ, 34ʳ, 37ᵛ, 42ʳ.
[125] Throughout the documents employed in the present study spellings of names are most often archaic and exceedingly inconsistent. While the original spellings have been maintained in direct quotations, modern Italian equivalents have been used in the course of the text for names frequently mentioned.
[126] SSA, DC, Vol. 198, fol. 304ᵛ. His signature (*Ego, Henricus de Flandria, cantore in San Giovanni*) is preserved in one of the Convent's Receipt Registers, dated October 31, 1491. SSA, *Ricevute*, Vol. 1050, fol. 126ᵛ.
[127] SSA, DC, Vol. 198, fol. 289ᵛ.

THE SINGERS OF SAN GIOVANNI IN FLORENCE 339

are also named as singers of San Giovanni. It is most likely that they too had been serving at the Baptistry for some time before joining the Cathedral chapel. Giovanni Pichardi is undoubtedly to be identified with the Iannes Piccardo (mentioned above) who was recorded at the Annunziata as early as February, 1482. He was probably a singer of San Giovanni as well.

With the exception of the last three, each of the singers was paid two florins a month for his services at the Cathedral. The others received one florin a month.

As previously stated, Guglielmo de Steynsel and Francesco Migliotti left Florence after August 1, 1485. Apparently Giovanni Pichardi also departed at the same time, for no payments are recorded to him in the subsequent Debit-Credit Register. Antonio Gabassoli is recorded at the Cathedral only until November 15, 1485.[128] His name disappears from the Annunziata's accounts at the same time. Gabriello Gabassoli left the Cathedral's service at the end of January, 1486.[129] The Annunziata's records, however, show that he continued to perform at that Church.[130]

The Cathedral chapel numbered only five singers until April 10, 1486, when Messer Giovanni degli Ans, identified as a singer in the Annunziata's accounts,[131] joined the group. His salary was fixed at two florins a month.[132] The presence of these six singers is then recorded through the month of December, 1486:[133]

Arrigo d'Ugo [Isaac]
Bartolomeo d'Arrigo [de Castris]
Giannes d'Angio
Messer Giovanni degli Ans
Messer Girolamo di Ser Antonio
Ser Niccolò di Lore.

Meanwhile the following had joined the Cathedral chapel during the closing months of 1486:[134]

Giorgio di Niccolò d'Austria, on October 1
Lorenzo di Giorgio, on October 1
Messer Piero Martini da Frigia,[135] on October 15
Frate Antonio da Vercelli, on November 1
Ugo di Parisetto di Champagnia de Reams, on November 15.

All named were paid a salary of two florins a month with the exception of the last two, who received one florin a month. But for Lorenzo di Giorgio these singers are also recorded as having begun services at the

[128] SMDF, QC, VIII, 1, 78, fol. 26ᵛ.
[129] SMDF, QC, VIII, 1, 78, fol. 27ᵛ.
[130] SSA, DC, Vol. 198, fol. 350ᵛ.
[131] SSA, EU, Vol. 247, fol. 277ʳ.
[132] SMDF, QC, VIII, 1, 78, fol. 81ʳ.
[133] SMDF, QC, VIII, 1, 79, fols. 75ᵛ-76ʳ.
[134] SMDF, QC, VIII, 1, 79, fols. 69ᵛ, 88ᵛ, 102ʳ.
[135] He was the brother of Johannes Martini. See Motta, *op. cit.*, p. 527.

340

Annunziata on approximately the same dates.[136] Each is named as a singer of San Giovanni in his first payment from the Annunziata.

Recorded at the Cathedral only for the month of January, 1487, is Giovanni d'Agnolo da Fiandra.[137] Identified as a singer of San Giovanni in the account books of the Annunziata, he had been serving at that Church since April 11, 1486.[138]

With the exception of Messer Piero Martini, who left the Cathedral's service on March 15, 1487, all the singers named above are recorded at the Cathedral through the month of June, 1487.[139] Martini, however, continued to be employed at the Annunziata until October 2 of the same year.[140]

It was now two years since the singers of San Giovanni had been re-admitted to the Cathedral chapel. The arrangement was proving so satisfactory that the overseers decided to increase the number of singers in the Cathedral's service:

July 27, 1487
Let it be known to all how the illustrious consuls of the *Arte della Lana* of the city of Florence, after due consideration etc., decided that in the future [up to the sum of] two hundred and forty gold florins can be spent each year by the overseers of the said *Opera* of Santa Maria del Fiore for the singers of San Giovanni and Santa Maria del Fiore of the city of Florence.

I, Paces Bambelli, a notary public of the said Guild, drew up and legalized this [document]. (Doc. 27)

It is of importance to note that every singer of San Giovanni recorded at the Annunziata after this time also served in the Cathedral chapel. On the other hand, several of the Cathedral's singers are not recorded at the Annunziata, and it is thus impossible to know whether they too were singers of San Giovanni.

The ten singers named above are recorded at the Cathedral through December, 1487.[141] New in the chapel on July 1 of that year were Ser Francesco Boscherini, the *tenorista* Giorgio di Giovanni d'Allemagna, a singer of San Giovanni who also began serving at the Annunziata on the same day,[142] and Bartolomeo d'Ugo da Fiandra.[143] The first two were paid one florin a month, the latter, two florins a month. He served only through the month of November. Joining the chapel on November 1 was another singer of San Giovanni, Lorenzo di Ghottifredo.[144] His salary was fixed at two florins a month.

During the month of December, 1487, the Cathedral chapel numbered

[136] SSA, *DC*, Vol. 198, fols. 233ᵛ, 234ᵛ.
[137] SMDF, *QC*, VIII, 1, 80, fol. 25ᵛ.
[138] SSA, *EU*, Vol. 247, fol. 264ᵛ.
[139] SMDF, *QC*, VIII, 1, 80, fols. 25ᵛ-26ʳ.
[140] SSA, *EU*, Vol. 699, fol. 65ᵛ.
[141] SMDF, *QC*, VIII, 1, 81, fols. 29ᵛ-30ʳ.
[142] SSA, *DC*, Vol. 198, fol. 248ᵛ.
[143] SMDF, *QC*, VIII, 1, 81, fols. 29ᵛ-30ʳ.
[144] SSA, *DC*, Vol. 198, fol. 257ᵛ.

thirteen singers, all of them, but for Boscherini and Lorenzo di Giorgio, singers of San Giovanni:[145]

Frate Antonio da Vercelli
Arrigo d'Ugo [Isaac]
Bartolomeo d'Arrigo [de Castris], contralto
Ser Francesco Boscherini, tenorista
Giannes d'Angio
Giorgio di Giovanni d'Allemagna, tenorista
Giorgio di Niccolò d'Austria, discantista
Messer Giovanni degli Ans
Piovano Girolamo di Ser Antonio
Lorenzo di Giorgio
Lorenzo di Gottifredo
Ser Niccolò di Lore, bass
Ugo di Parisetto, soprano.

This number was maintained until April 30, 1488, when Bartolomeo de Castris and Niccolò di Lore left Florence.[146] At the end of June both Giorgio di Niccolò and Lorenzo di Giorgio also departed.[147] Meanwhile, on June 15 another singer of San Giovanni, the contralto Giovanni Pintelli, joined the Cathedral chapel. His salary was fixed at one florin a month.[148] Thus on July 1, 1488, in addition to Giovanni d'Agnolo da Fiandra, who as on a previous occasion is recorded for only one month, the Cathedral chapel numbered ten singers.[149] On the following August 1 the soprano Cornelio di Lorenzo d'Anversa, Tassino d'Anversa, Thomaso Pintelli (all of them identified as singers of San Giovanni in the Annunziata's accounts),[150] and Lorenzo di Giovanni joined the Cathedral chapel. The first two received a salary of two florins a month, the others, one florin a month.[151] New in the chapel on September 1 was Giovanni di Pastore da Picchardia.[152] He received a salary of one florin a month, as did another Northerner, Beltramo di Giannot, who is recorded for the first time on November 18.[153] Beltramo di Giannot (Bertrandus Jannet) also served at the Annunziata, and is named as a singer of San Giovanni in his first payment from that church.[154]

By the end of December, 1488, the number of singers at the Cathedral was reduced to thirteen, owing to the departure of Giorgio di Giovanni, Lorenzo di Gottifredo, and Giovanni di Pastore.[155] Their departure was followed a month later by that of Lorenzo di Giovanni.[156]

[145] SMDF, *QC*, VIII, 1, 81, fols. 29ᵛ-30ʳ.
[146] SMDF, *QC*, VIII, 1, 82, fols. 28ᵛ-29ʳ.
[147] SMDF, *QC*, VIII, 1, 83, fols. 31ᵛ-32ʳ.
[148] *Loc. cit.*
[149] *Loc. cit.*
[150] SSA, *DC*, Vol. 198, fols. 270ᵛ, 271ᵛ.
[151] SMDF, *QC*, VIII, 1, 84, fols. 26ᵛ-27ʳ.
[152] *Loc. cit.*
[153] *Loc. cit.*
[154] SSA, *DC*, Vol. 198, fol. 271ᵛ.
[155] SMDF, *QC*, VIII, 1, 84, fols. 26ᵛ-27ʳ.
[156] *Loc. cit.*

Because of the imprecision of the records of 1489, it is not possible to state with certainty the exact dates of departures from the admissions to the Cathedral chapel. We can be sure that Ugo di Parisetto left Florence some time after April, for he is recorded in the Papal chapel in June of the same year.[157] Thomaso Pintelli evidently left some time before July 1, for no payments are recorded to him after that time.[158] Tassino d'Anversa is no longer mentioned after December.[159] Guglielmo de Steynsel rejoined the chapel at the end of May as did Lorenzo di Giorgio and Gabriello Gabassoli on August 1.[160] New in the chapel during 1489 were Ser Michele di Bartolo Chricci, on October 1, and Messer Guglielmo Migliotti, on November 1.[161] The latter was paid two florins a month, while the former received but one-half a florin each month. Guglielmo Migliotti is identified as a singer of San Giovanni in the Annunziata's account books.[162] Thus during the month of January, 1490, the Cathedral chapel numbered fourteen singers, eleven of whom were also singers of San Giovanni:

Frate Antonio da Vercelli
Arrigo d'Ugo [Isaac]
Beltramo di Giannot
Cornelio di Lorenzo d'Anversa
Ser Francesco Boscherini
Gabriello Gabassoli
Giannes d'Angio
Piovano Girolamo di Ser Antonio
Giovanni Pintelli
Messer Giovanni degli Ans
Guglielmo d'Arnoldo [de Steynsel] d'Olanda
Lorenzo di Giorgio
Ser Michele di Bartolo Chricci
Messer Guglielmo Migliotti.

At the end of the month Lorenzo di Giorgio was replaced by the monk Lorenzo di Lansone.[163] His salary was fixed at one florin a month. Lansone is also recorded at the Annunziata but not named as a singer of San Giovanni.[164] Tassino is recorded as having served at the Cathedral during the month of March, 1490, thereby bringing the number of singers to fifteen.[165] He is gone, however, by April 1, as in Giovanni Pintelli.[166] Pietrichino Bonegli da Piccardia joined the chapel on the same day. He was given a salary of two florins a month.[167] He also served at the Annun-

[157] Haberl, *op. cit.*, p. 244.
[158] SMDF, QC, VIII, 1, 84, fols. 35ᵛ–36ʳ.
[159] SMDF, QC, VIII, 1, 85, fol. 31ʳ.
[160] SMDF, QC, VIII, 1, 85, fols. 28ʳ, 42ʳ, 61ʳ.
[161] SMDF, QC, VIII, 1, 85, fols. 64ʳ, 67ʳ.
[162] SSA, DC, Vol. 198, fol. 277ᵛ.
[163] SMDF, QC, VIII, 1, 86, fol. 54ᵛ.
[164] SSA, DC, Vol. 198, fol. 280ᵛ.
[165] SMDF, QC, VIII, 1, 86, fol. 35ʳ.
[166] *Loc. cit.*
[167] SMDF, QC, VIII, 1, 86, fol. 76ᵛ.

THE SINGERS OF SAN GIOVANNI IN FLORENCE 343

ziata, and his signature is preserved twice in the Convent's Receipt Registers, once on July 3, 1490 (Pietriquinus de Piccardia), and again on September 2, 1490 (Petrus Bonnel de Piccardia).[168] Michele Chricci left the Cathedral chapel on April 6, so that during the months of April, May, and June, 1490, there were thirteen singers.[169] Cornelio di Lorenzo and Guglielmo Migliotti left Florence on July 1;[170] thus only eleven singers are recorded through September 1, when Ugo di Parisetto rejoined the group.[171] He was followed on November 24 by the *tenorista* Piero Loba, "overo Pietrachione," who received a salary of two florins a month.[172] Loba is also recorded at the Annunziata but not named as a singer of San Giovanni.[173]

The Cathedral's Debit-Credit Register for the first six months of 1491 has not survived. That for the last six months of the same year shows that the following served during that time:[174]

Frate Antonio da Vercelli
Arrigo d'Ugo [Isaac]
Armanno de Atrio[175]
Cornelio di Guglielmo [de Climbert][176]

---

[168] SSA, *Ricevute*, Vol. 1050, fols. 96ʳ, 99ᵛ. He is undoubtedly to be identified with the composer Pietrequin, two of whose works (*Adieu Florence la yolye* and *Meschin che suis secretement*) are preserved in manuscripts of the National Library in Florence. See B. Becherini, *Catalogo dei manoscritti musicali della Biblioteca Nazionale di Firenze* (Kassel, 1959), pp. 26, 77. Becherini (p. 174) assumes that Pietrequin is Pierre de la Rue.

[169] SMDF, QC, VIII, 1, 86, fol. 35ʳ.

[170] SMDF, QC, VIII, 1, 86, fol. 76ʳ. Cornelio had been in the chapel of Duke Ercole I of Ferrara before going to Florence. On March 16, 1484, the Duke had a letter written to his ambassador in Florence requesting him to find Cornelio as soon as possible and "to tell him in our behalf to send us without delay the new L'homme Armé Mass by Philippon." See B. Murray, "New Light on Jacob Obrecht's Development—A Biographical Study," *Musical Quarterly* XLIII (1957), p. 509. Another of the Duke's letters, dated August 27, 1484, was addressed directly to Cornelio. The letter is interesting, not only because it reveals that Obrecht's music was well known in Florence at that time, but also because it shows how much competition there was among the various Italian courts to obtain the services of the best musicians:

DELICTISSIME NOSTER!

The Mass of Jacob Obrecht which you sent has been gratefully received, and we have seen it and accepted it most willingly and with delight, and thus we thank you and commend you very much. For the moment we have not made any decision about re-establishing (*ritornare*) our chapel, and for this reason we cannot answer you with regard to that soprano, whom you say you'd risk your soul to send here....
(Printed in A. Cappelli, "Lettere di Lorenzo de'Medici detto il Magnifico conservate nell' Archivio Palatino di Modena con notizie tratte dai carteggi diplomatici degli Oratori Estensi a Firenze," *Atti e memorie delle deputazioni di storia patria per le provincie modenesi e parmensi*, Vol. I [1863], p. 41.)

[171] SMDF, QC, VIII, 1, 87, fol. 30ʳ.
[172] SMDF, QC, VIII, 1, 87, fol. 54ʳ.
[173] SSA, DC, Vol. 198, fol. 295ᵛ.
[174] SMDF, QC, VIII, 1, 88, fols. 18ᵛ-19ʳ.
[175] He also served at the Annunziata, but is not named as a singer of San Giovanni. SSA, DC, Vol. 198, fol. 320ᵛ.
[176] Although not a singer of San Giovanni. His signature (Cornelio Willyelmi

Ser Francesco Boscherini
Gabriello Gabassoli
Giannes d'Angio
Messer Giovanni degli Ans
Piovano Girolamo di Ser Antonio
Guglielmo d'Arnoldo de Steynsel
Giovanni d'Arrigo[177]
Ser Michele di Bartolo Chricci
Piero Loba da Brabante
Thomaso Pintelli.

The last named is recorded only until the end of September. New in the Cathedral chapel on October 1 were Alessandro Agricola (with a salary of four florins a month) and Carlo di Piero Francioso (with a salary of two florins a month).[178] Although both are also recorded at the Annunziata, only Carlo di Piero is named as a singer of San Giovanni.[179] His signature, *Karolus de Launoy*, is preserved several times in the Annunziata's Receipt Registers.[180]

All these singers are recorded at the Cathedral from November 1, 1491, through the end of June, 1492.[181] Beltramo di Giannot rejoined the group during that time, thus bringing the number of singers serving in the chapel to fifteen.[182]

In the meantime, a brilliant epoch in Florentine history had come to a close with the death of Lorenzo the Magnificent on April 8, 1492. Lorenzo's passing was to bring about great changes, not only in Florentine politics but in the affairs of all Italy. For the time being, however, the power of the Medici was such that the reins of government passed peacefully to Lorenzo's politically incompetent son, Piero. But if Piero possessed none of his father's gifts for diplomacy and politics, he had nevertheless inherited the Medici love for music and the fine arts. That he con-

---

de Climbert) is preserved in one of the Convent's Receipt Registers. SSA, *Ricevute*, Vol. 1050, fol. 117ʳ.

[177] He is recorded only during the month of July.

[178] SMDF, QC, VIII, 1, 88, fol. 61ʳ. Agricola had been in Florence before that time, however. Duke Galeazzo Maria Sforza of Milan had sent him with a letter of recommendation to Lorenzo de'Medici on March 23, 1474. See Motta, *op. cit.*, p. 532. A letter written by Agricola to the Duke, dated Florence, July 7, 1474, is printed in C. Sartori, "Organs, Organ-Builders, and Organists in Milan, 1450-1476: New and Unpublished Documents," *Musical Quarterly* XLIII (1957), p. 64.

[179] SSA, DC, Vol. 198, fols. 325ᵛ, 326ᵛ.

[180] SSA, *Ricevute*, Vol. 1050, fols. 117ʳ, 128ʳ. Launoy had been associated first with the court of Ferrara and then with the court chapel in Mantua before going to Florence, and had departed from the court without the permission of the Marchesa Isabella d'Este-Gonzaga. In a letter written to Isabella shortly after that time the composer Johannes Martini sought to justify Launoy's departure by stating that Launoy had left to accompany Alexander. See A. Bertolotti, *Musici alla Corte dei Gonzaga in Mantova dal secolo XIV al secolo XVII* (Milan, 1890), pp. 14 ff. The Alexander mentioned in the letter was undoubutedly Agricola, for the documents indicate that the two musicians arrived in Florence together.

[181] SMDF, QC, VIII, 1, 89, fols. 36ᵛ-37ʳ.

[182] SMDF, QC, VIII, 1, 89, fol. 75ᵛ.

THE SINGERS OF SAN GIOVANNI IN FLORENCE 345

tinued his father's policies regarding the singers of San Giovanni is evident from the following letter,[183] apparently written to him shortly after Lorenzo's death by the Papal singer Johannes Petit, alias Baltazar:

MY LORD, I COMMEND MYSELF MOST HUMBLY TO YOUR GOOD GRACE!

I have received the letters which it pleased you to write me [and] by which you let me know of your kind grace [and] of the great and good offers and promises—which are more than I merit—to the effect that I should come to reside in your chapel at Florence, for which I do not know how to thank you enough. My Lord, may it please you to know that I would have never come to this court if I had not had the hope of obtaining some benefice in my native land, [and that] in order to help me provide for myself when it is time for me to cease singing and leave youth. On several occasions I have been offered by different chapels a much larger salary than what I have here, but I have never wanted to accept because it would grieve me greatly to leave Rome without obtaining some considerable advantage, the more so since I have been resident here now for five years and have somehow got used to it. Also, a few days ago the Pope told my associates and me that he intended to provide for us in a way that would make us happy. May it please God, in short, that he keep his promise, because if I had a provision such as I would like, there is no other prince nor other lord to whom I would rather submit myself than to you. . . .

Several changes are noted in the Cathedral chapel after June 1, 1492. The departure from Florence at that time of Alessandro Agricola and Giovanni degli Ans was followed a month later by that of Armanno de Atrio.[184] Payments to Francesco Boscherini for serving in the chapel are no longer recorded after September 1, even though he was associated with the Cathedral for many years afterwards.[185] On October 1 Verbonetto di Giovanni joined the chapel, with a salary of three and one half florins a month.[186] He also served at the Annunziata, and his signature, *Johannes Ghiselin alias Verbonnet*, is found several times in the Convent's Receipt Registers.[187] Rejoining the Cathedral chapel during the same month were four singers of San Giovanni: Ser Niccolò di Lore, Bartolomeo de Castris, Giovanni Pintelli, and Ser Arnolfo da Francia.[188] Thus during November and December, 1492, the Cathedral chapel numbered the following singers:[189]

Frate Antonio da Vercelli
Messer Arnolfo da Francia
Arrigo d'Ugo [Isaac] da Fiandra
Bartolomeo d'Arrigo [de Castris] da Fiandra
Beltramo di Giannot
Carlo di Piero Francioso [de Launoy]
Gabriello Gabassoli

[183] Printed in Becherini, "Relazioni," pp. 111f.
[184] SMDF, QC, VIII, 1, 90, fols. 40ᵛ-41ʳ.
[185] SMDF, QC, VIII, 1, 90, fol. 56ᵛ.
[186] SMDF, QC, VIII, 1, 90, fol. 75ʳ. Ghiselin had been in the service of the Ferrarese court before going to Florence. See Bertolotti, *op. cit.*, p. 16.
[187] SSA, *Ricevute*, Vol. 1050, fols. 161ʳ, 163ʳ.
[188] SMDF, QC, VIII, 1, 90, fols. 78ᵛ-79ʳ.
[189] *Loc. cit.*

Giannes d'Angio
Giovanni Pintelli
Piovano Girolamo di Ser Antonio da Firenze
Guglielmo d'Arnoldo [de Steynsel] d'Olanda
Ser Michele di Bartolo Chricci
Ser Niccolò di Lore da Firenze
Piero Loba da Brabante
Pietrichino Bonegli da Piccardia
Verbonetto di Giovanni [Ghiselin] da Piccardia.

Messer Arnolfo left the chapel at the end of December.[190] He was immediately replaced by Messer Ghuasparre Siciliano,[191] who is also recorded at the Annunziata, though not named as a singer of San Giovanni.[192] Frate Francesco d'Antonio d'Androagli began serving at the Cathedral on January 1, 1493, and thus during the months of January and February, 1493, the chapel counted eighteen singers, the largest number ever recorded at the Cathedral.[193] Of these, at least twelve are known to have been singers of San Giovanni.

This unprecedented number of singers at the Cathedral was reached only during the final months of the chapel's existence. Frate Francesco d'Antonio is already gone by March 1, and on March 15 both Guglielmo de Steynsel and Piero Loba departed. The remaining singers are recorded through the month of March, after which payments to the singers abruptly cease, even though the Debit-Credit Register continues to record payments to other Cathedral employees for the rest of the semester.[194] Payments to the singers are also abruptly terminated in the Annunziata's account books at the end of March, 1493, so that there seems to be little doubt that the singers of San Giovanni were disbanded at that time.[195]

The surviving documents give no reasons for the sudden disbanding of the singers. Yet it seems certain that the move is to be connected with the political decline of the Medici during the early 1490's. Indeed, Piero's political ineptitude, arrogance, and princely manners, which even before his father's death had excited the worst suspicions among the people, were to result in the family's banishment on November 4, 1494. Nevertheless, in March of 1493, Piero still wielded considerable influence in the affairs of the State, and it would appear that he consented to the dismissal of the singers only in order to gain the approbation of a new popular leader in Florence, Fra Girolamo Savonarola.

Savonarola's influence in Florentine history dates from 1490, when he took up residence in the city, apparently at the request of Lorenzo

[190] SMDF, QC, VIII, 1, 91, fol. 12ʳ.
[191] SMDF, QC, VIII, 1, 91, fol. 30ʳ.
[192] SSA, DC, Vol. 198, fol. 365ᵛ.
[193] SMDF, QC, VIII, 1, 91, fol. 30ʳ.
[194] SMDF, QC, VIII, 1, 91, fols. 48ᵛ-49ʳ.
[195] The Annunziata continued to employ organists after that time, however. Two contracts, dated January 5, 1495, and November 28, 1497, name the Convent's organists during those years: Ser Matteo di Piero and the composer Alessandro Coppini. SSA: Ricord., Vol. 49, fol. 224ʳ; Ricord., Vol. 50, fol. 40ᵛ.

de'Medici himself.[196] Savonarola's inspired oratory against the luxury, paganism, and corruption of the times, and his earnestness in proclaiming his doctrines of chastisement and regeneration created a sensation. So large were the crowds which flocked to the Convent of St. Mark's to hear him preach that the church could not contain them. His popularity led to an invitation to preach at the Cathedral, and during the Lenten season of 1491, he delivered his first sermons from the pulpit of Santa Maria del Fiore, with even greater success. Enthusiasm for his teaching virtually swept through the city. By the time of Lorenzo's death Savonarola had become a force to be reckoned with in Florentine politics.

Savonarola's views on music have been discussed frequently, and it is well known that he was vitally concerned with music insofar as it affected the well-being of the soul. He was not opposed to music *per se*, for he recognized its value as a means of increasing the spiritual devotion of the people. He himself, in fact, is known to have composed religious texts, *laude*, which were sung to several of the most popular tunes of the day.[197] But Savonarola was violently opposed to the ribald and often lascivious secular music that was so diffused in Florence at that time. During the years of Lorenzo's rule the Carnival season had become infused with an almost pagan spirit, and the music sung by the people on those occasions, the *canti carnascialeschi*, contributed not a little to the debauched atmosphere of the season. Ridding the city of its carnival excesses and particularly of the carnival music became an important part of Savonarola's reform program. That he actually succeeded in transforming the traditional Florentine Carnival into a *religious* festival is an indication of the influence which he exercised over men's minds.

Savonarola's attitude was equally severe toward the use in religious services of polyphony, which, he felt, interfered with man's communion with God:

figural music is sooner injurious in church than useful, because there one must contemplate and pray to God with the mind and with the intellect, and figural music does nothing but charm the ear and the senses. . . .[198]

In Savonarola's mind polyphony was inextricably connected with the worst abuses of those external forms of devotion that were all too often made to serve as substitutes for true piety:

with this I want to say, in effect, that men today receive the sacraments through habit and for external appearances, not because of the fervor of their

---

[196] Information on Savonarola is derived from the following: P. Villari, *La storia di Girolamo Savonarola e de' suoi tempi* (Florence, 1859-61); R. Ridolfi, *Vita di Girolamo Savonarola* (Rome, 1952); M. Ferrara, *Savonarola* (Florence, 1952).

[197] L. Parigi, *Laurentiana* (Florence, 1954), p. 91; Ferrara, *op. cit.*, pp. 182ff. Savonarola's *laude* are printed in *Poesie di Fra Girolamo Savonarola con l'aggiunta di una canzone pel bruciamento delle vanità e precedute da notizie storiche di C. Guasti e I. del Lungo* (Lanciano, 1914).

[198] P. Villari and E. Casanova, eds., *Scelta di prediche e scritte di Fra Girolamo Savonarola* (Florence, 1898), p. 144. (Sermon of March 23, 1495.)

faith nor for the true belief which comes from within; and the more one becomes addicted to this habit, the worse it becomes, because, as I have told you, men grow more evil and thus it provokes God's wrath upon us all the more. . . . The Lord says: your sins and your iniquities have provoked my wrath. You think to placate me by going to Mass, by playing the organs, with embellishments and other ceremonies: you do nothing of the kind. . . . Come leaders of the Church, come priests, come monks, come laymen! Come everybody, come singers, those I say, who drink well first and then sing the Mass! Up, come everybody! Let us have a beautiful feast with organs, with adornments, with ceremonies: these have no value without that which is within. . . . O Rome, O Italy, what shall I tell you? . . . You have provoked the wrath of God upon us. . . .[199]

More deplorable to Savonarola, however, was the prominent position given polyphony in the liturgy of the leading Florentine churches. As a result, feast day services at the Cathedral and the Baptistry had become a means of entertaining the people; and the clergy, rather than objecting to this transgression of spiritual propriety, had concurred. Indeed, we have an indication of the importance which both the ecclesiastical and secular administrators of the Cathedral attached to the use of polyphony in the liturgy from the record of their decision to re-establish the chapel a few years after Savonarola's death. They state that a chapel would not only be "to the honor of God and the Church," but would bring "satisfaction and universal contentment to all the city as well."[200] The Medici, who had always been most sensitive to Florentine civic pride, had realized this, and wisely turned it to their own advantage by allowing their musicians to serve in the principal churches.

Savonarola had been a keen observer of the Medici policy. No record survives of what he may have said about it during the time they were still in power. But his feelings on the subject were so strong even a year and a half after the banishment of the Medici that he found no difficulty in alluding to them in one of his most stinging denunciations of polyphony:

God says: Take away all your beautiful figural music; *these gentlemen have chapels of singers which seem like a rabble* . . . because there stands a singer with a large voice like a calf's, and the others howl around him like dogs, and no one understands what they are saying. Let figural music go, and sing the plainchant ordered by the Church! You also want the organs played. You go to church to hear the organs. God says: I don't hear your organs, but yet you refuse to understand. . . .[201] [italics mine]

There seems to be little doubt that it was Savonarola's insistent preaching against polyphony that brought about the abolition of the chapels in the city's three leading churches. While it is true that all his surviving statements regarding polyphony date from well after that time, it is never-

---

[199] G. Savonarola, *Prediche italiane ai Fiorentini*, ed. R. Palmarocchi (Florence, 1933), Vol. III, pp. 280ff. (Sermon of March 1, 1496.)

[200] SMDF, *Agnus Dei*, I, 3, 1, fols. 100ᵛ-102ᵛ. A part of the document is printed in Seay, *op. cit.*, p. 55.

[201] G. Savonarola, *Prediche italiane ai Fiorentini*, Vol. III, pp. 389f. (Sermon of March 6, 1496.)

theless most likely that he had been promulgating his views since coming to Florence. His sermons make it clear, furthermore, that from the start he never wavered in attributing the existing corruption in church and society to the Medicean regime. It follows as a matter of course then that Savonarola would have carried his ringing appeals for reform directly to the head of the government and principal patron of the singers of San Giovanni, Piero de'Medici. That Piero should have sought to conciliate the reformer by consenting to the dismissal of the singers is in itself a good indication of the supine manner with which he met every crisis in the affairs of the State.

Apparently all forms of vocal polyphony, with the exception of *laude*,[202] were excluded from the Cathedral's services during the years of Savonarola's spiritual dictatorship. That dictatorship lasted only a short while, however, for Savonarola's excommunication by the Borgian Pontiff Alexander VI eventually succeeded in turning the majority of his supporters away from him. By order of the Florentine government Savonarola was arrested on April 8, 1498 (Palm Sunday), and executed on the following May 23.

It is significant that polyphony was reintroduced into the services at the Cathedral only three days after Savonarola's arrest. This document, dating from a few weeks before his death, records the provision made at that time for the musicians, most of them, evidently, former members of the Cathedral's boys' choir:

April 27, 1498
A copy of the law made in the council of the *Arte della Lana* stipulating the salaries to be given the singers [who perform] on holy days.
Item the fifth. So that the choir of our church of Santa Maria del Fiore be more embellished in honor of Omnipotent God, and to the satisfaction of the populace frequenting the said [church], [the consuls decided] that the eight choristers should each be paid one florin a year (for a beret for each of them), and the four *tenoristae* or *contra[tenoristae]*, four *lire* each. These [salaries] should be understood to have begun on Easter just past, and the first payment should have been made starting on the said Easter as above, since the said choristers, *tenoristae*, and *contra[tenoristae] sang on the said Easter and [during] Holy Week*, and did all that they were supposed to do. [These singers] are obliged to sing at solemn Masses and at Vespers during Holy Week, and on other feasts, in that way and manner as the other choristers and priests of our chapels in the said church used to sing. . . . [italics mine] (Doc. 28)

These musicians continued to perform at the Cathedral until December 1, 1501, when the adult chapel, comprised for the most part of chaplains

---

[202] From another of Savonarola's sermons, it seems certain that *laude* were performed daily at the Cathedral during those years:

> And now children, let us talk to you a bit. Listen to me: you sing *laude* here every morning and that's fine; but once in a while I'd also like to hear you sing the *canti* of the church such as the *Ave maris stella* or the *Veni creator Spiritus;* and it wouldn't hurt if the people were to sing the responses; and if I were to come to the pulpit and find that you were singing that *Ave maris stella*, I'd probably sing also. . . .

(G. Savonarola, *Prediche italiane ai Fiorentini*, Vol. III, p. 437.)

associated with the Church, was re-established.[203] The reorganization of the chapels at the Baptistry and the Santissima Annunziata followed shortly afterwards.[204] At that time the previous arrangement of using the same singers for the separately administered chapels of the three churches was put into effect once again. It is interesting to note that only by order of the first Grand Duke of Tuscany, Cosimo de'Medici, were the separate administrations united, and the system restored that had been instituted by the first Cosimo de'Medici almost one hundred years earlier.[205]

As a conclusion to this account of the singers of San Giovanni it seems fitting to add a final word on the Medici's role in Florentine musical history of the 15th century. Because of their policies, necessitated, to be sure, by political reasons, music in Florence did not exist under an exclusive court patronage as at Rome, Naples, Milan, Ferrara, and other principal Italian cities. Thus reflecting the democratic aspirations of the city, polyphony in Florence lost its restrictive associations and eventually came to form a part of even the ordinary citizen's cultural interests. Indeed, the public enthusiasm for polyphony was so keen that not even the compelling admonitions of Savonarola could destroy it. During the years of his theocratic regime the accomplishments of nearly half a century were almost completely obliterated. That polyphony had become so entrenched in the cultural life of Florence that it survived that period so effectively was the final vindication of the Medici's policies.

The striking feature of the chapel established on December 1, 1501, was that almost to a man it was made up of local musicians. The situation was indicative of the fact that polyphony in Florence would no longer be directly dependent upon the North. The emergence in the early 16th century of a Florentine school of composition headed by such figures as Bartolomeo Fiorentino, Bernardo Pisano, and Francesco Corteccia was the most important result of the intense musical activity in Medicean Florence.[206] The singers of San Giovanni, in addition to fulfilling their immediate functions as performers, had ultimately performed a didactic role: through them the future growth and practice of polyphonic music in Florence was assured.

---

[203] Seay, *op. cit.*, p. 55. The singers appointed to the chapel at that time were Ser Francesco Boscherini, Ser Zenobi di Felice, and Ser Davit d'Alessandro, tenors; Ser Iacopo di Bonaiuto, and Ser Antonio da Pescia, basses; Ser Giovanfrancesco d'Antonio and Carlo di Launoy, contraltos; Ser Leone, Ser Raffaelo di Piero, and as many choristers as were available, sopranos; in addition, there were two teachers of figural music, Ser Franco d'Andrea and Ser Giovanni Serragli, who also sang with the group. SMDF, *Delib.*, II, 2, 9, fol. 41^r.

[204] ASF, Arte di Calimala, *Delib.*, Vol. 23, fols. 78^v-79^r; SSA, *Ricord.*, Vol. 51, fols. 201^v-202^r.

[205] Baccini, *op. cit.*, pp. 29f.

[206] Studies of the life and works of Bartolomeo Fiorentino and Bernardo Pisano are now being prepared for publication.

THE SINGERS OF SAN GIOVANNI IN FLORENCE 351

APPENDIX

Documents

Doc. 1 (SMDF, *Delib.*, II, 2, 2, fol. 49ʳ)
[*in margin:* commixio eligendi cantores in Laurentium de Medicis]
Dicta Die Sexta Decembris 1438
Actendentes ad virtutem et prudentiam infrascripti Laurentii de Medicis, ad presens oratoris pro Comuni Florentie ad summum pontificem, et optantes iusta posse quod divinus cultus augeatur et quod ecclesia S. Marie del Fiore in honore omnibus aliis precellat et sit hornata, et considerantes quod honorabile et preclarum esset continue ad servitium dicte ecclesie retinere cantores et ideo [gap] desiderantes honorem ecclesie augeri, deliberaverunt quod scribatur honorabili viro Laurentio Johannis Biccii de Medicis, oratori Comunis Florentie ad summum pontificem, ad presens Ferrarie existenti, quod conetur iusta posse si habere possit unum magistrum capelle cum tribus cantoribus et pluribus prout expedit capelle, et quod habeat commixionem expendendi pro dictis cantoribus pro anno quolibet usque in florenis ducentis.

Doc. 2 (SMDF, *Allogazioni*, I, 1, 4, fol. 3ᵛ)
1438
Item postea eisdem anno et indictione, die nona mensis Decembris . . . Dominus Ugholinus olim Filippi de Giugnis, canonichus Florentinus, vigore commissionis sibi facte per dominos operarios Opere Sancte Marie del Fiore . . . conduxit ad canendum . . . in maiori ecclesia Florentina diebus festivis in dicta ecclesia, in vesperis tantum:

Magistrum Benottum de Ferraria, cum salario librarum quinque parvorum pro quolibet mense, L. 5.
Fratem Beltramum ordinis Sancti Agustini, cum salario librarum quatuor parvorum pro quolibet mense, L. 4.
Iannes de Monte de Ferraria, cum salario librarum quatuor parvorum pro quolibet mense, L. 4.
Francischum Bartoli, cum salario librarum trium et solidorum sex parvorum [pro]quolibet mense, L. 3 s. 6.
In totum inter omnes pro quolibet mense L. XVI. S. VI parvorum. Qui cantores stare debent pro eo tempore et prout et sicut videbitur operariis dicte Opere pro tempore existentibus et maiori parte ipsorum, et maxime dictis diebus prout requiritur.

Doc. 3 (SMDF, *Stanz.*, II, 4, 16, fol. 84ʳ)
29 Aprile 1439
Magistro Benotto, magistro cappelle Sancti Iohannis, L. 3 s. 6 parvorum pro suo et suorum sociorum labore in canendo in vesperis in maiori ecclesia in die translationis facte de corpore beati Zenobii. L. 3 s. 6.

Doc. 4 (ASF, Arte di Calimala, *Delib.*, Vol. 21, fol. 65ʳ)
19 Novembre 1504
Prefati domini consules et offitiales musaici pro dicta arte ecclesia et opera Sancti Johannis Baptiste insimul adunati . . . deliberaverunt . . . quod ditti cantores omnes teneantur et obligati sint . . . canere . . . in ditta ecclesia Santi Johannis . . . qualibet die, de mane, qua magnifici et excelsi domini domini priores libertatis populi florentini faciunt eorum introytum quolibet bimestri, videlicet prima

IV

die mensis Ianuarii, Martii, Maii, Iulii, Settenbris et Novenbris, et dum ditti magnifici domini sunt in dicta ecclesia S. Johannis prout antiquitus consuetum est diebus predictis congregati in dicta ecclesia pro audienda missa solemni et alia divina officia. . . .

Doc. 5 (SMDF, *Stanz.*, II, 4, 17, fol. 133ᵛ)
Die 28 Februarii 1446 [1447]
Magistro Benotto et quinque sociis cantoribus noviter conductis Flor. auri 27 sunt pro eorum salario et pagha 4 mensium cum dimidio initorum die 15 Ottobris proxime preteriti qua die finivit officium cantorum preteritorum. Fl. XXVII.

Doc. 6 (ASF, Arte della Lana, *Partiti*, Vol. 220, fols. 156ʳ-156ᵛ)
Die XXVI mensium Augusti, 1475
Supradicti domini consules invicem omnes in palatio dicte artis in loco eorum solite audientie more solito collegialiter et in sufficienti numero congregati. . . .
Item audita et intellecta quandam [sic] reformatione et constitutione facta per dictam artem et capitulum cathedralis ecclesie florentine predicte, continente in effecta quod consules dicte artis et due [sic] partes eorum, aliis etiam absentibus . . . possint eligere et deputare predicatores, chantores, sonatores orghanorum, clericos et campanarios et alios ministros cathedralis ecclesie Sancte Marie del Fiore de Florentia, ipsamque auctoritatem commicendi in operarios opere predicte pro eo tempore et termine quibus et prout et sicut eis et duobus partibus eorum in concordia videbitur et placebit; quapropter premisso et facto inter eos solepni et secreto scruptinio . . . commiserunt et remiserunt in operarios opere Sancte Marie del Fiore de Florentia, pro tempore duratoro hunc ad per totum mensem Ianuarii proxime futuri 1476, eligendi chantores, sonatores orghanorum, clericos et campanarios dicte ecclesie, ipsosque et quemlibet capssendi et removendi et alium seu alios denuvo eligendi et presentandi, et eo modo et forma quibus et prout et sicut eis in concordia videbitur et placebit.

Doc. 7 (ASF, Arte di Calimala, *Delib.*, Vol. 20, fol. 4ᵛ)
[*in margin:* cassatio Benozii]
Die XXIII Ianuarii 1447 [1448]
Prefati consules . . . audito Benozio [gap], cantore in ecclesia S. Johannis, dicente et velle recedere a dicto exercitio cantare et nolle amplius in dicta ecclesia cantare, servatis servandis, providerunt et deliberaverunt quod dictum Benozium possit et debeat recedere et quando vult vadat et quod amplius se non intromictat in officinando in dicta ecclesia. Et ex nunc ad cautelam ipsum Benozium tanquam inhutilem dicte ecclesie cassaverunt et removerunt a dicto exercitio cantandi in dicta ecclesia. Et quod sibi possit et debeat solvi de suo salario usque ad per totum presentem diem.

Doc. 8 (ASF, Arte di Calimala, *Delib.*, Vol. 20, fol. 60ᵛ)
[*in margin:* electio cantorum]
31 Marzo 1449
Item prefati consules et consiliarii informati quod in Ecclesia S. Johannis Baptiste ad presens non sunt pro electis vero nisi tres cantores, et quod ipsi non sufficient ad honorem dicte Ecclesie, et iam sunt plures menses elassi servientes in cantando in dicta ecclesia
Petrus Petri) et sine aliqua
Guglelmus Ver . . . [illegible]) electione de ipsis
facta, cum spe quod eis provideatur de eorum labore. . . . Et volent simul honori dicte Ecclesie providere et dictis cantoribus promissa servare . . .

elegerunt dictos Pierum et Guglelmum in cantores in dicta Ecclesia cum provisione et aliis usitatis et quam et que habent alii cantores. . . .

Doc. 9 (ASF, Arte di Calimala, *Delib.*, Vol. 20, fol. 61ʳ)
31 Marzo 1449
Item quod . . . liceat deliberare et stantiare cantoribus supra noviter electis eorum provisionem et salarium eisdem debitum pro tempore preterito quo servierunt in cantando usque ad per totum presentem mensem Martii non obstante quod non essent electi.

Doc. 10 (ASF, Arte di Calimala, *Petizioni e Stanziamenti*, Vol. 17 bis, fol. LXXIʳ)
[*in margin:* pro cantoribus]
Die V Julii 1449
Sit omnibus manifestum qualiter constituti in presentia nobilis viri Bartholomei Niccolai de Martellis, unius ex presentibus dominis consulibus dicte Artis, et Iohannis Leonardi de Altovitis, et mei Francisci, notarii dicte Artis, Perettus [gap] et Florentinus [gap], cantores in ecclesia S. Johannis, pro se et pro aliis eorum sociis cantoribus in dicta ecclesia, petierunt a dicto Bartholomeo licentiam discendendi a civitate Florentie et redeundi ad propriam patriam dummodo sibi solveretur et satisfieret de provisione eisdem debite pro mense Iunii proxime preteriti et pro benandata fieret eis aliquod donum . . . et remanserunt cum dicto Bartholomeo in hac concordia, videlicet, quod eisdem solvantur pro uno mense finito die ultimo dicti mensis Junii proxime preteriti, et flor. tres pro quolibet pro benandata et dono. Et ipsi promiserunt dicto Bartholomeo quod quandocunque ipsi vel aliquis ipsorum requirerentur a consulibus qui pro tempore fuerint dicte Artis, redire ad servitia dicte ecclesie S. Johannis dummodo dicti consules teneantur solvere expensas itineris et fiendas in redeundo, usque in quantitatem florenorum viginti pro quolibet ipsorum cantorum. Et quod facta solutione de dictis provisione et benandata, fieret eisdem lictera bene serviti. Et sic dictus Bartholomeus fecit solvere dicto Peretto fl. octo eidem tangentes, et dictus Florentinus . . . recepit pro se et pro Cornelio, eius socio, flor. sedicem. . . .

Doc. 11 (ASF, Signori, Legazioni e Commissarie, Vol. 13, fol. 17ᵛ)
27 Maggio 1451
Noi qui non habiamo altro che scrivere se non che qui s'attende ad ordinare una bella festa per celebrare il giorno del nostro protectore San Giovanni. Sichè se gli cantori regii verrano, sarà iocondissimo a tucto il nostro, et veduti volentieri da questa signoria. . . .

Doc. 12 (ASF, Signori, Legazioni e Commissarie, Vol. 13, fol. 19ʳ)
5 Giugno 1451
Ne agiugneremo altro se non che tucto il popolo con grande desiderio aspecta quelli regii cantori, adornamento della solennità del Baptista e letitia della città nostra, i quali saranno per più rispecti, et maxime per contemplatione del principe al quale servono, da noi benignamente ricevuti. Et tu del giorno che partono darai aviso. . . .

Doc. 13 (ASF, Signori, Legazioni e Commissarie, Vol. 13, fol. 20ᵛ)
11 Giugno 1451
Et i cantori aspectiamo di in hora in hora. Et saranno veduti volentieri per contemplatione di quel principe. . . .

Doc. 14 (SSA, *EU*, Vol. 689, fol. 103ʳ)
Sabato a dì XVIIII di Giugno 1451
A spese di ch'amangiare s. quindici sono per 25 melanzane e s. cinquanta quatro

354

per fiaschi VI di trebbiano a s. 9 el fiascho e s. dieci per 30 pani bianchi e s. dieci per frutte, le qua' cose comprano per fare honore a' cantori del re di 'ragona e conpagni. ... L.4 s. 9.

Doc. 15 (SSA, *EU*, Vol. 689, fol. 130^v)
Lunedì a dì XXI di Giugno 1451
A spese straordinarie s. sei, portò frate decto [Biagio] disse aveva pagato per fare arecare e riportare l'organetto d'Antonio. Fu quando e cantori del re di 'ragona vennoro a cantare la messa. ... S. 6.

Doc. 16 (ASF, Stinche, Vol. 98, fol. 20^v)
Die 1 Novembris 1467
Johannes Franciosus alias l'Abate, cantore in S. Giovanni, presentatus fuit captus dictis superstitibus per ser Marianum de Pistorio, capitaneum familie dominorum, ad petitionem Pieri Cosimi de Medicis de numero Decem Balie, et quod non relaissetur sine eius littera vel bulletta. Die 15 Novembris 1467 relassatus fuit Vigore licentie eidem concesse per dictum Pierum, de qua rogatum fuit ser Marianum de Pistorio sub dicta die.

Doc. 17 (ASF, Medici avanti il Principato, F. XXIII, c. 347)
[*verso:* Nobili viro Lorenzo di Piero di Chosimo de'Medici in Firenze 1471.
    da Filippotto chantore in Napoli. A dì VIII (*sic*) in Maggio.]
†Al Nome di Dio, adì XXVII di Maggio 1471.
Honorando viri tanquam pater e prudente karisimo, dopo le debite rechomandazioni etc. Kar^{mo} chompare, io no' v'ò scritto per lo pasato per non essere achaduto; e questi versi per dirvi chome in questo anno la maestà del S. Re mi mandò in Franc[i]a per menare de qua alchuno chantore, e pasai di chostì, ma fu mi fatto chomandamento ch'io no' vi dovesi fare motto, e per non disubidire pasai a dilungho, e chosì andai a fare la voluntà de' re. Di poi tornai e sono stato pocho rimeritato del servigio fatto. Niente di meno questo Re m'à chonceso ducati X d'oro il mese e V chane di pano fine per vestire, e terzo ducati XX d' ofetta l'anno, e più m'à donato una chapitaneria in Chalavria per uno anno, che n'ò da portatis ducati L, e tuto chon buono amore. Ma perchè la donna mia, disiderosa di tornare di chostà ala patria ongni giorno e ora mi stimola, e per questa chagione io sarei chontento tornare di chostà e farei che sempre aresti una buona avantagiata chapela, chon questo ch'io vorei che voi mi facesi avere uno spedale a mia vita, che fusi buona per me, e più ducati VI d'oro il mese. Sichè, karo chonpare, vedete se di chostà mi potete ripatriare, che sapete che sempre mai avete uno servidore; e rispondetemi e datemi la risposta a chi vi darà questa, e fate di tenere segreto e chauto, perchè se di qua fusi sentito io sarei disfatto. Altro non v'ò di dire, se non che sempre mi rachomando a voi. Che XPO. vi chonservi in felicie stato. Vostro servo.
    Filipotto de Dortenche, chantore dela Maestà del S. Re Ferando. i' Napoli.

Doc. 18 (ASF, Medici avanti il Principato, F. XXIX, c. 828)
[*verso:* Magnifico Laurentio Medici, in Cafaguolo
    1473. da Braccio Martelli, a dì III di Settembre.]
Arnolfo viene chostà pel bisogno suo che è d'essere condotto in Sancto Giovanni per cantore. Et io a sua contemplatione et per lo bisogno etiam dell'arte ti fo questa, rachomandandotelo et pregandoti che gli facci una lettera a Bernardo di Nichola Capponi che voglia operare cho' conpagni sia condocto. Sarebbe buono andare più là con lo scrivere, cioè tochagli il ricorreggere parte degli inconvenienti che vi sono, che ne sai parte, non tanto della cappella de' cantori quanto de' cappellani, che per caldo d'alchuno mandono sotto sopra quella chiesa; et io, che mi trovo hora là dipositario, lo veglio per pruova ogni dì. Quello Bernardo, maestro della capella, ha in somma tutti e cantori con quelli

che vi tiene ha tanto il mese, che Dio sa quanto e bene intese e il disagio ne riceve la capella. Credo farà anchora cantarvi e poveri che vanno achattando, per più avanzare. Tu se' savio, havendo a stare chostì tanto o quanto, sarebbe buono tocharne un motto al detto Bernardo Caponi. Et in ogni modo rachomanda Arnolfo, aportatore di questa; et io qui suplirò al resto. Vale.
      Tuus Br[accius] Martellus.

Doc. 19   (SMDF, *EU*, VIII, 3, 3, No. 14, fol. 22^v)
A dì 12 di Giugno 1479
A ser Antonio di Marcho da Montuchi, maestro de' fanciulli che chantano, L. dodici s. quindici per suo salario di mesi sei cominciati e finiti chome di sopra c. 67, L. 12 s. 15....

Doc. 20   (SMDF, *Delib.*, II, 2, 5, fol. 61^r)
11 Gennaio 1479 [1480]
[*in margin:* pro ser Antonio de Montughio]
Prefati operarii ... deliberaverunt quod camerarius ... det et solvat ... ser Antonio de Montughio, cappellano dicte ecclesie et magistro cantus figurati, L. duas s. duos d. quatuor pro eius labore in instruendo clericos canentes in dicta cappella cantus figurati....

Doc. 21   (SMDF, *Delib.*, II, 2, 6, fol. 24^v)
1483
Die septimo Aprilis. Item deliberaverunt et deliberando stantiaverunt infrascriptis clericis pro eorum remuneratione cantus figurati, et talis quantitas ponatur ad computum expensarum opere hoc modo, videlicet:

Francho Andree Franchi	Libras sedicim
Canti Bonasii cimatoris	parvorum in totum
Petro Phylippi Ciegia	et inter omnes et
Danieli Landini fornarii	sic L. duas cuilibet
Christophoro Gregorii muratoris	eorum, et hoc pro
Laurentio Georgii textoris	hac vice tantum et
Blaxio Andree mazerii	non secus vel ultra
Laurentio Salvatoris bambagiarii	ullo modo.

Doc. 22   (SMDF, *Delib.*, II, 2, 6, fol. 81^v)
19 Gennaio 1484 [1485]
Item viso quod meliores et doctiores cantores cantus figurati in eorum cappella Sancte Marie Floris se a dicto eorum exercitio cantus absentaverunt adeo quod sine illis dicta cappella restat inperfecta et sine suis partibus, et cognoscentes expensas que propterea fiunt esse vanas et sine utilitate aut ornatu aliquo dicte ecclesie causis predictis, omni meliori modo quo potuerunt eamdem cappellam anihilaverunt et nullam reddiderunt in omnibus suis partibus, et quod cantores ibidem canentibus vel canere solentibus solvi propterea non possunt per camerarium dicti officii sub pena solvendi de suo proprio dictus camerarius, et quod prefati cantores restent et remaneant in eo statu quo erant ante dictam electionem de eo factam. Et si quis ipsorum gauderet propterea aliqua immunitate vel beneficio ab eo intelligatur decedisse et ex nunc ipsum removunt et tollunt in omnibus et per omnia. Rogantes etc.

Doc. 23   (SSA, *Ricord.*, Vol. 49, fol. 27^r)
[*in margin:* Iannes Francioso per soprano a cantare]
1481 [1482]
Recordo chomo hozi questo dì 12 de Genaio 1481 [1482] in sabato, la matina circa hore 16, Ianesi Francioso infrascripto se obliga stare nel convento dela Anunciata per uno anno, ale spexe corporale del convento, e cantare in chiesia e

IV

in chapella e in convento sì chomo gli altri cantori. Con questo che'l priore e convento el debiano tenere e mantenere vestito e calzato e darli el mese mezo ducato d'oro, e a lui Ianes deto farli honesta e bone compagnia, e anche quando fusse infermo fare inverso de lui chomo fusse proprio frate del convento. E in chaso che'l dito Ianes cantore perdesse la voxe e non potesse canttare sovrano, non debia per questo essere licentiado avanti l'ano. . . .
Ego Iohannes Hurtault promitto et iuro sic observare ut supra plenius dicitur et scribitur, manu propria.

Doc. 24 (SSA, *Ricord.*, Vol. 49, fols. 33ʳ-34ʳ)
[*in margin:* Conventione con cantori della capella]
1482
In Xpi. nomin. amen
Notum sit presentes inspecturis qualiter infrascripti domini cantores hodie die prima Maii 1482 convenerunt . . . cantare in ecclesia Annuntiate et in capella ipsius Annuntiate secundum consuetudinem iam inceptam con pactis et condictionibus infrascriptis. Primo et ante omnia quod cantores infrascripti et quilibet ipsorum servare debeant honestatem in dicta ecclesia et capella quando cantant, ita et taliter quod loquendo aut ridendo non faciant scandalum aut strepitum, sub pena duorum soldorum pro quolibet et pro qualibet vice.
Item similiter in refectorio debeant servare honestatem et conformiter se habere con fratibus in mensa etc.
Item quod infrascripti cantores, una con aliis cantoribus conventus, sint obligati ante previdere que ipsi habent in ecclesia cantare sicut missam aut motetum aut magnificat etc., et hoc quotiens cantaturi sunt in ecclesia, non solum in diebus festis sed etiam ferialibus. Et si aliquis ipsorum defficiat, tunc punctetur et signetur in duobus solidis etc.
Item quod quotiens aliquis predictorum sive infrascriptorum cantorum defficeret in ecclesia aut in capella, sive in missa sive in vesperis sive in laudibus, si erit in die feriali incurrat penam unius carleni pro qualibet vice, et si in die festivo incurat penam duorum carlinorum. Et casu quod aliquis ipsorum cantorum vel omne quando defficiunt in ecclesia aut in capella in cantando, quia voluissent in alia ecclesia vel loco in illa hora cantare, tunc quilibet ipsorum incurat penam unius ducati de auro. Et predictis servandis servatis, possint ipsi cantores in qualibet loco honesto et in qualibet ecclesia cantare et docere et alia sibi placita facere.
Item . . . conventus se obligat dare cuilibet ipsorum pro quolibet mense unum ducatum auri cum dimidio. . . .
Et ultra dictum salarium debeant habere expensas sicut frates habent in refectoris, et ultra, si aliquis infirmaretur, debeat conventus providere de medico et medicinis.
Et in fidem predictorum omnium ego frater Antonius de Bononia, prior indignus conventus Annunciate civitatis Florentie, de manu mea omnia predicta scripsi con subscriptione ipsorum cantorum de manu eorum.
Ego Bartolomeo de Castris contentor in predictis scripturis.
Ego Iohannes Comitus contentor in scripturis predictis.
Ego Iohannes Vitine [?] contentor in scripturis predictis.
Notum sit qualiter, ultra predicta pacta . . . promissit dictus prior in spetiali Bartholomeo cantori, qui in cantando facit contraltum, sex ducatos pro una veste. . . .

Doc. 25 (SSA, *Ricord.*, Vol. 49, fol. 90ʳ)
1483 [1484]
In Xpi. nomine, adì 29 de Zanaio 1483 [1484]
Recordo chomo l'infrascriti cantori e homini da bene, cantori in Sancto

Giovane in Fiorenze, se obligano a cantare ala chapella dela Nuntiata el Sabbato matina la messa de canto figurato, perseverando tuto l'anno, servando in capella le bone cirimonie cum honestà. . . . E sia obligato el convento dare e achomadare le infrascrite cosse.
In prima, uno leto con lenzuola, matarassa, chapezale, colcina [sic], e coperta.
Item la lavatura de tuti i lloro pani lini.
Item el barbiere che li rada una volta la setimana bene e honorevolemente a loro contentamento e piacere.
Item oto para de scarpete e quatro para di pianele, secondo el bisogno loro, de tempo in tempo.
Item ala Pasqua de Quaresima, guarnello per uno farsetto.
Item per Santo Giovane, una breta per ciascaduno.
Item del mese de Setembre, pano bono per uno paio de calze.
Item per la Pasqua de Natale, diexe braza de bon pano per una vesta.
E in fede dele predite io frate Antonio da Bologna ho scrita questa ricordanza de mia mano chomo priore del convento, de volentà e comandamento deli nostri magnifici operarii. E a questa medesima ricordanza se sono soto scripti el piovano Girolamo, ser Arnolfo, Nicolò di Zovani da Fiorenze e Bartolomeo de Castris.
[Space left vacant for Piovano Girolamo's signature]
Io ser Arnolfo d' Arnolfo son contento a tute queste cose sopradicte, e però [sic: perciò] mi sono soto scripto di mia propria mano. Et ego Nicholaus Ihoannis hac die ut supradicta confirmo et contentus sum etc.
Ego Bartholomeus de Castris contentor in scripturis predictis.

Doc. 26   (SMDF, Delib., II, 2, 6, fol. 116ʳ)
[in margin: Copia deliberationis consulum pro cantoribus eligendis]
Die XXI Iunii 1485
Fit Fides Qualiter. Spectabiles consules artis lane civitatis Florentie servatis servandis etc. deliberaverunt quod possint eligi cantores S. Johannis et alios pro ecclesia Sancte Reparate cum pactis, salariis, et conditionibus, et aliis alios ordinandis, et quod in eis possint expendi usque ad summam Fl. ducentorum largorum quolibet anno. . . .

Doc. 27   (SMDF, Delib., II, 2, 7, fol. 5ʳ)
[in margin: Sumptus et copia deliberationis consulum pro cantoribus]
Die 27 Iulii 1487
Fit fides qualiter spectabiles consules Artis Lane civitatis Florentie servatis servandis etc. deliberaverunt quod in futurum cantoribus Sancti Ioannis et Sancte Marie del Fiore civit. Flor. per operarios dicte Opere Sancte Marie del Fiore possit solvi de pecunia dicte opere quolibet anno Fl. ducentos quadraginta largos de auro etc. Ego Paces Bambelli Pacis notarius in dicta arte rogatus scripsi.

Doc. 28   (SMDF, Delib., II, 2, 9, fols. 140ʳ-141ʳ)
27 Aprilis 1498
Copia legis desponentis de salario dando cantoribus ebdomoda sancta, facte in arte lane et in consilio.
Item quinto, ut corus ecclesie nostro Sancte Marie del Fiore ornatius reddatur in honorem omnipotentis Dei, et in satisfactionem populi frequentantis dictam [ecclesiam] quod de cetero solvatur et solvi possit otto clericis cantoribus quolibet anno L. 1 pro quolibet pro uno bireto. Et quatuor tenoristis et contra L. 4 pro quolibet et quolibet anno, qui inceptus esse intelligatur in proximo preterito Paschates resurrectionis et de dicto proximo preterito Paschate fieri debeat prima solutio ut supra: propterea quia dicti clerici tenoristi et contra in

IV

dicto Paschate et ebdomoda sancta cecinerunt et omnia fecerunt ad que tenebantur. Cum conditione tamen quod teneantur canere in missis solempnibus et in vesperis et in sancta ebdomoda et aliis solempnitatibus eo modo et forma et prout et sicut alias solebant alii clerici et presbiteri cappelle nostratis in dicta ecclesia. . . .

V

LORENZO THE MAGNIFICENT AND MUSIC

Within the last decade a number of important books have appeared which, among other things, consider aspects of musical patronage during the Renaissance in such diverse cities as Ferrara, Bruges, Naples and Mantua. Each has added a good deal to our knowledge of the practice and politics of music in those places, and collectively they have furnished several useful avenues of approach to a subject which, in Renaissance musical studies at least, is still in its infancy. Rather less has been done for Florence, particularly during its golden age under Lorenzo the Magnificent, although Luigi Parigi's *Laurentiana*, published almost four decades ago, furnished some very valuable insights into Lorenzo's relationship with the Florentine musical world of his day.[1] In the intervening years a number of scholars, including the present writer, have contributed a good deal to our knowledge of Florentine music in that period. But there has been no systematic attempt to bring this research together and to relate it to Lorenzo and his role as a musical patron. One of my principal aims in the present study is to rectify this situation. In doing so I shall also raise attendant issues that have a bearing not only on Lorenzo's patronage and practice of music but also on some of the more general aspects of musical performance and repertories in late Quattrocento Florence.

At least four principal types of musical patronage were evident during that time. Although these systems of patronage assumed

---

[1] L. PARIGI, *Laurentiana: Lorenzo dei Medici cultore della musica*, Florence 1954; see, in addition, the chapter «Il Magnifico e la società musicale» in E. BARFUCCI's *Lorenzo de' Medici e la società artistica del suo tempo*, Florence 1945, pp. 87ff. A. ROCHON also devotes a number of pages to a discussion of Lorenzo and music in his *La jeunesse de Laurent de Médicis (1449-1478)*, Paris 1963, pp. 42-44, 69-70, 436-438, 444-447, 461-464, 474.

different forms, ultimately they were all dependent upon and guided by individuals, and Lorenzo, as might be expected, played a leading, if not dominant role, in all of them. They were:

1) Private patronage, especially that of the great families such as the Medici, the Strozzi and the Rucellai, who maintained composers, singers, and instrumentalists on a formal as well as on a casual basis.

2) Church patronage, especially of large establishments such as the Cathedral and the Baptistry (which shared a musical chapel for much of the 15th century) and the Santissima Annunziata, which for a time also employed many of the same musicians as the Cathedral and the Baptistry; church patronage in the case of these latter churches is inextricably tied to corporate patronage, and to a certain extent, because of the Medici, to private patronage, a point I shall consider in a moment.

3) Corporate patronage, especially of guilds such as the Arte della Lana and the Calimala which, acting through their representatives on the various governing boards, were responsible for the administration of Duomo and the Baptistry; but also corporate patronage of the companies which directed religious confraternities such as those at Orsanmichele, San Zanobi and San Piero Martire, which had a long history of employing performers.

4) State patronage, particularly of permanently employed instrumental groups, such as the *trombetti* and the *pifferi* who served the Signoria at the Palazzo Vecchio, as well as of individual *araldi* and *cantori*, who were employed there both on a permanent and a casual basis.

The various kinds of musicians and repertories which can be associated with these forms of patronage may be classified according to accepted or traditional norms, though identification with one group does not necessarily exclude inclusion in another. To the first two categories belong, almost exclusively, those singers, composers and on occasion, instrumentalists, particularly organists, many if not all of them Northerners except for the organists, who may be identified with ongoing traditions, new developments and contemporary performance practices of written polyphony, that is, with the high art music of the day.[2] Most members of the musical

---

[2] Their presence is documented in my *The Singers of San Giovanni in Florence during the 15th Century*, «Journal of the American Musicological Society», 14, 1961, pp. 307-358.

chapels were professionals, often though not always clergymen or men connected with religious orders, people who earned their living by writing, copying, performing and sometimes teaching music, in churches, in courts and in private households. Their repertories would normally embrace music within the grand tradition of European polyphony, exemplified in Lorenzo's time by the Burgundian or French chanson and by settings, which sometimes might incorporate local practices, of liturgical and paraliturgical texts, suitable for church services and for private music making as well. The names of singers of polyphony who were privately employed by Lorenzo have not come down to us. Their presence in his household, however, is confirmed by an undated list of his retainers who accompanied him on one of his trips to the thermal baths, undoubtedly during the last decade of his life. In addition to his personal chaplain, his barber, his cook, two of his chancellors and others, there were his instrumental accompanist «El compare,» the Cathedral organist Antonio Squarcialupi, and two unnamed «cantori».[3] Judging from the names of those in Piero de' Medici's entourage when he visited Rome in 1493, it appears that singers of polyphony privately employed by the Medici were normally drawn from the Florentine chapel.[4]

Although the origins of the laudesi companies, the third category, were decidedly popular and offered genuine venues for popular devotion, by Lorenzo's time the larger of the Florentine companies were wealthy institutions, run by prominent people, which often vied with one another in the splendor of their services.[5] The wealthier religious confraternities employed professional organists, string players and other instrumentalists as well as occasional professional singers, but the usual corps of musicians – the performers of laudi – were men and youths who earned their living as artisans and craftsmen or in some other way, people who for want of a better description might best be called semi-professionals. How

---

[3] The list was compiled by Lorenzo's chancellor Piero Dovizi da Bibbiena, who sent it to Matteo Franco. It is published in I. DEL LUNGO, ed., *Un viaggio di Clarice Orsini de' Medici nel 1485 descritto da Ser Matteo Franco*, Bologna 1868, p. 7. For «El compare» della viola see note 45 below.

[4] See below, note 54.

[5] On music and the role of musicians in the companies' services see B. WILSON, *Music and Merchants. The Laudesi Companies of Republican Forence*, Oxford 1992, particularly chapters 3 and 4, pp. 74-182 and particularly p. 214.

many of them received formal training in music, that is, whether they relied solely on oral traditions and learned what they did by ear and by rote, or whether they also had some training in reading polyphony, as seems likely, are matters that have to be decided on an individual basis according to the evidence.

In a sense the repertories of the laudesi were as diverse as the people who performed them. There were well-known or traditional monophonic melodies, whose origins might have lain in the art music of the time or of a by-gone era, or melodies that might have been composed by musicians working outside that tradition, but melodies in any case which were known and sung by people from every walk of life, music that was in the popular consciousness. But there was also polyphonic music, sometimes adapted or rearranged in simpler guise, that sprang from ballatas, chansons or carnival music, as the «cantasi come» rubrics show, that is, rubrics which tell the performer what melody or melodies the laudi texts were to be sung to.[6] The crossover or interaction between these repertories is analogous to the kinds of musicians who were employed as laudesi and to the wider audiences who themselves sang many of the tunes.

Within the fourth category may be placed the brass and wind players, percussionists and the players of other instruments such as the lute and the viola who were employed at the Palazzo Vecchio and who performed at various public ceremonies and at entertainments within the Palace.[7] Fanfares and other types of ceremonial music as well as music suitable for entertainment at dinner or afterwards formed the principal part of their repertories. Many of these musicians, who as a rule were laymen, supplemented

---

[6] The process of adapting laudi texts to pre-existent music has been discussed by G. CATTIN in a number of studies, among them, *Contributi alla storia della lauda spirituale*, «Quadrivium», 2, 1958, pp. 45-78; *I 'cantasi come' in una stampa di laude della Biblioteca Riccardiana (Ed. r. 196)*, ibid., 19, 1978, p. 5-52; *Musiche per le laude di Castellano Castellani*, «Rivista italiana di musicologia», 12, 1977, pp. 185-206; *Contrafacta internazionali: musiche europee per laude italiane*, in *Musik und Text in der Mehrstimmigkeit des 14. und 15. Jahrhunderts*, eds. U. GÜNTHER and K. VON FISCHER, Kassel 1984, pp. 411-442. See also F. LUISI, *Laudario giustinianeo*, 2 vols., Venice 1983, I, passim; and F. GHISI, *Strambotti e laude nel travestimento spirituale della poesia musicale del Quattrocento*, «Collectanea historiae musicae», 1, 1953, pp. 45-78. A comprehensive view of the laude and contrafacta is given by WILSON, *Music and Merchants* cit., pp. 170-180.

[7] For the instrumentalists employed at the Palazzo Vecchio, see G. ZIPPEL, *I suonatori della Signoria di Firenze*, Trent 1892; L. CELLESI, *Documenti per la storia musicale di Firenze*, «Rivista musicale italiana», 34, 1927, pp. 579-602; 35, 1928, pp. 553-582; and K. POLK, *Civic Patronage and Instrumental Ensembles in Renaissance Florence*, «Augsburger Jahrbuch für Musikwissenschaft», 3, 1986, pp. 51-68.

their incomes, whenever it was possible for them to do so, by playing at private functions, and it is obvious that they also played a pivotal role in dance music. In this respect, however, they must have had a good deal of competition, for there were any number of independently employed – what we might call free-lance – instrumentalists who made a living by performing at the many social functions at which music was required in Florentine society. Some of these latter also set up shop as teachers to the bourgeois families who sought to emulate their social betters.[8] Trained in their own traditions, all of these musicians had repertories designed for listening and for dancing, both written and unwritten, which required years of practice and experience to master. The appearance in late 15th-century sources from Florence and elsewhere of pieces, either adapted, with a few modifications, from pre-existent vocal music or composed in a manner akin to it, which formed part of a written instrumental repertory, implies that many instrumentalists were by then receiving the kind of training that enabled them to master the intricacies of the traditional notational system.

Similar observations regarding musical training may be raised about the poet-improvisers and other singers who performed for the delectation of the Signoria during or after meals at the Palazzo Vecchio and who also entertained at state functions. Florentine heralds, like their counterparts elsewhere, were state employees.[9] They were called upon to celebrate in verse, and perhaps song, a variety of subjects ranging from the political to the personal. Others of their kind, the elite of the professional improvisers such as Niccolò Ciecho d'Arezzo, went from city to city and court to court in search of ever more lucrative invitations.[10] Complementing them, on a more popular level, especially in Florence, were the *canterini* or *cantimpanche*, like Lorenzo's great favorite Antonio di Guido, who gave public recitations in the Piazza San Martino to the delight of

---

[8] To cite but one of the free-lance musicians: «Mariotto di Bastiano di Francesco, suona l'arpa» who reported in the Catasto of 1446 that he rented a room for the purpose of teaching dancing (ASF, Catasto 655, 1446, S. Spirito, Drago, f. 745).

[9] R. C. Trexler's *The Libro Cerimoniale of the Florentine Republic*, Geneva 1978 offers definitive word on the duties of Florentine heralds.

[10] See D. De Robertis, *L'esperienza poetica del Quattrocento*, in *Storia della letteratura italiana*, III: *Il Quattrocento e l'Ariosto*, eds. E. Cecchi and N. Sapegno, Milan 1966, pp. 402 ff.

attentive and appreciative audiences.[11] In addition to being extraordinarily gifted narrators and versifyers, many of these poet-improvisers had a smattering of musical training.[12] Not a few are reported also as having accompanied themselves on the lute, the lira or the viola, testimony to their having had some kind of musical instruction.[13] Then, too, there were the virtuoso instrumentalists – lutenists and others employed by the government and courts elsewhere and by private families – who performed both at informal gatherings and under more formal conditions that we today would call concerts. These performers were assuredly musicians of the highest professional calibre. We know from occasional references, such as a Sienese report from 1475 of «two players, a harpist and a [lute?] player of Lorenzo de' Medici», that performers of this type were also found in his household.[14] Thus, for their various needs and delectation the Florentine institutions and families which patronized music in Lorenzo's time employed several types of professional and semiprofessional musicians, performers who had assuredly had diverse kinds of training in traditions which may or may not have

---

[11] For Antonio di Guido see F. FLAMINI, *La lirica toscana del Rinascimento anteriore ai tempi del Magnifico*, Pisa 1891, pp. 162 ff. and B. BECHERINI, *Un canta in panca Fiorentino, Antonio di Guido*, «Rivista musicale italiana», 50, 1948, pp. 241-247. Flamini discusses Antonio's surviving literary production, including four laudi, a sirventese, «Nel verde tempo della vita nostra», and the «Vangeli in ottava rima», which were composed for Santa Maria Nuova (*ibid.*, pp. 168-172). An interesting point about Antonio's working methods is illustrated by Flamini who cites a report that Feo Belcari lent Antonio books and tracts from which the young poet-singer, drew materials for his improvisations. The borrowed materials included a Dialogue of St. Gregory, «which Antonio returned with a letter and a sonnet», saying he would sing of it «in versi».

[12] See, DE ROBERTIS, *L'esperienza poetica* cit., p. 403, for a summary of their repertories, which comprised subjects drawn from chivalric romances, classical fables and myths, ancient history, sacred legends, contemporary events, all of which were extemporized in traditionals forms such as ottave rime, capitoli, canzoni, laudi and sonnets. Adept at gauging public taste and possessed of extraordinary abilities at versifying, the poet-improvisers, with their facile imaginations and the effects of their delivery, were able to engage their audiences in a way that is almost impossible for us to reenact, or imagine, today. An outstanding predecessor of Antonio di Guido was Cristoforo Fiorentino called Altissimo, who sang in ottava rima all ninety stanzas of his *Primo libro de' Reali*, taken from the romance of the same name.

[13] Sometimes the poet-improvisers employed others to sing their verses, as may be inferred from a report which cites a performance in San Martino on 8 March 1450 by a young boy who had a «gentil pronunzia». But the public preferred improvisation, real or apparent, and the facility with which the singer went effortlessly from verse to verse (further, see FLAMINI, *La lirica toscana* cit., pp. 242, 600 and BECHERINI, *Una canta in panca* cit., 242).

[14] ASS, Concistoro 641, f. 59v. They were among the many musicians who were in Siena on August 15th of that year to perform at the annual Assumption Day festivities. A chronological survey of the various forces assembled for those celebrations can be found in G. CECCHINI's, *Palio e Contrade nella loro evoluzione storica*, Siena 1958 and Milan 1982).

been related and who came to making music with different experiences and different repertories. It is not always clear in some situations, such as the various functions and ceremonies at the Palazzo Vecchio or in the paraliturgical services of the laudesi, or for that matter in private music making at home, how and where the lines of demarcation between the types of performers and repertories were drawn.

Lorenzo was intimately connected in one way or another with all of these categories of Florentine musical patronage. During his later years he was in fact the very personification of the enlightened Renaissance patron, one whose broad musical interests reflected not only his own tastes and predilections but also the wider needs of a vibrant and complex society in which music was present at every level. He was uniquely qualified for the role because of his privileged political position, his love of music and his knowledge of the art. Lorenzo's activities as a patron of music and musicians and as a champion of musical performance in all of its varied aspects, indeed even his own talents as a performer, have perhaps been overshadowed by the accomplishments of his second son, Giovanni. As Pope Leo X, Giovanni, who himself was something of a composer, brought musical performance at the Vatican to heights never achieved before his time.[15] The Pope's love of music and his patronage of many of the great musicians of his time were commented upon, celebrated and criticized even in his own day. Giovanni, however, would clearly never have become such a discriminating patron of music without the training, encouragement and example provided by his father.

Lorenzo, too, had his parents and others in his family to thank for his broad musical background and for fostering his interest in all kinds of music. His grandfather Cosimo was responsible for instituting musical chapels in the city's major churches. Almost from the outset these employed Northern musicians, the purveyors of the new polyphony, and Medici agents in France and the Lowlands,

---

[15] A. PIRRO, *Leo X and Music*, «The Musical Quarterly», 21, 1935, pp. 1-16 has a particularly sympathetic account of the Pope's relations with musicians. For Leo and musicians in Rome during his papacy see H. W. FREY, *Regesten zur päpstlichen Kapelle unter Leo X und zu seiner Privatkapelle*, «Die Musikforschung», 8, 1955, pp. 58-73, 178-199, 412-437; 9, 1956, pp. 46-57, 139-156, 411-419. An account of the celebrations and musical performances attendent on Giovanni's election to the papacy and his trip to Florence in 1515 is given by A. M. CUMMINGS, *The Politicized Muse*, Princeton 1992, pp. 42-53, 67-82.

acting with Cosimo's approval and using the resources of his bank, were often instrumental in recruiting many of them.[16] Cosimo may very well have been behind the commission from Guillaume Dufay, one of the new stars in the musical firmament, of the ceremonial motet «Nuper rosarum flores», which was performed at the consecration of the Florentine cathedral in 1434, an event presided over by Pope Eugene IV, in whose chapel Dufay was then serving. The friendship struck up at the time with Dufay endured for decades, as several letters in Medici archives attest.[17] Piero and Giovanni, Cosimo's sons, were passionately interested in music, and Giovanni, who owned instruments which he himself played, apparently had musicians in his private employ.[18] Piero, too, as can be inferred from his subsequent activities with regard to the musical

---

[16] See my *The Singers of San Giovanni* cit., especially pp. 315ff.

[17] See particularly the letter (ASF, MAP VI, 776) from Dufay (1452) in which he announced that he would be sending them his newly composed Lamentations on the fall of Constantinople. The letter is published in B. BECHERINI, *Relazioni di musici fiamminghi con la corte dei Medici*, «La Rinascita», 4, 1941, p. 87 and in English translation in my *The Singers of San Giovanni* cit., pp. 318f. Also telling is the letter Squarcialupi wrote Dufay on 1 May 1467, where among other things, he thanked him for sending the newly arrived chapel singers to Florence, «the best of your church, just as you wrote». The letter (ASF, MAP VIII, 131) is published in G. GAYE, *Carteggio inedito di artisti*, Florence 1830, I, pp. 208f. and in English translation in *The Singers of San Giovanni* cit., p. 322.

[18] On Giovanni and music see V. ROSSI, *L'indole e gli studi di Giovanni di Cosimo de' Medici*, «Rendiconti della Reale Accademia dei Lincei», V s., 2, 1893, pp. 38-60, 129-150. Of immediate interest are the letters from 13 January and 20 February 1445 (ASF, MAP V, 273 and MAP VI, 194, cited by ROSSI, *op. cit.*, p. 46) concerning two of Giovanni's lutes that had been had lent out, and another (ASF, MAP VI, 75) from 29 March 1448 written by Piero de' Ricci, who reports that he was about to buy him another «which is one of the most beautiful things you've ever seen» (ROSSI, *op. cit.*, p. 44: «che è una de le più belle cose che tu vedessi mai»). FLAMINI, *La lirica toscana* cit., p. 279, note 1, mentions a viola which Rosello sent to Giovanni and Piero. Flamini also cites (p. 279, note 3) various letters which attest to a lively exchange of poetry and music between Rosello Roselli and Giovanni. Roselli sent Giovanni a ballata on 6 March 1445 (ASF, MAP VII, 20) and other verses four days later (ASF, MAP VII, 28). On the 23rd of the same month he followed these up with some music, which he urged Giovanni to try out with his own singers, adding that the singers with him had found it pleasing. Roselli says he had also given a copy of this latter to ser Francesco so that he could teach it to Lucrezia, Giovanni's sister-in-law (ASF, MAP VII, 39: «Vedi tu se s'è ben servuto con cotesti cantori; questi di qua mi dicono che sta bene. Io ne ho dato la copia a ser Francesco perché l'insegni alla Lucrezia»). In April 1447 Giovanni sent Rosello a canzonetta, which Rosello had had sung, and shortly afterwards Rosello returned the compliment by sending Giovanni a ballata, which he said «sings magnificently» (ASF, MAP VII, 24: «qui è suta intonata e cantasi magnificamente»). Also noteworthy is the letter to Giovanni written by his half-brother Carlo at Ferrara on 12 July 1445, in which Carlo recommended a certain ser Lino, «who is expert in dance, song and a thousand other pleasant things» (ASF, MAP IX, 168, quoted in ROSSI, *op. cit.*, p. 50 and in G. PIERACCINI, *La stirpe de' Medici di Cafaggiolo*, 4 vols., Florence 1924 and Florence 1986, I, p. 78).

chapels, also had some kind of formal musical training, as shown by the music books in his possession.[19] Perhaps the best indication we have of the extent of Piero's training and of his discriminating taste comes from the letter written in 1467 by the great Florentine organist Antonio Squarcialupi to his good friend Guillaume Dufay, by then a renowned composer and venerable canon of Cambrai, in which he repeated Piero's prohetic words «that you, [that is, Dufay,] are the greatest ornament of our age».[20]

The Medici obviously owed a good deal of their musical sophistication to Antonio Squarcialupi, an early recipient of the family's generosity. Squarcialupi was a child prodigy who had his first professional job at the age of fourteen as an organist for the laudesi at Orsanmichele.[21] He was soon picked up by Cosimo, and even though his official post was that of organist at the Cathedral, he seems to have spent a good deal of his time in the family's company. He was a good friend of Giovanni di Cosimo, for whom he scouted out and bought instruments.[22] More tangible evidence of

---

[19] See F. AMES-LEWIS, *The Inventories of Piero di Cosimo de' Medici's Library*, «La Bibliofilia», 84, 1982, pp. 103-142 for music books listed in the two surviving inventories from 1456 and from 1464/65. In the earlier inventory three items, no. 104, «uno libro di musicha piccolo»; no. 105, «uno libro di musica grande in membrane»; and no. 106, «uno libro di musica grande in papiro», were recorded by the first compiler; two of these items (nos. 105, 106) were also cited among the three (nos. 148-150) recorded by the second compiler, who worked as late as 1463 on the same inventory. In the later inventory from 1464/65 three items (nos. 120-122) are again mentioned, including a «liber musice parvus» (the same as no. 104, no. 150 in 1456); a «liber musice novus in papiro coperta violacia» (perhaps identical to no. 106 in 1456) and a «liber musice in membranis antiquis coperta celestina», which is no. 149 of the earlier inventory and may also be no. 105 of the same inventory. Ames-Lewis makes the improbable suggestion that this latter may be BAV, MS Urb. lat. 1411. That volume, copied between 1440-1450, was given by Piero as a gift to Piero di Angelo de' Bonaventuri of Urbino (see the *Census-Catalogue of Manuscript Sources of Polyphonic Music 1400-1500*, IV, American Institute of Musicology 1988, p. 68 for further details). Of the 19 works in BAV, MS Urb. lat. 1411, 15 are chansons (12 by Binchois, 2 by Dufay, 1 anon.) and 4 are settings of Italian texts («O rosa bella» in the versions by Ciconia and Bedingham, Dufay's «La dolce vista», and the anonymous «Con dollia me ne vo»). The volume undoubtedly preserves examples of the kinds of pieces favored by musical circles among the Florentine upper classes. In this regard, it is interesting to recall Dufay's connections with the Medici. For further information about French chansons in Florentine sources of the later 15th century see A. ATLAS, *The Cappella Giulia Chansonnier*, 2 vols., Brooklyn 1975, particularly I, pp. 233 ff.

[20] See note 17 above.

[21] See my *Antonio Squarcialupi alla luce di documenti inediti*, «Chigiana», 23, 1966, pp. 3-24, and the biographal entry by K. VON FISCHER in *The New Grove Dictionary of Music and Musicians*, ed. S. SADIE, XVIII, 1980, pp. 28f.

[22] On 26 November 1450 Squarcialupi wrote to Giovanni from Siena extolling the qualities of a reed organ owned by the King of Naples and said that he would soon have Giovanni hear another instrument that he was sure to like. The letter (ASF, MAP VIII, 127) is published in GAYE, *Carteggio inedito d'artisti* cit., I, pp. 160f.

their relationship is revealed in a letter of 3 April 1445 from Ugo della Stufa to Giovanni, who was then in Rome. Della Stufa writing from Florence says: «it's truly delightful, sometimes we go to Careggi, sometimes to Bivigliano... fleeing our cares as much as we can. Antonio plays the organ all the time and gives us much pleasure». Ugo continues: «You will have received since last I wrote you the song which [Antonio] worked so hard on» and says that the company rejoiced when the composer completed his work because of the difficulty he had experienced writing it. Ugo reports that he lent Squarcialupi one of his own books of songs to study in order to help him in his efforts.[23] It is evident that Squarcialupi was aware of Giovanni's exacting tastes, for in a follow-up letter from two weeks later, Ugo writes to Giovanni to say that he personally likes the ballata referred to in the previous letter and that Giovanni's sister-in-law Lucrezia had learned it in three days and was now singing it. Ugo goes on to say, however, that Squarcialupi, was dissatisfied with his ballata because he had «promised to send it to you perfect» and that he planned to rewrite the piece so that Giovanni would find the setting «in a better guise than in its present state» when he returned.[24]

[23] The letter (ASF, MAP V, 590), has been cited or quoted in part by ROSSI, *L'indole e gli studi* cit., p. 45, PIERACCINI, *La stirpe de' Medici di Cafaggiolo* cit., I, 79 and BECHERINI, *Relazioni di musici fiamminghi con la corte dei Medici* cit., pp. 89f., among others: «No' siamo quagiù et non domandare con quanto diletto stiamo. Hora la facciamo a Careggi hora a Bivigliano... fugiendo i pensieri più potiamo. Antonio ancor cogli organi ci dà piacere asai che sono forniti quegli di que' sofoli che altro non voresti udire, che co' mantaci non si può soperire alla volontà d'Antonio di sonare quando gli ha tra mano... Da poi ti schrissi arai auto la canzona intonata che questo tristo ha tanto penato a fare, che ti so dire et gioia che tutti si vorebono casare ch'è per merito della fatica durammo per lui. Et ci lascia adrieto per parecchi[e] nebie [?], che perché e' facesi la tua gli prestai u' mio libro de canti che me l'ano tutto copiato et poi la darò a messer Rosello te-lla mandi. La quale come tu l'arai auta, avisa se sta a tuo modo. Et se scrivi a messer Rosello biasimala, non sia tenuta buona costà».

[24] The letter (ASF, MAP V, 605), from 17 April 1445, has been cited or quoted in part by ROSSI, *L'indole e gli studi* cit., p. 45, PIERACCINI, *La stirpe de' Medici* di *Carfaggiolo* cit., I, p. 81, and BECHERINI, *Relazioni di musici fiamminghi con la corte dei Medici* cit., pp. 89 f., among others: «Piacemi la ballata riesca buona e sì t'aviso la Lucrezia l'ha compiuto d'aparare 3 dì sono e sì la canta. Maestro Antonio isdegnò per tal modo di questa ballata, perché avendoti promesso mandartela perfetta e che la proverebbe, che a fatica la potessi vedere a lume di lucierna una sera senza udirla cantare, che in veruno modo ne vole fare nulla. Ma bene vole che alla tornata tua la truovi rintonata da altri migliore che cotesta; che vi vole metere hogni diligenza et insieme con quel benoto [?] e col manacordo. Li dà l'animo apresarsi non c'altro ma ab introis [?] et io a ciò lo conforto, po' che vego non n'ha il capo a 'mparare; quelle farai tu poi seguitare quelle che melgio ti pare». Mention should also be made of the ballata which Ugo della Stufa sent Giovanni on 10 April 1445, and of a sealed scroll containing polyphonic songs, which John, Earl of Worcester, sent to Giovanni on 17 December 1460 (the letters accompanying the music, all of which is now lost, ASF, MAP IX, 146 and VI, 520,

I have quoted the letter at length not so much because it paints such a charming picture of the carefree, proverbially informal atmosphere that prevailed in the Medici household[25] but because it provides so much information about the accomplishments of the Medici generation before Lorenzo and also reveals a bit about the musical experiences of some of the people in their circle, like Ugo della Stufa. The latter's training and background – he referred to one of his own music books, obviously kept for performance – was apparently sufficient to allow him to discuss a newly composed piece of music with Giovanni, himself a performing musician whose refined tastes were well known to Squarcialupi. More important, however, is the knowledge that Lorenzo's mother, Lucrezia Tornabuoni, a gifted poetess of exquisite religious sensibilities, was also a trained musician, capable of learning a new piece in three days.[26] To our knowledge of Lucrezia's influence on Lorenzo in other matters must now be added the encouragement and influence she had on his musical education and the formation of his musical tastes. Her efforts were not lavished on Lorenzo alone, however. A recently published report of a visit to Florence in 1460 by Pope Pius II and his entourage recounts how some members of the Papal party were entertained by Lorenzo's sister Bianca, who played several pieces on an organ that had been given to Squarcialupi by King Alfonso of Naples.[27] Later in the evening, after the company had

are cited by Rossi, *L'indole e gli studi* cit., p. 47; the second letter is published in full, with an English summary, in my *A Late 15th-Century Sienese Sacred Repertory: MS K. I. 2 of the Biblioteca Comunale, Siena*, «Musica Disciplina», 37, 1983, pp. 149f.).

[25] Music making clearly played an important part in the family's everyday life, even outside the home. Witness Piero's letter to his father, Cosimo, written some ten years earlier (1455) from the thermal baths at Macereto, where he was staying. Piero reports that he had been well received, that the six-year old Lorenzo was everyone's favorite and that when they were not taking the cure, the company did nothing but sing, dance and play instruments («Qui e dallo stare nel bagno infuori non s'attende se non a ballare, chantare e sonare»). The letter (ASF, MAP XII, 210) is quoted by Pieraccini, *La stirpe dei Medici di Cafaggiolo* cit., I, pp. 82f.

[26] See also note 18 above for reference to the letter in which Rosello Roselli told Giovanni de' Medici that he had given a copy of a piece to ser Francesco, who was apparently a musician, so that he could teach it to Lucrezia. Perhaps this was the same piece as the one referred to in della Stufa's lettera.

[27] The report has been published by W. F. Prizer, *Games of Venus: Secular Vocal Music in the Late Quattrocento and Early Cinquecento*, «The Journal of Musicology», 9, 1991, pp. 3ff. (At the time the Pope was returning to Rome from the Council of Mantua). It is interesting to note that the writer said a propos of the gift that the king remarked «that he was giving him [Squarcialupi] this instrument because he was the best [organist] he had ever heard, or would ever». Squarcialupi recounted his visit to the Neapolitan court in the letter to Giovan-

danced balletti, saltarelli and a ballata, Bianca and her younger sister Nannina also sang a song, as did another young woman. Their repertory included courtly French chansons, two of them by Binchois, an Italian piece perhaps of the Venetian type that was then in fashion and another piece, described by the writer, as «an angelic song», by which he might have meant a lauda.[28] These kinds of pieces fit in well with what we know about Florentine taste in general in this period and find corroboration in one of Giannozzo Manetti's reports from Venice in 1448 where he mentions that the Florentine exiles there sang polyphonic French, Venetian and Sicilian songs.[29]

Though barely documented, Squarcialupi's influence in forming the musical tastes of the young Lorenzo was enormous. Whether he actually gave Lorenzo music lessons is another matter, but there is no doubt that Lorenzo sought his counsel in musical matters even when he was an adult. This much is apparent from Squarcialupi's letter to Dufay of 1467, mentioned earlier.[30] Squarcialupi's immediate reason for writing at that time was to request Dufay to set one of Lorenzo's poems to music. He went on to say that «because of the excellence of his divine talent, [Lorenzo] enjoys

---

ni from Siena, dated 2 November 1450, mentioned in note 22 above. Squarcialupi's reputation at Naples, and elsewhere in Italy, was such that King Ferrante wrote to Lorenzo, 5 February 1473, recommending the son of his counsellor, the Count of Altavilla, who wished to go to Florence so that he might study with Squarcialupi (ASF, MAP XLV, 82, published in E. PONTIERI, *La dinastia aragonese di Napoli e la casa de' Medici di Firenze*, «Archivio storico per le province napoletane», n.s., 26, 1940, p. 300). In view of this it seems reasonable to suppose that Squarcialupi taught organ to the Medici children. In addition to this report of Bianca's playing, there is the remark made by the young Gian Galeazzo Sforza in a letter to his father to the effect that Cosimo had had Piero's oldest daughter play, which was a graceful thing to hear, and that she had done so every day since the prince's arrival in Florence, where he was staying as the Medici's guest (The passage, in a letter dated 19 April 1459, is printed by B. BUSER, *Die Beziehungen der Mediceer zu Frankreich während der Jahre 1434-1494*, Leipzig 1879, p. 374 and is quoted by F. T. PERRENS, *Histoire de Florence*, I, 1888, p. 197. It is also cited by, among others, PIERACCINI, *La stirpe de' Medici di Cafaggiolo* cit., I, p. 151).

[28] More specifically, the chansons were «Dueil engoisseux», «Mon cuer chante joyeusement», both by Binchois; and an unspecified «Fortune», which Prizer suggests might be Bedyngham's «Fortune helas». Prizer (*Games of Venus* cit., p. 6) also points out that both this latter and «Dueil engoisseux» exist in intabulations in the Buxheim organ book and that Bianca may have played organ arrangements of them without singing at all. But she did sing the canzonetta with her sister, as well as «the angelic song», and the other woman sang «Mon cuer».

[29] The passage is given by A. DELLA TORRE, *Storia dell'Accademia Platonica di Firenze*, Florence 1902, p. 282, note 2, and is quoted by W. RUBSAMEN, *The Justiniane or Viniziane of the 15th Century*, «Acta Musicologica», 29, 1957, p. 173.

[30] See note 17 above.

quality in all of the arts, and thus he delights exceedingly in the greater refinement of your music, and for that reason he admires your art and respects you as a father». No musical setting of «Amor c'hai visto ciascun mio pensiero» survives to indicate whether Dufay was able to grant Lorenzo his wish. But the letter and evidence from other sources leaves no doubt that even as a youth Lorenzo knew a good deal about northern polyphony in its various forms and that he had learned early on to look to Squarcialupi for guidance and expert advice in matters of repertory as well as of performance. Lorenzo would later remember his mentor by having a bust of the organist placed in the Duomo, the only Florentine musician ever so honored.[31]

According to contemporary reports, Lorenzo was a knowledgeable and discriminating music lover, a person who, in the words of one writer, enjoyed the company «of all good singer».[32] He himself sang and improvised, both for his own pleasure and that of his friends. One can just as easily imagine him holding his own part in a polyphonic piece in the company of northern Cathedral singers as singing and improvising to his viola in the manner of the *cantimpanche* or in the perhaps more arcane manner practiced by Ficino and his circle. How much Lorenzo and his friends made music a part of their everyday lives is vividly recounted by Poliziano in a letter, dated 8 April 1476, to Lorenzo's wife Clarice from San Miniato, where Lorenzo and his party, en route from Florence to Pisa, had stopped off for a few days. Poliziano recounts how the group had sung all the way on the trip, occasionally breaking off «to discuss some sacred thing, so as not to forget that it was Lent». That night, after dinner, he says, they read a bit of St. Augustine and followed it with «some music making and in taking up and trying to

---

[31] For poetry by Poliziano, Ficino and Lorenzo, among others, written on Squarcialupi's death see A. M. BANDINI, *Catalogus codicum latinorum Bibliothecae Mediceae Laurentianae*, III, Florence 1755, p. 248, and BECHERINI, *Un canta in panca* cit., p. 246, n. 5.

[32] N. VALORI, *Laurentii Medicei Vita*, ed. L. MEHUS, Florence 1749, p. 337. I have seen the Italian translation of the passage which reads «Lorenzo in questa arte della Musica sempre si compiacque e per havere ingegno universale, ne habbe tanta notizia che gl'era equale a ogn'altro, e tutti i buoni cantori gl'erano accetti, e dilettandosi non solo nelle liberali, ma etiandio nelle pratiche, fu studiosissimo della Architettura» (*Il Magnifico Lorenzo di Niccolò Valori patrizio fiorentino*, ed. P. COLAPRICO, Milano 1982, p. 65). This and another apparently similar passage by Redditi, in BML, Ms. Laur. XLVII, 21, f. 7v, are cited by DELLA TORRE, *Storia dell'Accademia Platonica* cit., p. 791, n. 8).

refine a certain skillful dancer of local fame».[33] A propos of dancing, I might note that Lorenzo and his siblings, like others of their social class throughout Italy, were taught fashionable courtly dances from their earliest years and that Lorenzo's name is associated with the steps for two bassadanze, «Venus» and «Lauro», both of which are preserved in the well-known treatise of the famous Jewish dancing master Guglielmo Ebreo, known after his conversion to Christianity as Giovan Ambrosio da Pesaro. Some months before his wedding to Clarice Orsini on 4 June 1469 Lorenzo was in touch with Giovan Ambrosio and others about the matter of choreographing new dances for the festivities, and several years later the two were again in correspondence about the possibility of Giovan Ambrosio's coming to Florence to do choreographies for the carnival season, perhaps that of 1477.[34] Lorenzo's mother, aunt and sisters were no strangers to traditional Florentine dancing either, as the letter of the young Galeazzo Sforza from 1459 indicates.[35]

References abound from throughout Lorenzo's life to his singing the kind of music that Nino Pirrotta so aptly described as belonging to the unwritten tradition, that is, to the improvised song that was very much the fashion in late Quattrocento Italy.[36] In the case of Florence it is perhaps necessary to distinguish between the kinds of improvised singing practiced by professional poet-improvisers such as Antonio di Guido, which was undoubtedly emulated by amateurs throughout the city, and to the more arcane kind of improvised, or

---

[33] The letter is published by I. DEL LUNGO in his edition of POLIZIANO's *Prose volgari inedite e poesie latine e greche*, Florence 1867, p. 47. The elegant English translation of the passage is from N. PIRROTTA, *Music in Italy from Poliziano to Monteverdi*, Cambridge 1982, p. 23. Other testimony to the importance of music in the everyday life of Lorenzo and his friends is illustrated by an earlier letter dated 27 April 1465 to Lorenzo, who was then in Milan, from his friend Braccio Martelli in which Martelli recounts how he and their circle of friends, which included a «Lo Spagnolo sonator di liuto», had enjoyed themselves singing and dancing at one of their recent gatherings. The letter, partly in cipher, is printed by I. DEL LUNGO, *Gli amori del Magnifico Lorenzo*, Florence 1923, pp. 33-39. Another reference from this letter is given below, in note 45.

[34] See J. McGEE, *Dancing Masters and the Medici Court in the 15th Century*, «Studi musicali», 17, 1988, pp. 218-224.

[35] BUSER, *Die Beziehungen der Mediceer* cit., p. 374; PERRENS, *Histoire de Florence* cit., I, p. 198; a portion of the same letter regarding Antonio di Guido's improvisations is also cited by E. MOTTA, *Musici alla corte degli Sforza*, Milan 1887 and Geneva 1977, p. 58.

[36] Among the many studies Pirrotta has devoted to this theme may be cited his *Ars Nova and Stil Novo*, *The Oral and Written Traditions of Music*, and *Music and Cultural Tendencies*, all of which are now reprinted as Chapters, 3, 6 and 7 of *Music and Culture in Italy from the Middle Ages to the Baroque*, Cambridge, Mass. 1984, pp. 26-38, 72-79, 80-112.

perhaps quasi-improvised singing that was practiced by Ficino and to which Lorenzo must have been introduced at an early age by his renowned tutor. Ficino made a cult of singing the Orphic hymns to the accompaniment of what was described then as an Orphic lyre, an instrument he apparently played with a good deal of skill. We know little about the actual instrument and the melodic style he adopted for singing the hymns, except, perhaps, as D. P. Walker and others have suggested, that it was monodic and that it probably resembled enraptured psalm-singing.[37] Expressiveness and conveying the effect of the text were the ideals Ficino espoused and he wrote that on occasion he had heard «our own Lorenzo sing to the accompaniment of a lira certain songs similar to these [laudi]», as though possessed «by a divine frenzy».[38]

How similar Ficino's improvised ritualistic singing was to courtly or popular forms of improvising is a matter of speculation. Suffice it to say that I use these latter terms merely to distinguish the improvised performances of poetry in courtly or private chambers from what was performed in public piazzas, without taking into account any differences there might have been in melodic style, literary content or the instruments that may or may not have been used by the singer to accompany himself or by others who might have assisted him in the accompaniment. As far as Lorenzo and his circle are concerned, there are a few pieces that come down to us which may reflect the kinds of music they performed. Among them is an anonymous 4-voice setting in a Milan manuscript from ca. 1510 of a strambotto text, «La morte tu mi dai per mio servire», that has been attributed to Baccio Ugolini[39] (Example 1). Ugolini, a poet and improviser who was a particular favorite of Lorenzo, created the title role in the Mantuan production of Poliziano's «Orfeo». Notable in the example is the recitational style of melody, hovering around the

---

[37] D. P. WALKER, *Spiritual and Demonic Magic: from Ficino to Campanella*, London 1958, p. 20; J. WARDEN, *Orpheus and Ficino*, in *Orpheus: The Metamorphoses of A Myth*, ed. J. WARDEN, Toronto 1982, pp. 94ff.; M. ALLEN, *Summoning Plotinus: Ficino, Smoke, and the Strangled Chickens*, in *Reconsidering the Renaissance: Papers from the Twenty-Sixth Annual CEMERS Conference*, ed. M. DI CESARE, Binghamton, N.Y. 1992, pp. 63-88.

[38] The quotation, from FICINO's *Opera*, Bâle 1576, I, p. 665, is given by A. DELLA TORRE, *Storia dell'Accademia Platonica di Firenze* cit., p. 792. Della Torre also cites documentation regarding Ficino's singing and playing the lira (*ibid.*, pp. 790ff.).

[39] Modern edition in R. GIAZOTTO, *Onde musicali nella corrente poetica di Serafino dall'Aquila*, in *Musurgia Nova*, Milan 1959, p. 36; K. JEPPESEN, *La Frottola*, III, Aarhus 1970, pp. 209-210, and most recently in PIRROTTA, *Music and Theater* cit., p. 35.

Ex. 1 - Milan, Biblioteca Trivulziana, Ms 44, ff. 15v-16r

dominant A, which sets the opening line of the text and the contrast this provides with the more fluid and balanced phrases that bring the second line to a cadence on the tonic. In contemporary practice the setting of the first two lines of the text were used, with appropriate adjustments, for the remaining six lines of the the stanzas. There is also a recently recovered version from ca. 1499-1515 of a melody of decidedly popular origin that must have been used to sing some if not all of the stanzas in ottava rima of Lorenzo's «Nencia da Barberino» and perhaps of the many verses written in emulation of it[40] (Example 2). Much of the material used by Lorenzo and his

---

[40] F. CARBONI and A. ZIINO, *Una nuova testimonianza musicale per la 'Nencia da Barberino'*, in *Musica popolare e musica d'arte nel tardo Medioevo*, Testi della I Giornata di Studi sulla Musica Medievale, Palermo, maggio 1981 (estratto della sezione Contributi di Schede Medievali, 3, 1982), pp. 253-280. The example given here is after the version published by Carboni and Ziino. The melody is found as a tenor in two polyphonic settings by Johannes Martini and Johannes Japart that are only loosely associated with the poem, but it appears in a perhaps more authentic version in a manuscript in Rome's Angelica Library, where it is given as a monophonic tune devoid of measure and with the text of one of Lorenzo's stanzas. As Carboni and Ziino remark, however, it is impossible to determine whether the melody, which is assuredly of popular origins, really served as an accompaniment to one stanza or several, or indeed all of the stanzas, whether the melody was used to accompany the Nencia from the very beginning – having been fished out, as it were, of the vast repertoire of popular tunes by Lo-

LORENZO AND MUSIC

Nen - cioz - za mi - a ch'i' vo' sa - ba - t'an - da - re

sin a Fio - ren - za_a ven - der do so - mel - le

Ex. 2 - F. Carboni - A. Ziino, *Una nuova testimonianza musicale per la «Nencia da Barberino»* cit., p. 270.

friends was doubtless like this, a melodic pattern of a few bars length which could be adjusted to accomodate the number of syllables in each verse and to which might be added extempore embellishment and cadential flourishes in the course of performance. Similar in this respect is the simple melody of «Hora è di maggio», which forms the basis of Heinrich Isaac's four-voice setting of the text (Example 3).

Ho - ra_è di Mag - gio che rin - ver - di - sce_o-gni_her - ba

Fi - gliuol del re fac - ti_al la fi - ne - strel - la

Et mi - ra_et sguar - da_e qual è la più bel - la.

Ex. 3 - Florence, Biblioteca Nazionale Centrale, Ms Magl. XIX, 164-167, No. 7.

The melody, repeated a number of times throughout the piece, also furnishes the basis for motives used by Isaac in the construction of his magnificent contrapuntal scaffolding.[41] Another notable example is provided by a three-voice setting that carries the text of Lucrezia de' Medici's lauda, «Ecco il Messia», published as late as 1563 by Serafino Razzi (Example 4). Earlier rubrics, more or less contemporaneous with Lucrezia's poem, say that the text was sung

---

renzo or some one else – or whether it was only later associated with Lorenzo's poems as it gained more popularity.

[41] The piece is published in H. ISAAC, *Weltliche Werke*, ed. J. WOLF, Vienna 1909 and Graz 1959, pp. 206f.

Ex. 4 - Serafino Razzi, *Primo libro delle laudi spirituali*, Venezia 1563, f. 15v.

to the tune of Poliziano's May-Song, «Ben venga Maggio»,[42] and recent research shows that the tune is that of a popular dance-song of the later Quattrocento.[43] The setting of the tune printed by Razzi is notable for the delicate chordal accompaniment and harmonically functioning bass line, which may be contemporaneous. Although we cannot be absolutely certain that any of these melodies are ones that were actually sung by Lorenzo and his friends, they come from a period close enough in time to furnish, at the very least, a glimpse of the kinds of music that might have been used by him and his friends when they sang to the viola. However, I think it important to bear in mind that whatever popular or courtly aspects of the improvising tradition Lorenzo practiced were tempered by solid training and by a thorough knowledge of the art music of the north and of his own native land.[44]

Lorenzo himself excelled in the kind of improvisation that Florentines of his day would have heard in Piazza San Martino and elsewhere, which is to say that he was exceedingly clever at

---

[42] Since Lucrezia died in 1482, Poliziano's text and its musical setting, which furnished the model for Lucrezia's travestimento spirituale, must be from before that time. A version of the piece with Poliziano's text reinstated can be found in PIRROTTA, *Music and Theater* cit., p. 30, and in J. J. GALLUCCI, *Florentine Festival Music, 1480-1520*, Madison 1981, p. 1.

[43] Francesco Luisi communicated his discovery in a paper read at a conference commemorating the 500th anniversary of Lorenzo's death sponsored by the Italian Musicological Society. The paper will be published in the proceedings of the conference.

[44] Interesting in this regard is Poliziano's letter of 17 October 1477 to Lorenzo who was then in Pisa. Poliziano reports that «today maestro Antonio degli Organi [Squarcialupi] tried out signor Ludovico [Sforza]'s lutenist, who seems to satisfy him so much that he'll recommend him to Davitte as well as to Pierbono» (the letter, which has been cited on numerous occasions, is published in DEL LUNGO's edition of POLIZIANO's *Prose volgari* cit., p. 54). On Pietrobono see particularly the chapter, «Pietrobono and the Improvisatory Tradition» in L. LOCKWOOD, *Music in Renaissance Ferrara, 1400-1505*, Cambridge, Mass. 1984, pp. 95-108.

versifying and that he was able, in the course of a recitation, to exchange quick, witty remarks on the spot. He was, in other words, adept at engaging in a kind of poetic, intellectual and musical repartee that is perhaps difficult for us to imagine today, although those of us who know some of Lorenzo's spiritual Florentine descendents do not find the idea too far-fetched. Although there is evidence that Lorenzo and his friends enjoyed the company of an unnamed «compare della viola», that is, of an accompanist on the viola or lute, who was a skilled improviser in his own right, there is also evidence to show that Lorenzo was an accomplished enough musician to be able to accompany himself.[45] He had in fact had lessons on the viola with Giuliano «sopradetto Catellaccio», and on those few occasions when he was without his own instrument, he had no hesitation in sending for it.[46] This much is evident from a letter he wrote from Cafaggiolo to Niccolò Michelozzi in Florence in early August 1472. Lorenzo, it seems, had gone to his country house without his viola, probably a viola da braccio, which he was eagerly awaiting, and he told Michelozzi to make sure to bring the instrument with him when he came.[47] Another of Lorenzo's letters to Michelozzi from the following year, when he was staying in

---

[45] The identity of this unnamed «compare della viola», whose presence in Lorenzo's circle in 1473 is amply documented, has excited the attention of literary historians because of his possible connections with the composition of two of Lorenzo's works which exemplify the improvised tradition, the *Uccellagione di starne* (dedicated to the «compare» in one redaction) and *La Nencia da Barberino*. The matter has been discussed by ROCHON, *La jeunesse de Laurent de Médicis* cit., pp. 436ff. and by P. ORVIETO, *Angelo Poliziano 'Compare' della brigata laurenziana*, «Lettere Italiane», 25, 1973, pp. 301-318. Orvieto's identification of Poliziano as the «compare della viola» has been questioned by C. DEMPSEY in his forthcoming *The Portrayal of Love, Botticelli's Primavera and Florentine Humanistic Culture*, Princeton. Dempsey also notes that Lorenzo «Certainly had many accompanists in his employ during his lifetime», and cites the letter, mentioned above in note 33, written partially in cipher by Braccio Martelli to Lorenzo, in which Braccio describes how Costanza Rucellai and another woman sang together to the accompaniment of the compare Lo Spagnuolo. Lo Spagnuolo has yet to be identified (see DEL LUNGO, *Gli amori del Magnifico Lorenzo* cit., p. 38).

[46] Catellaccio identifies himself as Lorenzo's viola teacher in a letter (ASF, MAP XXIII, 92) he wrote him on 1 December 1466. I am grateful to Prof. F. William Kent for calling my attention to this document and to Dr. Gino Corti for transcribing it.

[47] *Lettere*, I, 110, p. 391f. In an earlier letter, dated 24 May 1466, Filippo Martelli wrote to Lorenzo from Rome to say that by then Piero della Luna would have brought him a lute he had sent. The letter (ASF, MAP XX, 210) is cited by ROCHON, *La jeunesse de Laurent de Médicis* cit., p. 69, n. 307. Another letter to Lorenzo at Cafaggiolo, written by Luigi Pulci on 8 August 1468, says that his viola and his books have been sent to him. The letter (Paris, Bibliothèque Nationale, Ms It. 2033, No. 32) has been published by F. BRAMBILLA AGENO, *Una nuova lettera di Luigi Pulci a Lorenzo de' Medici*, «Giornale storico della letteratura italiana», 141, 1964, pp. 106f.

Vallombrosa, instructed Michelozzi to seek out maestro Antonio della Viuola, that is, Antonio di Guido, and invite him to join Lorenzo there, as Lorenzo himself had already done in a sonnet he was sending Antonio.[48] Clearly, on occasions such as these Lorenzo exchanged rhymes and sang and played his own works with the most accomplished Florentine improviser of the day. Almost twenty years later, on 28 May 1489, Zanobi da Ameria wrote to Lorenzo to say that he wanted Lorenzo to have the viola that had been left him by Clarice, Lorenzo's wife, for after their recent visit it occurred to him how much Lorenzo appreciated the instrument, which he knew Lorenzo played better than he did.[49] From 1490 comes a letter to Lorenzo's son Piero written by Alessandro degli Alessandri, when he was attending Lorenzo at the spa at Vignone. Alessandri recounts how it «brought a bit of consolation» to his friends to hear him sing and that «he will probably sing more now because of the arrival last night of Baccio Ugolini who will keep him company».[50]

Lorenzo's children were all given an extensive musical education, one which included instruction in performing all of the kinds of music that Lorenzo himself so delighted in. A letter of Poliziano's from 5 June 1490 leaves no doubt that Lorenzo's eldest son Piero had inherited his father's gift for improvisation. «The night before last», writes Poliziano, «I heard our Piero sing impromptu, when he came to assail me at home with all of these improvisers». Poliziano was quite pleased with his pupil's performance, especially with «his jokes and his retorts» which he delivered with ease and good diction, so much so that Poliziano thought he was seeing and hearing Lorenzo himself.[51] From these remarks it is obvious that Poliziano

---

[48] *Lettere*, I, 144, p. 467f. Michelozzi was also instructed to make sure that the maestro's trip be made comfortable. Michelozzi's reply from the next day informed Lorenzo that Antonio would arrive within a day, even though he was somewhat hesitant about traveling. Antonio apparently liked Lorenzo's sonnet but said there were references in the text he hadn't quite understood. See G. VOLPI, *Lorenzo il Magnifico e Vallombrosa*, «Archivio storico italiano», VII s., 22, 1935, pp. 122f, and M. MARTELLI, *Studi laurenziani*, Florence 1965, p. 122.

[49] The letter (ASF, MAP XLI, 137) is quoted by MARTELLI, *Studi laurenziani* cit., p. 189.

[50] The letter, dated 12 May 1490 (ASF, MAP XVIII, 22), is quoted in part by DEL LUNGO, *Florentia* cit., p. 307, and mentioned by BARFUCCI, *Lorenzo de' Medici e la società artistica* cit., p. 107.

[51] POLIZIANO, *Prose volgari inedite*, ed. cit., p. 78, and more recently in MARTELLI, *Studi laurenziani* cit., p. 46: «udii Piero nostro cantar improviso, che mi venne a casa con tutti questi provisanti, satisfecemi a maraviglia, et presertim ne' motti e ne 'l rimbeccare, e nella facilità e pronunzia, che mi pareva tutta via vedere e udire V.M.». The English translation is from PIRROTTA, *Music and Theater* cit., p. 23, n. 4.

appreciated above all facility with words and ease of declamation rather than musical ability.[52] As for Piero's knowledge of the other kind of music, that is, music of the written tradition, not only do we have it, again on Poliziano's word, that he could read music,[53] but there are also indications that, doubtless following in his father's footsteps, he kept a number of the Northern chapel singers in his own household. Three of them, in fact, were in his entourage when he visited Rome in 1493, as were his viola accompanists.[54] Piero also took over his father's informal role as musical advisor to the chapel, about which I shall have more to say in a moment, and he was sufficiently well informed about the singers' repertory to be able to furnish Isabella d'Este in Mantua with copies of some of the polyphonic Masses they were performing.[55] The musical accomplishments of Lorenzo's second son, Giovanni, who as Pope Leo X was perhaps the most knowledgeable musical patron ever to occupy the chair of St. Peter, have already been noted and need no further comment here. Giuliano, Lorenzo's youngest son was also

---

[52] PIRROTTA, *Music and Theater* cit., p. 22, makes a point of noting that Poliziano probably knew little about polyphony and its theory and that because of his prejudices, he was, like other humanists, «less than prepared to understand or appreciate the little» he did know. Lorenzo and his children, it seems clear, had precisely the kind of training in polyphony that enabled them to perform and to appreciate both kinds of music.

[53] Most notably in letter to Pico in which he said that Piero sang written music, that is, polyphony, as well as songs to the lute: «Canit etiam, vel notas musicas vel ad cytharam carmen» (the letter is published in *Epistole inedite di Angelo Poliziano*, ed. L. D'AMORE, Naples 1901, pp. 38-40).

[54] The chapel singers were Heinrich Isaac, Pietrequin Bonnel and Colinet de Lannoy, the accompanists, «il chonpare della viola, il chardiere della viola». The chapel singers are mentioned in my *Some Neglected Composers in the Florentine Chapels, ca. 1475-1525*, «Viator», 1, 1970, p. 273; the accompanists are cited by M. WARBURG, *Bildniskunst und Florentinisches Bürgertum*, in *Ausgewählte Schriften und Würdigungen*, ed. D. WUTTKE, Baden-Baden 1980, p. 96. Il Cardiere was highly praised for his improvised singing to the lira and is said to have performed almost every night in Piero's house: «Praticava in casa di Piero un certo, chiamato per soprannome Cardiere, del quale il Magnifico molto piacer si pigliava per cantare in sulla lira all'improvviso meravigliosamente, del che anch'egli profession faceva; sicché quasi ogni sera dopo cena in ciò si esercitava» (the passage, from A. CONDIVI's *Vita di Michelangelo*, Rome, Antonio Blado 1553, paragraph 14, is quoted by PARIGI, *Laurentiana* cit., p. 103, n. 6).

[55] The letter accompanying the music destined for Isabella, written by Manfredo di Manfredi from Florence on 29 June 1493, says that the gift was comprised of three quinternions of new Masses and that they were being sent only now because it required some time to copy them. («Mando a la Signoria Vostro certo libro de canti, che sono tri quinterni de messe nove, quale questo giorno me ha dato el Magnifico Piero de Medici, che sono per parte de la promessa che in suo nome feci questi giorni passati a la Signoria Vostra. Più presto non si è mandato per haver bisognato farlo transcrivere et notare come la vedera»). The passage is quoted from S. DAVARI, *La musica in Mantova*, «Rivista storica mantovana», 1, 1885, pp. 65f, n. 3.

proficient in performing, as is attested by the music books he owned and by his purported remarks in Castiglione's discourse on music in *Il Cortegiano*.[56]

Although I have yet to trace the source of the traditional view that Piero, his brother Giovanni and the other children in the Medici household received musical instruction from Heinrich Isaac, there is little reason to doubt that this was the case, considering the high regard Lorenzo had for the composer and also the concern that Giovanni showed for Isaac's welfare after he became pope. We know precious little about the way music was taught to youngsters in Florence at this time. A School of Chant and Grammar had been established at the Cathedral by Pope Eugene IV in 1432, but polyphony was not officially established as a part of the curriculum until 1479, when ser Antonio di Montughi, a composer and organist at San Lorenzo, was appointed as the first teacher of figural music, a post that was ever after retained at the Cathedral.[57] The larger monasteries also instituted instruction in polyphony around this time, and the Santissima Annunziata even appointed a teacher of laudi. There is no reason to doubt that theory teachers, particularly Franco-Netherlanders such as the singer-composer Arnolfo Giliardi, who taught in these places might not also have engaged in private teaching.[58] No reports of the typical musical curriculum have survived, but it seems reasonable to assume that solmization and methods of vocal production, the basic principles of mensural notation and perhaps even some elementary counterpoint were taught to youngsters. The same kinds of materials must have been taught to Florentine children who were not destined for careers as professional musicians, if we can judge from a letter written by the young Guido Machiavelli to his father Niccolò in 1505, when the boy reported that he would resume his lessons «singing, playing and

---

[56] It is possible that one of the surviving Medici chansonniers was compiled for or owned by Giuliano, who also owned other books of music. See A. ATLAS, *The Cappella Giulia Chansonnier*, 2 vols., Brooklyn 1975-1976, particularly I, pp. 29ff. For the remarks about music attributed to Giuliano by Baldassare Castiglione, who knew him from the time, after 1503, when they both sojourned in Urbino, see note 82 below.

[57] On the establishment of the school and ser Antonio's appointment, see A. SEAY, *The 15th-Century Cappella at Santa Maria del Fiore in Florence*, «Journal of the American Musicological Society», 11, 1958, pp. 45ff; see also *The Singers of San Giovanni* cit., p. 329.

[58] Ser Arnolfo Giliardi, a Franco-Netherlandish composer and singer who also taught music for a while at the Santissima Annunziata, was a great favorite of Lorenzo's (see my *Some Neglected Composers in the Florentine Chapels* cit., p. 266).

writing 3-part counterpoint» as soon as his teacher, Bartolomeo degli Organi, the Cathedral organist, was recovered from his illness.[59] This was, of course, a quarter of a century after the time the young Medici children received instruction in figural music, but whatever they were taught and whoever their teacher, at least one of them, Giovanni, was trained well enough that he was able to realize a natural talent for composition.

With their musical background, performing abilities and firsthand experience with some of the greatest musicians of the age it is small wonder that Lorenzo and his children after him were so knowledgeable about various kinds of music and could become so involved with the musical institutions and the kinds of patronage mentioned earlier. Here, I shall consider Lorenzo's patronage of the Florentine chapel last, since this is best documented of his activities. We know rather less about his involvement with the instrumental groups that were employed at the Palazzo Vecchio, although I suspect that once all of the pertinent records are examined, we shall learn that his influence was felt as strongly even in that quarter. This is hinted at in private correspondence, too, such as the letter a friend of Lorenzo's wrote to him about a shawm player employed at the Palazzo Pubblico in Siena who was so good that he thought Lorenzo ought to lure him away.[60] Minutes of Lorenzo's correspondence from 23 April 1477 show him instructing Giovanni Lanfredini to facilitate the travel of a group of Venetian shawm players to Florence.[61] A few months later, on 7 September 1477, Antonio de' Medici was instructed to transfer funds to the Florentine branch of the Medici bank on behalf of certain trombonists.[62] Writing from Mantua on 22 January 1478, Leonardo piffero, promised that he would send Lorenzo a shawmist who was particularly adept at playing the soprano part in ensemble music,[63] and twelve years later, in 1489, the German shawmist Michele d'Alemagna wrote from Modena

---

[59] See my *Alessandro Coppini and Bartolomeo degli Organi: Two Florentine Composers of the Renaissance*, «Analecta Musicologica», 4, 1967, p. 53.

[60] The letter (ASF, MAP XX, 397) was written by Mario de' Nobili in Florence on 29 January 1469.

[61] *Protocolli*, p. 5.

[62] *Protocolli*, p. 22.

[63] The letter (ASF, MAP XXXV, 104) is published in BECHERINI, *Relazioni di musici fiamminghi con la corte dei Medici* cit., p. 105.

recommending his brother Agostino trombone.[64] Presumably, both musicians would have been appointed to the Palace wind band. Not all of Lorenzo's recruitment efforts bore fruit, however, as is illustrated by the letter written by Bartolomeo tromboncino from Mantua on 15 June 1489 in which he excused himself for not being able to accept Lorenzo's invitation to transfer to Florentine service.[65]

The laudesi companies may also prove to have benefitted from Lorenzo's endeavors, not only with regard to policies initiated by the governing boards of the principal institutions – often comprised of Lorenzo's partisans, but also with regard to performers, few of whom, particularly the gifted ones, could have escaped Lorenzo's attention, or would have wished to.[66] I would suspect in this instance, however, that Lorenzo's principal contributions lay in his encouragement of the dramatic presentations offered by the companies and in his contributions to the genre, that is to the laudi texts he himself composed, either to pre-existing tunes or for which he commissioned new musical settings. One of Lorenzo's laudi, «Quant'è grande la bellezza», has come down to us in a 2-voice setting in a Florentine manuscript from 1522 and in a version, published by Razzi, which adds a third part to the other two. Recent research has established that the music of one or the other of these versions was also used for Lorenzo's famous carnival song, The Triumph of Bacchus and Ariadne, which begins «Quant'è bella giovinezza». The text of the Triumph was composed for carnival of 1490, so it must be that the music of the laude to which it was adapted comes from before that time.[67]

When Lorenzo assumed the reins of government there was a long-established policy of Medici direction of musical matters at the

---

[64] ASF, MAP XLI, 158; see BARFUCCI, *op. cit.* Michele piffero, listed among the musicians employed by Duke Ercole d'Este of Ferrara, from 1488-1491, was a much sought after musician, who occasionally worked at the nearby court of Mantua. See LOCKWOOD, *Music in Renaissance Ferrara* cit., pp. 183, 282.

[65] ASF, MAP XLI, 167; published in DEL LUNGO, *Florentia* cit., p. 305; also in JEPPESEN, *La Frottola* cit., I, p. 145, with a facsimile of the letter on p. 151.

[66] See WILSON, *Music and Merchants* cit., pp. 92, 126, 134, 219 for remarks about Lorenzo's direct involvement with some of the laudesi companies. ROCHON, *La jeunesse de Laurent de Médicis* cit., pp. 43ff. provides an interesting account of Lorenzo's ties to the Confraternity of St. Paul.

[67] See W. RUBSAMEN, *The Music for 'Quant'è bella giovinezza' and other carnival songs by Lorenzo de' Medici*, in *Art, Science, and History in the Renaissance*, ed. C. SINGLETON, Baltimore 1968, pp. 163-184. The music is also published in modern edition by GALLUCCI, *Florentine Festival Music* cit., pp. 6f.

Cathedral and at the Baptistry. From the outset musicians were appointed by the overseers with the approval of the appropriate clergy and chapel expenses were drawn from the operating budgets of both churches. Loans, salary advances and perhaps supplementary stipends for private service were provided by the Medici, though there are no records extant regarding this last. It was in any case a complex system of institutional patronage and private support that permitted the chapel's maintenance, and while there were variations in appointment processes, the amount of support contributed by the Medici, guild activities and church participation, the Florentines established a policy of maintaining some of the finest musicians on the international scene during the middle decades of the 15th century.

Although there are a number of records pointing to Lorenzo's interest in the chapel in the later 1470s – witness the letter to him from Ludovico Sforza in 1477 saying he was sending Lorenzo certain polyphonic Masses because he had learned of Lorenzo's desire to have them, presumably for performance by the chapel – it seems that Lorenzo did not give his full attention to musical matters until the early 1480s, when, freed from the threat of war with Naples and having consolidated his regime at home, he was able to fulfill plans that had been put in abeyance by the Pazzi conspiracy and its aftermath.[68]

Thus it happened that during the last decade of his life and for a few years after his death the Florentine chapel, whose musicians at first performed only at the Baptistry, but then at the Cathedral and at the Santissima Annunziata, became one of the best institutions of its kind in all of Europe. At its apogee it was employing at least eighteen singers, among whom were some of the best known Franco-Netherlanders of the time. Names such as Heinrich Isaac, Pietrequin Bonnel, Colinet de Lannoy, graced the chapel's rolls as the trend from ensemble to large-scale choral performance gained momentum. Lorenzo's own letters, such as those written to messer Antonio, a singer of the Duke of Ferrara in 1482 and 1483, telling him to send one of his companions to Florence in order to let Lorenzo know whether they would in fact join the Florentine chapel,

---

[68] *The Singers of San Giovanni* cit., p. 326. The letter from Ludovico Sforza (ASF, MAP XXXV, 893) was written at Calci on 30 November 1477.

are indicative of his interest in personnel matters.[69] An indication of how enmeshed the chapel's expenses were with Lorenzo's own finances is furnished by one of Lorenzo's letters from 12 July 1488 to Gaspare Bonciani instructing him to pay from Medici funds the 20 or 25 ducats needed by the two singers who were come to Florence from Flanders.[70] In this respect Lorenzo was like the other Italian princes, who often vied with one another to obtain the services of the best musicians. The court of Rome, with its ability to confer benefices led the way, though it was established policy for many secular rulers such as the Sforza and the Este, to enter into the fray. Lorenzo was no less adept at pulling strings and seeking benefices for favored musicians, as is illustrated by a letter dated 4 September 1487 to Giovanni Lanfredini in Rome instructing him to pay whatever expenses were necessary in order to get a benefice at Verdun confirmed for the singer Iannes, who was a great favorite of Lorenzo's.[71]

The one musician for whom Lorenzo could not seek benefices was Heinrich Isaac, who nevertheless must have been the recipient of Medici largesse in ways only barely hinted at in surviving records from Lorenzo's time. Isaac had come to Florence expressly at Lorenzo's invitation, if we may believe Niccolò Pitti, who said that Lorenzo sent «as far away as Flanders» to bring him to Florence, «where», adds Pitti, «he gave him a wife».[72] Although there are as of yet no known documents which clarify Isaac's position in the Medici household, what evidence there is leaves little doubt of how highly Lorenzo valued Isaac's music. Witness his remarks in a letter of 25 June 1491 to Piero Alamanni in Rome, instructing him to thank the

---

[69] Minutes of these letters, respectively, from 17 December 1482, and the following 16 January, are published in *Protocolli*, pp. 218, 222.

[70] A record of the letter is published in *Protocolli*, p. 377. Also interesting in this regard in the record of another letter from March 1485 to Tommaso Portinari in Bruges instructing him to credit 50 or 60 ducats to the account of Bartolomeo de Castris, who was one of the mainstays of the Florentine chapel (*ibid.*, p. 343).

[71] In addition to the letter (ASF, MAP LVII, 100), there are the minutes of letters written on 25 March 1488 to Lanfredini, Giovanni Tornabuoni, Nofri Tornabuoni and Clarice, Lorenzo's wife, «per Giannes cantore», cited in *Protocolli*, p. 372. I am unable to identify positively this Iannes, but it is possible that he was the composer Jannes or Johannes Japart, who made a 4-part polyphonic arrangement of the tune, mentioned above, associated with some stanzas of Lorenzo's *Nencia da Barberino*. Japart's piece, *Nenciozza mia*, is published in modern edition in H. M. Brown, *A Florentine Chansonnier from the Time of Lorenzo the Magnificent*, 2 vols., Chicago 1983, II, pp. 208ff.

[72] See my *Heinrich Isaac in Florence: New and Unpublished Documents*, «The Musical Quarterly», 49, 1963, pp. 464-483, particularly p. 473.

Venetian ambassador for having asked for some songs by Isaac, songs which Lorenzo arranged to have sent by the next post. «Had I known what manner of song pleases him», adds Lorenzo, «I should better have been able to serve him because Arrigo Isach, their composer, has made some of various kinds, grave and sweet, skillful and full of ingenuity».[73] How we wish that Lorenzo had spoken at greater length about those qualities in Isaac's music that pleased him so much! Yet, even these few remarks are sufficient to indicate that Lorenzo had a real appreciation for polyphony, that he was aware of Isaac's superior abilities as a contrapuntist and harmonist and above all that he was moved by the expressive qualities of Isaac's songs.

But what were these songs? If we take Lorenzo's use of the word «canti» literally and interpret it to mean secular vocal music, then there can be little doubt that he was referring to Isaac's chansons. For to judge from the evidence of the surviving Florentine sources from Lorenzo's time or shortly afterwards, these constituted the bulk of Isaac's secular production during his Florentine years. This, of course, is not surprising, given our knowledge of the popularity of the French chanson from the mid-15th century onwards among the Florentine upper classes, amply illustrated in the case of the Medici by surviving documents such as those mentioned earlier.[74] One of the great monuments of Florentine music, the manuscript Banco Rari 229, copied by 1491, presents a lavish feast of the chansons that

---

[73] ASF, Medici-Tornaquinci III, 123 («Se sapessi di che maniera si dilecta più, l'avrei meglio servito, perché Arrigho Jsach componitore di essi, ne ha facto di diverse maniere et gravi et dolci et anchora ropti et artificiosi»); quoted in this English translation in RUBSAMEN, *The Music for 'Quant'è bella giovinezza'* cit., p. 184. Rubsamen (*loc. cit.*) cites another letter to Alamanni from 9 July 1491 (ASF, Medici-Tornaquinci III, 126), in which Lorenzo announced that a book of Isaac's music had been sent for presentation to the Venetian ambassador.

[74] In terms of musical evidence suffice it to say that there are at least three Florentine manuscripts from Lorenzo's lifetime that contain more than 150 chansons and about 40 Italian texted pieces dating from as early as mid-century, notably, BNF, Ms Magl. XIX, 176; Florence, Biblioteca Riccardiana, Ms 2356; and Paris, Bibliothèque Nationale, Ms fonds fr. 15123 («Pixerecourt»). Allan Atlas has advanced compelling reasons for dating the three manuscripts from the late 1470s and early 1480s, and argues that all of them betray some trace of Neapolitan influence with respect to their repertories and readings. Florentine manuscripts from the 1490s include BNF, Banco Rari 229, about which more below, Bologna, Civico Museo bibliografico musicale, Ms Q 17, BNF, Magl. XIX, 178 and the Cappella Giulia chansonnier, BAV, C. G. XIII, 27. These include some three hundred chansons and a scattering of Italian texted pieces (see ATLAS's *The Cappella Giulia Chansonnier* cit., I, pp. 236ff., 254ff., 258). The chansons and Italian texted pieces performed and heard by Lorenzo and his Florentine contemporaries form the subject of a soon-to-be published paper by Howard Mayer Brown, originally read at the Conference honoring Lorenzo that was held at the Wolfe Institute of Brooklyn College in May 1992.

were current in the city during Lorenzo's time, and undoubtedly preserves some of his personal favorites. In his brilliant analysis of the chanson style of various composers represented in Banco Rari 229, Howard Mayer Brown calls particular attention to Isaac's mastery of imitation and its preeminence as the principal structural feature in his music, a trait which marks him, in Brown's words, «as one of the earliest composers of the new style» of chanson writing in the later 15th century.[75] Noteworthy also are Isaac's sophisticated use of texture, his control of form, his sure sense of melody and his clearly directed tonal plans. Undoubtedly, works such as those found in Banco Rari 229 must exemplify what Lorenzo had in mind when he spoke of the varied qualities of Isaac's canti.

But was Lorenzo thinking only of Isaac's chansons when he mentioned canti? Perhaps, though it is also possible that he was using the word in a wider sense and was referring to Isaac's polyphonic production in general, to his Masses and motets, to his instrumental pieces and to his settings of Italian carnival songs and ballatas.[76] Two of the latter, «Un dì lieto già mai» and «Questo mostrarsi adirato di fuore», are in fact settings of texts by, respectively, Lorenzo and Poliziano.[77] This music, too, after all was part of Lorenzo's musical world, music that he heard when he went to church or that he perhaps heard even in the privacy of the Medici Palace chapel, music that he heard at carnival festivities and other public celebrations, music that he and his family may have performed themselves or had performed for them. Like the chansons many of Isaac's surviving works in these genres must have been written expressly for Lorenzo and for his family and friends, although it is exceedingly difficult to prove this, given the lack of sources containing these particular repertories from Lorenzo's time.[78]

---

[75] *A Florentine Chansonnier from the Time of Lorenzo the Magnificent* cit., I, p. 96.

[76] Banco Rari 299, conceived in the classical chansonnier format, the contents of which were defined by a tradition that admitted only an occasional Latin, Spanish, Italian or Flemish texted work, offers little or no testimony to Isaac's contributions in these areas, nor should we expect it to.

[77] They are published in modern edition in ISAAC, *Weltliche Werke* cit., pp. 44, 42. This volume and the supplement mentioned above in note 41 contain all of Isaac's surviving vocal and instrumental secular works with Italian and Latin texts or titles.

[78] Florentine sources of sacred music from Lorenzo's time, which would have reflected the repertories performed at the Cathedral, the Baptistry and the Santissima Annunziata, have all disappeared. The Cathedral's sources from this period were apparently replaced with newer works by Francesco Corteccia and others of his generation and later beginning in the 1530s. These are the oldest manuscripts mentioned in the earliest surviving inventory of Ca-

For example, a few of Isaac's carnival songs and ballate, together with several other contemporaneous settings, survive in a collection dating from the second decade of the 16th century and later.[79] It is doubtful that this preserves all of Isaac's contributions to either form. So too with Isaac's sacred music, for the bulk of what comes down to us comprises music composed for his Austrian and German patrons, long after Lorenzo's death.[80] Nevertheless, a number of works in the various genres can be traced to Lorenzo's time, among them, the «Alla Battaglia», composed for the installation of Niccolò Orsini as Florentine commander in 1487, the carnival song «Hora è di maggio» the *Missa Salve nos*, portions of which Isaac used in his setting of Poliziano's threnody on Lorenzo's death, «Quis dabit capiti meo aquam», the Medici heraldic piece, «Palle, Palle» and the motet «Prophetarum maxime» in honor of Florence's patron saint, John the Baptist.[81] The motet's text includes a non-scriptural passage as well as the words of an antiphon for St. John's Day, June 23. It would thus have been appropriate for one of the festivities, civic or sacred, that marked observance of the day in Florence, although it may be that it had a more specific function and was composed for the ceremony that took place at the Baptistry when Giovanni publicly received his cardinal's hat in March 1492. Clearly, one would need more specific reference than what is found in the motet's text to relate it to this latter event, but just as Giovanni's elevation was celebrated with a triumph and a musical setting of a text by Agnolo Dovizio da Bibbiena for the occasion, so too might Isaac have been commissioned to write an appropriate piece for the celebration, which had long been anticipated.

Which leads back to the question of Lorenzo's musical training

---

thedral musical holdings, dating from 1632. The Florentine chansonniers from Lorenzo's time include a few sacred pieces, notably, the Benedictus from Isaac's «Missa Quant j'ai», and Isaac's «Salve regina».

[79] This is reproduced in my *Florence, Biblioteca Nazionale Centrale, MS Banco Rari 230*, New York and London 1986.

[80] Other lost works of Isaac include his «missa supra J'ay pris amours», which had been «recently composed», according to the singer Cornelio di Lorenzo of Antwerp, when he wrote to Duke Ercole of Ferrara from Florence on 11 March 1490. Cornelio sent the Mass to the Duke two months later, on 12 May 1490. See LOCKWOOD, *Music in Renaissance Ferrara* cit., pp. 164f.

[81] For the dating of «Alla Battaglia», see T. J. MCGEE, *'Alla Battaglia': Music and Ceremony in Fifteenth-Century Florence*, «Journal of the American Musicological Society», 36, 1983, pp. 287-302; on «Palle, Palle», see A. ATLAS, *Heinrich Isaac's Palle, Palle: A New Interpretation*, «Analecta Musicologica», 9, 1974, pp. 17-25.

and his patronage of music and musicians. Some of the questions one might pose regarding Lorenzo and musical patronage in late 15th-century Florence are so general and so basic that it is probably useless even to speculate about what their answers might be. We might ask, for instance, whether the history of Florentine art music – and ultimately, therefore, of Italian secular music – would have been any different if he hadn't hired Heinrich Isaac and put him to work, as later generations would recount it, at revivifying the carnival music that had been sung in Florence since time immemorial. In attempting to make a suitable response, we would doubtless have to ask whether Isaac, in turn, was influenced by the traditional Florentine *canti carnascialeschi* models (of which little or no trace apparently remains) that he was called upon to refine so that they would be more pleasing to contemporary taste. To frame the question another way, perhaps too generally, might we not ask whether late 16th- and 17th-century Italian music (and subsequently European music which it so profoundly influenced) would have been what it became had not Lorenzo and other like-minded individuals brought all of those *oltremontani* to Italy in the late 15th century and had them compose and perform music, both secular and sacred, that was intended for groups of people whose tastes and experiences were necessarily different from those of similar classes of listeners and musical consumers in northern Europe.

The Franco-Netherlanders, reared in the polyphonic traditions of the great *maîtrises* of the north, brought their remarkable skills to the peninsula, where many of them spent long and fruitful years. As a consequence much, though not all, of the music, they wrote for Italian audiences (a good deal of it preserved, not coincidentally, only in manuscripts and prints of Italian origin) was naturally influenced by Italian concepts, both musical and philosophical. In the case of Josquin, who is documented in Italy as early as 1459, when he was perhaps no more than eighteen or nineteen years old, it is easy to think of his music as being the product of the two cultures, of the north where he was born and had his earliest training and to which he later returned, and of the south, where he reached artistic maturity and spent many of the most productive years of his life.

Josquin's influence on the music of his contemporaries and successors seems so obvious and has been commented upon so many times that it hardly needs restating. Isaac too had his followers, and not only in Germany, where he had a seminal role in the production of sacred music. For Isaac was the founder of what I have called the «new» Florentine school, two generations of composers, all of whom in some fashion or another were indebted to his music, both sacred and secular. Specifically, one can cite the earlier composers of this group, Bartolomeo degli Organi and Alessandro Coppini, who in their ballate and canti carnascialeschi emulated Isaac's penchant for elegant and expressive melody, for artfully articulated and well-balanced phrases, for clearly defined goals within a restricted tonal compass and for the flexibility and contrast provided by the succession of metrically diverse passages. A later generation includes Francesco Corteccia, whose fondness for canonic and imitative devices and quotation of pre-existent material, in both his sacred and secular music, stem directly from Isaac's practices; and Mattia Rampollini, whose preoccupation with proportions, though somewhat anachronistic in the madrigal genre of the 1540's, clearly derives its inspiration from Isaac's earlier models. And on a broader level, it is undeniable that the early madrigals of Bernardo Pisano, Francesco de Layolle, and Philippe Verdelot, to name the Florentine contributors to the new genre, could not have come about without the musical and conceptual fusion, exemplified in Florence by Isaac's work, that was a byproduct of the two traditions. Doubtless the same can be said about the music of early madrigal composers in other important centers, but it is also fair to say that manifestations of this fusion first appeared in Florence and Rome at a time when fortune was once again smiling on Lorenzo's children and grandchildren. Thus Lorenzo's patronage of the *oltremontani* can be connected in a general but neverthless very real way to the grand strides made by Italian musicians in the second quarter of the 16th century and later, when they took the lead in musical matters and began to set the standards that would prevail throughout Europe for the next one hundred and fifty years, just as their Franco-Netherlandish teachers had done in the previous century.

To sum up: All of the evidence points to an involvement with music on Lorenzo's part that was genuine and not born from a desire merely to compete with other princes or to show the world how cultured he and his family were, although the prestige factor among the upper classes in late Quattrocento Italy should never be discounted. It sprang, to judge from all available records, from an innate love of music, from a talent for making music and from an ability, acquired from his earliest years through solid training, self-discipline and wide experience, to appreciate many different kinds of music. This clearly is not the profile of a dilettante, of someone who sponsored polyphony for the prestige it might bring him or for any number of other reasons one might care to consider. It is, rather, the profile of a person who was well trained in it, capable of performing it, and who was passionately involved in it, a person, to paraphrase Castiglione's words, for whom music was both an ornament and a necessity.[82] There is no doubt that promoting musical performances in the city's churches and at the Palazzo Vecchio and arranging for musical accompaniments to carnival festivities and other civic and religious celebrations were activities that complemented Lorenzo's own ambitions for the arts and enhanced his political programs. But considerations such as these should not detract from his enormous contributions to the development of all forms of music in late Quattrocento Florence. His efforts on behalf of public institutions and his own private support were prime factors in the dissemination of the many kinds of music that reached all levels of society. Having said this, I should add a caveat and say that I am not suggesting that Lorenzo or any of the Medici was solely responsible for the remarkable flowering of polyphony that occurred in Florence in the late Quattrocento any more than he or any one of them was solely responsible for Florentine achievements, intellectual, artistic and otherwise, that occurred during the period when he was at the helm of the state. But what I will suggest is that from the 1480s onward, in music's case, Lorenzo took the lead in promoting polyphony on an unprecedented scale at both official and unofficial levels and that by doing so he set a splendid example for others to follow. It was an example which his son Giovanni never forgot after he became Pope and presided over one of the most memorable moments in Italian and European musical history.

---

[82] Lorenzo's attitude about music may have been best expressed by Castiglione in one of the passages in his *Il Cortegiano*, when he had Lorenzo's son Giuliano say, in response to a remark by Gaspare Pallavicino to the effect that music, like other vanities, was more suitable for women than for real men, that he was not at all in agreement and that on the contrary he believed that «music is not only an ornament but a necessity to the Courtier» (B. CASTIGLIONE, *The Book of the Courtier*, translated by C. Singleton, New York 1959, pp. 75, 77).

VI

SACRED MUSIC IN FLORENCE IN SAVONAROLA'S TIME

When Savonarola returned to Florence in 1489, he encountered a musical culture whose vitality and diversity were equalled by few other places in Italy at the time. What a wealth of music there was to be heard! Religious services on Sundays and feast days were now celebrated with chant and organ playing at all of the city's major churches, while vocal polyphony, performed by highly trained chapels of singers, could be heard at the Cathedral, the Baptistry and the Santissima Annunziata. At the Palazzo Vecchio two corps of trumpeters signalled the Signoria's public appearances and called the populace to witness the arrival or departure of important personages. Within its public rooms and private chambers, the town's wind band played for the delectation of the Signoria and its distinguished visitors. At the seats of the greater guilds and the Parte Guelfa other instrumentalists provided similar kinds of entertainments and fanfares for high ranking officials and their guests. During the meetings of the confraternities, particularly the wealthier ones, the monophonic melodies sung by members themselves were enhanced by performances of motets and polyphonic laude by instrumentalists and singers, many of whom were of semi-professional or professional status. In the squares the cantimpanche sang their witty and moralizing texts, as they narrated stories based on classical mythology, medieval lore, holy scripture and contemporary events. The more raucous festivities at Calen di Maggio and Carnival, celebrated in typically Florentine fashion, saw singers and perhaps instrumentalists furnishing the music that accompanied the elaborately decorated carri and fancifully costumed revelers as they processed through the city. Public celebrations for the feast of San Giovanni, though of a more solemn and rather more political nature, were no less lavish in their use of music. This was the public or near public side of it[1].

---

1. The principal studies from which this discussion is drawn include: F. Ghisi, *I canti car-*

Private music making and performance by professionals and amateurs alike was no less pervasive and reached most if not all ranks of society. No festive evening was complete without dancing and the music that accompanied it[2]. Though the city lacked all the trappings of a reigning court, Medici encouragement and patronage was as active as politics and finances allowed. Social custom may have hindered their having large personal musical entourages such as those maintained by the Milanese and Ferrarese dukes, the Neapolitan kings and the popes at Rome, but Medici involvement in musical matters was as sustained and as consistent, circumstances permitting, as those of any monarch. Musicians ostensibly hired to perform in public places could also lend their services to private patrons, a situation the Medici exploited to its fullest, as did other leading families. Polyphonic French chansons and Italian texted songs, instrumental pieces, and the satirical, amorous or politically-charged verses of the poet-improvisors formed the principal kinds of music heard in the privacy of the palace and the intimacy of the home. Often, the performers were professional musicians, many of whom composed music for their Florentine patrons, who themselves began as never before to take an active role in music making.

Within the rarified atmosphere of the Florentine upper classes an ability to sing or play an instrument had become a much prized social asset and musical instruction now formed an important part of the education of the young. Musical instruction, moreover, was available not only to children of

---

nascialeschi nelle fonti musicali del XV e XVI secolo, Florence 1937 (rist. 1970); Id., *Strambotti e laude nel travestimento spirituale della poesia musicale del Quattrocento*, "Collectanea Historiae Musicae", 1, 1953, pp. 45-78; F. A. D'Accone, *The Singers of San Giovanni in Florence During the 15th Century*, "Journal of the American Musicological Society", 14, 1961, pp. 307-358; Id., *Alcune note sulle Compagnie fiorentine dei laudesi durante il Quattrocento*, "Rivista Italiana di Musicologia", 10, 1975, pp. 86-114; A. W. Atlas, *The Cappella Giulia Chansonnier: Rome, Biblioteca Vaticana, MS Cappella Giulia XIII.27*, voll. 2, Brooklyn 1975-76; H. M. Brown, *A Florentine Chansonnier from the Time of Lorenzo the Magnificent*, voll. 2, 7, Chicago and London 1983; K. Polk, *Civic Patronage and Instrumental Ensembles in Renaissance Florence*, "Augsburger Jahrbuch für Musikwissenschaft", 3, 1986, pp. 83-92; F. A. D'Accone, *Lorenzo il Magnifico e la musica*, in *La musica a Firenze al tempo di Lorenzo il Magnifico*, ed. P. Gargiulo, Florence 1993, pp. 219-248, and the English version of this study, in *Lorenzo the Magnificent and Music*, in *Lorenzo il Magnifico e il suo mondo. Convegno internazionale di studi, Firenze, 9-13 giugno 1992*, ed. G. C. Garfagnini, Florence, 1994, pp. 259-290.

2. Witness Savonarola's own remark a propos of dancing in a sermon he delivered on 7 March 1496, three years after the Medici were banished: "Ancora per le ville si fanno balli el dì delle feste". G. Savonarola, *Prediche italiane ai Fiorentini*, ed. R. Palmarocchi, Florence 1933, voll. 3, III, 1, p. 388). Another allusion to dancing occurs in the same sermon "Qui canitis ad vocem psalterii sicut Davit; putaverunt se habere vasa cantici; questi sono li suoni e balli che fate doppo e' conviti, e vostri organi e vostri canti; questi sono ancora quelli che appropriano alli uomini li psalmi fatti in onore di Dio" (*ibid.*, p. 436).

wealth and station, but also, thanks to church schools and private teachers, to the sons and daughters of the middle classes and of the artisans and others in the lesser guilds, the classes from which later sprang the principal figures in the city's renascent school of composers, among them, Alessandro Coppini, Bartolomeo degli Organi, Bernardo Pisano, Francesco de Layolle and Francesco Corteccia. Thus, music, in all of its forms, monophonic, polyphonic, vocal, instrumental, sacred, devotional and secular, had come to form a fundamental part of the daily life of Florentines of all ages and classes, and the city itself – the Florence of Savonarola's day – it seems clear, had become one of the musical capitals of Europe.

This musical effloresence, to be sure, had not come about by chance. Rather, it was the result of formal and informal systems of public and private support, some of them more than a century old, some of more recent institution. In the later Trecento intellectual and aesthetic preferences of noble and upperclass ecclesiastics and laymen had largely defined Florentine musical horizons. But after the turn of the new century, as the Renaissance gathered momentum and pride in the city's accomplishments grew at a concommitant pace, expanded musical programs, the reinvigoration of existing ones, and a greater interest in musical performance on the part of an ever-widening circle of amateurs converged to provide a broad societal impetus and a sound fiscal basis for the cultivation of music and musical performance never before experienced.

Savonarola, who had previously spent the greater part of the 1480s in the city, was acutely aware of the pervading presence of music in Florentine life, and he did not like much of what he heard. We do not know what he said about it before he became a dominant voice in Florentine politics, but when the time was ripe, he had no hesitation in condemning current practices, reserving some of his most scathing remarks about what he had earlier witnessed for his Lenten sermons of 1496. In those and other sermons he also stated his preferences regarding the kind of music he thought was needed in a well-ordered Christian community[3]. He loved the traditional chants of the church, particularly the more familiar hymns and antiphons, whose melodies and texts were often sung by the faithful of all ages and stations. When it

---

3. Sermon of 7 March 1496: "voi cantate qua delle laude la mattina e sta bene; ma io vorrei ancora che voi cantassi qualche volta de' canti della Chiesa come è *Ave maris stella*, o *Veni creator spiritus*, e non saria anche male nessuno che il popolo rispondesse, e quando io vengo in pergamo, se io trovassi che voi cantassi quella *Ave maris stella*, canterei forse ancora io" (Savonarola, *Prediche italiane* cit., III, 1, p. 437).

came to non-liturgical music, he preferred monophonic tunes set to devotional texts, both because these were easily learned and accessible even to the musically illiterate and because he saw them as a means of increasing popular piety. Thus, he encouraged the singing of laude as well as the traditional chants of the church, and he himself wrote texts for a number of laude, most of which, like many other devotional texts, were sung to popular tunes or to previously composed pieces in part-music[4]. The latter were generally simple homophonic settings, easy of execution – pieces much like the hymns of a later day – whose chordal textures made for easy understanding of the text. Apparently, this was the reason why Savonarola countenanced any kind of part-music at all, though he may also have tolerated these simply harmonized tunes because learning to sing them required little beyond the basic musical training that was available in many Florentine schools[5].

The part-music that was being sung in chapels at the Cathedral, the Baptistry and the Santissima Annunziata was another matter. This was usually, if not always, composed by Franco-Flemish masters and their imitators in the most advanced style of the time. It was music that characteristically featured several parts weaving and interweaving melodic patterns amongst themselves within artfully conceived structures that often concealed esoteric polyphonic devices. With varying degrees of success, depending, of course, on an individual composer's talents and imagination, the music's shifting textures, lustrous harmonies and fluid formal designs effectively served to convey the mood and meaning of the text. At its best, it was music whose technical bravura and expressive qualities unmistakably placed it among the highest of the "high art" forms of the time. There could be no denying that it was music composed for a cultural élite who had the education and taste to recognize its technical achievements and formal subtleties and to appreciate its intellectual as well as its sensual appeal. Savonarola's sincere conviction was that this music was as distracting as it was meaningless and that, like other exterior forms of worship, it could be a hindrance to direct communion

---

4. The most recent study of the practices is P. Macey's *Bonfire Songs: Savonarola's Musical Legacy*, Oxford 1998, particularly pp. 98-117.

5. Support for this supposition comes from a remark Savonarola made when he preached his ideas about the education of the young in his sermon of 7 March 1496. Though he went on at some length about which authors should or should not be taught in grammar classes, when he came to discussing music, he merely mentioned, almost in passing, the "tanti canti figurati che voi gl'insegnate a questi novizi". Though I find it difficult to determine exactly what he meant, I am assuming he was in this instance referring to the essentials of singing and music theory that were then being taught in places such as the Cathedral School (Savonarola, *Prediche italiane* cit., III, 1, p. 438).

SACRED MUSIC IN FLORENCE IN SAVONAROLA'S TIME

with God[6]. It was inevitable that he would also detest this music because in Florence it was inextricably connected to the Medici and the mores of the political and social world they embodied[7].

This was also music whose performance required highly specialized singers, many of whom, like the composers, had been trained in schools attached to the great cathedrals of northern France and the Low Countries. These Franco-Flemish singers were much in demand throughout Europe, perhaps nowhere more than in Italy, where popes and princes – and the Medici – went to great lengths to secure their services. Many of the leading singers were also clerics who came to Italy in search not only of fame and fortune but also of the benefices – to be obtained through the good offices of a powerful prince or prelate, or the pope himself – that would ensure continuing comfort in old age. The lucky ones did obtain ecclesiastical preferments, for by all accounts it was a singers' market and star singers were often as pampered and favored as were the operatic divas of a later day. It should come as no surprise to learn that the behavior of some of these star singers often left much to be desired, and this despite their clerical status. In Florence, even before Savonarola's day, there are records of rowdy singers and others serving jail time, and the situation cannot have been much different in the 1480s and 1490s. For his part Savonarola found the conduct of

---

6. "Il culto del cristiano è interiore e esteriore, ma lo esteriore è ordinato all'interiore [...] E però nelle orazioni, che sono culto esteriore, tanto debba l'uomo procedere, quanto le sono aiutorio al culto interiore, e non più in là, secondo che dice San Tommaso. E quando tu sentissi che queste orazioni esteriori ti togliessino o impedissino lo interiore, si debbano resecare e lasciarle, e stare saldo nella elevazione della mente e nel culto interiore. E però si dice che li canti figurati sono più presto nocivi nella chiesa, che utili, perché quivi si debbe orare e contemplare Dio colla mente e coll'intelletto, e e' canti figurati non fanno altro che dilettare il senso e l'orecchio" (G. Savonarola, *Prediche sopra Giobbe*, ed. R. Ridolfi, Rome 1957, voll. 2, i, p. 393). Earlier, in his Lenten sermons of 1491, delivered from the Cathedral pulpit, Savonarola spoke of evils abounding in the church, though he did not mention polyphony at the time. See D. Weinstein, *Savonarola and Florence*, Princeton 1970, p. 94.

7. "Praeterea il tiranno tiene nelle chiese alcuna volta, non per onore di Dio, ma per suo piacere cantori imbriaconi che come sono ben pieni di vino, vanno a cantare la messa a Cristo, e pagali delli danari del comune" (Sermon of 24 February 1496; Savonarola, *Prediche italiane* cit., III, 1, p. 191). Also relevant in this respect is a passage from a sermon of 7 March 1496 in which he not only alluded to the Medici but also to his impression of the Franco-Flemish music, in this case probably a cantus-firmus setting of a Mass: "Il Signore non vuole queste cose [...] dice Dio: lieva via quelli tuoi belli canti figurati. Egli hanno questi signori la capella de' cantori che bene pare proprio uno tumulto, come dice qui el profeta, perchè vi sta là un cantore con una voce grossa che pare un vitello e li altri gli cridono atorno come cani e non intende cosa che dichino.Lasciate andare e' canti figurati, e cantate e' canti fermi ordinati dalla Chiesa; voi volete pur sonare organi; voi andare alla chiesa per udire organi. Dice Dio: io non odo e' vostri organi" (Savonarola, *Prediche italiane* cit., III, 1, pp. 388-389). Savonarola's attitude towards vocal polyphony is illustrated and discussed by Macey, *Bonfire Songs* cit., pp. 92-98.

some singers as distasteful as the music they performed, and he was no less stinging in his denunciation of them than he was of their repertory[8].

Many of the activities that defined the flourishing musical culture of fin-de-siècle Florence disappeared during the years of Savonarola's ascendency. His rigid attitudes towards the kinds of music performed at public functions, whether secular or sacred, were, it is quite clear, influential in forming public opinion as well as government policy, both before and during the time he became the leading force in Florentine political life. After the Medici were banished the vigor of his teachings was such that carnival and other festivities where music played a very prominent role were done away with, and entire repertories of secular song, including the canti carnascialeschi, were consigned to the bonfires of the vanities[9]. There is, however, only indirect evidence regarding the disbanding of the chapels at the Cathedral, the Baptistry and the Santissima Annunziata in the spring of 1493, for at the time forces sympathetic to the friar were not yet in control of the government. But even allowing for the instability of Piero de' Medici's regime and perhaps for a lack of a clear consensus as how best to continue supporting the chapels in troubled times, there can be little doubt that Savonarola's hostitlity toward these institutions furnished the direct reason for their suppression. The abolition of the position of teacher of figural music in the Cathedral school and with it the boys' choir at the end of 1494, a month after the Medici expulsion, can perhaps be laid more directly to Savonarola's influence. Perhaps the reason for retaining a teacher up to that time rested on the premise that some training in part music was necessary for teaching young people how to sing laude[10].

The end of the story is well known. Despite the fervor and alacrity with which Savonarola's teachings were embraced, they were, insofar as they in-

---

8. In addition to the passage quoted in the previous note, the following offers another illustration of Savonarola's attitude towards polyphony and its practictioners: "Voglio in effetto dire per questo che li uomini oggi si sono dati alli sacramenti della Chiesa per una usanza e per culto esteriore, non per vivacità di fede né per culto interiore [...] Questo si pruova in molti luoghi della Scrittura [...] El signore dice: ecco, li vostri peccati e le vostre iniquità hanno provocato l'ira mia. Voi credete placarmi per andare a messe, fare organi e paramenti e altre cerimonie: voi non farete nulla. Però dice il Signore irrisoriamente: venite A Bethel, il quale è interpretato domus Dei, idest casa di Dio. Venite alla casa mia a sacrificarmi con vostre cerimonie [...] Venite, capi della Chiesa, venite preti, venite frati, venite secolari. Venga ognuno, venite cantori; quelli dico, che beano prima molto bene poi cantano la messa. Su, venite ognuno, facciamo una bella festa d'organi, di drappelloni, di cerimonie: queste non vagliano nulla sanza quel di dentro" (Sermon of 28 February 1496; Savonarola, *Prediche italiane* cit., III, 1, pp. 280-281).

9. The latest account of the bonfires is in Macey, *Bonfire Songs* cit., pp. 73-82, 86-87.

10. In support of this hypothesis is the remark, quoted above in note 5, that Savonarola made when he preached his ideas about the education of the young.

fluenced Florentine musicians, at best transitory. Though laude singing, and particularly his own laude texts and some of the music to which they were adapted – carnival songs at that – continued to lead an underground existence for decades after his death, finally to resurface in Serafino Razzi's publications, his lasting effect on the course of the further development of polyphonic music in Florence was, to put it bluntly, negligible[11]. The Florentine situation, in fact, offers quite a contrast to the long-lasting influence and dissemination of his signature tune, *Ecce quam bonum*, and the ever-widening circle of composers throughout Europe who were led to compose music inspired by his meditations. All of the notable Florentine composers of the 16th century, with one exception, shunned Savonarolan teachings and any music associated with his legacy[12].

Before illustrating this paradox, I shall give, in the following pages, a more detailed account, most of it based on previously unpublished material, of the state of music in the city's churches before and after Savonarola's rise and fall. I have purposely confined my remarks to the churches because they were the institutions that employed the city's leading musicians during and after the Savonarolan interregnum, thus nurturing the careers of those who were destined to form the nucleus of the new Florentine school of composers. A few remarks about the Florentine sacred repertory of the late 15th century and the question of whether Savonarola should be held accountable for its disappearance will fill in this picture of how polyphony triumphed in Florence in the years after the friar's death.

During the 1480's the singing chapels at the Cathedral and the Baptistry, founded under Medici auspices decades earlier, were experiencing renewed

---

11. For particulars see Macey, *Bonfire Songs* cit., pp. 39-58, which contains a pertinent bibliography of works devoted to the subject.
12. The one notable exception, Giovanni Animuccia, published a setting of the tune sung to Savonarola's laude *Ecce quam bonum*. Though Animuccia was born in Florence, he spent the most productive years of his professional musical life in Rome [A discussion of Animuccia's career there is provided by Iain Fenlon in his article in this volume]. Another exception, though I have yet to determine its connection, if any, with the friar of San Marco, is an anonymous 4-voice setting of *Ecce quam bonum*, together with a number of other texts set for 2-voices, appropriate to services on Maundy Thursday, that appear in several sources of the Opera del Duomo in Florence (modern edition in P. Verdelot, *Opera Omnia*, ed. A. M. Bragard, 1973, voll. 3, II, pp. 132-136). These sources, among them, Seconda Serie, ms. 45, ms. 6 and ms. 13, suggest that the settings formed part of the Cathedral's liturgy from at least the 1530s and perhaps even earlier (Further on these, see Gabriele Giacomelli's article in this volume). Marco da Gagliano's setting of the same text, like the earlier one, unrelated to the melody of *Ecce quam bonum* associated with Savonarola, was probably composed as replacement for the earlier piece. I rather doubt that either musical setting was conceived as a tribute, commemoration or celebration of Savonarola, but rather that each offers further testimony to the practice, already well established at the Florentine Duomo by the turn of the 16th century, of embellishing various services during the Triduum Sacrum with polyphony.

vitality as a result of an ambitious policy of expansion recently inaugurated under the guidance of Lorenzo the Magnificent. At the Cathedral, a group of four adult singers and a number of boys, which performed from January 1482 through December 1484, was replaced in March 1485 by a boys' choir and, additionally, in July of the same year by a newly reorganized adult chapel. The boys' choir, with the assistance of their teacher and perhaps of one or two other adults, would henceforth sing polyphony every Saturday morning at the Mass of the Madonna. Another result of the 1485 reorganization was that the adult chapel began to draw most, if not all, of its personnel from among the singers employed at the Baptistry. A similar policy had been adopted several years earlier at the Servite convent church of the Santissima Annunziata. What this meant, in effect, was that most of the singers now formed part of a larger group – which I have called the Florentine chapel – that even then was known as "i cantori di San Giovanni", perhaps because special significance was attached to their services at the Baptistry. Since the singers usually performed at different times in the three churches – Masses on Sundays and holidays at the Baptistry, Vespers on Sundays and holidays, as well as during Holy Week at the Cathedral, and Saturday morning Masses at the Annunziata – it was relatively easy to divide the group into smaller units on the few occasions throughout the year when polyphony was called for at services held simultaneously in the three churches.

An elaborate system of patronage supported the enterprise, one which, though few particulars are available, saw the governing bodies of the three churches, the Arte della Lana and the Arte dei Mercatanti – respectively, the patronal guilds of the Cathedral and the Baptistry – the Cathedral Chapter and the Medici contributing in one form or another to the financing and management of the group. It was a very effective arrangement, for it made possible the employment of larger numbers of singers than might otherwise have been engaged had each of the churches gone it alone. At the same time this cooperative effort allowed each church to set its own priorities. Thus the Annunziata employed several of its own monks, and the Cathedral, one or two of its own chaplains, alongside the many Franco-Flemish musicians who constituted the backbone of the chapel.

It was evidently the Baptistry that took the lead during the late 1470s in welcoming the *oltremontani* to Florence. Though its records are lost, data from the Cathedral and the Santissima Annunziata provide some idea of the forces employed there. In late 1484 there were eleven cantori di San Giovanni among the eighteen singers employed at the Annunziata. Seven of the ten singers initially appointed to the Cathedral chapel in 1485 were also cantori di San Giovanni, a pattern repeated in later years at the Cathedral, for example, in December 1487, when eleven of them were among the thirteen recorded, and in February 1493, when twelve were cited among the eighteen. Apparently, the Baptistry's musical forces were equal to or even greater than those of the other churches, for the other churches generally did not employ all of the singers of San Giovanni[13].

That the singers' duties at the Baptistry were more demanding than in the other churches is suggested by a statement made many years later by Niccolò Pitti, who reported that in Lorenzo the Magnificent's time, the singers each received monthly salaries of three florins from the Baptistry, two from the Cathedral and one from the Santissima Annunziata[14]. Though this information may have been relevant only to Heinrich Isaac, on whose behalf Pitti was supplying it, records from the two latter churches show that the singers were in fact paid the sums he mentioned. Florentine salaries, it would seem, were not as high as those paid by the Sforza dukes in Milan, the kings of Naples, or the Popes in Rome, and fringe benefits and additional income from service to private parties may or may not have been as lucrative. But Florentine compensation was clearly competitive, as can be seen by the large numbers of foreigners, who, perhaps because of Lorenzo's reputation or his recruitment efforts, were drawn to service in the chapel. In sum, from the time Savonarola first arrived in Florence in 1482, through his departure in 1487 and then again on his return in 1489, three of the city's churches were offering musical programs of vocal polyphony and organ music that rivalled those anywhere in Italy or on the continent, for that matter. This state of affairs would last until March 1493, when the chapel was abruptly disbanded.

These were not the only churches in Florence where polyphony could be heard. Records from conventual and collegiate churches, large and small alike, testify to the prominent role of organ music at services on Sundays and holidays, and in some cases to the teaching of figural music and with it, the introduction of Franco-Flemish vocal polyphony. The fame of the legendary Antonio Squarcialupi, organist at the Cathedral and the Baptistry for most of the 15th century, has tended to obscure the presence of outstanding musicians in the city's other churches throughout his lifetime and during that

---

13. See my *The Singers of San Giovanni* cit., pp. 335-346, for particulars.
14. See my *Heinrich Isaac in Florence: New and Unpublished Documents*, "The Musical Quarterly", 49, 1983, pp. 464-483.

of his son and successor Francesco[15]. The careers of Francesco and Antonio, however, though the most well known and well documented, are in a sense emblematic of those of the other, lesser known musicians, many of whom contributed in no small way to the prevailing culture of polyphony in Florentine churches and convents. Documentation is not always available for all churches, San Marco being the most conspicuous of those whose records for the period are lacking, but enough has survived to give a good idea of the norm. Besides San Marco, the major churches for which no late 15th-century records are available include Santa Trinita, seat of the Vallombrosan Order, and Santa Croce, the principal Franciscan establishment in the city. Organists are regularly recorded at Santa Trinita in the early 15th century, and when payments to them begin reappearing in the 1520s, the impression is that there was no change in previous practice[16]. A similar situation prevailed at Santa Croce, the bulk of whose documentation comes from after the 1540s. The presence there in 1461 of the monk Giovanni, an organ tuner who is cited as having worked on the organ at the hospital of Santa Maria Nuova's church of Sant'Egidio, and mention of another organist taking a post at Santa Croce in 1499, are certain indications that organ polyphony flourished there as well[17].

At Sant'Egidio payments to organists for playing at services from the early 1440s offer testimony to the antiquity of the practice there[18]. In the 1480s its organists included Girolamo d'Andrea (January 1480 [81]-April 1482); Gismondo di Iacopo di Maestro Agnolo (mid-April 1482-December 1486); Gherardo di Giovanni (1487-July 1497). Gherardo, who was also an illuminator, had previously served as organist in 1478. His successor, the

---

15. See G. Giacomelli, *Antonio Squarcialupi e la tradizione organaria in Toscana. Testimonianze documentarie iconografiche ed organologiche del Quattrocento all'Ottocento*, Rome 1992, particularly pp. 9-14; and G. Giacomelli and E. Settesoldi, *Gli organi di S. Maria del Fiore di Firenze*, Florence 1993, particularly pp. 29, 37f-38, 42, for Antonio's influence in introducing specifications from northern European models to the Cathedral organ and in helping to establish a Tuscan tradition that endured to this century.

16. See my *Music and Musicians at the Florentine Monastery of Santa Trinita, 1360-1363*, in *Memorie e contributi alla musica dal medioevo all'età moderna offerti a F. Ghisi nel settantesimo compleanno (1901-1971)*, voll. 2 = "Quadrivium", 11-12 (Bologna 1971), I, pp. 131-152. A few of the later documents are in the Corporazioni Religiose Soppresse archives of the Archivio di Stato, Florence. I cite them in the Appendix, under No. 11.

17. In my account of musicians and musical activities at the churches in question, I confine myself to citing the names of musicians employed around and immediately after Savonarola's time, though in the documentary appendices I include earlier and later samplings of documents so as to illustrate the indubitable continuity of Florentine practices.

18. The relevant documents are in the Appendix, No. 1.

Servite friar and composer, Alessandro Coppini, is cited from September 1497- November 1500, when Ser Andrea di Giovanni da Prato is mentioned. From that time forward organists are mentioned throughout the remainder of the century. Though I have yet to find references to singers at Sant'Egidio, it is interesting to note that the largest Florentine collection of Holy Week music of the early 16th century, Florence, Biblioteca nazionale centrale, ms. BR II. I. 350, hails from that church's library.

Mention of the Servite friar Alessandro Coppini inevitably leads to the parent church and convent of the order, the Santissima Annunziata, which was one of the three places where the Florentine chapel performed. That church also had a venerable tradition of its own, both in vocal polyphony and in organ playing, that can be traced to the late 14th century, when fra Andrea de' Servi served there as organist and also taught keyboard playing to several of the convent's friars. After his time an unbroken succession of organists ensured that the Santissima Annunziata remained as one of the city's principal venues for the performance of organ music, and later of polyphonic laudi and figural music. The most renowned of the convent's organists in the mid- 15th century was frate Biagio d'Alberto da Firenze, recorded from mid-December 1450 through the end of December 1471[19]. His pupil and successor, Frate Bernardo di Luca da Firenze, is cited from mid-June 1471 through August 1480, and then, after a gap of ten years from October 1490 through the end of April 1493. Several other organists are cited at the Annunziata during Frate Bernardo's long tenure. They include Bernardino di Messer Iacopo (January-March 1480), Ser Piero di Giovanni d'Arezzo (January 1481-mid October 1484), Frate Piero di Domenico d'Arezzo (November, 1485; January 1486), Frate Benedetto d'Antonio da Bologna (September 1483; April 1486-July 1488), Bartolomeo da Pavia (August 1486), Frate Alessandro da Bologna of the Augustinian Order (April 1486-mid March 1492), and Frate Girolamo d'Antonio da Bologna (27 June 1487-April 1488). Alessandro Coppini, who was the convent's teacher of figural music as well as organist, served first from August 1489 through April 1493 and then again from December 1497 through the end of May 1510. The second organist during this time was another Frate Bernardo, cited from July 1499 through mid-December 1511.

---

19. The relevant documents are in the Appendix, No. 2. During the first years of Fra Biagio's tenure, the previous organist, Piero d'Andrea Vaiaio continued to play as well. Vaiaio was employed from November 1445 through May 1456.

At the Florentine Badia, the earliest extant accounts from the 1440s point to a tradition of organ playing on Sundays, major feast days and the eves of other feasts from well before that time. In 1471 and 1472 the Badia's organist was the previously mentioned Servite friar and teacher, Frate Bernardo di Luca di Firenze. His successor, Maestro Antonio, a canon of Fiesole, served through August 1473 and perhaps later. There is a gap in the records until October 1489, when Piero d'Andrea Mazzi is mentioned, his tenure lasting through April 1502. Piero's immediate successors were Michele di Bartolomeo Mazzi, first cited in 1502, and the composer Bartolomeo degli Organi, who began serving in 1505. As with all of the other Florentine monastic churches, organists are recorded at the Badia throughout the 16th century[20].

Although organ music was already a regular feature of services in the convent church of Santa Felicita by the end of the 14th century, no documentation survives from after that time until a century later, when Ser Guido di Ser Nicolao, "notaio in vescovado e nostro organista", is mentioned in various payments from November 1492 through May 1493. Among his successors were Ser Nicolao di Matteo della Colomba da Pisa (July - December 1493); Ser Giorgio de Alamania (January through September 1494); Piero di Francesco da Poggibonsi (October 1494 - 15 December 1495); Ser Andrea di Niccolò (May 1496); Ser Mariano di Paolo Tucci (January 1500); and Ser Pellegrino da Prato (15 August 1500). Many other organists are recorded after the turn of the century, testifying to a performance tradition which by then had endured for over 150 years[21].

During the late 1480s vocal polyphony was introduced into the Augustinian convent church of Santo Spirito, whose priors are more renowned in the annals of Florentine history for their spiritual and intellectual leadership than for an interest in musical performance. Documentation, though incomplete, is sufficient to show that by that time the convent was employing northern singers to teach figural music to its novitiates. The northerners included Carlo de Burgis in 1486-87 and in 1488 Giovanni Pintelli, a composer who sang at the Florentine Cathedral, at Siena Cathedral and at the Vatican. Both teachers were obliged to perform polyphony with their students at various services. More evidence pointing to the performance of vocal

---

20. The relevant documents are in the Appendix, No. 3.
21. See my *Giovanni Mazzuoli, A late representative of the Italian Ars Nova*, "L'Ars Nova Italiana del Trecento", 2, Certaldo 1968, pp. 23-38, and the documents in the Appendix, No. 4.

polyphony in Santo Spirito comes from the record of a payment of three florins, L. 18 s. 18, on 20 March 1488, for "a book of figural music." Organists were also present during those years, though documentation, as in the case of the music teachers, is spotty. The convent was certainly not lacking an organ, for a few documents indicate that the instrument was either rebuilt or built anew by 15 February 1475. But names of organists are lacking until the late 1480s and later, when the accounts mention Ser Guido (through September 1490), Benedetto da Peretola (September 1490-September 1493); Frate Agostino da Fivizzano (January 1496-October 1497); and Ser Damiano da Lucca (November 1497-January 1498)[22].

Lest it be thought that the introduction of vocal polyphony into services at Santo Spirito was a short-lived experiment without any lasting effect, let me note that singers of polyphony are again reported there after the turn of the 16th century. From 29 December 1501 comes a payment of L. 8 to Frate Martino and Frate Piero, singers, "for having gone to the Misericordia," while in April and June of 1503, an unspecified number of singers and the organist were paid for performing at Tenebrae services. This practice is recorded as late as July 1522 when singers were paid L. 14 "for having performed Lamentations at Tenebrae services." And with regard to instruction in polyphony, suffice it to cite a document from June 1509 which states that such teaching was now a part of the organist's duties[23].

An organ is mentioned in the Carmelite convent church of Santa Maria del Carmine from as early as 1335, and one monk from Florence, the organist Frate Bartolomeo Duccini, is cited in a necrology of 1341. In the intervening years other documents report the teaching of chant and organ to the novices, the restoration of the organ in the early 15th century, and the presence of a lay organist, Piero Del Pace in 1452-53[24]. The death of Frate Niccolò di Simone da Empoli, cited as organist in extant payments from 1475 through June 1479, is reported on 22 November 1491. It is possible that he held the post to within a few years of that time, for a new organist, Frate Alberto de' Boccacci da Cremona, is mentioned only on 1 December 1489. Alberto's contract stipulated that he was to give organ lessons to one of the novices, Frate Piero di Giovanni da Colonia. This Frate Piero is apparently the same person as the organist Fra Pietro Bianco who became the Carmine's organist on 1 July

---

22. See the documents in the appendix, No. 5.
23. For the full text, see the documents in the appendix, No. 5.
24. A. Sabbatini, *Memorie nei secoli degli organi organari organisti della basilica del Carmine di Firenze*, "L'Organo", 10, 1972, pp. 168-197, especially pp. 167-173.

1490. A payment to him from 11 June 1495 names him organist and master of the novices, an indication that the fundamentals of figural music may have also figured in the Carmine's teaching program[25].

At San Pancrazio, which boasted an organ constructed in 1445-46 by the famed organ builder Matteo da Prato, little information is available from before 1478, when the organist Messer Antonio is mentioned. A contract signed with ser Zanobi di Giovanni Lenzi, dated 7 July 1490, reveals that the organist was required to play at Massers and Vespers on all Sundays and feast days and also on the eves of certain feasts, with the added stipulation that should he be required to perform on extraordinary occasions, he was to have dinner with the monks. Ser Zanobi is mentioned through the end of November 1499. The next known organist was the Servite friar Frate Ambrosio di Maestro Gismondo da Cortona, who served from January through June 1501. Several organists are recorded in quick succession in the following months, among them, Ambrosio's teacher the Servite friar Bernardo (June) and the Florentine priest, Ser Girolamo d'Andrea d'Arrigo (July-August 1501). In September of the same year, 1501, Frate Alessandro di Giovanni da Bologna, also recorded earlier at the Santissima Annunziata, began his tenure, which lasted through his death on 25 april 1505. From that time forward, a succession of organists through the end of the 16th century, all of whom were required, as was Zanobi Lenzi in 1490, to play on Sundays and feast days throughout the year[26].

At the main Dominican church in Florence, Santa Maria Novella, there was a centuries' old tradition for performing both laudi and organ music. As regards the former, suffice it to say that the Compagnia di San Piero Martire, which held its meetings in Santa Maria Novella, employed singers and instrumentalists throughout the 14th- and 15th centuries. By the mid 1450s, the Company employed singers to perform every evening and others to perform on feast days. There were seven of them by 1479, when the program was revised to include performances only on feast days. A group of seven singers, described in one document from 1483 as "sette fanciulli che cantano le laude", is then recorded throughout the 1480s, 1490s and through the first decades of the 16th century[27].

---

25. See the documents in the appendix, No. 6. For information about later organists at the Carmine, see my *The Florentine Fra Mauros. A Dynasty of Musical Friars*, "Musica Disciplina", 33, 1979, pp. 80-84.
26. See the relevant documents in the Appendix, No. 7.
27. See my *Alcune note sulle compagnie fiorentine dei laudesi* cit., pp. 88-92.

Documentation regarding organists is not so plentiful from earlier in the 15th century, but the first extant payments form the late 1470s indicate that Santa Maria Novella normally employed them. Mentioned in October 1478, is frate Filippo sonatore, cited through 17 April 1480. His successor, Ser Stefano, had a long tenure and is recorded from July 1480 through 8 August 1494. He was succeeded by the young Bartolomeo degli Organi, who held the post until 19 December 1502. Next came Ser Girolamo d'Andrea, whose 25-year tenure, from February 1503 through the end of January 1528, was exceptional. Girolamo had several successors through the end of the century, when Frate Tommaso Minerbetti took over the post and personally helped usher in one of the most brilliant moments in Santa Maria Novella's musical history[28].

A few reports note that the organ at Sant'Ambrogio was repaired in 1453 by Matteo da Prato, though extant payments to organists begin only in 1470, when Carlo di Giovanni was mentioned. From mid-May 1484 through mid-June 1492 the organist was Piero di Matteo. Another long-time holder of the organist's post was Ser Carlo di Jacopo del Maestro Agnolo, recorded from mid-March 1495 through mid-February 1505. His successors included Lorenzo di Donato, 1510-1513; Ser Bastiano di Girolamo, 1513-1515, and a host of others throughout the remaining years of the 16th century[29].

A venerable tradition for organ playing at the collegiate church of San Lorenzo may be traced to the time of Francesco Landini and even before then[30]. In the early 15th century another composer, Piero di Giovanni Mazzuoli, served as organist[31], and in the later 15th century, when San Lorenzo had become the family church of the Medici, the incumbent was the same Ser Antonio di Marco, mentioned above, who taught polyphony in the Cathedral school[32]. Ser Antonio (December 1481 through 1489, perhaps

---

28. See the documents in the Appendix, No. 8 and also my *Repertory and Performance Practice in Santa Maria Novella at the Turn of the 17th Century, A Festschrift for Albert Seay*, ed. M. D. Grace, Colorado Springs 1982, pp. 71-136.

29. See the documents in the Appendix, No. 9.

30. On Landini at San Lorenzo see my *Music and Musicians at the Florentine Monastery* cit., pp. 135-137, and F. A. Gallo, *Lorenzo Masini e Francesco degli Organi in S. Lorenzo*, "Studi Musicali", 4, 1975, pp. 57-63. One of Landini's predecessors, the organist Filippo, is mentioned in accounts from November 1347 through March 1348. See my *Una nuova fonte dell'Ars nova italiana: il codice di San Lorenzo, 2211*, "Studi Musicali", 13, 1984, p. 20, note 29.

31. For Mazzuoli, *ibid.*, pp. 15-18. Further attesting to the place of music in San Lorenzo's liturgy in the mid-15th century is an inventory of 1457, which mentions "Uno libriciuolo di canti per gl'orghani". See F. Baldasseroni and P. D'Ancona, *La biblioteca della basilica fiorentina di S. Lorenzo nei secoli XIV e XV*, Prato-Florence 1906, pp. 18-19.

32. See the documents in the Appendix, No. 10.

later) was followed by Ser Zanobi Guidetti, who served from sometime before May 1496 through the end of January 1499, when he left to become organist at Santa Croce. Zanobi's successors included Andrea da Prato detto Galloria (February 1499) and the much sought-after Alessandro Coppini, who served through 1505. For most of these years the Cathedral singer and music copyist Ser Matteo di Pagolo resided within San Lorenzo's walls, though no mention is made of his singing at services. From 1459 onwards San Lorenzo also employed a "master of the novices" who taught plainchant and grammar to the twelve clerks under his tutelage. There is little evidence that figural music formed part of their curriculum, though I am now inclined to believe, given the church's history of employing composers and singers who lived within its precincts, that vocal polyphony of some kind must have been performed at the votive Mass of Our Lady that the clerks were obliged to sing daily. This was certainly true after 1515, when Matteo Rampollini was engaged to teach the clerks figural music[33]. A report from 1519 regarding the performance in polyphony of Lamentations and responsories during Holy Week indicates that similar performances had been given in past years.

As for the other principal companies of laudesi, I shall mention here two others, the Company of San Zanobi, whose members met at the Cathedral, and the Company of the Madonna di Orsanmichele. The earlier of the two, San Zanobi, founded in 1281, employed singers and instrumentalists to perform on special feast days throughout the Trecento. During the following century, as at San Piero Martire, two types of singers were employed, those who performed every evening and those who performed on feast days. After a period of decline, the company's forces were reinvigorated in May 1480 with the hiring of five "sovrani" and three "tenoristi," the same number of personnel also being reported three years later, in December 1483. By July 1491 the group was enlarged to include nine laudesi, headed by Piero da San Giorgio, and similar forces are cited from the early 1490s through 1502[34].

At Orsanmichele, the company of laudesi founded in 1291 eventually became the richest of all such Florentine organizations. Throughout the Trecento and well into the Quattrocento it employed large numbers of singers

---

33. See my *Mattia Rampollini and His Petrarchan Canzoni Cycles*, "Musica Disciplina", 27, 1973, pp. 65-106, especially p. 69, note 12, p. 72, and D. Moreni, *Continuazione delle memorie istoriche dell'ambrosiana imperial basilica di S. Lorenzo in Firenze*, Florence 1816, I, pp. 53-64.

34. In addition to my *Alcune note su alcune compagnie fiorentine dei laudesi* cit., see also my *Le compagnie dei laudesi in Firenze durante L'Ars Nova*, "L'Ars Nova Italiana del Trecento", 3, Certaldo 1970, pp. 253-280.

and instrumentalists who performed at the confratelli's various services. The company also employed organists, and in 1453 the post was held by no less a figure than Antonio Squarcialupi, who is mentioned together with four other instrumentalists and twelve singers. A gap in the records permits us only to speculate on the size of the group of performers employed at Orsanmichele in the later decades of the 15th century. When records again become avilable in 1508, musical forces by then included six tenoristas, nine sovrani and the organist, Ser Alessandro di Matteo Bastiani. Similar numbers of singers and an organist are reported in the following years through 1530[35].

This account of activities and personnel at Florentine churches during Savonarola's time and shortly afterwards confirms both the continuity of established musical programs and the presence of a good many professional organists and teachers in the city throughout those years. Whatever effect Savonarola's condemnation of vocal polyphony may have had on the Florentine chapel, his remarks about the organ fell on deaf ears. At the same time performances of polyphonic laudi continued to form part of the services held by two major companies, with the more than likely possibility that this was true also of the third, Orsanmichele. Given Savonarola's musical tastes, the unbroken record of performances by the laudesi is hardly surprising. The retention of organ playing in all churches, on the other hand, is remarkable in view of the scorn he expressed for the instrument. But perhaps it is not so remarkable when one considers the practical reasons for retaining its use. It was so firmly entrenched in the liturgy, especially in those churches where the organist performed in alternatim with singers of the chant, that its removal would assuredly have caused unwanted disruption in celebrating divine services. Then, too, the solo repertory of the organist, devoid of text and heard for the most part during breaks in the liturgy, such as at Elevation or while communion was being served at Mass, would hardly have been construed by many clergy as detracting from the Christian message or as interefering with that interior form of worship that Savonarola preached as being so essential a link between man and his Creator.

It is not difficult to understand why such an accomodation would have been acceptable to most of the Florentine clergy, if not to Savonarola himself. The main burden of his charges against sacred music practices of the time fell on the repertories performed by the chapel singers. His few pro-

---

35. *Le compagnie dei laudesi in Firenze* cit., pp. 105-107. Among the documents I cite there is one from 26 February 1518 attesting to the longevity of service of the tenorista Sano di Giovanni, who by that time had served Orsanmichele as a singer for more than fifty years.

nouncements regarding Franco-Flemish vocal polyphony show that his principal objections stemmed from his conviction that it served as a powerful distraction during worship. Moreover, the compositional techniques on which most vocal polyphony of the time was based – contrapuntal elaboration of a cantus firmus, pervasive imitation, canon – must have seemed to him as obstacles to an understanding of the text, even in the works of the most gifted composers. Whether his hostility towards this kind of music was exacerbated by problems of actual performance such as poor diction and inappropriate tempos or by virtuoso vocal displays remains a matter of speculation, though I tend to doubt that this was so, given the highly professional nature of the Florentine chapel. But there is no doubt that his unfavorable attitude was exacerbated by the habitual drunkeness and unseemly behavior of some of the singers at religious services. He made no such charges against organists and had nothing to say about their repertories or performances.

A musical style that prized contrapuntal artifice at the seeming expense of divinely inspired text could only earn the wrath of a reformer like Savonarola, whose main concern was the salvation of souls and the reform of society. In contrast, the music of the Florentine laude, based it was on a chordal or on an essentially homophonic texture, employed a style of polyphony that was both easily grasped and virtually guaranteed intelligibility of the text. The friar of San Marco would understandably have embraced a kind of music that exemplified his programmatic ideals. Furthermore, laudi singing, whether polyphonic or monophonic, had the added virtue of being essentially classless. Though many of the Florentine élite were members of the confraternities, the music sung at their services was of a decidedly popular nature, its melodies known to all. That some of these would have been elaborated on with part music that was sung or accompanied by professional musicians was hardly a reason for banning that repertory.

This, of course, was not true of the Franco-Flemish music performed by the chapels at the Cathedral, the Baptistry and the Santissima Annunziata. The glories of that music, as attractive and pleasing as it might be, could only be truly appreciated by the cognoscenti, by a musically literate audience comprised of the rich and the powerful in Florentine society. Or so it appeared to Savonarola. Even allowing for the sincerity of his objections to the distractions of vocal polyphony and the singers' behavior, there is no reason to doubt that the deep revulsion he felt was in no small part due to his perception of the chapels as creations of the Medici and their supporters, and his suspicion, justified or not, that they were not averse to using public funds to support institutions that catered to their personal tastes and sensibilities.

Further evidence of Savonarola's hostility toward the chapels might be adduced from the fact that Florentine sources of sacred music from the later 15th century seem not to have survived – I say "seem" because I am convinced that there are manuscripts still awaiting discovery. For the moment we know nothing about their fate, and if they are altogether lost, the question arises as to whether Savonarola is to blame for this loss. One might be tempted to answer in the affirmative, given his public statements about the chapel singers and their music. But I believe that factors other than his remarks about the prevailing style of church polyphony contributed to the loss of these sources, this despite the strong case that has traditionally been made for his encouraging the destruction of canti carnascialeschi and other kinds of secular polyphony. Before putting forth this defense, a few comments and citation of some contemporary reports about the music that was performed by the Florentine chapel will be useful.

From at least the 1470s onwards the Cathedral, the Baptistry and the Santissima Annunziata owned comprehensive repertories of polyphonic Masses, hymns, Magnificats, motets and music for Holy Week. These repertories included works by Dufay – who a few decades earlier had himself sent some of his music to the Medici – as well as works by younger composers such as Philippon Basiron, whose new *Missa L'homme armé* was specifically requested from a Florentine singer, Cornelio di Lorenzo, in March 1484 by the Ferrarese Duke Ercole d'Este. Later, in August of the same year, Ercole thanked the same singer for having sent one of Jacob Obrecht's Masses, another indication that the production of the latest wave of Franco-Flemish composers was known in Florence, even those composers who like Obrecht were not employed in the city. Much of the new sacred music that was not composed in Florence or brought there by resident composers such as Arnolfo Giliardi, Isaac, Alexander Agricola, Pintelli and Johannes Ghiselin, or by earlier itinerants such as Johannes Stochem, reached the city from Milan and from Rome[36]. The Roman connections will be cited presently.

---

36. The latter were in the city for very brief periods. Stochem sang at the Santissima Annunziata during the months of July and August 1486, when he was en route to Rome. See my *Some Neglected Composers in the Florentine Chapels, ca. 1475-1525*, "Viator", 1, 1970, p. 272. His signature, signifying receipt of a monthly salary of one gold ducat, is preserved twice in convent records: Archivio di Stato, Firenze, Corporazioni Religiose Soppresse 119, SS Annunziata, vol. 1050, *Ricevute, 1486-1493*, f. 6v : "Ego Johannes Stochem recipi 31 julii [1486] ducato 1)", and f. 8v: "Ego Johannes Stochem recipi ducato 1 [5 settembre 1486]").

The evidence for Milan is provided by a letter of Lodovico Sforza to Lorenzo de' Medici in November 1477, when Sforza wrote that he was sending a set of Masses that Lorenzo had requested[37].

Turning specifically to the question of repertories at the three churches where the chapel sang, it is possible to have some idea of the music perfomed at the Cathedral and at the Santissima Annunziata because several of their acquisitions of music can be traced through records in extant account books. The loss of the Baptistry's accounts presents a serious drawback in this regard. As the singers' principal place of employment and the place where they sang Masses on Sundays and feast days, that church would have had an extensive library of works, both old and new, as suggested by the just-mentioned Masses by Basiron and Obrecht. Though the singers performed at Vespers on Sundays and feast days at the Cathedral, and at occasional Masses on special feasts, there is no mention of works appropriate to those services in surviving Cathedral records. This is true also of the the Mass music that was sung by the boys' choir on Saturday mornings. Instead, what little there is regards the commissioning of music for the last three days of Holy Week, when Matins and Lauds were anticipated and celebrated with great solemnity. One record cites a payment to the San Lorenzo chaplain and Cathedral singer Arnolfo Giliardi "for his work in composing chanti" in late March 1479, just before Holy Week. A report from the following year, 1480, notes that another San Lorenzo chaplain, the singer Ser Matteo di Pagolo, was paid "for texts and notation of figural music for the Lamentations of Jermiah and responsories for the same Lamentations and other things composed for the days of Holy Week"[38]. In both instances none of the music survives.

After 1480 I find no further reference to musical acquisitions in Cathedral records until 1514, when the then-chapelmaster Bernardo Pisano was engaged to copy music, which may or may not have included his own re-

---

37. See my *Lorenzo the Magnificent and Music* cit., p. 283 and for the full text of Sforza's letter, my *Lorenzo il Magnifico e la musica* cit. p. 239.

38. The just-cited payment regarding Arnolfo ("per sua faticha di chonporre canti") and the one for Ser Matteo di Pagolo ("pro scripturis et intonaturis cantus figurati pro Lamentationibus Hieremie et responsis ipsarum lamentationem et aliarum rerum compositarum [sic] pro diebus ebdomode sancte"] are given in my *Some Neglected Composers* cit., p. 266 and p. 279. See my *Bernardo Pisano, an Introduction to His Life and Works*, "Musica Disciplina", 17, 1963, pp. 115-135, especially p. 133, note 64 for the documents regarding the commissions from Matteo. Earlier, on 23 July 1475 and 21 April 1475, Matteo was paid a total of 2 florins by the Santissima Annunziata "for his work notating certain quaternions of large bolognese [folios]" and "for notating Masses and other things in figural music for the Annunziata's chapel." On 26 April 1476 Matteo received another florin "for the rest of the notating of 11 quaternions of figural music he notated for the chapel". The citations are in the Appendix, No. 2, items 5 and 7b.

sponsories for Holy Week. Pisano was cited again in connection with music books in 1515 and 1516[39]. In that latter year fra Arrigo di Bartolomo di Santa Croce, was also paid "for having copied a book of figural music"[40]. Pisano's responsories, like those of Arnolfo, were still being performed at the Cathedral in the late 1520s, as Francesco Corteccia pointed out in the preface to his own book of Responsoria, which though not published until 1570, contained works already composed by 1544[41]. I cite the early 16th-century references to Cathedral music books because, as is the case with the late 15th-century sources just mentioned, none, including Pisano's responsories, is listed in the earliest surviving inventory of polyphonic music owned by the Cathedral from 1651[42].

Reports from the Santissima Annunziata in the later 15th century are more plentiful and give a clear picture of how and when sacred repertories were acquired for that church. From 1479 come several payments to Ser Antonio da Montughi, who was then teaching at the convent, one of them specifying that he copied two quaternions of music "notated in figural music for those who are learning to sing," while on 28 June 1481 a payment of one ducat is cited to the Hungarian priest Ser Biagio di Giovanni, "for part of book of figural music he sold to the convent"[43]. Some idea of the provenance of newly acquired works and how they were transmitted from other cities is provided by a record from March 1483 that mentions three florins reimbursed to the convent's prior "when he went to Rome, for having five Masses, three motets and laudi notated, and for giving dinner to the pope's singers, who furnished the copies of the said Masses and songs."

Among a number of other records testifying to the purchase of new polyphonic works by the Santissima Annunziata are a payment, dated 8 May 1483, that mentions disbursement of L. 2 to the singer Matteo Tedesco "because he brought [us] two Masses in figural music," and another that both reaffirms Rome's central position as a source of new polyphony while giving proof of compositional activity within the convent. This latter, from 3 June 1483, notes that L. 2 were paid to the singer Iannes (last name problematic)

---

39. See my *Bernardo Pisano* cit., p. 133, note 63 for the documents regarding the commissions.
40. *Ibid.*
41. See the Introduction to my edition of Francesco Corteccia, *Music for the Triduum Sacrum*, *Music of the Florentine Renaissance*, vol. 11, American Institute of Musicology 1985.
42. See my *The Sources of Luca Bati's Sacred Music*, in *Altro Polo, Essays on Italian Music in the Cinquecento*, ed. R. Charteris, Sydney 1990, pp. 159-177, especially p. 162 and p. 174, note 3.
43. Documentation for all of the citations regarding the Annunziata's music books are in the Appendix, No. 2, items 10, 11, 12.

"for two Masses he brought [us] from Rome and for other songs [he] composed here in the convent". Finally, I cite a record from 7 April 1484 that reports an expenditure of "s. 7 for one quinternion of mid-size Bolognese folios for notating the Mass we got from Lorenzo", as an indication of how seriously the Medici themselves were involved in the affairs of the chapel, to the point of procuring or furnishing music for the singers.

The "songs" mentioned in the Annunziata's records were probably motets, though they could also have been Magnificats, which, along with Masses, were the other polyphonic items specified for performance in a contract signed by several singers and the convent's prior in 1482[44]. Leaving aside the question of the position occupied by motets in the Florentine liturgy of this time, there is, as just mentioned, a good deal of evidence, both contemporary and of later date, pointing to the use of polyphonic settings of responsories, Lamentations, psalms and hymns for the Tenebrae services of Holy Week, though the earliest extant Florentine ones are those of Pisano from ca. 1512-1520. Like the motets, hymns and psalms that were assuredly sung at Vespers at the Cathedral and the Masses and motets sung at the Baptistry, none of the musical items cited in the Annunziata's accounts survives.

It is noteworthy that references to works by Isaac, the Florentine composer par excellence of this time, are conspicuously lacking in extant accounts at the Duomo and at the Annunziata. Whether this is because they were commissioned privately by the Medici and then made available to the chapels, as the just-mentioned report from the Annunziata suggests, or because payments for them were mentioned in records now lost, or because they furnished gratis by the composer – which I doubt – is a matter of speculation. Conspicuous also is the low survival rate of Isaac's works in Florence, this despite his close association with the city, before, during and after Savonarola's time. Apart from a few Masses and a scattering of single Mass movements and a motet honoring St. John, which I believe was written for Giovanni de' Medici's investiture in 1490, it would seem that most of Isaac's extant sacred music dates from the time he spent in imperial service.

So how can one account for the disappearance of an important body of works that, like the others just mentioned, must have constituted a good part of the Florentine sacred repertory of the late 15th century? Does this loss mean that these collections were purposely destroyed during Savonarola's time because of his resentment toward Franco-Flemish polyphonic music? I

---

44. See my *The Singers of San Giovanni* cit., p. 333.

rather doubt it. Instead, I believe that this repertory has disappeared for the simple reason that it went out of fashion. As it was superseded by newer works, this music was either put away or stored in archives, to be dealt with at a later time. Some of it may subsequently have been destroyed for any number of reasons, among which might be cited the Tridentine reforms. Some of it, as I suggest, may still be awaiting discovery. Some of it may have been recycled and put to other uses. As we know from several recent discoveries, if the leaves of a manuscript were in good enough condition, they were reused in the bindings of new books. In the Cathedral's case there is also the more remote possibility that some manuscripts were discarded because the boys and men in its newly reconstituted chapel of 1501 were incapable of performing the more difficult music sung by the previous group. Corteccia implied as much in his just-cited preface when he noted that Bernardo Pisano had taken vocal ranges and capabilities of existing personnel into account when he composed his responsories, works that by Corteccia's day were considered to be too slow in places and too tiring for the singers. A lack of performers of professional calibre, though, as a reason for destroying repertories seems a rather lame explanation, especially when weighed against the reinstitution of chapels at the Baptistry – and with it a growth in personnel – and at the Santissima Annunziata within the following decade.

Perhaps, then, the simplest reason for the loss of late 15th-century sources of Florentine sacred music is also the most logical one. As the years went by, music that was no longer current or no longer met the Cathedral's needs was generally put aside, though not necessarily destroyed. When the Cathedral and Baptistry chapels were reconstituted for the second time in 1540, under Duke Cosimo I, a conscious effort was made by the new chapelmaster, Francesco Corteccia, to supply the singers with new settings of hymns, motets, responsories, passions and perhaps even Masses, with music that was meant to supplant the mid- and late 15th century works that were no longer fashionable or deemed suitable for performance. Corteccia's efforts were supplemented by the acquisition of a good deal of new music for the chapel's use during the next several decades, as witnessed by a large number of payments to music copyists in Cathedral archives[45]. It is perhaps symptomatic of Florentine attitudes towards polyphony that many of Corteccia's

---

45. A sampling of documents relating to acquistions and music copying at Santa Maria del Fiore is in the Appendix, No. 12.

works and those of his contemporaries were themselves replaced by settings of the same or similarly suitable texts by Marco da Gagliano at the turn of the 17th century. But unlike the earlier works, some of Corteccia's works were kept and are in fact listed in the Cathedral inventory of 1651.

Savonarola's attitudes towards polyphony, while not ambivalent, were not totally negative. He clearly favored limiting the kind of music performed at church services to Gregorian chant. Neither was he averse to laudi singing, nor, as it turns out, to organ playing, and this despite his occasionally scathing references to the instrument. And though he has often been blamed for the loss of Florentine polyphonic musical sources of the later 15th century, the claim is not tenable insofar as sacred music is concerned. However devastating his reforms were to the Florentine musical establishment in the short term, in the long run they proved to be nothing if not epehemeral. How epehemeral they were is illustrated by a provision, made a few weeks before his death, for the resumption of performances of polyphonic music at the Cathedral. On 27 April 1498, after noting that a group of four adults and eight boys had sung during Holy Week and Easter just past, the Cathedral overseers reappointed the singers to serve in future at Masses, at Vespers and during Holy Week. It was this group that formed the nucleus of the new Cathedral chapel that came into being on 1 December 1501, to be followed, as I have noted, by reinstitution of chapels at the Baptistry and the Santissima Annunziata within a few years.

The lasting effect of Savonarola's preaching on the future development of Florentine polyphonic music was equally negligible. Though a rich legacy of polyphony in the form of canti carnascialeschi, ballate and others was purposely destroyed – a few examples of it, of course, do survive – extant sources from the early 16th century show that Florentine secular music was back on course within the decade after his death. In fact, polyphony was so deeply entrenched in the city's cultural life that when Carnival was resumed and private patrons once again began encouraging the production of music, new works by Coppini and Barolomeo degli Organi were so much in the spirit of earlier works by Isaac and others that it has not always been easy for modern-day scholars to distinguish between the two. Coppini's and Bartolomeo's secular music, though not plentiful, amply illustrates how the tradition continued even as it progressed and diversified. Moreover, an examination of their works, and of those of the next generation which included Bernardo Pisano and the young Francesco de Layolle, confirms that Florentine secular music pursued a course of its own, proceeding almost independently of contemporaneous developments in the north- Italian frottola production while remaining firmly grounded in earlier indigenous practice. Similarly, later, mature works, sacred as well as secular, by Layolle, Francesco Corteccia and Mattia Rampollini betray the continuing influence of Isaac as well as of their older Florentine contemporaries and offer further testimony to the vitality of that practice. These composers, as I remarked earlier, never had recourse to any of the musical legacy of Savonarola, nor were they inspired by his meditations, as were other composers throughout Europe[46]. It seems then that Florentine music developed in spite of the Savonarolan interlude. And if, as I believe, the early Cinquecento madrigal as exemplified by Verdelot's works, stemmed from Florentine musico-aesthetic principles and from Florentine musical practices such as the polyphonic canti carnascialeschi, ballate, dialogues and canzoni of Coppini, Bartolomeo and Pisano, then the impact of Savonarola's teachings must be seen as having imposed a fleeting and totally ineffectual respite within that development.

46. Most of the sacred works of the composers mentioned here are available in my *Music of the Florentine Renaissance*, American Institute of Musicology 1965); the few that are not will appear in future volumes of the series. On the continuing influence of Savonarola-inspired texts and music, see Macey, *Bonfire Songs* cit.

Appendix of Documents

(ASF=Archivio di Stato, Firenze)

No. 1

ASF, Archivio del R. Arcispedale di Santa Maria Nuova
1) Vol. 4503, Uscita, 1460-1462, f. 49v
A frate Giovanni, frate di Santa Chrocie, Fl. 6 larghi, e quali ebe insino adì 19 d'aprile 1461 per la sua faticha di temperare gli orgahni di San Gilio [...]
2) Vol. 4514, Uscita, 1477-1479, f. 112r
11 aprile 1478
A Gherardo di Giovanni, miniatore e nostro sonatore d'organi, Fl. quattro d'oro larghi, portò lui a libro segnato D, c. 16. Fl. 4
3) Vol. 5875, Libro mastro D, 1476-1487
a) f. 144r Spese di salari di questo spedale deono dare [...]
E a Girolamo d'Andrea cherico adì 7 d'aprile 1482 L. quarantuna s. X, dal quaderno salari c. 98, posto debbi avere in questo c. 212, per suo salaro per chericho e sonare gli orghani d'anni 2, mesi 2, dì 20, L. 41 s. 10.
b) f. 299v
Gismondo di Iachopo del maestro Angnolo, nostro sonatore d'orghani, inchominciò adì 8 d'aprile 1482, de' dare Fl. uno largo, portò e' detto insino adì XV di luglio 1482 [...]
4) Vol. 5683, Giornale e Ricordi A, f. 447v
1487
Gherardo di Giovanni di Miniato che ci suona gl'orghani nella nostra chiesa di San Gilio, chominciò a dì 24 di diciembre 1486, che insino a ttal dì tenemo Gismondo di Iacopo di maestro Agnolo, come si vede a libro biancho A, c. 143, cioè inchominciò a ssonare gl'orghani nella nostra chiesa di San Gilio a dì 24 di diciembre 1486 et dobbianli dare per suo salaro [gap] a libro biancho A, c. 174, apare il suo conto.
5) Vol. 5878, Libro mastro azzuro C, 1492-1496, f. 86r
Gherardo di Giovanni di Miniato, nostro orghanista [...]
E de' avere L. 320, sono per suo servito d'anni otto à sonato gl'orghani, cioè da dì XXIIII di dicembre 1486 insino a questo dì XXIIII di dicembre 1498, d'achordo cho' lui [...] L. 320
6) Vol. 5879, Libro mastro azzuro C, 1495-1497, f. 213r
Gherardo di Miniato nostro horganista de' avere [...]
E adì 3 d'agosto 1497 Fl. 10 d'oro in oro, paghati a Monte suo fratello e ereda chome della piensione della servita [...]
7) Vol. 5880, Libro mastro rosso D, 1497-1501, ff. 18v-19r
Frate Alessandro di Bartolomo di Marchione, fratte de' Servi, nostro chapelano e organista, de' dare L. X s. V d. XVIII piccioli per tantto debi avere [...]

Fratte Alessandro di Bartolomeo di chontro venne a servire nostro ispedale 6 di settembre 1497 e abi per chapellano e organisto e avere per suo salaro Fl. dieci larghi d'oro in oro l'anno.

E de' avere L. dieci quali sono per suo salaro di mesi tre serviti per sonare [...]

8) Vol. 4516, Uscita, 1504-1506

a) f. 2r 10 luglio 1504

A messer Andrea di Giovanni da Prato nostro organista L. ventuno e s. otto d. quattro, portò e' detto contanti, a libro rosso segnato 2 D, c. 225. Fl. 3 s. 4

b) f. 23v 29 ottobre 1504

A maestro Alessandro di Bartolomeo nostro organista Fl. dua d'oro in oro, L. 1 s. 8 piccioli, portò contanti a librso segnato A c. 125. Fl. 2. 1. 8

c) f. 35v 20 dicembre 1504

A frate Alessandro di Bartolomeo nostro organista Fl. dua d'oro in oro, portò e' detto contanti a libro giallo A, c. 125. Fl. 2

d) f. 104v 31 dicembre 1505

A nostra chiesa di Sancto Egidio L. 6 piccioli e per llei a maestro Pellegrino, frate de' Servi di Firenze, portò contanti frate Pagolo di Bernardo, frate in detto convento che ci suona gli organi, sono per limosina a detto maestro di sua predicationi, a libro giallo A c. 236. L. 6

No. 2

ASF, Corporazioni Religiose Soppresse, 119, Santissima Annunziata

1) Vol. 277, Giornale, 1450-1462

a) f. 8r 1450

Frate Biagio, organista, de' dare a dì 19 di dicembre Fl. cinque d. quattro [...]

b) f. 20v 1452 [1453]

Frate Biagio, organista, de' dare a dì 2 di gennaio per pagare l'organo ebi da llui in prestanze, L. 10

2) Vol. 689, Entrata & Uscita, 1451-1456

a) f. 96r 11 maggio 1451

A llimosine L. dodici, portò frate Biagio di Berto, organista e maestro de' novizi, portò de' dare a libro nero [...] sono per limosina gli fa el convento acioché possi soplize a bisogni della sua madre, e questo si fa pel sonare l'organo che egli fa in chasa; e questo è la limosina di gennaio, febraio e marzo 1450 e d'aprile 1451 a L. 3 el mese [...]

b) f. 247v 30 aprile 1455

A llimosina L. sei, portò frate Biagio, organista [...] per limosina di sonare l'organo in casa [...] L. 6

c) f. 268r 8 novembre 1455

Alla sagrestia Fl. uno largho, portò Piero d'Andrea vaiaio [...] sono per parte di magior somma de' avere di suo salario di sonare l'organo di casa a L. quattro s. 5 el mese [...]

d) f. 278r 22 febbrario 1455 [1456]
Alla sagrestia L. 5 s. 6, portò Piero d'Andrea vaiaio, organista [...]
e) f. 286r 29 maggio 1456
A Piero d'Andrea vaiaio L. 11 s. 8 à servito la casa a sonare l'organo [...]
3) Vol. 690, Entrata & Uscita, 1462-1469
a) f. 112r 30 aprile 1463
A frate Biagio d'Alberto da Firenze L. trentasei sono per salario gli dà el convento di mesi undici a L. tre al mese, cominciati a dì primo di giugno 1462, finiti per tutto aprile 1463, sono per sonare horgano in casa [...]
b) f. 134v 28 maggio 1464
A frate Biagio d'Alberto da Firenze L. trentasei, portò e' detto, sono per salario di uno anno per sonare l'organo in casa [...]
c) f. 254r 13 dicembre 1467
A frate Biagio d'Alberto da Firenze L. undici s. 8 [...] sono per sonare l'organo [...]
4) Vol. 691, Entrata & Uscita, 1469-1472
a) f. 40v 30 giugno 1470
A vestimento a dì decto L. otto s. dodici sono per resto del vestimento di frate Biagio d'Alberto di primo anno finito di giugno 1470, e L. diciotto, sono per resto della limosina gli dà l'anno il convento per l'organo a L. trentasei l'anno [...]
b) f. 98r 29 dicembre 1471
A vestimento a dì detto Fl. due larghi, portò frate Biagio organista, sono per parte di suo vestimento, L. 11.
A limosina a dì detto L. venti sono per limosina di mesi sei proximi passati per sonare l'organo in casa a L. quaranta l'anno, L. 20.
5) Vol. 693, Entrata & Uscita, 1475-1476
a) f. 18r luglio 1475
A Matteo cherico che canta adì 23 Fl. uno largho, è per lui a frate Alfonso, sono per parte di suo fadigha di notare certi quaderni grandi bolognesi di note [...] L. 5.13
b) f. 38r 13 april 1476
A Matteo chericho adì detto Fl. uno portò e' detto al q. c. 71, sono per resto di notatura di quaderni 11 di canto figurato à notati per la capella in casa, a libro rosso segnato B. L. 5. 13
6) Vol. 694, Entrata & Uscita, 1472-1473, f. 71r
3 febbraio 1472 [1473]
A frate Bernardo da Firenze a dì detto Fl. quattro larghi sono per parte di fl. dieci larghi et per suo vestimento di sonare l'organo, come apare a lib. Rosa s. B, c 89, portò lui detto contanti, L. 22.
7) Vol. 695, Entrata & Uscita, 1474-1475
a) f. 71r dicembre 1474
A frate Bernardo di Lucha da Firenze a dì 24 di detto Fl. due larghi sono per parte di limosina gli dà l'anno el convento per sonare l'organo [...]
b) f. 78r aprile 1475

A spese straordinarie a dì 21 di detto Fl. uno largho portò Matteo di Pagholo, chericho in San Giovanni, sono per sua faticha di notare messe e altre chose in chanto fighurato per la chappella della Nunziata, al quad. e a libro rosso., c. 179, L. 5. 12

8) Vol. 696, Entrata & Uscita, 1476-1477

a) f. 22r luglio 1476

A frate Bernardo L. 3 e s. 6 d. 8 a dì primo d'aghosto per sua limosina del mese passato si gli danno perché suona l'organo [...]

b) f. 40v aprile 1477

A llimosina a dì 30 decto L. Nove e s. Nove e d. 4 sono per limosina si gli dà per sonare l'organo del convento, portò frate Bernardo di Lucha [...]

9) Vol. 698, Giornale del Camerlengo, 1477-1479, f. 59r settembre 1478

A frate Bernardo di Lucha da Firenze a dì 11 di detto Fl. Tre larghi, portò lui detto in quatrini, presente el padre priore, sono per suo salario dell'organo, L. 17. 5

10) Vol. 246, Entrata & Uscita, 1479-82

a) f. 78r 19 marzo 1478/79

A ser Antonio, maestro di musica, a dì detto, L. quattro per chonto di canti notati e di suo salario d'insegnare in chasa chantare a' noviti et altri, a lib. s. G. c. 59, L. 4

b) f. 88v 5 giugno 1479

A straordinario a dì detto L. tre si dettono a ser Antonio di Marcho, chappellano in Santa Maria del Fiore, per sua fatica per avere schritto due quinterni notati di chanto figurato per quelli che 'nparano a chantare portò lui detto contanti in quatrini, a lib. s. G, c. 59, L. 3

[...]

A ser Antonio di Matteo [sic] a dì detto L. tre per resto di quinterni di canto figurato al convento, portò lui detto a lib. s. G c. 59, L. 3

11) Vol. 197, Debitori & Creditori, 1478-84, f, 223r

Ser Biagio di Giovanni prete ungharo de' dare a dì 28 di giugno 1481 L. tre per parte d'uno libro di chanto fighurato vendè al chonvento per pregio d'uno duchato a Usc. s. C, c. 203, L. 3. E adì 27 di luglio, L. 3 [...]

12) Vol. 247, Entrata & Uscita, 1482-86

a) f. 78v 8 maggio [1483]

A spese strasordinarie a dì detto L. due portò Matteo tedescho et cantore [sic] perché recò duo messe in canto figurato [...] L. 2

b) f. 81r marzo 1483

A spese strasordinarie Fl. tre larghi d'oro in oro per e quali pagò maestro Antonio [d'Alberto Alabante] sopradetto, quando era a Roma per fare notare cinque messe e tre mottetti e laudi et per far una collatione a' chantori del papa i quali dettono la chopia di dette messe e chanti [...] L. 18. 3

c) f. 83r 3 giugno [1483]

A spese strasordinarie a dì detto L. due per Iannes Vitine [?] cantore per duo messe recò da Roma e per più canti composti qui in convento [...] L. 2

(d) f. 130v 7 aprile 1484:

A spese di noviti a dì detto s. sette, portò il Grasso, sono per uno quinterno di fogli mezzani bolognesi per notare la messa s'ebe da Lorenzo [...] S. 7

VI

No. 3

ASF, Corporazioni Religiose Soppresse, 78, Badia di Firenze

1) Vol. 78, Debitori & Creditori, 1450-1460, f. 394r

Frate Biagio di Ruberto [sic, Alberto] de' frati di Santa Maria de' Servi di Firenze, suona gli organi nostri, de' avere L. quaranta otto di piccioli per suo salario e provisione d'uno anno cominciato a dì primo d'ottobre 1456 e finito a dì primo detto, 1457. E quali organi debbe sonare per le solepnità di che siamo d'accordo per una scripta nella nostra sacrestia e che lui tiene la copia. Et con questi pacti che per caso di moria la maggior parte de' monaci s'avessino a partire in modo che sonare non bisognassi, gliele dobbiamo manifestare et da quello dì in là non pagarlo, chome d'acchordo fu col nostra abbate don Luca et don Francesco, e cche appare a Ricordanze s. C, c. 121, L. 48.

2) Vol. 79, Debitori & Creditori, 1460-1471, f. 276r

Frate Biagio di [gap], frate di monasterio di Santa Maria de' Servi, sonatore de' nostri organi, deve avere a dì XXI di marzo 1468 [1469] L. quarantotto piccioli sono per suo provisione e salaro per sonare e nostri organi per uno anno cominciato fino a dì primo di gennaio 1468 [1469] e finito per tutto dicembre 1469, apare a lib. S. E, c. 46.

Dopo la morte d'Antonio di Mino, tintore, che prima gli sonava come appare in questo, L. 48.

E de' avere L. 48 piccioli sono per suo salario e provisione del sonare e nostri organi per uno anno incominciato a dì primo di gennaio 1469 [1470] e finito per tutto dicembre 1470, alla sagrestia a c. 71, L. 48.

E de' avere L. 48 piccioli per suo salaro d'uno anno per tutto dicembre 1471, L. 48.

3) Vol. 80, Debitori & Creditori, 1471-1482

a) f. 73r

Frate Bernardo di Luca da Firenze, frate di Santa Maria de' Servi, che suona li nostri organi, de' avere L. Quaranta otto piccioli, per tanti posto debba dare al libro verde segnato C, c. 276, dove di tanti ne restava creditore fatto creditore del suo salario per tutto dicembre 1471 a L. 48 piccioli per ciascuno anno, et dicieva la partita in frate Biagio d'Alberto.

b) f. 72v

Nota che lo sopradetto frate Bernardo non ci serve più perché gli fu necessario sonare alla sua chiesa di Santa Maria de' Servi.

c) f. 160v

Messer Antonio di [gap], canonico fesulano, de' avere Fl. dodici di sugello, sono per sua provisione overo salaro di uno anno finirà per tutto dì XIIII d'aghosto 1473 che ci à sonato li nostri organi di chiesa. Et confermo d'accordo co' llui che quello tempo servirà la casa in sonare detti organi, noi gli dobbiamo dare ciascuno anno di salaro Fl. XII di sugello [...]

4) Vol. 81, Debitori & Creditori, 1491-1506

a) f. 104r
Piero d'Andrea Mazzi, nostro sonatore dell'organo, de' avere Fl. 17 [...] sono per suo salario di uno anno comincaito a dì primo d'ottobre 1489 a ragione di Fl. Diciasette di sugello l'anno [...]
b) f. 332v
Piero d'Andrea Mazzi, nostro sonatore dell'organo [...] Nota che il sopradetto Piero passò di questa vita addì primo d'aprile 1502.
c) f. 373v
Michele di Bartolomeo Mazzi, nostro nuovo organista [...] per la sua provisione del sonare el nostro orghano di mese septe finiti per tutto ottobre proximo passato 1502, a ragione di Fl. Dodici larghi di grossi per qualunque anno, come si li è promesso nella nuova reconductione fatta a detto Michele per cagione della morte di maestro Piero Mazzi suo zio, ne' modi e co' patti che pienamente si dicono et appariscono alla ricordanze segnate H, c. 79. Nota che detto Michele morì a dì 11 di maggio 1505. Requiescat in pace.

No. 4

ASF, Corporazioni Religiose Soppresse, 83, Santa Felicita

1) Vol. 71, Debitori & Creditori B, 1492-1495
a) f. 36r 1492
Ser Ghuido di ser Nicholao notaio in vescovado e nostro organista de' avere a dì primo di novembre L. 22 per resto di suo conto [...] L. 22
E de' avere L. 20 sono per suo servito di mesi otto a ragione di L. 30 l'anno, cioè da dì primo di novembre 1492 per infino infino [sic] tuto dì trenta di giugno 1493 d'acordo insieme con ser Antonio di ser Nicolao suo fratello questo dì 29 di novembre 1493[...] L. 20
b) ff. 65 left and right 1493
Ser Nicolao di Matheo della Colomba da Pisa nostro orghanista de' dare a dì 13 di dicembre 1493 Fl. uno largho d'oro in oro, a lui detti contanti [...]
Ser Nicolao di Matteo nostro organista al incontro de' avere a dì 26 di dicembre 1493 L. 13 s. 2, sono per suo servito di sonare l'orghano per mesi 5 e mezo, cioè da dì 10 di luglio passato per infino a detto dì [...] L. 13. 2
c) ff. 65 left and right 1493 [1494]
Ser Giorgio di [gap] prete & orghanista della Magna [in margin: per infino] de' dare a dì 5 di gennaio 1493 [1494] L. una s. 10, contanti a lui per parte di suo salario [...] L. 1. 10
Ser Giorgio dalla Magna organista rincontro de' avere a dì primo d'ottobre 1494 L. 27, le quali sono per suo servito dell'orghano nostro di mesi nove, cioè da dì primo di gennaio 1493 [1494] per infino a detto dì, a ragione di L. 3 per mese [...] L. 27

VI

d) ff. 79 left and right 1494

Piero di Francescho di Nanni da Poggibonzi, tessitore di panilini e sonatore d'orghani, de' dare a dì 31 d'ottobre 1494 L. 2 piccioli [...] L. 2

Piero di Francescho nostro orghanista a rincontro de' avere a dì 31 d'ottobre 1494 L. 2 piccioli, le quali sono per suo servito del presente mese à sonato gli organi nostri che di tanti restano d'achordo.

E de' avere a dì ultimo d'aprile 1495 L. 12 piccioli per suo servito di mesi sei, cioè da dì primo di novembre 1494 per infino a detto dì 30 d'aprile 1495 [...] L. 12

2) Vol. 72, Debitori & Creditori C, 1495-1502

a) f. 39 right 1495

Piero di Francesco di Nanni da Poggibonzi nostro orghanista de' avere a dì primo di maggio 1495 L. 2 [...]L. 2

E de' avere a dì 15 di dicembre 1495 L. Quindici, sono per suo servito di mesi 7 e mezo, cioè da dì primo di maggio 1495 infino a detto dì, L. 15

b) ff. 120 left and right 1500

Ser Pellegrino del Monachetto da Prato, nostro sonatore d'orghani e capellano in chasa, de' dare a dì 21 di novembre 1500 L. otto piccioli [...]L. 8

Ser Pellegrino del Monachetto da Prato nostro capellano e sonatore de' avere L. 13 s. 4 piccioli per suo servito di mesi 4 e dì [gap], a ragione di L. 40 l'anno [...] L. 13. 4

3) Vol. 115, Ricordanze, 1485-1528

a) f. 26v 1493 [1494]

[margin: Ricordo di ser giorgio orghanista, posto a lib. Debitori e creditori s. B, a c. 63]

Ricordo chome oggi questo dì primo di gennaio 1493 [1494] togliemo per nostro organista per uno anno incominciando detto dì prete Giorgio di [gap] de Alamania al quale promettiamo dare per suo salario lire trentasei piccioli per detto anno. El quale ha promesso sonare nella chiesa nostra a uso di buon sonatore ne' tempi consueti secondo l'uso degli altri sonatori e così restamo d'acordo insieme.

Stette al servigio di detto organo mesi 9, cioè per tutto dì 30 di settembre decto.

b) f. 29r 1494

[margin: Ricordo di Piero da Pogibonsi orghanista]

Ricordo chome per insino a dì primo d'ottobre 1494 togliemo per nostro sonatore de'orghani Piero di [gap] et tessitore di panni lini, al quale siamo tenuti dare per suo salario L. due el mese, cioè L. 2 piccioli et così siamo restati d'acordo, chomiciò a sonare detto dì, cioè cominciò il tempo di suo salario.

c) f. 36r 1496

[margin: ser Andrea orghanista]

Ricordo come oggi questo dì primo di maggio 1496 ser Andrea di Niccolò cominciò a sonare gli orghani nostri di chiesa per anno uno, al quale siamo tenuti dare per suo servito di detto anno L. venti piccioli e così siamo restati d'acordo insieme questo dì 24 di maggio 1496.

d) f. 36v 1497

[margin: ser Raphaello]

Ricordo chome a dì 2 d'aprile 1497 venne a stare per chappellano di chasa in casa ser Raphaello prete fiorentino, ne' modi e patti e conventioni e salarii che gli altri chapellani con questo inteso per gratia e amore insegni a cherichuzi che servino la chiesa a leggere e a chantare et di tanto fare ha promesso di sua propria volontà.

Et a dì 20 di giugno 1497 si partì e andò a stare per capellano in Sancta Maria Nuova [...]

e) f. 41v 1499 [1500]

[margin: ser Mariano orghanista]

Ricordo chome per insino a dì primo di gennaio 1499 [1500] Mariano di Paolo Tucci nostro organista inchominciò a sonare l'orghano nostro in chiesa, al quale siamo contenti dare per suo salario ciaschun anno L. trenta et d'acordo insieme con detto [...]

[margin: ser Pellegrino da Prato]

Ricordo chome a dì 15 d'aghosto 1500 venne a stare in casa per capellano e sonatore degli orghani ser Pellegrino del Monachetto da Prato, el quale venne a stare a uso degli altri capellani di casa et sonare gli orghani, al quale si gli à a dare per suo salario L. quaranta piccioli ciaschun anno.

Partisse detto ser Pellegrino a dì 31 di dicembre 1500.

f) f. 43v 1500 [1501]

[margin: ser Antonio orghanista]

Ricordo come questo dì primo di gennaio 1500 [1501] venne a stare per chappellano di casa a uso degli altri ser Antonio Chroccia da Pistoia [...]

Partisse 20 d'ottobre 1509.

h) fol. 82v 1510

[margin: ser Tadeo da Pistoia capellano]

Ricordo come ser Tadeo di marioto da Pistoia venne per capellano et organista in Sancta Felicita per salario di L. quaranta l'anno et venne[...] a dì primo di dicembre 1509 [...]

Partì a dì 30 di giugno 1516.

No. 5

ASF, Corporazioni Religiose Soppresse, 122, Santo Spirito

1) Vol. 1, Libro Campione A, 1475-1494

a) ff. 118v-119r

Ricordo come Carlo de Burgis venne a stare con noi a dì primo di septembre 1486 per mezzo di frate Giovanni, pater noster, con patto ch'egli insegnassi a' novitii canto fermo e figurato e cantare in chiesa con loro, con salario di quatro lire il mese, che monta un anno lire quarantotto.

Carlo de Burgis de' dare a dì 16 di febraio 1486 [1497] lire una s. dieci per parte di sua ragione [...]

VI

E de' dare a dì 10 di gennaio 1487 [1488] lire tre e soldi tre per ogni suo resto avessi avuto affare col convento [...] L. 3 s. 3

b) ff. 178v-179r

Ricordo chome per insino a dì 19 di gebraio 1487 [1488] venne a stare con noi Giovanni Pintelli francioso per magistro del canto e per insegnare a' novitii canto figurato e per cantare insieme cogli altri, dandogli per ciascheduno mese lire quatro colle spese e la tornata di chasa servata cum honestate conventus.

Giovanni Pintelli francioso de' dare a dì [gap] di maggio 1488 Fl. Uno d'oro in oro per parte di suo salario valse lire sei soldi sette [...]

E de' dare a dì 20 di septembre 1488 lire nove e soldi dieci [...]

[margin: stette per insino a dì 20 di giugno 1488]

c) f. 196v

Frate Benedetto da Perettola sonatore degli organi de' avere da dì primo d'octobre 1490 per insino a dì ultimo di septembre 1491 lire trentasei per sonare gli organi a ragione di tre lire el mese. L. 36 [...]

E de' dare per l'anno 1493 per tutto septembre, L. 36

2) Vol. 8, Entrata & Uscita A, 1488-1496

a) f. 79v marzo 1487 [1488]

Item a dì 20 a frate Agnolo di Certaldo fl. tre d'oro in oro e per lui dua a frate Francesco e uno a bacciellere cathelario per uno libro di chanto figurato, valsono lire diciotto e soldi diciotto.

b) f. 91r septembre 1490

Inprima [a dì primo] a ser Guido lire quattro soldi dua per salario di mesi tre per sonare gli organi.

c) f. 115r gennaio 1495 [1496]

Inprima a dì 8 a frate Agostino sonatore lire dua al suo conto a libro segnato B, c. 59, L. 2.

d) f. 135r octobre 1497

Item per insino a dì 8 del mese passato a frate Agostino da Fivizano lire quaranta soldi uno per ogni suo resto avesse avuto affare del convento, cioè sonare gli organi e la predica di Certaldo, a suo conto a libro s. B, c. 59 in due partite, L. 40. 1

e) f. 137v gennaio 1497 [1498]

Item a dì detto [22] a ser Damiano da Lucha sonatore lire sei soldi quattordici per parte di sonatura di mesi due e mezo a lire tre el mese, L. 6. 14.

3) Vol. 9, Entrata & Uscita, 1498-1506

a) f. 77v dicembre 1501

Item a dì 20 a frate Martino e a frate Piero cantori, lire octo per l'andata alla Misericordia, L. 8

b) f. 86r 30 marzo 1502 [1503]

Item a Giovanni sonatore lire quatordici per parte di sonare li organi.

c) f. 87r 28 aprile 1503

Item al sacrestano lire dicianove soldi undi per comprare palme et uliva, pagare e cantori, el diacono et altre cose a sua entrata.

d) f. 88r giugno 1503
Item a dì per insino a dì 7 per la piatanza del mercholedì che furono le quattro tempore et per venerdì et sabato et per spese facte per cantori, sonatore, lire sette.

e) f. 107r 28 gennaio 1504 [1505]
Item a Baccino sonatore Fl. uno d'oro in oro per salario suo di dua mesi passati [...]

f) f. 108r 27 marzo 1505
Item a' cantori e al diacono lire tre.

g) f. 112r 1 novembre 1505
Item a Baccino sonatore Fl. uno d'oro in oro per ogni suo resto di sonare gli organi [...]

h) f. 116r luglio 1505
In primo a frate Andrea cantore lire sette, L. 7
Item a fra Benedetto sonatore lire sette, L. 7

4) Vol. 10, Entrata & Uscita, 1506-1512, f. 79r giugno 1509
Item a dì 6 a frate Giovanbaptista da Pisa lire trentauna soldi sedici danari nove per salario suo dell'organo e per insegnare noviti cantare, L. 31.16.9

5) Vol. 12, Entrata & Uscita, 1521-1526, f. 109r
resta della uscita di luglio 1522
Item a' cantori che cantarono le lamentationi e dì santi lire quatordici di contanti, L. 14

6) Vol. 127, Debitori & Creditori dell'Opera, 1471-1481, ff. 90v-91r
Maestro Bernardo priore del convento di Santo Spirito de' avere a dì 15 di febbraio 1474 [1475] L. cento s. XVI piccioli per deliberazione degli operai, rogate ser Francesco Siri sotto dì 23 di febbraio [...]che sono pe' gli orghani della chiesa. L. 100 s. 16

No. 6

ASF, Corporazioni Religiose Soppresse, 113, Santa Maria del Carmine

1) Vol. 87, Uscita, 1470-1478, f. 110r
Dicembre 1477
A frate Nicholò di Simone da Empoli per resto del salario di sonare l'orghano uno anno, cioè da dì primo di novembre 1476 per insino a dì primo di novembre 1477 lire dodici, sono del fitto del podere tien da noi a vvita posto all'entrata s. B, c. 240 [...]

2) Vol. 149, Debitori & Creditori, 1462-1490
a) f. 27r Salario de' cantori
Frate Nichlaio di Lanzalaglio e frate Giovanni cherico deno avere per fare la cantoria soldi dieci per uno, e quali cominciarono addì primo di maggio 1481, come apare in questo a c. 63. L. 1

b) f. 45r 1479

Fra Nicholò di Symone da Empoli ogi questo dì 9 di giugno 1479 ò fatto saldo oggi questo dì detto cho' Mateo di Francesco da Terzolla di tutto el grano à portato di qua a macinare [...]

c) f. 138r

Frate Nicholò di simone organista de' havere l'anno di salario per la sonatura dell'organo lire diciotto d'acordo cominciando oggi questo dì primo di novembre 1476, come apare in questo a c. 33, L. 18.

Et a dì 7 di dicembre 1477 L. quindici per resto di questo anno, chome apare di suo mano alle portate segnato A a c. 6 [...]

d) f. 151r

Fra Piero Biancho cominciò a sonare l'organo a dì primo di luglio 1490 per pregio di L. una el mese, sono l'anno L. dodici, et più una lire el mese quando desse a uno per imparare e non altro.

E anne avuto a dì 29 di luglio 1490 L. due [...]

Anne avuto a dì 23 di gennaio 1491 [1492] L. dua [...]

e) f. 153r YHS 1489

Sia noto e manifesto come ogi questo dì 30 di novembre 1489 el priore insieme co' distretti [e] con consentimento del padre provinciale concedono e son contenti dare a frate Alberto de' Bochacci da Chremona a sonare l'orghano nostro per uno anno cominciando a dì primo di dicembre 1489 seguendo per insino adì detto 1490. Con questi patti, cioè per suo salario L. ventiquattro, cioè L. 24 piccioli, pagando di mese in mese s. quaramta. Et più l'uificiatura della capella di san Jacopo per L. una il mese e lui è contento oltre al sonare l'orghano nostro a insegnare gratis per decto tempo a frate Piero di Giovanni da colonia o a un altro de' nostri se lui morissi o non volessi inparare. Et decto fra Piero s'obliga e sia obligato dare al decto frate Alberto ducati dua d'oro, cioè L. Una el mese. E più d'acompagnarlo alla capella e a quello medesimo sarà obligato quello che a llui succedessi morendo o non volendo imparare el decto fra Piero [...]

f) f. 324v Sabato a dì 9 di novembre 1497

A fra Piero sonatore degli organi e maestro de' novitii L. sei sono per parte di spesi de' noviti, a salario, L. 6

g) fol. 342r Mercholedì a dì 27 di giugno 1498

A fra Piero maestro de' novitii L. cinque s. quattordici per fare le spesi a' novitii.

No. 7

ASF, Corporazioni Religiose Soppresse, 88, San Pancrazio

1) Vol. 1, Memoriale A, 1478-1492, f. 2r

Messer Antonio che suona gli orghani qui a noi de' dare a dì 31 d'ottobre [1478] L. 4 s. 10, sono per valuta di barili 3 di vino vermiglio ebbe da noi, chome si vede al giornale segnato A a c. 5. L. 4 s. 1

2) Vol. 65, Ricordanze, 1475-1492, f. 37v

Richordo chome oggi questo dì VII di luglio 1490 abbiamo tolto per sonare l'orghano della badia nostra di san Panchratio ser Zanobi di Giovanni Lenzi per uno anno avenire, debbe chominciare a dì primo d'aghosto prossimo futuro 1490 chome seghue; e debbe avere in detto anno per suo salario e faticha di sonare L. trentatsei piccioli d'achordo chon detto ser Zanobi chon questi patti e modi: che detto ser Zanobi sia tenuto e debba sonare detto orghano o fare sonare quando fussi ochupata a altra persona che sappia quanto lui o più alla messa e al vespro in tutti i dì delle feste chomandate per lla santa chiesa chosì dì santi chome Domeniche e anchora debbe sonare nelle infrascritte solenità, cioè nella festività di santo antonio, di san Bastiano, di san Fabiano, di san Gregorio papa, di san Benedetto, di san Giovanni in porta latina, nella vittoria di san Michelagnolo, di san Panchratio, la visitatione della Vergine maria, di san Giovanni Ghualberto, di san Cosimo e Damiano, di san Geronimo, la traslatione di san Giovanni Gualberto, di san Salvadore, di santa chaterina, di santo Jacopho interciso, di san Bernardo veschovo, di san Nicholò, la concietione della Vergine maria, del agnolo Raffaello, e in questi e in altre feste s'avesino a fare in detta badia, cioè non sono chomandate per lla santa chiesa possi detto ser Zanobi la mattina desinare in chonvento cho' monaci, e anchora è tenuto detto ser Zanobi venire a sonare in alchune vigilie in fra l'anno, chome delle paschue e altre principale solenità secondo quando gli sarà mandato a dir dall'abate o sachrestano, et a fede di ciò perciò osservare l'uno a l'altro si soscriverà detto ser Zanobi qui da pie di sua propria mano.

Io do' Gregorio kamerlingho ò fatto questo cho' voluntà di messer Innocentio abbate di detto monastero al presente.

Io ser Zanobi di Giovanni Lenzi sono chontento ad quanto di sopra si chontiene e per fede di ciò mi sono soscripto di mia propria mano anno e mese e dì detto di sopra.

3) Vol. 39, Debitori & Creditori, 1493-1527
   a) ff. 13v-14r
Ser Zanobi di Giovanni Lenzi sonatore d'organi de' dare L. Dicianove piccioli ... per sua ragione d'anni due finiti insino a dì primo d'agosto 1492 ...
Ser Zanobi di Giovanni Lenzi di chontro de' avere L. Trentasei sono per suo salario d'uno anno à sonato gli orghani in casa finito a dì prima d'agosto 1493 ...
E de' avere a dì XXX d'aprile 1495 L. Ventisette per suo salario del sonare di mesi 9 finiti a detto dì che si partì ... L. 27
   b) ff. 39v-40r
Zanobi di Domenico di Zanobi nostro sonatore del orgahno [...] de' dare a dì XV d'agosto 1495 fl. uno largo d'oro in oro [...]
Zanobi di domenicho di contro de' avere L. XXXII s. XVII sono per sua faticha del sonare l'orghano che finì el tempo d'aprile 1496 [...]
   c) ff. 53v-54r
Zanobi di Domenicho che suona l'orghano [...] de' avere L. trentasei sono per suo salario d'uno anno che chominciò a dì primo di novembre 1498 e finità a dì primo detto 1499 [...]

d) ff. 77v-78r
Frate Ambrosio di maestro Gismondo da chortona frate in Santa maria dei Servi di Firenze e sonatore d'organi de' avere L. XXXX per suo salario e faticha di sonare l'organo nella nostra chiesa di San Pancrazio per uno anno chominciato a dì primo di gennaio 1500 [1501] e finiti per tutto il mese dicembre 1501 per tenpo secondo che arà guadagnato, e lui debbe venire a sonare mattine e dì di tutte le feste chomandate e vigilie di pasche e altre feste di divotioni sechondo che sarà richiesto chome si vede alle ricordanze segnato B c. 29. L. 40

Partissi detto frate Ambrogio del mese di giugno 1501, fornì di sonare detto mese frate Bernardo, già suo maestro che avea avere per detto mese L. 6[...]

4) Vol. 2, Ricordi B, 1493-1527, f. 91r

Ser Girolamo prete, d'Andrea d'Arigho da Firenze, sonatore d'organo nella nostra chiesa di San Pancrazio, de' avere L. Quaranta, sono per suo salario di sonare el nostro organo per uno anno per insino adì primo di luglio proximo passato 1501 [...]

Licenziosi detto ser Girolamo adì 8 di settembre [...] et però si chanciella [...]

No. 8

ASF, Corporazioni Religiose Soppresse, 102, Santa Maria Novella

1) Appendice Vol. 16, Entrata & Uscita, 1478-1488
a) f. 73v novembre [1478]
A frate Filippo sonatore a dì 24 Fl. tre larghi sono per parte di suo salario [...]
b) f. 75v
A frate Flippo sonatore a dì 12 di maggio 1479, L. undici s. dodici per parte di suo salario [...]
c) f. 80v
A ser Stefano che suona gli orghani a dì primo di luglio 1480 L. tre per parte di suo salario dell'orghano [...]
d) f. 95v
A ser Stefano sonatore a dì 20 luglio 1483 s. 10 sono per parte di suo salario [...]

2) Appendice, Vol. 19, Entrata & Uscita, 1488-1497
a) f. 64v febbraio 1488 [1489]
A ser Stefano sonatore a dì 13 detto Fl. uno largho d'oro in oro in moneta per la valuta sono per parte di suo salario degli orghani.
b) f. 104v 1494
A ser Stefano sonatore a dì 8 d'aghosto L. cinque s. tredici sono per ogni suo resto dal salario avuto a fare cholla sagrestia per insino a dì 5 d'aghosto 1494, chome apare alle ricordanze c. 17, L. 5.17
c) f. 109r 1494 [1495]
A Bacino nostro sonatore d'orghani per insino a dì 23 dì febbraio Fl. sei larghi d'oro in oro, i quali ebbe in tre volte lui contanti, L. 39. 12

d) f. 110v
A Baccino organista dì 19 di dicembre 1502 Fl. Due larghi d'oro in oro sono per parte i suo salario [...]
e) f. 111r
A ser Girolamo d'Andrea nostro organista a dì 23 di febbraio 1502 [1503] L. otto, sono per parte di suo salario alle ricordanze c. 54.
f) f. 116r [1504]
A ser Girolamo sonatore per insino a dì 4 d'aprile L. quattordici sono per parte di suo salario [...]
A Baccio di Michelagnolo per insino a dì 4 d'aprile 1504 L. 14 per noi da frate Piero di Benedetto [...]
g) fol. 166v 1510
A ser Girolamo sonatore a dì 30 di marzo L. sette [...]
3) Appendice, Vol. 1, Ricordanze 1510-1527
a) f. 50r 1512 [1513]
A ser Girolamo orghanista a dì 22 di febbraio L. quatordici per parte di suo salario [...]
b) f. 55r 1524
Ser Girolamo nostro organista ha havuto dalla nostra sagrestia maggiore oggi questo dì 25 di maggio 1524 L. sette piccioli, sono per parte di suo salario degli orghani [...]
A ser Girolamo detto a dì 3 di novembre 1526 L. quattordici piccioli sono per parte di suo conto [...]
c) f. 57r 1526 [1527]
Ser Girolamo nostro orghanista ha havuto della nostra sagrestia a dì 12 di gennayo 1526 [1527] L. sette piccioli per parte di suo salario [...]
anne hauto oggi questo dì 24 di gennaio 1527 [1528] il sopradecto ser Girolamo L. quatordici per parte di suo conto [...]

No. 9

ASF, Corporazioni Religiose Soppresse, 79, Sant'Ambrogio

1) Vol. 21, Entrata & Uscita, 1469-1471
a) fol. 62v Uscita 1470
A prete Karlo di Giovanni sonatore a dì 22 detto [luglio] fiorino uno largho portò e' detto contanti a libro I a c. 163. L. 5 s. 10
b) fol. 63v 1470
A prete Karlo di Giovanni sonatore degli orghani a dì 23 di settembre fiorino uno largo portò contanti a libro segnato C a c. 168. L. 5. 9
2) Vol. 57, Debitori & Creditori, 1481-1487, ff. 109 left and right
Piero di Matteo orghanistro nostro de' dare a dì 2 di luglio 1484 Fl. uno s. quatro, portò e' detto chontanti, avuta E c. 158 [...]

VI

Piero di Matteo dirinchontro, nostro organistro, de' avere a dì 15 di maggio 1484 Fl. otto di sugiello e quali sono per la sua faticha per sonare detto orghano che chosì abbiamo per obrigho di dare anno per anno [...]

E de' avere da dì 14 di magio 1485 per sino a dì 15 di magio 1487 che sono anni dua Fl. sedici di sugiello [...]

3) Vol. 58, Debitori & Creditori, 1487-1492, f. 62 left
1487

Piero di Matteo nostro organistro de' avere dal nostro munistero anno per anno per sua faticha per sonare l'orghano della nostra chiesa tutti e dì chonsueti Fl. otto di sugiello. . . .

E de' avere per tutto dì 15 d'aprile 1490 che sono mesi cinque e dì quindici Fl. tre s. tredici d. 4 [...]

Piero di Matteo organista de' havere [...] per resto di suo servito per insino a dì 11 di giugno 1492 [...]

4) Vol. 59, Debitori & Creditori G, 1492-1508, ff. 185 left and right
1495

Ser Carlo di Jacopo del maestro agnolo nostro organista de' dare a dì 12 di luglio 1495 L. sei piccioli [...]

Ser Carlo di Jacopo del maestro Agnolo de' havere Fl. otto di sugiello, sono per suo provisione per sonare l'organì primo anno cominciato a dì 12 di marzo 1494 [1495] [...]

E a dì 24 di giugno 1503 L. ventuno [...]

5) Vol. 60, Debitori & Creditori H, 1501-1512, f. 112 right

Ser Carlo di Iachopo del maestro Angniolo nostro orghanista [...] de' avere L. trentacinque s. XVIII d. 8, sono per suo servito di mesi undeci, cioè per tutto dì 12 di febraio 1504 [1505] e detto dì finì il tempo suo. L. 35. 18. 8

No. 10

Firenze, Biblioteca Medicea Laurenziana, Archivio Capitolare di San Lorenzo

1) Vol. 2467, Entrata & Uscita dal 1451 al 1453
a) f. 22r 1451
Uscita di vino
Al maestro Matteo organista nostro barili sei di vino [...] L. 5 s. 8
b) f. 121v [1451]
La sagrestia di Sancto Lorenzo de' avere [...]
A me avuto paghato a Maestro Matteo che suona gli orghani in chasa [...] L. 3 s. 15
2) Vol. 1927[1], Libro di sagrestia segnato G, 1472, f. 37r
Piero d'Andrea organista de' avere l'anno di suo salario lire sessanta. L. LX
3) Vol. 1928[1], Libro di sagrestia segnato L, 1476, f. 35r
organista

SACRED MUSIC IN FLORENCE IN SAVONAROLA'S TIME 351

Piero d'Andrea rigattiere de' avere l'anno per suo salario lire sexanta.
organista
Ser Domenico, capellano in Orzanmichiele, cominciò a servire adì 15 di dicembre, per pregio di lire sexanta l'anno [...] L. 60

4) Vol. 1928^2, Libro di sagrestia segnato M, 1477, f. 41r
Ser Domenico d'Andrea de' avere l'anno per sonatura dell'organo lire sessanta. L. 60
Partissi adì 25 di dicembre
Ricordo chome adì primo di gennaio [1478] venne a stare per sonatore d'organo Antonio di Marco, de' avere per suo salario lire 48 l'anno. L. 48

5) Vol. 1929^1, Libro di sagrestia segnato O, 1479, f. 55v
Antonio di Marcho Lippi, nostro sonatore, de' havere l'anno per suo salario lire quarantotto. L. 48

6) Vol. 2366, Partiti A. 2, 1482-1501
a) f. 3r 1482
[margin: Acresiamento del salario dell'organista]
Addì 26 di dicembre 1482 si vinse capitularmente che ser Antonio organista dovesse havere per suo salario ogn'anno lire sessanta dalla sagrestia cominciando detto salario addì primo di gennaio 1482 [1483].

b) f. 26v 1488
Adì 20 d'octobre 1488 ordinammo il salario a ser Antonio di Marco organista, nostro organista, di lire cento l'anno cominciando decto salario adì primo di novembre proximo futuro, con questo che non faccia sonare ad altri sanza licentia sotto la pena di quella apuntatura parrà al priore e così quando mancassi et non fussi al porto.

c) f. 52r 1494
Ricordo come adì 5 di septembre 1494 per cagione di certa differentia exorta fra 'l capitolo nostro e ser Matteo di Pagolo, cappellano di San Lorenzo al titolo a cappella di San Lorenzo, per sè come cappellano di dicta e predicta cappella o non cappellanea d'accordo feciono generale compromesso [...]

d) f. 57v 1496 Maggio
[margin: Substitutione di ser Zanobi organista]
Adì 27 di decto in Capitolo per loro partito vinto sustituirono alla cappella di ser Antonio da Prato Vechio per la messa piana [...] ser Zanobi di Ludovico Guidetti, nostro organista, debba cominciare adì primo di giugno 1497 e seguire al loro beneplacido, celebrando ogni mattina debba havere per sua helemonsina dal decto ser Antonio per ciascuno anno lire sessanta piccioli.

e) f. 74v 1498
[in margin: Electione dell'organista]
Item adì 31 di gennaio [1499] congregato el nostro capitolo ut supra et avendo notitia come ser Zanobi Guidetti, al presente nostro sonatore del nostro organo, cioè novamente era stato electo sonatore dell'organo di Santa Crocie, come da llui piena rilatione avemmo, in suo luogo e per nostro sonatore elegemmo ser Andrea di [gap]

da Prato detto Galloria, degno e sufficiente sonatore col medesimo salario. Sanza rogò.

f) f. 77r 1499

Item adì 10 di decto [giugno] si fermò el salario di lire cento a prete Andrea Galloria l'anno per la sonatura dell'organo incominciando decto salario adì prima di decto.

g) f. 77v 1499

Item dicto dì [10 luglio] si die licentia a ser Matteo di Pagolo nostro cappellano d'andare al bagno Monte Catini, lasciando ongni dì la messa in suo luogo.

h) f. 88v Die 30 novembris 1500

[margin: Renuntio dell'organista/ Electio dell'organista]

Essendo congregato el nostro capitolo ut supra venne in capitolo prete andrea da Prato decto Galloria, sonatore d'organi, interamente e di suo propria volontà renuntiò al sonare del nostro organo che più tempo era stato nostro sonatore.

Et statim sine intervallo in luogo del predetto eleggiemmo per sonatore del nostro organo col medesimo salario che aveva el sopradecto, maestro Alexandro di [gap] de' Servi. Sanza rogò.

7) Vol. 2181, Partiti, A. 3, 1501-1516

a) f. 25r Die 12 novembris 1503

[margin: Privatio & electio organista]

Congregato el nostro capitolo ut supra et essendo a quello noto publice come maestro Alexandro, frate de' Servi, nostro sonatore dell'organo, molto male ci serviva del sonare in modo che al Capitolo e a nostri parrochiani generava grande schandolo, onde per essere meglio servito la nostra chiesa e per levar via la spese grande e essere mal serviti, capitularmente decto maestro Alexandro fu privato della sonatura del nostro organo; in luogo di questo statim fu dal Capitolo nostro electo ser Mariotto di [gap], prete allenatosi nel monastero di S. Niccolò di Cafaggio di Firenze, con salario ciascun anno di L. 60 e à a sonare tutte le feste comandate e molte altre secondo la nota glisarà data.

b) f. 76r 5 settembre 1511

Essendo stato richiesto el Capitolo nostro da più persone e più volte d'uno sonatore pel nostro organo maxime perché messer Mariotto, presente nostro sonatore è stato facto piovano di Rubbiano, e per levarsi noi da questa molestia e per non esser ongnidì per ciò ricerchi, capitularmente eleggiemmo in futuro sonatore Bastiano di Gherardo, decto el Pretino, per L. 48 ciascuno anno per suo salario e questa s'intenda quando el decto messer Mariotto non volesse più sonare lui.

8) Vol. 1, Partiti B, 1516 (-1544)

f. 25r Die XI Maij 1519

Coadunato Capitolo fu vincto uno partito per omnium fabas nigras per il quale fu data comessione al K[amerleng]o che paghassi li cantori che havevano cantato le Lamentationi et li riponsi questa Septimana Sancta passata secondo che havevano havuto li altri anni [...]

No. 11

ASF, Corporazioni Religiose Soppresse 89, Santa Trinita

1) Vol. 50, Ricordi, 1519-1566, f. 18r

Ricordo come io don Vincentio, abbate di Santa Trinita, per conservatione del nostro organo mi sono convenuto con Mariano di domenico di Mariano d'Arezzo di darli lire XIIII l'anno et lui sia obligato mantenerci l'organo, cioè accordarlo e prepararlo ogni volta sia di bisogno, cioè a requisitione del organista, et per fede di suo proprio mano ho scripto questo ricordo oggi questo dì 16 di septembre 1525.

2) Vol. 72 Debitori & Creditori di Chiesa, Entrata & Uscita della Sagrestia, 1522-1548

a) f. 3v

Ser Lexandro detto el Gragniolo, nostro organista, de' dare L. sette, portò contanti per parte di suo salario a dì 13 di augusto 1522, a uscita segnato R, c. 80. L. 7
[...] E a dì 23 di septembre 1526, L. 14. L. 14

b) f. 36v

Frate Martino di Martino, frate di Santa Maria de' Servi, al presente habitante in San jacopo Canpo Cartolini, ha tolto a sonare el nostro organo nel modo consueto per pretio di L. sessanta per ciaschuno anno da incominciarsi questo dì 24 di dicembre 1531, pagandolo di uno mese in mese come segue posto in questo c. 48.

c) f. 67r 1541

Io fra Martino, frate de' Servi et organista di Santa Trinita, ho ricevuto questo dì 24 di novembre L. settanta piccioli, e quali ho ricevuto per resto di mio servito per sonare l'organo per tutto il tempo ch'io ho servito per infino a detto dì, sono stati anni 10 et di tanto mi chiamo contento [...]

No. 12

Firenze, Archivio dell'Opera di Santa Maria del Fiore

1) VIII. 3. 120, Entrata & Uscita, 1540, f. 30v

A paramenti d'Opera, L. 22. 10 p[iccio]li, per lui a messer Francesco Corteccia, sono per uno libro di musica, sciolto, venuto da Lione per Sua Excellenza. L. 22.10

2) VIII. 3. 121, Entrata & Uscita, 1541, f. 32r

A ser Giovampiero di Niccolò Masacconi, adì detto [1 ottobre] lire 14, portò contanti a buon conto, per avere scripto music. L. 14

3) VIII. 3. 124, Entrata & Uscita, 1542 [43], f. 30r

A ser Gianpiero Masacconi L. 21 p[iccio]li, per conto della musica che scrive per Sua Excellenza, per tanti fattonelo creditore al quaderno, a c. 32. L. 21

4) VIII. 1. 228, Quaderno di cassa, 1565, f. 61, left and right sides

Ser G[i]anpiero Masachoni, iscrivano di cappella, de' dare L. 192, consegniatocelo el quaderno 5o da c. 72, posto avere in questo, c. 74. L. 192

E de' dare addì 28 d'agosto lire ottantasette s. XII d. VIII, portò contanti, per resto di questo contto. L. 87 s. 12 d. 7

Ser G[i]anpiero di contro de' avere adì 28 d'agosto lire dugentosetantanove s. XII f. VIII, se gli fanno buoni per ispese d'opera, e sono per le notte [recte, note] d'uno libro di moteti e uno di magnifichate e uno di passi, fatici a S. XVIII l'una delle carte, e sono cartte 307, e per 4 quaderni di fogli, per lire 3.6.8, per n° 33. L. 279.12.8

5) VIII. 3.169, Entrata & Uscita, 1565, f. 42r

A dì 8 agosto

A spese d'opera L. 279 s. 12 d. 8 è per loro a maestro Gianpiero Masachoni, che L. 276 s. 6 d. 6 sono per la condotta di 307 carte iscritte in un libro di mottetti e uno libro di magnificat covertato di nero e l'altro in g[i]allo iscrittoci e uno libro di pasi[oni] e mottetti iscrittoci tutto per s. 19, e L. 3. 6. 8 per valuta di 4 quaderni di fogli per detti libri. L. 279.12.8

6) VIII. 3. 170, Entrata & Uscita, 1566, f 45v

A dì 27 aprile 1566

A spese d'opera L. 105. 10 a maestro Gianpiero di Niccolò Masaconi per avere iscritto 14 charte di musica, cioè 7 di messe di congiunto e 7 di motteti. L. 105. 10

7) VIII. 3. 175, Entrata & Uscita, 1568, f. 47r

A dì 20 novembre 1568

A spese d'opera L. 5 s. 8 a ser Gianpiero di Nicholò Masachoni e sono per 6 charte iscritte di musicha a s. 18 la charta per motteti in chiesa. L. 5.8

8) VIII. 3. 180, Entrata & Uscita, 1570 [71], f. 47r

A dì 16 febraio

A spese d'opera L. 145 a ser Gianpiero di Nicholò Massachoni sono per aver iscritto e rigato un libro di messe di musicha per la chapella di N° 116, a L. 1 s. 5 la charta. L. 145

VII

HEINRICH ISAAC IN FLORENCE: NEW AND UNPUBLISHED DOCUMENTS

WELL over three decades ago in an article for *Grove's Dictionary* Charles Sanford Terry drew a biographical sketch of Heinrich Isaac that, because of its logical deductions and lucid prose style, may still be regarded as the definitive and most readable account of the composer's life in any language.[1] Since Terry's time increasing interest in Isaac's music has occasioned further publication and study of his works. Surprisingly, however, little has been added to our knowledge of his biography. The year and place of his birth in Flanders, for example, as well as the cathedral school at which he was trained are still not known. The present study, based for the most part on unpublished Florentine documents, attempts only to bring into focus the events of the last thirty years of his life, from the time he is first mentioned in Florence until his death there in 1517. His activities during the years preceding his association with Florence must remain unknown for the time being, pending further research in the archives of his homeland.

In the course of a recent article Claudio Sartori raised the possibility that Isaac may have resided in Florence several years before the commonly accepted date of his arrival there, c. 1484.[2] Sartori's suggestion

[1] *Grove's Dictionary of Music and Musicians*, 3rd ed., London, 1927, II, 739 ff. In the present study all information based on non-Florentine sources is taken from Terry's article, where reference is made to the publications in which the original documents first appeared. For the sources and modern editions of Isaac's music see G. Reese, *Music in the Renaissance*, rev. ed., New York, 1959, pp. 169 ff., 212 ff., 647 ff.

The following abbreviations are used in this article:
ASF   Archivio di Stato, Firenze
MAP   ASF, Medici avanti il Principato
NAC   ASF, Notarile ante-cosimiano
SMDF   Archivio dell' Opera di Santa Maria del Fiore, Firenze
SMN   ASF, Archivio del R. Arcispedale di Santa Maria Nuova
SSA   ASF, Corporazioni Religiose Soppresse No. 119, Santissima Annunziata

[2] C. Sartori, *Organs, Organ-Builders, and Organists in Milan, 1450-1476: New and Unpublished Documents*, in *The Musical Quarterly*, XLIII (1957), 63.

was based on a passing remark made in a letter written by the Milanese organist Passino di Eustachio to Duke Galeazzo Maria Sforza on February 14, 1474 — namely, that a certain *Misser Ysacch* had been the pupil of Maestro Antonio del Bessa of Florence.[3] If the *Ysacch* in question were in fact the composer, there would be little doubt that he was in Florence at least a decade before he is first mentioned in the surviving Florentine documents. The possibility would also exist that he had received his training from some Florentine master, rather than at a cathedral school in the north. Both possibilities, however, seem highly unlikely to this writer. What is more probable is that the *Ysacch* referred to in the letter, which was after all written by an organist who was concerned with other organists and organ builders, was none other than the Greek-Florentine organist Isac. Argyropoulo.[4] As Sartori has shown, Argyropoulo was associated with the Milanese court just around that time and was certainly known to both Passino and the Duke. Furthermore, as will be noted below, the Florentine documents make it quite clear that the composer was a singer by profession, not an organist.

Documents indicating the exact date of Isaac's arrival in Florence have not come down to us. But he must have arrived there to take up a permanent post sometime during the late fall of 1484, for he is recorded as having passed through Innsbruck on his way south during the middle of September of that year. Though he may have visited or even worked in Italy before, the Innsbruck document suggests that at the time he was traveling to Florence directly from his northern home-

[3] Sartori, *loc. cit.*, believes del Bessa to be the organist Antonio Squarcialupi. Although Sartori's deduction seems logical, it should be noted that Florentine documents of the period never refer to Squarcialupi by that name, but rather as Antonio di [the son of] Bartolomeo or Antonio degli Organi. It is also worth noting that the account books of one Florentine church, the Badia, record a Lionardo di Bartolomeo *vocato il Besso*, an organist who received a payment from that church for several months' service on November 8, 1444. (ASF, Corporazioni Religiose Soppresse No. 78, Badia di Firenze, *Debitori e Creditori*, Vol. 77, fol. 244ʳ.)

[4] On Argyropoulo, see A. Cappelli, *Giovanni ed Isacco Argiropulo*, in *Archivio storico lombardo*, Serie II, VIII (1891), 168 ff. An undated letter to Lorenzo de' Medici from someone named *Isac*—undoubtedly Argyropoulo—also suggests that the Greek had studied with Squarcialupi, and thus helps to support Sartori's assumption regarding the identity of Maestro Antonio del Bessa. In the letter (most recent publication in B. Becherini, *Un Canta in Panca Fiorentino, Antonio di Guido*, in *Rivista musicale italiana*, L [1948], 247) the writer apologizes for not yet having found time to repair Lorenzo's clavichord, and adds that not even Maestro Antonio, who was then ill and away at the baths, had been able to repair the instrument. Argyropoulo was apparently a great favorite of Lorenzo, who wrote letters in his behalf on May 9, 1477; January 29, 1478; and February 4, 1478. See M. del Piazzo (ed.), *Protocolli del Carteggio di Lorenzo il Magnifico per gli anni 1473-74, 1477-92* ("Deputazione di storia patria per la Toscana," Documenti di storia italiana, Serie II, II), 8, 36, 37.

land and that he had stopped en route before resuming his journey. Indeed, a letter written in his behalf some thirty years later informs us that Lorenzo de' Medici had sent "as far away as Flanders" to call the composer to Florence.[5]

It is not surprising to learn that Lorenzo was personally responsible for bringing Isaac to Florence. Since shortly after their rise to power, the Medici had consistently pursued a policy of engaging foreign musicians for the chapels at the city's Cathedral and Baptistry, as well as for their own private chapel.[6] And Lorenzo's predilection for music surpassed even that of his father and grandfather. How eagerly and with what enthusiasm Lorenzo entered into the lively competition of securing the services of the best musicians of the day! The success of his endeavors is revealed by the names of singers employed in Florence during the closing years of the century, among them Piero Martini, Niccolò di Lore, Eustache Havresse, Johannes Stochem, Cornelio di Lorenzo, Tommaso and Giovanni Pintelli, Charles de Launoy, Pietrequin, Johannes Ghiselin, and Alexander Agricola.[7] But despite the arrival of so many illustrious musicians, Isaac remained the unique ornament of the Florentine chapel, held in the highest esteem and affection by his patrons and the populace alike.[8]

Historians have assumed that Isaac's duties in Florence also comprised those of music master to Lorenzo's two eldest sons, Piero and Giovanni (later Pope Leo X). The assumption, though not corroborated by any of the existing documents, seems reasonable in view of Leo X's excellent musical background. Isaac remains the most logical candidate for the position of music master to the future pope simply by virtue of his protracted stay in Florence. But the concern that Leo displayed for Isaac's welfare in later years also points to a close bond between the two. And that bond undoubtedly had its roots in the days when Leo, still under the paternal roof, had received encouragement in his musical aspirations and a thorough training as well from the foreigner so esteemed by his father.

Tradition has it that Isaac provided music for one of Lorenzo's principal poetic works, the religious drama *La Rappresentazione di San*

---

[5] The letter, written by the Florentine Niccolò de' Pitti on May 13, 1514, is given in translation below.

[6] See my *The Singers of San Giovanni in Florence during the 15th Century*, in *Journal of the American Musicological Society*, XIV (1961), 314 ff.

[7] *Ibid.*, p. 331 ff.

[8] See Niccolò de' Pitti's letter below. See also F. Ghisi, *I Canti carnascialeschi nelle fonti musicali del XV e XVI secolo*, Florence, 1937, 41, for reference to a letter of June 25, 1491, in which Lorenzo speaks of his high regard for Isaac's music.

Giovanni e Paolo. Although the music has not survived, a setting by Isaac of one of Lorenzo's *canzoni a ballo, Un dì lieto giammai,* testifies to the artistic collaboration between musician and patron. Indeed, in the preface to one of the earliest printed collections of *canti carnascialeschi,* edited by Il Lasca in 1559, Isaac was credited with having composed the first polyphonic setting of a carnival text by Lorenzo that was sung in Florence.[9] Il Lasca also reports that Isaac was master of the chapel at the Baptistry of San Giovanni during the time of Lorenzo de' Medici.[10] And since the Baptistry's singers performed at the Cathedral also, Isaac must have directed the chapel at that church as well. There is no proof that Il Lasca's report is correct, but there is also no proof to the contrary.

Isaac is first mentioned in Cathedral archives in a list of the singers of San Giovanni who were readmitted to the Cathedral's service in July 1485. In that document he is called Arrigo da Fiandra, *chantore.*[11] He was employed at the Cathedral until the end of March 1493, and in all subsequent payments from that church he is referred to as either *chantore* or *chonponitore,* but never as *maestro di cappella* (Docs. 1-5).[12] But neither is any other singer named as master of the chapel during these years. The same situation prevails in the account books of the Santissima Annunziata, the third church at which the singers of San Giovanni performed.[13] Now it may be that the scribes who recorded the payments simply did not bother to qualify Isaac's position among the singers of San Giovanni. Or it may be that his duties were specified in other documents now lost. Certainly, the close rapport that he maintained with the Medici as well as the length of his stay in Florence suggest that Il Lasca was not mistaken in naming him master of the Florentine chapel.

It is clear from the same account books, however, that Isaac never

---

[9] Quoted in F. Ghisi, *op cit.,* p. 2.

[10] *Ibid.*

[11] D'Accone, *op cit.,* 338. It should be noted that Florentine documents of the period refer to Isaac as Arrigo da Fiandra or Arrigo di Ugo da Fiandra. He himself used the latinized form of his name, Henricus Yzac de Flandria, when acknowledging payment of salary in the Santissima Annunziata's receipt registers. (SSA, *Ricevute,* Vol. 1050, fols. 114ᵛ, 126ᵛ, 163ʳ.) See the illustration.

[12] The documents will be found in the Appendix to this article.

[13] D'Accone, *loc. cit.* Isaac was late in joining the chapel at the Santissima Annunziata, for it is only in 1491 that his name begins to appear regularly in that church's account books (Doc. 6). Since San Giovanni's account books from these years are lost, it is impossible to know when Isaac began serving there. But it cannot have been any earlier than November 1484, the approximate date of his arrival in Florence.

served as organist at any of the three churches mentioned above. Nor is he mentioned in that capacity in the existing account books of any other major Florentine church. Since documentary sources concerning the Cathedral's organists were employed some twenty-five years ago in an article by Emilio Sanesi, it is surprising to find that recent biographies of Isaac continue to speak of him as organist at that church.[14] Sanesi correctly reported that Antonio Squarcialupi was succeeded as organist at the Cathedral by his son Francesco, who held the post until his death on December 12, 1509. The composer Bartolomeo di Michelangelo was then appointed to the position, and he remained associated with the church for the next thirty years. At the Baptistry Antonio Squarcialupi was followed by Ser Feo di Giuliano, who in turn was succeeded in 1501 by Ser Zanobi Ghuidetti, musicians otherwise unknown to historians.[15] During the period that Isaac was in Florence the Santissima Annunziata employed eight organists, the most famous of whom was Alessandro Coppini.[16] It is obvious therefore that the assumption that Isaac was employed as organist at the major Florentine churches is without any documentary foundation whatsoever.

Isaac's marriage to Bartolomea, daughter of a Florentine butcher named Piero Bello, must have taken place sometime during the late 1480s. The record of the marriage tax paid to the city, which would have given the marriage date, has not survived. Neither has the marriage contract. In the notes accompanying the publication of Isaac's last will Gaetano Milanesi reported that Bartolomea had brought one half of a small farm with a gentleman's and tenant's house as her dowry.[17] Nevertheless, in a tax report filed for the Florentine government in 1480 Piero Bello declared that his daughter Bartolomea, then approaching her sixteenth birthday, was "without a dowry and without a husband."[18] In Florence Piero Bello and his family lived in a modest house on the Via del Ariento in the parish of San Lorenzo, a stone's throw from the

---

[14] E. Sanesi, *Maestri d' organo in Santa Maria del Fiore, 1436-1600*, in *Note d' archivio*, XIV (1937), 171 ff.

[15] ASF, Archivio dell' Arte di Calimala, *Deliberazioni*, Vol. 28, fol. 11^v; *Deliberazioni*, Vol. 58, fol. 32^v.

[16] SSA, *Entrata e Uscita*, Vol. 246, fols. 131^r, 148^r, 173^v; *Entrata e Uscita*, Vol. 247, fols. 106^r, 261^r; *Entrata e Uscita*, Vol. 699, fols. 36^r, 49^r, 84^r; *Vestimenti*, Vol. 857, fols. 88^r, 137^r.

[17] G. Milanesi, *Communicazione: Maestro Arrigo Isach*, in *Rivista critica della letteratura italiana*, III (1886), 187.

[18] ASF, Archivio del Catasto, *Campione delle Portate dei Cittadini: San Giovanni, Leon d'Oro, 1480*, Vol. 1017, fol. 315^r. Bartolomea's baptismal date is given as Wednesday, May 16, 1464, in Cathedral archives. (SMDF, *Libro Battesimi, Maschi e Femmine: 1460-1466*, fol. 104^r.)

Medici palace. And his farm outside the city was in the neighborhood of Careggi, the seat of one of the Medici's country estates. He must have been a friend of the Medici, for the letter referred to above informs us that Lorenzo arranged for Isaac's marriage to Bartolomea. Another of Piero Bello's daughters, Margherita, was also given in marriage to a musician, the Frenchman Charles de Launoy. Isaac's marriage was apparently a happy one, for several documents from the following years attest to his concern that his wife, who, following the custom of the times, was evidently a good many years younger than he, should be well provided for after his death.

On February 13, 1489, Isaac's name appears for the first time in the notary acts of the Florentine lawyer Ser Giovanni Carsidone. All legal documents that the composer had drawn up during his years in Florence were subsequently handled by Carsidone. In this first document it is recorded that Isaac and a certain Lorenzo Gianberti had agreed to name a third party, Piero Buonaveri, as arbiter in the settlement of their financial differences (Doc. 7). The agreement was nullified only two weeks later when, in a document dated February 27, 1489, Gianberti acknowledged a debt of over one hundred and twenty lire to Isaac, and agreed to pay it in full within the year (Doc. 8).

Isaac's favored position in Florence was not destined to last long. The death of Lorenzo de' Medici on April 8, 1492, was followed less than a year later by the disbanding of the city's chapels, at the instigation of the religious reformer Fra Girolamo Savonarola.[19] This curtailment of public musical activities diminished Isaac's income considerably. His fortunes suffered a further reverse in November 1494, when Lorenzo's sons were declared traitors and banished from Florence. But despite the downfall of his patrons, Isaac chose to remain in the city, and his presence there is recorded in two legal documents of January 1495. In the first of these, dated the 19th of that month, Piero Bello acknowledged a debt to Isaac of fifty gold florins, a sum the composer had spent in Piero's name in restituting the dowry of a certain Donna Piera (Doc. 9). Neither the reason why Piero was obliged to refund the lady's dowry nor her relationship to the Bello family is explained in the document. At the same time Piero acknowledged an additional debt of forty gold florins that Isaac had spent, at Piero's request, in having the walls repaired and other improvements made on the farm at Careggi. That Isaac was able to lend the princely sum of ninety gold florins at a

---

[19] D'Accone, *op. cit.*, p. 346 ff.

time when he was unemployed shows that he had managed to put away a considerable nest egg while in Florence.

Isaac's concern that his wife be well provided for in the event of his death is demonstrated in a document dated the very next day (Doc. 10). At that time he transferred credit for the total debt owed him by his father-in-law to Mona Bartolomea, with the stipulation, however, that the bequest be invalidated should she die before him. In the absence of any other documents from this time we may assume that Isaac made the bequest because he was planning to leave the city and wished to put his affairs in order before doing so. It is significant that on the previous day Piero Bello had promised to pay his debt to Isaac within the month, sending the money to Pisa if necessary. By that time it must have become apparent even to the Medici's staunchest supporters that their cause in the city was lost. And as all hope of a Medici restoration faded, Isaac's thoughts must have turned to the problems of finding employment elsewhere.

The opportunity to do so presented itself with the arrival in Pisa during October 1496 of the Emperor Maximilian. After a successful interview with this sovereign, Isaac was directed to proceed to Vienna along with the other members of the imperial chapel and await further instructions. It may be that he even journeyed north with the imperial court, for Maximilian's intervention in the Italian wars was short-lived. Upon arrival in Innsbruck Isaac was given a formal appointment as *Hofcomponist,* with a salary of one hundred fifty gulden per annum. His new duties — other than a promise to devote his art to the imperial chapel and to do all that might be required of a faithful composer — are not specified in the contract that he signed on April 3, 1497. We may assume therefore that residence at the imperial court was not obligatory. And it is because of this assumption that his whereabouts during the next five years, until he is mentioned again in Florence, have to the present time remained largely a matter of conjecture. It is possible, as Terry has suggested, that he made Innsbruck his headquarters for a while. He may have also sojourned in the vicinity of the Augustinian monastery at Neustift, of which he eventually became an associate. But a document from the archives of the Florentine hospital of Santa Maria Nuova shows that only two years after his imperial appointment Isaac had returned to Florence to take up residence there once again (Doc. 11).

The document, dated September 25, 1499, records an agreement made between Isaac and the hospital's director. In return for a donation of one hundred and four gold florins "to the hospital's poor" Isaac and his wife were to receive once each year for the rest of their lives twenty-four bushels of grain, five barrels of summer wine, one barrel of olive oil, and one hundred pounds of salted meat. It is also stated that the hospital was to begin sending the provisions during the following month of October. The investment proved to be a wise one, for Mona Bartolomea survived her husband by seventeen years, and the hospital's records show that she continued to receive the provisions until the time of her death.

During the next few years Isaac is reputed to have negotiated with Duke Ercole I for a position at the court of Ferrara. He may have even visited that city for a while. But he apparently continued to use Florence as his base of operations, for his presence in the city is attested to by several documents. On April 9, 1502, it is recorded that he personally brought forty gold florins to Santa Maria Nuova, a payment on the investment he had made two and a half years previously (Doc. 12). And on the following August 15 he had his first will drawn up.[20] After "humbly commending his soul to Omnipotent God, His most glorious Mother Mary ever Virgin and all the saints in paradise" and donating three lire to the city's various building projects — a tax paid by all persons filing wills in Florence — Isaac bequeathed the entire bulk of his estate to "his beloved wife, Bartolomea." Since Bartolomea was named as the sole beneficiary, it would appear that the couple had never had any children.

From evidence in Sicher's *Orgelbuch* it has been adduced that Isaac was in Constance sometime before Whitsuntide 1504. Isaac's name is nevertheless recorded twice during this time in the account books of Santa Maria Nuova (Docs. 13-14). The documents do not specify, however, whether he was in the city. But a legal transaction recorded by Ser Giovanni Carsidone on July 4, 1506, definitely places Isaac in Florence on that date (Doc. 15). At the time his sister-in-law Margherita, described in the document as the widow of the singer Charles de Launoy, was to be married to a Florentine, Michele Gaudenti. Since Piero Bello was now dead, Isaac was acting as Margherita's guardian, and it is recorded that he had deposited one hundred gold florins in the Florentine State Bank and given thirty gold florins in cash as her dowry. Provision was also made at that time for Isaac's niece Maria, the daughter of Charles de Launoy (Doc. 16). She was eventually to share

---

[20] NAC, *Protocollo di Testamenti di Ser Giovanni Carsidone*, Vol. C 195, fols. 81ʳ-81ᵛ. Since this document is almost identical to the third will published by Milanesi, it is not reproduced in the Appendix.

in Isaac's estate through a legacy from Bartolomea. Another document from the same day records a debt of seven gold florins owed Isaac by Michele Gaudenti, repayable by January 4, 1508 (Doc. 17).

During the next five years there is little record of Isaac's activities. In a letter dated January 17, 1508, Niccolò Machiavelli, who was then on a diplomatic mission to the imperial court for the Florentine government, stated that while in Constance he had been to visit "Arrigo the composer, who has his wife here."[21] On August 7, 1509, it is reported that twenty-four bushels of grain were delivered to Isaac's home, and it may be assumed that the couple had by that time returned to Florence (Doc. 18).

Two deeds drawn up on January 4, 1512, show that on that day Isaac and Bartolomea arranged to exchange their house on the Via del Ariento for a smaller one on the Via del Cocomero, presently the Via Ricasoli (Docs. 19-20). On November 16 of the same year he named Ser Andrea di Pasquino, a chaplain in San Lorenzo, as his proxy (Doc. 21). Five days later Isaac had his second will drawn up.[22] Bartolomea was again named sole beneficiary. These arrangements suggest that he was contemplating another trip to the imperial court and again wished to settle his affairs before attempting the journey. And the reason for his making the trip is not difficult to deduce in the light of military-political events of the summer of that year.

Thanks to the might of the combined Spanish-papal armies the Medici were restored on September 1, 1512, to their former position as "principal citizens" of Florence. Their hold on the city was further strengthened when, on March 13 of the following year, Cardinal Giovanni de' Medici was elected to the papacy as Leo X. Just as the new political climate in Florence sharpened Isaac's desire to pass the remaining years of his life there, the sudden turn in his friends' fortune encouraged him to seek the means to make that desire possible. And when the matter was brought to Leo's attention, he apparently lost no time in seeking to provide for the aging composer in a manner befitting one who had been a faithful servant of his family for over twenty years. The following letter to Leo's nephew Lorenzo, who was at the time representing the family's interests in Florence, was written at the Pope's request by his younger brother Giuliano (Doc. 22):

[21] O. Tommasini, *La Vita e gli scritti di Niccolò Machiavelli nelle loro relazioni col Machiavellismo*, Turin, 1883, I, 101.

[22] NAC, *Protocollo di Testamenti di Ser Giovanni Carsidone*, Vol. C 195, fols. 148^r-148^v. This will is also similar to the one published by Milanesi.

VII

473   Heinrich Isaac in Florence

Magnificent Lord and Honored Nephew!
I understand that Maestro Henrico Isaac, a musician and an old servant of our House, is back there again, and because he is old and has a wife and children [sic] there, he would like to settle down and stay if some provision were to be made for him. And since I wish to gratify him as much as I possibly can, out of consideration for his faithful service of many years — dating from the time of our father — and, no less, for his worthy talents, I pray Your Magnificent Lordship, for these reasons and for your love of me, to be kind to him and do everything possible so that a provision be made him. He had [such a provision] at one time as a singer of San Giovanni, and it could now be drawn from the same source. Any favor and benefit you do him will be worthily placed in a deserving person. You could not do anything that I would appreciate more. I commend myself to you.
From the Apostolic Palace at Rome, on the tenth day of May, 1514.

Giuliano de' Medici

That the Pope had had a direct hand in the matter is confirmed by a letter written two days later, addressed this time to Lorenzo by the latter's secretary, Balthassare Turini da Pescia (Doc. 23):

[Rome, May 12, 1514]
My Magnificent Lord and Patron, after continued commendations!
In my last letter I forgot to tell Your Lordship that the most Reverend Monsignor ordered me to recommend Henrico Ysac to you and to tell you that Our Lord [the Pope] had had a letter written in his behalf, and also that the Magnificent Giuliano had written about him to Your Lordship [requesting] that he be confirmed in the provision he used to have when he was first there, which Your Lordship will have done willingly since you delight so in music and since you have him staying there...

The letter the Pope had caused to be written to his nephew in behalf of Isaac has also survived:[23]

My Magnificent and Most Honored Lorenzo, greetings!
His Holiness the Pope has instructed the Magnificent Giuliano de' Medici to write you in favor of Arrigo Ysac, a singer and a most singular composer, as well as a most beloved servant of the blessed memory of Lorenzo de' Medici, who sent as far away as Flanders for him, and then in Florence gave him a wife who is still living. Now because the poor soul has grown old and would regret having to return north, His Holiness the Pope, as mentioned above, has asked the Magnificent Giuliano to write and recommend him to you so that the poor soul may be given the provision he used to have during the time of the blessed memory of Lorenzo de' Medici, that is, the one he had when he was a singer of San Giovanni. The provision is this: that the *Arte de' Mercatanti* should give him five gold ducats, the *Opera di Santa Reparata* two gold ducats and the Annunziata one gold ducat;[24] and this was the provision that each of the singers used

---

[23] MAP, Filza CXI, fol. 322; printed in F. Ghisi, *op. cit.*, p. 43 ff.

[24] The *Arte de' Mercatanti* or *Arte di Calimala*, one of the city's largest merchant guilds, was charged with the secular administration of the Baptistry. The

to have at the time of the blessed memory of Lorenzo de' Medici. As mentioned above, the Pope will be pleased that he be made such a provision, since he was always [loyal to your] House. And I, who am a creature of your House, always grateful to the Pope and to the Magnificent Giuliano, am recommending him to you at their instruction. You will be doing something pleasing to all Florence because Arrigo is well liked by everybody. I shall say nothing else. May God maintain you in prosperity and in good health.
Rome, May 13, 1514

>Niccolò de' Pitti, singer and prior of the papal chapel

The Cathedral's overseers did not delay in complying with the Pope's request (Doc. 24):

May 30, 1514
The above said lord overseers, all in agreement, after due consideration, etc. . . . decided that Magister Arrigus the singer, newly appointed provost of the chapel of figural music, should have two gold florins monthly for each month that he is at the head of the said chapel, beginning at the time and for that length of time in which the *Arte di Calimala* of the city of Florence pays the same Magister [Arrigus].

Payments to Isaac from the Santissima Annunziata were also begun a short time after the Pope's request (Doc. 25):

August 19, 1514
To Arigo d' Isach the singer, on the said day, 14 lire, which are given to him at the wish of the Pope: one ducat each month; and these [fourteen lire] are for two months, June and July. . .

Notwithstanding the wording of the Cathedral's overseers' deliberation it is doubtful that Isaac ever assisted again in any of the chapels in question. Successive payments recorded under his name in the Cathedral's account books usually refer to him as *proposto alla cappella* or *presidente della cappella,* implying that his position was purely honorific (Docs. 26-27). And since after this time the chapel continued under the direction of its twenty-three-year-old master, Bernardo Pisano, there is every reason to believe that the payments were exactly what the Pope had intended them to be, retirement benefits in recognition of many years of faithful service.[25] His future in Florence thus secure, Isaac accordingly undertook the journey to Vienna in order to seek his

---

Cathedral of Santa Maria del Fiore had formerly been dedicated to Saint Reparata, and the habit of referring to the church by its original name persisted well into the 16th century. The *Opera* was the institution responsible for the Cathedral's secular administration and building works. (See D'Accone, *op. cit.,* 309, n. 7; 310, n. 8.)

[25] For information about Bernardo Pisano see my study in *Musica Disciplina,* XVII (1963), 111 ff.

release from the Emperor's service. There on January 27, 1515, he was granted permission to reside permanently in Florence. Maximilian also settled a generous allowance of one hundred fifty gulden per annum on him.

On November 10, 1515, Isaac is recorded as personally receiving his monthly stipend from the Cathedral (Doc. 28). Thus he must have been on hand to participate in the many festivities the Florentines arranged in honor of Leo X's visit to the city during that month. It may be that Isaac's works were also performed during the services in San Lorenzo at which the Pope officiated (Doc. 29):

Expenditures made for the coming of His Holiness Pope Leo X de' Medici, our principal and most exalted patron, to this his beloved church of San Lorenzo of Florence...

On November 6, 1515, it pleased our patroness, Madonna Alfonsina Orsini, widow of the Magnificent Piero di Lorenzo de' Medici, and many other men of good will to have part of the choir of our church dismantled and reduced to one level so as to accommodate more people, one greater in width which can be and is in every respect appropriate for use as a papal chapel, because it was thus designated while His Holiness was in Florence... And every morning the Pope's singers performed a beautiful Mass of figural [music] at the altar of the said Holy Sacrament, and this church was very much frequented by the populace out of respect for the Pope and [because of] the magnificence [of the services.]

Isaac had his third and final testament drawn up on December 4, 1516, again naming Bartolomea the sole beneficiary.[26] He died only a few months later, on March 26, 1517, the day on which payments to him from the Cathedral cease (Doc. 30). The date of his death is confirmed also by an entry in an account book from the sacristy of the Santissima Annunziata (Doc. 31):

March 27, 1517

On the said day [we received] an offering of four lire for having gone to the funeral of Maestro Arrigho *decto* Isaach, a Flemish singer; they were received by Maestro Andrea Francioso; and in addition, ten lire were given for the Mass of St. Gregory and for an Office said for his soul. And this was done at the request of his wife...

In his last will Isaac had requested Bartolomea to have a Mass sung at the Santissima Annunziata "for the repose of his soul, each year for ten years, with thirty monks or other ecclesiastics celebrating the Mass." Several entries in that church's account books reveal that Bartolomea fulfilled her husband's request.[27] It was also his wish that he be buried

---

[26] NAC, *Protocollo di Testamenti di Ser Giovanni Carsidone*, Vol. C 195, fols. 161ʳ-161ᵛ; published in G. Milanesi, *loc. cit.*

[27] SSA, *Libro di Uffici di Morti*, Vol. 813, without pagination, entry dated 29 April 1532; *Libro di Uffici di Morti*, Vol. 814, fol. 47ᵛ.

in the chapel of St. Barbara at the Santissima Annunziata, the traditional burial place of the city's Flemish residents. The search for his tomb has proved fruitless, however. During the course of a restoration of the church in the 19th century many of the old tombs were removed, among them, apparently, that of Isaac.[28]

The documents assembled in the present study make it clear that Isaac passed much more time in Florence than has hitherto been suspected. And as a result of this knowledge, we may safely assume that most of the works from the last thirty years of his life were actually composed in that city. There is no doubt now that his secular works with French and Italian texts, as well as a good many of his instrumental pieces — preserved almost exclusively in Florentine sources — were written for his Florentine friends and patrons. It is still impossible, however, to tell which of his many Masses and motets that exist in sources elsewhere were written originally for the city's chapels, since, with a few exceptions, the Florentine sources of sacred music have not come down to us. A point, nevertheless, may be made with regard to the date and place of composition of the monumental *Choralis Constantinus,* left unfinished at the time of his death. Even though the work was commissioned in Constance in 1508 and undoubtedly initiated there as well, it would now appear that the major portion of it was composed in Florence, where, but for a brief trip to the imperial court, the composer resided from the summer of 1509 until his death in 1517.

Ultimately, however, the significance of Isaac's years in Florence must be judged not by the number of works he might have composed there, but by the contribution he made, through his teaching and personal influence, to the dissemination of the highly developed musical techniques of the north. The history of Florentine music boasts of a succession of distinguished composers, starting with Dufay and ending only a century later with Verdelot, who brought their northern training and techniques to the city, and who in turn were influenced by its ideals and sensibilities. By the very length of his stay in Florence Isaac may be named among the principal figures in that glorious tradition of cultural and artistic reciprocity that was to ensure for Italy the first place among musical nations in the late 16th century.

[28] Mona Bartolomea survived her husband by seventeen years, dying just a few weeks after her seventieth birthday, on May 30, 1534. (SMN, *Libro dei Commessi,* Vol. 5825, fol. 306ʳ.) Under the terms of her will, filed on February 3, 1521, her estate was divided between her younger sister Antonia and her niece Maria. (ASF, *Testamenti e Contratti di Ser Lorenzo Poggini,* Vol. P 494, fols. 182ʳ-182ᵛ.)

VII

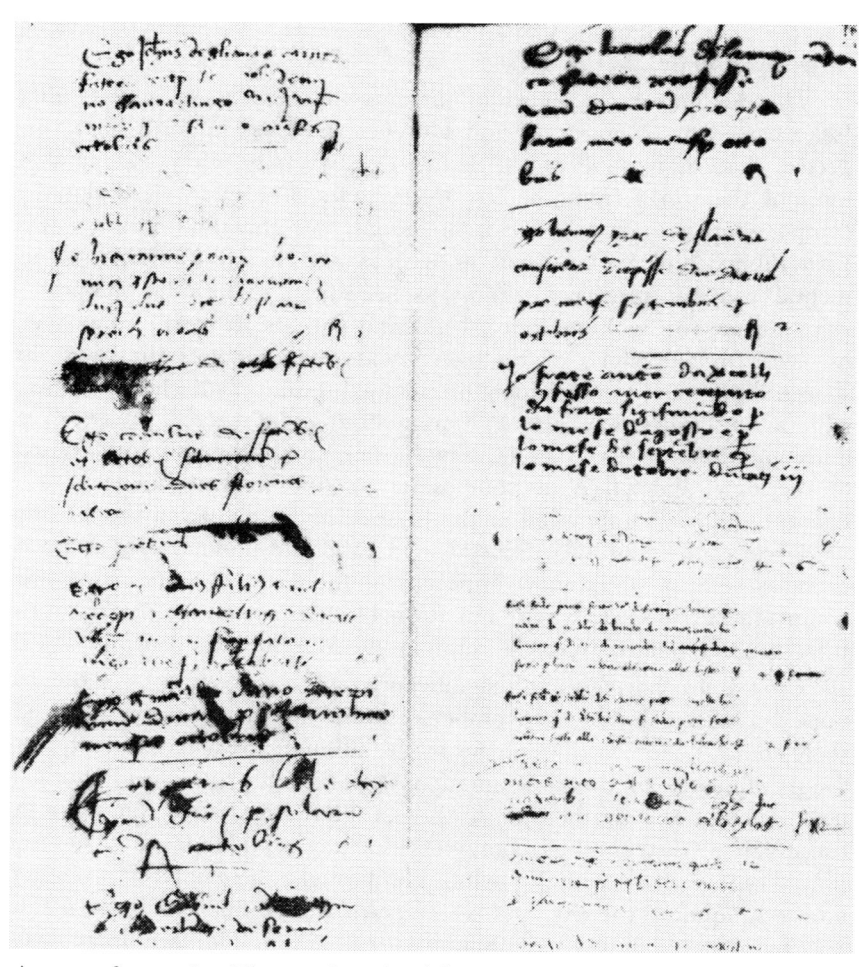

A page from the Florentine Archives (SSA, *Ricevute,* Vol. 1050, f. 163r) showing Isaac's signature in the second entry of the right-hand column

VII

Letter from Giuliano de' Medici to his nephew Lorenzo in behalf of Isaac (see Document 22)

Heinrich Isaac in Florence

APPENDIX
Documents[29]

Doc. 1   (SMDF, *Quaderni Cassa,* VIII. 1. 79, fol. 75^v)
[30 dicembre 1486]
Spese della chappella del chanto fichurato di Duomo... E de' dare a dì detto Fl. quattro larghi d' oro in oro per loro: Fl. due larghi d'oro in oro a Arrigho d'Ugho di Fiandra, chantore overo chonponitore...

Doc. 2   (SMDF, *Quaderni Cassa,* VIII. 1. 82, fol. 28^v)
[1488]
La chappella del chanto figurato di Santa Maria del Fiore de' ' dare a dì 4 di febbraio Fl. quattro larghi d'oro in oro pagati a Arrigho di Ugho da Fiandra, chonponitore del chanto nella chapella.

Doc. 3   (SMDF, *Quaderni Cassa,* VIII. 1. 86, fol. 54^v)
[1490]
La chapella del chanto fighurato... E a dì 7 di magio Fl. due larghi d'oro in oro per loro a Arrigho d'Ugho di Fiandra, chantore, per suo salario del mese d'aprile; è per lui a Giuliano di Lorenzo de' Medici; portò Simone di Francesco.

Doc. 4   (SMDF, *Quaderni Cassa,* VIII. 1. 88, fol. 80^v)
[1492]
Capella dei cantori de' dare... E a dì 23 di gennaio Fl. due larghi d'oro in oro per loro a Arrigho d'Ugho, chantore, pel mese d'ottobre; è per lui a Lorenzo de' Medici.

Doc. 5   (SMDF, *Quaderni Cassa,* VIII. 1. 91, fol. 48^v)
[1493]
La chapella del chanto fighurato... E de' dare a dì 30 di marzo Fl. due larghi d'oro in oro a Arigho d'Ugho, chantore, per suo salario del mese di marzo.

Doc. 6   (SSA, *Debitori e Creditori,* Vol. 198, fol. 304^v)
[1491]
Maestro Arigho d' Isach, chantore, de' dare a dì XXX d'aprile Fl. due larghi...

Doc. 7   (NAC, *Atti di Ser Giovanni Carsidone,* Vol. C 193, I, fol. 154^v)
1488 [1489]
Item postea, dictis anno, indictione et die XIII^a februarii. Actum in populo S. Laurentii de Florentia, presentibus... testibus etc.

    Arrigus Ugonis de Fiandra, cantor S. Joannis de Florentia, ex parte una, et Laurentius Francisci Blasii Gianberti, populi S. Trinitatis de Florentia, ex parte alia, omnes eorum lites etc. compromiserunt in Pierum Honofrii Gimignani

---

[29] The Florentine new year began on March 25, and as a result documents recorded before that day usually carry the date of the preceding year. In the course of the text such dates have been changed to conform to our modern system. Punctuation and accent marks, lacking in the original documents, have been added by the present writer.

VII

478

Buonaveris, populi S. Trinitatis predicte, presentem tanquam in eorum arbitrum etc. dantes etc. auctoritatem laudandi etc. . . .

Doc. 8   (NAC, *Atti di Ser Giovanni Carsidone,* Vol. C 193, I, fol. 156ʳ)
1488 [1489]
Item postea, dictis anno, indictione et die XXVIIª presentis mensis februarii. Actum in populo S. Laurentii de Florentia, presentibus . . . testibus etc.

Laurentius olim Francisci Blaxii Gianberti, populi S. Trinitatis de Florentia, sponte etc. omni modo etc. fuit confessus et publice recognovit se debitorem etc. Arrigi olim Ugonis de Fiandra, ad presens cantoris S. Ioannis de Florentia, ibidem presentis etc. in summa et quantitate L. 120 s. 13 pp. ex causa veri et gratuiti mutui. . . Quas quidem L. 120 s. 13 pp. dictus Laurentius promisit reddere et solvere dicto Arrigo presenti etc. hinc ad per totum mensem februarii anni 1489 absque aliqua exceptione. . .

Suprascriptus Laurentius, ex parte una, et Arrighus, ex alia, omni modo renumptiando quilibet eorum prius et ante omnia et singula cuidam compromisso alias et sub die XIIIª presentis mensis facto per dictas partes in Pierum Honofrii Gimignani Buonaveris, rogato manu mei notarii infrascripti, quod quidem compromissum cum omnibus in eo contentis irritum et inane esse voluerunt. . .

Doc. 9   (NAC, *Atti di Ser Giovanni Carsidone,* Vol. C 193, II, fol. 73ʳ)
1494 [1495]
Item postea, dictis anno, indictione et die XVIIIIª ianuarii. Actum in populo. S. Laurentii de Florentia, presentibus . . . testibus etc.

Pierus olim Joannis, alias Piero Bello, becharius dicti populi, sponte etc. omni modo etc. recognovit se debitorem etc. Arrigi Ugonis de Fiandra ibidem presentis . . . in et de summa et quantitate fl. quinquagintorum auri largorum de auro in auro et lib. quindecim et s. XIII pp., quia sic et tamque . . . dictus Arrigus solvit et mutuavit pro dicto Piero cuidam domine Piere, uxore olim [gap], pro dote ipsius domine Piere ad cuius dotis restitutionem tenebatur et obligatus erat dictus Pierus. . . Ac etiam dictus Pierus recognovit se debitorem etc. dicti Arrigi presentis et ut supra recipientis etc. in et de summa et quantitate fl. quadraginta quatuor auri largorum de auro in auro et lib. quadraginta et s. XVIIII et d. IIII pp. pro tantis expensis facti super . . . podere ipsius Pieri Belli positum in populo S. Petri a Chareggi. . . Quas quantitates et summas . . . dictus Pierus, alias Piero Bello, promisit eidem Arrigo reddere et solvere etc. hinc ad per totum presentem mensem ianuarii, absque aliqua exceptione, Florentie Pisis etc. . . .

Doc. 10   (NAC, *Atti di Ser Giovanni Carsidone,* Vol. C 193, II, fols. 73ᵛ-74ʳ)
1494 [1495]
Item postea, dictis anno, indictione et die XXª ianuarii. Actum in ecclesia Sancte Marie del Fiore de Florentia, presentibus . . . testibus etc.

Arrigus olim Ugonis de Fiandra, habitator ad presens in populo S. Laurentii de Florentia, ex certa scientia etc. sponte etc. et causa donationis inter vivos, omni modo etc. donavit etc. Bartolomee eius uxori et filie dicti Pieri Ioannis becharii . . . dictum suprascriptum creditum dictorum fl. quinquaginta auri largorum in auro et lib. XV et s. XIII pp., et dictum creditum dictorum fl. quadraginta quatuor auri largorum in auro et lib. quadraginta et s. XVIIII et d. IIII pp., de quibus supra in proximo precedenti contractu fit mentio. . . . Cum hac tamen conditione, quod si dicta domina Bartolomea eius uxor et donataria predicta predecederet ipsum Arrigum, tunc et eo casu dicta donatio intelligatur esse et sit ipso iure nulla. . .

Doc. 11 (SMN, *Giornale "D,"* Vol. 5686, fol. 107ʳ)
Mercholedì e addì 25 di settembre 1499
Arrigho d'Ugho di Fiandra, chantore, e mona Bartolomea, sua donna e figluola fu di Piero di Bello bechaio, deono avere ogni anno una volta sola e non più durante la vita loro e chi di loro due sopraviverà et non d' altri, staia XXIIII di grano buono et chomunale, barili V di vino d'estate, buono et durabile, et barili uno d'olio dolce, libbre 100 di carne salata. Et tutte le decte cose s' à a porre alla chasa della loro abitazione a ogni spesa di questo spedale. Le quali chose dà et conciede loro messer Giovanni dall'Antella, nostro spedalingho. E chosì vuole sia loro oservato per l'avenire pe' sua successori chome di sopra, pe' rimunerazione d'una limosina fatta pe' detti a' poveri di questo spedale di Fl. cientoquattro d'oro in oro, chome apare a Entrata segnata D, c. 69.
E àssi a chominciare mandare loro le prime chose e'l vino del mese d'ottobre prossimo avenire 1499, e di poi seguendo di mandare l'altre chose in que' tenpi che s'usa di mandare agl' altri simili.

Doc. 12 (SMN, *Libro Maestro Rosso "D,"* Vol. 5880, fol. 121ʳ)
1502
Arigho d'arigho [sic] di Fiandra, chantore, de' avere a dì 9 d'aprile 1502 Fl. quaranta larghi d'oro in oro; rechò e' detto; disse per parte di Fl. C quatro in oro vol' dare a pocho a pocho per fare una chomessione per sè e per mona Bartolomea, sua dona; a Entrata segnata D, c. 30.

Doc. 13 (SMN, *Libro Maestro "F,"* Vol. 5882, fol. 26ʳ)
1504
Arigho d'arigho [sic] di Fiandra de' avere Fl. 40 larghi d'oro in oro, per tanti debba dare a libro rosso segnato 2 D, c. 121, e quali danari vuole fare chomessione per sè e per mona Bartolomea, sua donna, et chosì per ll'avenire di quelli redassi, Fl. 40 d'oro.

Doc.14 (SMN, *Libro Maestro "F,"* Vol. 5882, fol. 333ʳ)
1504
E deono avere Fl. quaranta larghi d'oro in oro . . . da Aricho d'aricho [sic] da Fiandra. . .

Doc. 15 (NAC, *Atti di Ser Giovanni Carsidone,* Vol. C 194, I, fol. 475ʳ)
[1506, die IIIIª iulii]
Item postea, dictis anno, indictione, die et loco, et coram testibus suprascriptis . . .
  Prefatus Michael sponte etc. omni modo etc. fuit confessus etc. habuisse etc. pro dote domine Margherite eius uxoris et filie olim Pieri Johannis, alias Piero

Bello, bechaio populi S. Laurentii de Florentia, et iam uxor Caroli cantoris, Fl. centum de creditis dotium de tribus pro centenario, qui sunt descripti super libro Montis Communis Florentie sub nomine dicti Michaelis, et Fl. triginta auri de sigillo ab Arrigho Ugonis de Fiandra, professore musice, infra denarios et donamenta communi concordia inter partes extimata...

Doc. 16 (NAC, *Atti di Ser Giovanni Carsidone,* Vol. C 194, I, fol. 475ᵛ)
[1506, die IIIIª iulii]
Item postea, incontinenti etc.
 Suprascriptus Michael sponte etc. omni modo etc. promisit etc. suprascripto Arrigho et mihi notario infrascripto recipienti etc. pro Maria, filia dicti olim Caroli cantoris et dicte domine Margherite, ipsam Mariam tenere in domo sua et penes se eidem dare et prestare victum et vestitum condecentem usque ad etatem annorum XVIII° completorum, gratis et absque aliqua inpensa...

Doc. 17 (NAC, *Atti di Ser Giovanni Carsidone,* Vol. C 194, I, fol. 475ᵛ)
[1506, die IIIIª iulii]
Item incontinenti etc.
 Suprascriptus Michael omni modo etc. recognovit se debitorem suprascripti Arrigi in et de summa et quantitate Fl. septem auri largorum in auro ... quos Fl. septem largos in auro solvere promisit etc. dicto Arrigho presenti et acceptanti etc. hinc ad per totam diem IIII ianuarii 1507 libere et absque aliqua exceptione...

Doc. 18 (SMN, *Giornale "C,"* Vol. 5690, fol. 116ʳ)
7 agosto 1509
Arigo d'Ugo di Fiandra a dì detto: 24 staia di grano grosso; portò Romolo, nostro vetturale.

Doc. 19 (NAC, *Atti di Ser Giovanni Carsidone,* Vol. C 194, I, fols. 311ʳ-311ᵛ)
1511 [1512]
Item postea, dictis anno, indictione et die IIIIª ianuarii...
 Certum esse dicitur quod de anno Domini 1509 ... dominus Albertus Pieri de Bertinis, clericus florentino ... dedit et concessit ser Francisco Benedicti Joannis cartolarii clerico florentino, ibidem presenti, et pro se et suprascripta domina Marietta eius sorore ... ad vitam tamen ... recipienti et acceptanti, unam domunculam positam in populo S. Marci de Florentia in via dicta del Cocomero... Unde hodie, hac presenti suprascripta die prefati ser Franciscus et dicta domina Marietta cum consensu dicti sui mundualdi etc. et legitime certificata etc ... de licentia tamen et consensu prefati domini Alberti de Bertinis... dederunt et vendiderunt etc. magistro Arrigho Ughonis de Flandria, musice professori excellentissimo, et domine Bartholomee uxori dicti Arrigi ... habitatoribus ad presens in populo S. Laurentii de Florentia ... dictam suprascriptam domum cum suis pertinentis et positam ut supra in loco et infra confines predicti vel alios veriores... Quam venditionem etc. fecerunt etc. pro pretio etc. lib. centum quadraginta pp., quod pretium et quas L. 140 dictus Arrigus pro se et dicta domina Bartholomea actualiter dedit solvit et numeravit dicto venditori presenti...

481 Heinrich Isaac in Florence

Doc. 20 (NAC, *Atti di Ser Giovanni Carsidone,* Vol. C 194, I, fols. 312ʳ-312ᵛ)
1511 [1512, die IIII* ianuarii]
Item postea, dictis anno, indictione et die et loco...
 Prefata domina Bartholomea, cum consensu et certificata etc. et dictus **Arrigus** et quilibet eorum in solidum etc. omni modo etc. dederunt et vendiderunt etc. suprascripto ser Francisco ibidem presenti et recipienti etc... unam domum cum suis pertinentis positam in populo S. Laurentii et in via dell' Ariento... Et predictam venditionem etc. fecerunt etc. pro pretio et nomine pretii L. centum quadraginta pp., quod pretium dictus ser Franciscus actualiter solvit et numeravit dictis venditoribus...

Doc. 21 (NAC, *Atti di Ser Giovanni Carsidone,* Vol. C 194, I, fol. 396ᵛ)
1512
Item postea, dictis anno, indictione et die XVI* novembris...
 Arrighus olim Ugonis de Flandria, musice professor excellentissimus, habitator in populo S. Marci de Florentia, omni modo etc. non revocando etc. fecit et constituit etc. suum procuratorem etc. venerabilem virum presbitum Andream Pasquini Andree clericum florentinum et cappellanum in ecclesia S. Laurentii de Florentia, presenti etc. generaliter ad agendum etc.

Doc. 22 (MAP, Filza CVIII, fol. 53)
Magnifice Domine & Nepos Honorande
Io intendo che maestro Henrico Isaac, musico et antico servitore di Casa nostra, si rritruova al presente costì, e per essere homai vecchio e havervi la moglie et figliuoli, desiderrebbe fermarsi e riposare, quando li fusse fatto qualche partito. Onde desiderando io gratificarlo di quanto per me si può, hauto rispetto alla fedele sua servitute et antica sino dal tempo di nostro Patre, et non meno alle digne sue virtute, prego La M. V. per detti rispetti et per amor mio, lo voglia havere a cuore, et faccia ogni opera, che li sia constituita una provisione. La quale già hebbe come cantore di S. Giovanni, et si cavi donde si solea, che oltre locarà ogni piacere et beneficio li faccia, dignamente, et in persona meritoria, a me non me potrebbe fare cosa più grata, et a quella mi raccomando.
Romae ex palatio apostolico die X maii MDXIIII
 Iulianus de Medicis s[crip]s[it])

Doc. 23 (MAP, Filza CII, fol. 24)
Magnifice vir patrone mi obser.ᵐᵉ Commen.
Per l'ultima mia me scordai dire ad V. S. come Monsignore Reverendissimo me haveva commisso gli racommandassi Henrico Ysac et gli dicessi che Nostro Signore ne haveva facto scrivere et lo Magnifico Juliano anchora lui ne haveva scripto ad V. S. che lui fussi recognosciuto da quella della provisione che haveva in quel tempo che stava li, il che V. S. doverrà fare volentieri delectandosi de musica, et havendo lui ad stare li per stantia...
Romae die XII maii MDXIIII
 Hmll. S.ᵒʳ Balthassare Iu[rini]

Doc. 24 (SMDF, *Deliberazioni,* II. 2. 11, fol. 167ᵛ)
Die 30 maii 1514
Supradicti domini operarii omnes in concordia et servatis servandis etc. . . . .

deliberaverunt quod magistro Arrigo cantori et denovo preposito Cappelle canctus figuratus, singulis mensibus dum preerit dicte cappelle habere debeat Fl. duos auri largos in auro mense quolibet initiando temporibus et terminis quibus et prout eidem magistro solvere incipiet ars et universitas mercatorum civitatis Florentie.

Doc. 25   (SSA, *Entrata e Uscita*, Vol. 795, fol. 130^r)
19 agosto 1514

A Arigo d'Isach, chantore, a dì detto L. 14, sono che tanti se gli danno di volontà del Ponteficie ogni mese uno duchato; che sono per due mesi, giugno e luglio, portò lui contanti.

Doc. 26   (SMDF, *Entrata e Uscita*, VIII. 3. 70, fol. 28^r)
[luglio-dicembre, 1514]

A maestro Arrigo d'Ugo di Fiandra, chantore proposto alla capella del chanto fighurato, L. ottantaquatro per suo salario in detto tempo aragione di Fl. due larghi d'oro in oro il mese.

Doc. 27   (SMDF, *Entrata e Uscita*, VIII. 3. 72, fol. 37^r)
[gennaio-giugno, 1516]

A maestro Arrigho d'Ugho di Fiandra, presidente della capella, L. 84 per suo salario in detto tempo, avuto al Q. C. 58, c. 123.

Doc. 28   (SMDF, *Quaderni Cassa*, VIII. 1. 133, fol. 58^v)

Maestro Arrigho d'Ugho di Fiandra, maestro del chanto fighurato, de' dare addì 23 d'aghosto 1515 L. ventotto piccioli; portò lui conto di suo salario, come disse Bartolo di Filichaia. L. 28

E de' dare addì 10 di novembre L. ventotto per lui et per ser Bernardo [Pisano], maestro della cappella; portò lui detto conto. L. 28

Doc. 29   (Firenze, Archivio Capitolare di San Lorenzo, *Giornale "A"*
                                                  della Sagrestia dal 1506-1521, fol. 305^r)
1515

Spese facte per la venuta della Sanctità di Papa Leone X° de' Medici, nostro precipuo et maximo patrone, in questa sua dilecta chiesa di Sancto Lorenzo di Firenze. . .

A dì 6 di novembre 1515 è piaciuto a madonna Anfolsina [sic] Orsina et donna che fu del magnifico Piero di Lorenzo de' Medici, nostra patrona, et a molti altri huomini da bene disfare parte del nostro choro et ridurlo a uno bello piano in modo sia capace di più gente, uno con più largheza che si può, et che esia [sic] con ogni facilità acto a essere capella di Papa, perchè così fu disegnato in mentre stava Sua Sanctità in Firenze questa chiesa sia capella Papale. . . Et ogni mattina cantarano e cantori del Papa la bellissima messa di figurato allo altare di decto sacramento et era questa chiesa molto frequentata da populi per rispecto del Papa et di tante magnificentie.

VII

Heinrich Isaac in Florence

Doc. 30 (SMDF, *Entrata e Uscita*, VIII. 3. 74, fol. 32^v)
[gennaio-giugno, 1517]
A maestro Arrigho d'Ugho di Fiandra L. trentanove s. 13 d. 4 piccioli, sono per suo salario di mesi II e dì XXV, dalli primo di gennaio addì 26 di marzo, 1517, aragione de Fl. II d'oro il mese, per esser presiede alla sopradetta capella. . .

Doc. 31[30] (Firenze, Archivio del Convento della Santissima Annunziata, *Entrata e Uscita della Sagrestia*, Vol. II, fol. 8^r)
27 marzo 1517
A dì decto lire quattro, sono per limosina per esser iti al mortoio di maestro Arrigho decto Isaach, cantore fiammingho, portò maestro Andrea Francioso; e più lire dieci, sono queste limosina per lle messe di Sancto Gregorio, e per uno ufizio facto per l'anima sua; e questo fece fare la sua donna. . .

---

[30] I am indebted to Father Eugenio Casalini, curator of the Convent's private archives, for the transcription of this document.

VIII

SOME NEGLECTED COMPOSERS IN THE FLORENTINE CHAPELS, CA. 1475-1525

Chapels of polyphonic music, emulating those of northern Europe, were first established at the Florentine cathedral and baptistry in 1438. During the next century, despite brief periods of inactivity, these institutions provided a focal point around which much of the public musical life of Renaissance Florence revolved. Though modestly staffed at first, the chapels grew steadily both in numbers and in prestige, for under the enlightened patronage of the Medici no effort was spared in securing the services of the finest musicians of the day, foreign as well as Italian. The presence of these musicians, particularly those trained in the north, was to have a pround effect on the course of Florentine musical history. As a result of their contributions, not only did the new polyphonic style of the Franco-Netherlanders gain wide acceptance in the city's cultural life, but native forms, such as the carnival song and the ballata, were also further developed. More important, however, was the didactic role these musicians played, since it was through their teaching and influence that the foundations were laid for later Florentine schools of polyphonic composition.[1]

A particularly brilliant moment in the history of the chapels was reached during the closing decades of the fifteenth century, when several musicians of international reputation found employment in Florence. Chief among these were the composers Heinrich Isaac, Alexander Agricola and Johannes Ghiselin. The moment was short-lived, however, for with Savonarola's rise to power the chapels were disbanded, and most musicians were forced to leave the city in search of positions elsewhere. Reestablished early in the sixteenth century, the chapels were to continue as independent institutions until the end of the Republic. In these years they were staffed for the most part with local musicians. Nevertheless, a semblance of former glory was

---

[1] For further information on the musicians employed in the Florentine chapels, see my "The Singers of San Giovanni in Florence during the Fifteenth Century," *Journal of the American Musicological Society* 14 (1961) 307-358. (Hereinafter the article is referred to as "Singers.")

regained under the leadership of such younger composers as Bernardo Pisano, Mattia Rampollini and, above all, Philippe Verdelot.[2]

In addition to these well-known figures, there were a number of composers of lesser fame associated with the Florentine chapels during this period of fluctuating splendor and decline. A few of them are known to have composed several works. Others are not so well represented. According to extant documents, however, all of them played an active part in the city's musical life. My purpose here is to bring together all of the known materials relating to some of these composers and to give a survey of their surviving works. I pay particular attention to the compositions with Italian texts, which are without exception preserved in manuscripts of Florentine provenance and were doubtless written for Florentine audiences.

Ser Arnolfo Giliardi

A few works by one Arnolfo have come down to us in manuscripts of the late fifteenth and early sixteenth centuries. All but one of these sources give the composer's first name only, the exception being MS Magliabechi XIX, 176 of the National Library in Florence. In her catalogue of the library's holdings Bianca Becherini gives the name appearing on folio 127v of the manuscript as *Arnolfo Schard*.[3] Although her reading seems correct taken alone, a comparison between the script of this difficult spot and other more easily read portions of the manuscript indicates that the name is *Arnolfo Giliardi*.[4] This solution in turn fits in well with the initial of the composer's surname as given in the Vatican Library MS Cappella Giulia XIII, 27—also of Florentine origin— where he is referred to as *Arnolfo G*. An *Arnulphus Gilardus* is reported by the theorist Johannes Hothby, writing about 1480, to have been in the en-

---

[2] G. Reese's *Music in the Renaissance*, rev. ed. (New York 1959) gives excellent summaries of the lives and works of most of the musicians mentioned here. Other recent biographical studies include: A. Bragard, "Verdelot en Italie," *Revue belge de musicologie* 11 (1957) 109-124; C. Gottwald, "Johannes Ghiselin-Janne Verbonnet: Some Traces of His Life," *Musica disciplina* 15 (1961) 105-111; F. A. D'Accone "Bernardo Pisano—An Introduction to His Life and Works," *Musica disciplina* 17 (1963) 115-135; idem, "Heinrich Isaac in Florence: New and Unpublished Documents," *The Musical Quarterly* 49 (1963) 464-483; C. Sartori, "Rampollini, Mattia," *Die Musik in Geschichte und Gegenwart* 10.1913. Recent editions of music, all published by the American Institute of Musicology, include: Alexander Agricola, *Opera omnia*, ed. E. R. Lerner (4 vols. to date); Johannes Ghiselin—Verbonnet, *Opera omnia*, ed. C. Gottwald (3 vols. to date); Philippe Verdelot, *Opera omnia*, ed. A. Bragard (1 vol. to date); Bernardo Pisano, *Collected Works*, ed. F. A. D'Accone, Music of the Florentine Renaissance 1 (1966).

[3] Bianca Becherini, *Catalogo dei manoscritti musicali della Biblioteca nazionale di Firenze* (Kassel 1959) 75. Professor Becherini's reading of the surname has been questioned by a few scholars, but to my knowledge an alternate reading of it has yet to be advanced.

[4] I record here my thanks to Professor Gino Corti of Florence for his help in deciphering the name.

tourage of Cosimo de' Medici (d. 1464).[5] Is it possible that this Arnolfo and the composer are one and the same person? I am inclined to think so for several reasons. The presence of a composer in Cosimo's circle is not surprising in the light of our knowledge of Cosimo's interest in music. Other Florentine documents, moreover, reveal that a musician named Arnolfo was associated with the Florentine chapels over a number of years and that he was on friendly terms with Cosimo's grandson Lorenzo, whom he was later to assist in recruiting singers.

Among the documents that I have been able to uncover, Arnolfo's name is first mentioned in a letter written by Braccio Martelli to Lorenzo the Magnificent on 3 September 1473.[6] At the time Lorenzo was staying at the Medici villa in Caffagiolo, and Martelli's purpose in writing was to present Arnolfo, who was "coming there in order to be appointed as a singer in San Giovanni." Several other singers, apparently newly arrived from the north, were accompanying Arnolfo to Caffagiolo, and Martelli urged Lorenzo to expedite the appointment of all of them to the baptistry's chapel. Although Lorenzo was actively involved in the chapel's management, personnel matters had evidently got out of hand during his brief absence from Florence. Consequently, Martelli also exhorted him to write the responsible parties from Caffagiolo, while promising to do what he could in Florence: "In any case recommend Arnolfo, the bearer of this letter, and I shall attend to the rest here." From the tone of the letter it appears that Arnolfo himself had just arrived in the city. This does not lessen the possibility, however, that he is the same person as the Arnolfo who was in Cosimo's service some ten years earlier. Subsequent documents show that quite a few musicians, including Arnolfo, were in and out of Florence several times during the next two decades.

The baptistry's account books from the period under consideration are not extant, so we have no way of knowing the length of Arnolfo's service in the chapel at this time. Later records indicate that he was employed there again from 1483 to 1485.[7]

Arnolfo is first mentioned in extant documents from the Santissima Annunziata dated August 1478, though not in connection with the chapel.[8] His duties consisted of "teaching the [convent's] novices figural music," that is, the principles of reading, writing and performing polyphony.[9] This

---

[5] A. Seay, "The *Dialogus Johannis Ottobi Anglici in arte musica*," *Journal of the American Musicological Society* 8 (1955) 92, 99.

[6] The letter is printed with an English translation in "Singers" 326, 354-355.

[7] See n. 15.

[8] In the early 1480s, however, many of the musicians employed at the baptistry also began serving at the Annunziata. See "Singers" 331.

[9] Abbreviations used in citing documentary sources here and in the following notes are:
ASF   Archivio di Stato, Florence
AC   ASF, Archivio dell'Arte di Calimala

is a clear indication that Arnolfo was a composer as well as a performer, further substantiation of which is furnished in a document to be mentioned presently.

A few other records from the Annunziata, including receipts with his signature, show that Arnolfo retained his position there through the beginning of January 1479, when he was succeeded by ser Antonio di Marco da Montughi.[10] Previously, on 1 February 1478, *ser Arnolfo da Francia, contratenore*, had been engaged, along with ser Antonio and several other singers, to perform in the newly reconstituted chapel at the cathedral.[11] He left the cathedral's service in December of the same year.[12]

Further information about Arnolfo's activities during this period is provided by a document in the cathedral archives which states that on 26 March 1479 the cathedral's overseers directed that one florin be paid to "ser Arnolfo, a singer and chaplain in San Lorenzo, for his work in having composed vocal pieces."[13] Besides establishing the fact that singer and composer are the same person, the document reveals that meanwhile Arnolfo had also obtained a chaplaincy in the Medici's family church, doubtless as a result of Lorenzo's influence. Unfortunately, none of San Lorenzo's account books for the decade 1480-1490 which I was able to examine contains any reference to Arnolfo.

Arnolfo left Florence sometime during the year following the date of the cathedral document. The record of a letter written on 2 August 1480 states that Lorenzo requested him "to defer to another time sending the singers

---

SMDF   Archivio dell'Opera di Santa Maria del Fiore, Florence
SSA   ASF, Corporazioni Religiose Soppresse 119, Santissima Annunziata

The document recording Arnolfo's duties is found in SSA 697, *Entrata & Uscita, 1477-1478*, fol. 54v.

Agosto 1478

A ser Arnolfo, chantore, a dì 13 detto L. due sono per parte di suo salario per insegnare chantare a' novizi canto figurato.

[10] SSA 197, *Debitori & Creditori, 1478-1484*, fol. 30:

1478 [1479]

Ser Arnolfo di [gap], chantore.... de' avere a dì V di giennaio 1478 [1479] L. 8 s. X per tanto gli si dà d'achordo per insegnare a' nostri noviti chantare.

The Florentine new year began on March 25, and documents recorded before that day usually carry the date of the preceding year. In the course of the text such dates have been changed to conform to our modern system.

[11] A. Seay, "The Fifteenth-Century Capeplla at Santa Maria del Fiore in Florence," *Journal of the American Musicological Society* 11 (1958) 49.

[12] *Ibid.* 50.

[13] SMDF 8.1.65, *Quaderno Cassa, com. Gennaio, 1478/79*, fol. 55v:

Spese d'opera de' dare...

E de' dare a dì 26 di marzo [1479] Fl. uno largho per loro a ser Arnolfo di Arnolfo, chantore e chappellano di San Lorenzo, i quali gli danno gli operai per sua faticha di chonpore canti, porto e' detto. Fl. 1

Coming as it does a few weeks before Easter, which occurred on April 11 of that year, the payment suggests that the pieces were commissioned for use during Holy Week. Evidence that such works by Arnolfo were in the repertory of the cathedral chapel is given below.

here" (to Florence).[14] Whether this was merely a short trip in order to recruit singers for the chapels or one of longer duration is difficult to determine. Musical evidence—in this case a dedicatory motet—suggests that Arnolfo spent some time in Siena during these years, and it may well be that his sojourn there took place in this period. He was back in Florence serving in the baptistry's chapel sometime around the end of 1483. On 20 January 1484 it is recorded that *ser Arnolfo d'Arnolfo, cantore in San Giovanni*, signed an agreement with the Annunziata to sing polyphonic music there at Saturday morning mass throughout the year, in return for a room, clothing and personal services.[15] He received, in addition, a salary of one florin per month, payments of which are recorded in his name from 26 February 1484 to 2 July 1485.[16] The absence of further payments after the latter date and the record of another of Lorenzo's letters written shortly beforehand—a "general" one "in behalf of ser Arnolfo"—suggests that he once again departed from Florence.[17] He returned a few years later, rejoining the cathedral chapel on 1 October 1492.[18] This was the shortest of his stays, for he is recorded as being there only through the end of the following December.[19] After that time no further mention of him is made in the archives of the various Florentine musical establishments.

Arnolfo's works continued to be performed in Florence long after his departure, indeed, for almost a century after his death. Francesco Corteccia, in the preface to his *Responsoria* (Venice, Gardano, 1570), states that he had been "strongly urged" to have his own compositions for Holy Week printed

> because there were almost none of them left for us [to use here in Florence] except for those most ancient ones by a certain Arnolfo, which almost never cease insisting on the similarity of voices and for that reason are not very highly esteemed, since in everything, repetition is the mother of satiety.

In the light of Corteccia's remarks, unflattering as they are, it is surprising that none of Arnolfo's responsories seems to have survived either in Florentine or in other musical sources. In fact, only two of Arnolfo's sacred works, both settings of the Magnificat, are known at the present time. These simple pieces present an embellished version of the chant tone in the cantus, and in conformity with *alternatim* practice set only the even numbered verses of the canticle. The first setting, in the sixth tone, is for three voices of which

---

[14] M. del Piazzo, ed. *Protocolli del carteggio di Lorenzo il Magnifico per gli anni 1473-74, 1477-92*, Deputazione di storia patria per la Toscana, Documenti di storia italiana 2.2 (Florence 1956) 113.
[15] "Singers" 334-335, 356-357.
[16] *Ibid.* 335.
[17] M. del Piazzo 372.
[18] "Singers" 345.
[19] *Ibid.* 346.

the upper and lower only are written out.[20] The middle voice is to be improvised by the performer, as is indicated by the title "a faulx bourdon" and by the accompanying rubric "qui habet aures audiendi audiat." The second setting, in the eighth tone, is for four voices, all of them written out. Two versions of this piece survive in two manuscripts of north Italian origin dating from around the turn of the sixteenth century.[21] Perhaps this is an indication that Arnolfo spent some time in other Italian cities after leaving Florence.

Sena vetus, Arnolfo's paean to the glories of Siena and the beauty of its women, provides more direct evidence of his activities elsewhere in the peninsula. The piece, preserved in a handsomely decorated parchment manuscript of the late fifteenth century, was probably commissioned by the Sienese government or some civic minded patron, for its text also stresses the city's ancient tradition of liberty and its enjoyment of continuous and prosperous peace.[22] The three-part *Le Souvenir* is the only one of Arnolfo's works with French text known at the present time. It is found, as far as I can ascertain, in two manuscripts of Italian origin,[23] which suggests that it also dates from his years in Italy. The opening of Arnolfo's piece begins exactly like a setting of the same name by the mid-fifteenth century English composer Morton. If the pieces are nearly contemporaneous, as seems likely, Arnolfo's "is a very early example of the parody and represents a primitive stage in the development of that technique."[24]

Two of Arnolfo's works with Italian texts appear in the previously mentioned Florentine MS Magliabechi XIX, 176[25] (see musical supplement, nos. 1, 2). Though they present certain problems of interpretation and transcrip-

---

[20] The piece is preserved in MS Rés. Vm.[7] 676 of the National Library in Paris. See N. Bridgman, "Un manuscrit italien du début du xvie siècle à la Bibliothèque Nationale," *Annales musicologiques* 1 (1953) 183-184, 228-229.

[21] It appears anonymously in MS Rés. Vm.[7] 676 (*ibid*. 216-217), but with ascription to Arnolfo in MS Liber Capelle Franchini Gafori, vol. 1 of the Cathedral Archives in Milan. For the latter source see C. Sartori, *Le musiche della Cappella del Duomo di Milano, Catalogo* (Milan 1957) 44.

[22] The piece is printed in a faulty modern edition by S. A. Luciani, *La musica in Siena* (Siena 1942) 38-41.

[23] With ascription to Arnolfo in MS Cappella Giulia XIII, 27; anonymously in MS Q 16 of the Conservatory Library, Bologna. See A. Smijers, "Vijftiende en zestiende eeuwsche muziekhandschriften in Italië met werken van Nederlandsche componisten," *Tijdschrift der Vereeniging voor nederlandsche Muziekgeschiedenis* 14 (1935) 168.

[24] H. M. Brown, *Music in the French Secular Theater, 1400-1550* (Cambridge, Mass. 1963) 134.

[25] On fols. 40v-42 (*O invida fortuna*) and 127v-129 (*Piagneran gli occhi mey*) respectively. At one time the second piece also formed part of the contents of MS 2356 of the Riccardiana Library in Florence. See D. Plamenac, "The 'Second' Chansonnier of the Biblioteca Riccardiana," *Annales musicologique* 2 (1954) 112, 114. Both pieces are discussed briefly in B. Becherini, "Autori minori nel codice Fiorentino Magl. XIX, 176," *Revue belge de musicologie* 4 (1950) 24-25.

tion, both works are of great interest, poetically as well as musically, for the student of Italian quattrocento music. The three-part *Piagneran gli occhi mey* consists of two sections of music, the first marked "verte" at its close on the tonic, the second containing a *signum congruentiae* that indicates an ending on the dominant in bar 35, as well as another ending on the tonic in the next bar. As they stand, the musical structure of the sections and of their endings gives little indication of the form of the piece; nor does the poetry to which both sections are set.

The entire text consists of four strophes, each formed of four heptasyllabic lines with the rhyme scheme *a b b a*. In the first section one strophe is given line by line under the cantus part, a second strophe appears complete in the remaining space at the close of the contratenor part. The process is repeated for strophes three and four in the second section. Since textual continuity between strophes three and four is quite clear, a logical assumption is that the first two strophes are to be performed one after the other to the music of section one, the final two strophes to the music of section two, and that the piece is structured in an *A A B B* form. This solution, however, fails to take into account the "verte" marking at the end of section one, the two endings of section two (typical of the musical form of the trecento ballata) and the thought expressed in strophe two, which stands by itself as a closing apostrophe.

In my opinion the "verte" marking at the end of section one does not signify an immediate repetition of that section after strophe one. Rather, it serves as an indication that the performer is now to proceed to section two and continue with strophes three and four, utilizing the two different endings provided by the composer. Here, however, melodic and textual considerations point to the ending of the last bar as the appropriate close for strophe three, the ending at the *signum congruentiae* in bar 35 as that of strophe four.[26] After this a return is to be made to section one for the poetry of strophe two and the end of the piece. The text is thus treated as a ballata, though it is not one; and the musical form, thoroughly satisfying from a melodic, harmonic and structural point of view, also approximates that most widespread and enduring of all Italian polyphonic forms.

Quite apart from these problematic aspects, *Piagneran gli occhi mey* contains several passages of very beautiful music. At the opening of the piece, for example, the cantus presents a phrase on the syllable "pia" which encompasses the upward leap of a sixth and then comes almost immediately

---

[26] In returning to the opening of section two (for the text of strophe four) an awkward melodic interval (G-C-sharp) is avoided if strophe three ends on the A of the last bar. Furthermore, an ending on G at the *signum congruentiae* for strophe four ensures a smooth return to the opening note (A) of section one. With regard to the text, the last line of strophe three cannot be fitted easily to the last phrase of music if the ending is at the *signum congruentiae*.

to a cadence on the sharped leading tone. After a rest of one beat the phrase is resumed on the same syllable and the entire word, "piagneran," as well as the rest of the line follow. This abrupt halt in the middle of the first phrase not only serves to heighten the dramatic impact of the word, but also introduces almost literally into the musical structure the idea of a sob. The following phrase makes use of equally effective devices. Here the cantus rises in sequences of ascending fourths until it reaches a climax a full octave above its first note; it then descends to a deceptive cadence on the minor dominant, all the while having formed a series of poignant seven-six suspensions with the lower parts.

The composer's sensitivity to harmonic color is much in evidence throughout the rest of the piece. In the untransposed Aeolian mode on A, in which both sections begin and end, intermediary phrases are constructed so as to cadence on such widely divergent areas as e, a, B-flat and F; in the meantime ample use has also been made of notated chromatics such as G-sharp, C-sharp, B-flat and E-flat. Altogether, *Piagneran gli occhi mey* shows Arnolfo to have been a composer of no mean gifts, one who knew how to combine the clarity of Franco-Netherlandish part-writing with expressive Italian melody.

The three-part *O invida fortuna* also contains two musical sections, the first of which is marked "verte folium" at its close. The rubric in this case clearly means that the second section is to follow immediately upon the first. Both sections begin in the tonic, but only the second section ends there. The close of the first section, instead, first cadences deceptively on VI and then inconclusively on IV. This is another indication that the final cadence is that of the second section and that the musical form of the piece is a simple *A B*.

The poetry is divided into two sections which, like the music, must be read through from beginning to end. The first section consists of four lines with the rhyme scheme *a b b A*, the second of five lines with the rhyme scheme *c c d d C*.[27] Despite the fact that the first four lines form a complete statement and could be thought of as a ripresa, the poem cannot be classified as a ballata because none of the rhymes of the first section recurs in the second. Actually, as it is presented here, the poem does not correspond to any of the traditional Italian forms of the time. It is cast, rather, in a free scheme, one that is exactly mirrored in the straightforward structure of the music.

The only hindrance to a correct reading of the piece at first sight is caused by a copyist's errror. At the beginning of the second section lines five and six of the poetry should be sung to the same music. The copyist, however, neglected to repeat the music in his score, and it was apparently only after he finished that he realized his omission. Accordingly, he went back and placed one line of text below the other, with the clear intention of correcting his error. But in doing so he failed to give a sign of repetition in the musical score, with

---

[27] Lower case letters indicate heptasyllabic lines; capitals, lines of eleven syllables.

the result that, as it now stands, the piece seemingly does not have enough music to accomodate the text. By repeating the music of line five for line six of the text the mistake is easily rectified.

O invida fortuna is in the transposed Ionian mode on F, with all parts carrying a flat in the signature. Major cadential points occur on closely related degrees of the scale such as d and C, as well as on the tonic. The harmonic variety with which Arnolfo infused *Piagneran gli occhi mey* is not so apparent here, the only extra accidental introduced being an E-flat, which would have been supplied in any case by the performers because of the rules of *musica ficta*. Nevertheless, the piece is a worthy companion to its fellow, not only because of its well-designed contrapuntal passages and carefully planned harmonic scheme, but also because its phrase structure effectively reproduces the rhythms and accents of the text.

RUBINETTO, STOCHEM, PIETREQUIN

Only fragmentary information about these composers has survived in Florentine archives. *Rubinetto francioso, cantore*, is first recorded at the Santissima Annunziata on 7 February 1482, and payments to him for serving in the chapel there are listed in the convent's accounts until the end of the following April.[28] Two other payments, dated May 6 and 10 of the same year, give the expenses for a robe that the convent had had made for him.[29] There is no further mention of him after this time. Another "frate Rubinectus franciosus," who may or may not be the same person, is recorded in Florence twenty-four years later. This musician received an appointment to the cathedral chapel on 26 June 1506 and served there for a little over a year, leaving sometime before 13 August 1507.[30] One or the other of these men is probably the *F. Rubinet* to whom several chansons are ascribed in the Florentine manuscript Banco rari 229 and a few other manuscripts of the period.[31]

---

[28] "Singers" 332.
[29] SSA 246, *Entrata & Uscita, 1479-1482*, fol. 249v.
6 maggio 1482
A Rubinetto, cantore, a dì detto L. una s. sedici sono per cinque braccia di tella per fodrare la sua tonica e per fillo a cuxilla.
Ibid. fol. 250:
10 maggio 1482
A Rubinetto a dì detto L. una s. quattro sono per facitura dela sua tonica, portò il sarto.
[30] SMDF 2.2.9, *Deliberazioni, 1498-1507*, fol. 148v:
26 junii 1506
Item ... elegerunt in chantorem fratrem Rubinectum Franciosum loco Ciarles Premerani [?] pro contro alto et ad rationem L. quinque pro quolibet mense, prout solvebatur dicto Ciarles.
Rubinectus is not mentioned in a deliberation dated 13 August 1507, in which the chapel members are named. (*Ibid.* fol. 188).
[31] It is unclear whether Rubinet is the same composer as the Rubinus of the *Glogauer*

Johannes Stochem, whose works have come down to us in several well-known printed and manuscript collections of the time, was attached to the court of Matthias Corvinus, king of Hungary, during the early 1480s.[32] From 1487 to 1489 Stochem was in Rome, serving in the papal chapel of Innocent VIII.[33] While en route to Rome, Stochem stopped in Florence and received temporary employment in the Annunziata's chapel. Given the informal nature of his appointment, it is not surprising that his name is lacking in the account books that list the musicians regularly employed at the convent. His signature, however, appears twice in one of the Annunziata's receipt registers, under the entries for 31 July and 5 September 1486, in acknowledgement of his salary for the months of July and August 1486.[34] He must have left Florence shortly after this time, since he began serving in the papal chapel the following February.

Pierre Bonnel of Picardy, otherwise known as Pietrequin (Pietrachino), first arrived in Florence in the spring of 1490. He was employed at the Annunziata from 3 April of that year through 6 June 1491 and then again from 9 October 1492 to 20 March 1493.[35] His signature is also preserved in receipts from the convent's registers carrying the dates 3 July and 2 September 1490.[36] Although he is not identified as a singer of San Giovanni in the Annunziata's account books, it seems likely, given the length of his stay in Florence, that he was employed at the baptistry as well. Pietrequin joined the cathedral

---

Liederbuch. See G. Reese (n. 2 above) 48, 635. Five chansons, all of them apparently unique, are given to Rubinet in Banco rari 229. Another chanson, also attributed to him in this manuscript, is ascribed to Isaac in the Segovia manuscript and appears anonymously in Washington, Library of Congress, M2. 1. M6. A chanson by Stochem, preserved among other places in Banco rari 229 and the Cappella Giulia manuscript, is ascribed to Rubinet in MS Q 18 of the Conservatory Library, Bologna. I am indebted to Professor Howard M. Brown of the University of Chicago, who kindly communicated this information about Rubinet's works. Professor Brown's edition of MS Banco rari 229 is now in preparation and will be published by the University of Chicago Press in the "Monuments of Renaissance Music" series.

[32] For a summary of this composer's life and works see A. Seay, "Stochem, Johannes," *Die Musik in Geschichte und Gegenwart* 12.1392-1393.

[33] F. M. Haberl, "Die römische 'schola cantorum' und die päpstlichen Kapellsänger bis zur Mitte des 16. Jahrhunderts," *Vierteljahrsschrift für Musikwissenschaft* 3 (1887) 244.

[34] SSA 1050, *Ricevute, 1486-1493*, fol. 5v ("Ego Johannes Stochem recepi 31 julii ducato 1"); fol. 6v ("Ego Johannes Stochem recepi ducato 1").

[35] SSA 198, *Debitori & Creditori, 1488-1493*, fol. 279v:
Piero di Bonello, cantore, de' dare a dì 3 d'aprile 1490 Fl. uno largho. . . .
E de' dare a dì 6 di giugno 1491 Fl. uno largho.
Ibid. fol. 357v:
Pietro di Bonello, chantore, de' dare a dì 9 d'ottobre 1492 Fl. uno largho. . . .
E a dì 28 di marzo 1493 Fl. uno largho.

[36] SSA 1050, *Ricevute, 1486-1493*, fol. 96 ("Ego Pietrequinus de Piccardia recepi per sallario mensium III di aprile, maii, junius Fl. 3 la"); fol. 99v ("Ego Petrus Bonnel de Picardia recepi a di duo settembris duos ducatos pro salario mensium 2").

chapel on 1 April 1490 and served there through December of the same year.[37] After an absence of a few years he resumed service at the cathedral on 1 July 1492.[38]

Another glimpse of Pietrequin's activities at this time comes from an account recording the clothing expenses of the entourage that accompanied Piero de' Medici to Rome in September 1492, on the occasion of his journey there to congratulate the newly elected Pope Alexander VI. Apparently no expense was spared in providing suitable attire for the Medici party, which, among others, included three members of the Florentine chapels who also served as Piero's personal musicians:

> For the three singers, that is, Arigho [Isaac], Charletto [de Launoy] and Petrachino, for each of them a robe ... and a beret .. a tunic ... a hat ... the sum of 32 1/2 florins for each of them, in all Fl. 97 s. 10[39]

Besides indicating a hitherto unknown aspect of Pietrequin's activities while he was in Florence, the document is of great interest for the information it brings to bear on another point. It suggests that even at a time when the concept of choral polyphony was well established at public services in Florence, the Medici continued the time-honored, princely practice of retaining a smaller group of musicians for more intimate performances at home or in the family chapel.

Upon his return to Florence, Pietrequin rejoined the cathedral chapel, serving there until the end of March 1493, when the chapel was disbanded.[40] After that time he is no longer mentioned in Florentine musical archives. Six works are attributed to him in several manuscripts and a print of the late fifteenth and early sixteenth centuries. Among them is the delightful farewell chanson, *Adieu Florence la iolye*, a piece that perhaps was composed at the time of his trip to Rome.[41]

---

[37] "Singers" 342.
[38] SMDF 8.1.90, *Quaderno Cassa, com. Luglio, 1492*, fol. 40v:
La chapella del chanto fighurato de' dare. ... a dì 8 di detto [agosto] Fl. due larghi d'oro in oro per lui a Petrichino di Pichardia. ... per suo salario del mese di luglio. Fl. 2.
[39] ASF, Medici Avanti il Principato, 104, fol. 583:
Spese per vestire la famiglia del Mangnifico Piero per la gita di Roma. ... A' tre chantori, cioè Arigho, Charletto, Petrachino, a ciaschuno uno robone. ... e uno beretto. ... una robetta. ... uno chapello. ... somma Fl. 32 larghi e 1/2 per ciaschuno, monta in tutto Fl. 97 s. 10.
I am indebted to Professor Gino Corti of Florence for the transcription of this document.
[40] "Singers" 346.
[41] Four chansons are found in MS 2794 of the Riccardiana Library, Florence. See B. Becherini, "Alcuni canti dell' Odhecaton e del codice fiorentino 2794," *Bulletin de l'Institut historique belge de Rome* 22 (1950) 338-339; D. Plamenac (n. 25 above) 105-106. A fifth chanson, *Mais que ce fut secretement*, appears, among other places, in the Cappella

Pintelli

Two musicians, Giovanni di Giovanni Pintelli and his brother Tomaso di Giovanni, are recorded as having served in various Florentine chapels during the 1480s. Direct evidence is lacking as to which of them is the composer represented in musical sources by two works, the ballata *Questo mostrarsi adirata di fore* (text by Poliziano) and the mass *Gentilz gallans de France*. Unfortunately, only the composer's surname is given at the beginning of each of these works—a practice that is not unusual for the time. Nevertheless, for reasons to be cited below, extant Florentine documents make it appear that it was Giovanni who composed the works in question.

Due to the loss of the baptistry's accounts for the 1470s and 1480s, we cannot know exactly when Giovanni joined the chapel in San Giovanni. But he must have been employed there before entering the chapel at the Santissima Annunziata because in his first payment from that church, dated 10 October 1484, he is listed as *Giovanni di Giovanni Pintelli, cantore in San Giovanni*.[42] He was associated with the Annunziata over the next several years, the last record of payment in his name being issued on 5 February 1491.[43] Presumably, as with most other singers, he was simultaneously employed at the baptistry throughout these years. Meanwhile, on 15 June 1488, he had also become a member of the cathedral chapel, his tenure there continuing until 1 April 1490.[44] After the date of his last payment from the Annunziata his name does not appear again in the archives of the various chapels.

Tomaso di Giovanni Pintelli joined his brother in the cathedral chapel on 1 August 1488.[45] He was there for less than a year, leaving the church's service on or before 1 July 1489.[46] Several months earlier, on 2 December 1488, it is recorded that *Tomaso di Giovanni Pintelli, cantore in San Giovanni*, was appointed to the Annunziata's chapel.[47] He was employed there until

---

Giulia manuscript, Banco rari 229 and the *Odhecaton*, in the latter source with attribution to Compère. See H. Hewitt, ed., *Harmonice Musices Odhecaton* (Cambridge, Mass. 1942) 165-166, 400. *Adieu Florence la iolye* is preserved in Banco rari 229; MS Magliabechi XIX, 178 of the National Library, Florence; and MSS 328-331 of the University Library, Munich (communication from Professor H. M. Brown).

[42] "Singers" 336.
[43] SSA 198, *Debitori & Creditori, 1488-1493*, fol. 149v:
Giovanni di Giovanni, chantore, de' dare....
E a dì 5 di febbraio [1491] de' dare Fl. uno largho.
[44] "Singers" 341-342.
[45] *Ibid.*
[46] *Ibid.*
[47] SSA 198, *Debitori & Creditori, 1488-1493*, fol. 270v:
Thomaxo Pintelli, cantore in San Giovanni, de' dare a dì 28 di dicembre 1488 Fl. uno largho.

15 October 1491.[48] As in the case of his brother, nothing further of him is known after the date of his last payment from the Annunziata.

Another question, that of the national origin of the Pintellis, should be considered before attempting to establish the composer's identity. Very little music by Italian composers from this period survives; the situation is echoed by archival sources, where lack of reference to native composers seems to indicate that around the middle of the fifteenth century creative musical activity on the peninsula went into an eclipse. Whatever the reasons for this,[49] recent scholarship has shown that toward the end of the century Italian composers began to appear on the scene once again. In Florence the emergence of a native school of composition at the turn of the sixteenth century is reflected in the works of Alessandro Coppini, Bartolomeo degli Organi and, slightly later, in those of Bernardo Pisano and Francesco de Layolle.[50]

One might suppose that Pintelli was an older member of this group. Certainly, the setting of a Florentine text by a composer with an Italian surname who lived and worked in Florence presents a convincing argument in favor of his Florentine, or at least Italian, origin. The Pintelli surname is even found in Florentine tax registers of the time.[51] I was not able, however, to locate the names of Giovanni and Tomaso in any documents pertaining to various branches of the Pintelli family.[52] There is, of course, the possibility that the brothers were priests and therefore not liable to be listed in tax registers; but the absence in their payments from the Annunziata and the cathedral of the titles "ser," "messer" or any other clerical distinction suggests otherwise. This perplexing situation was finally clarified by the chance discovery of a few documents from the convent church of Santo Spirito.

Surviving account books from the mid-1480s show that the musical establishment at Santo Spirito was hardly comparable to those of the baptistry or of the Annunziata. The Augustinian convent, however, did employ an organist, and there is some evidence that vocal polyphony was also performed

---

[48] *Ibid.* fol. 318v:
Tommaso Pintegli, cantore in San Giovanni, de' dare. . . . a dì XV d'ottobre [1491] Fl. mezzo largo.

[49] An excellent discussion of the problem is found in N. Pirrotta, "Music and Cultural Tendencies in Fifteenth-Century Italy," *Journal of the American Musicological Society* 19 (1966) 127-161.

[50] Modern editions of the collected works of these composers have been prepared by the present writer and are being published by the American Institute of Musicology in the series "Music of the Florentine Renaissance."

[51] For example, in ASF, Decima della Repubblica 6, *1498, Santo Spirito, Ferza*, fol. 253, wherein is found a tax report filed by Jachopo, Giovambatista, Gherardo, Bernardo and Piero, the sons of Piero di Jachopo Pintegli. The family had filed a previous report in 1481.

[52] Further information is found in Gargani's monumental *Poligrafo* no. 1566 ("Pintelli") in the National Library, Florence; in ASF, Archivio dell' Ancisa, HH. fols. 253v, 687; *ibid.* MM fol. 535v; and in ASF, Monte delle Graticole 977 fol. 259.

there. A payment in the convent's account books, dated 20 March 1488, for example, lists the cost of a "volume of figural music" for use by the choir.[53] Another entry shows that the novices were given instruction in music by a professional, who was also expected to assume the duties of *maestro di cappella:*

> I record that Carlo de Burgis came to stay with us [at the convent] on the 1st of September, 1486 at the instance of frate Giovanni, our prior, with the stipulation that he teach the novices plainchant and polyphony and sing in church with them, at a salary of four lire a month, which amounts to forty-eight lire a year.[54]

Payments to Carlo de Burgis are recorded until 10 January 1488, when it is stated that he received three lire and three soldi in severance pay.[55]

A little over a month later another musician was engaged to replace him:

> I record that on the 19th of February, 1488 *Giovanni Pintelli francioso* [italics mine] came to stay with us in the capacity of singing master and to teach the novices figural music and to sing with the others [in chapel] at a salary of four lire a month, with expenses and living quarters.[56]

The significance of the document is twofold: it suggests that Giovanni, by reason of his position as singing master and teacher of polyphonic music,

---

[53] ASF, Corporazioni Religiose Soppresse 127, Santo Spirito 8, *Entrata & Uscita A. 1488-1498*, fol. 79v;
marzo 1487 [1488]
Item a dì 20 a frate Agnolo di Certaldo Fl. tre d'oro in oro & per lui dua a frate Francesco & uno al baccielliere cathelario per uno libro di chanto figurato, valsono lire diciotto e soldi diciotto.

[54] Ibid. 1, *Libro campione AA, 1475-1494*, fol. 118v:
Ricordo come Carlo de Burgis venne a stare con noi a dì primo di septembre 1486 per mezzo di frate Giovanni, pater noster, con patto ch'egli insegnassi a' novitii canto fermo & figurato e cantare in chiesa con loro con salario di quatro lire il mese, che monta un anno lire quaranta otto.

[55] Ibid., *Entrata & Uscita A. 1488-1498*, fol. 78v:
gennaio 1487 [1488]
Item a dì 10 a maestro Carlo de Burgis lire tre e soldi tre per ogni suo resto avessi avuto a ffare col convento.

[56] Ibid. 1, *Libro campione AA, 1475-1494*, fol. 178v:
Ricordo chome per insino a dì 19 di febraio 1487 [1488] venne a stare con noi Giovanni Pintelli francioso per magistro del canto e per insegnare a' novitii canto figurato e per cantare insieme cogli altri, dandogli per ciascheduno mese lire quatro colle spese e la tornata di chasa.

Pintelli evidently remained at Santo Spirito for only a few months. In the continuation (fol. 179) of the above account, written in the margin are the words "stette per insino a dì 20 di giugno 1488." A payment to him, however, is listed below this with the date 20 September 1488.

was a composer as well as a performer; it also leaves no doubt that the Pintellis' origins were either French or Netherlandish. Clearly, whatever the original version of the name, its sound was familiar enough to Florentine ears to be Italianized into Pintelli.

Pintelli's four-part *Missa Gentilz gallans de France*, based in part on the tune of the same name, has survived, lacking portions of the first Kyrie and the Gloria, in an apparently unique source, MS Cappella Sistina 41 of the Vatican Library.[57] A few sections of the Mass also draw on the materials of two polyphonic chansons, the four-part *Gentil galans de Franza* of Prioris (?) and Agricola's three-part *Gentil galans*. The Patrem, for example, reproduces the duet between the cantus and altus (bars 3-6) of Prioris's chanson, first in its cantus and tenor, then in its altus and bassus, before enlarging upon the rest of the chanson's first phrase. Less obvious are the quotations, in the Sanctus and the Benedictus, of the descending fourth motive that appears at the opening and toward the close of the tenor of Agricola's chanson. Both of these chansons are preserved, among other places, in manuscripts of Florentine provenance,[58] and one might speculate that Pintelli drew on these materials because they were current in Florence at the time he was there.

The text of Pintelli's only known secular work, *Questo mostrarsi adirata di fore*, was also set by Isaac, who was his colleague in Florence for a number of years.[59] Pintelli's music, like Isaac's, was doubtless written for the court of Lorenzo the Magnificent and probably dates from the late 1480s. (The piece is given in the musical supplement, no. 3.) In its broad outlines it is similar to many of Isaac's Florentine works: it is in three parts, each of which is vocally conceived; its melodies, though simple, are constructed neatly and they closely follow the rhythms of the text; its prevailing duple meter is varied with the usual dancelike section in triple time appearing toward the end. Both Isaac's and Pintelli's settings are in the transposed Dorian mode on G. The music is provided with text only for the first stanza of the poem, the additional stanzas of which are written out at the close. Unlike Isaac's version, however, Pintelli's is through-composed. Frequent cadences, generally at the end of each line of text, occur on the tonic, the dominant and the submediant, with both ripresa and strophe beginning and ending in the tonic.

[57] See J. M. Llorens, *Capellae sixtinae codices* (Vatican City 1960) 81.
[58] The first is found anonymously in the Florentine manuscripts Banco rari 229 and Magliabechi XIX, 164-167, but with attribution to Prioris in manuscripts at Cortona and Regensburg and with attribution to Stappen in Petrucci's *Canti C*. Agricola's chanson is apparently preserved only in the Florentine manuscripts Magliabechi XIX, 178 and Banco rari 229.
[59] Both works are preserved in MS Banco rari 230 of the National Library, Florence. Isaac's setting is printed in a modern edition in J. Wolf, ed., *Heinrich Isaac: Weltliche Werke*, Denkmäler der Tonkunst in Österreich 14.1, 28.42.

Unity is obtained in the ripresa by stressing a rhythmic figure from the opening once again toward the close. The figure itself is first introduced in the tenor as part of a melodic sequence that is repeated three times in the first phrase. A sequential pattern also appears briefly in the setting of the volta and provides, perhaps fortuitously, a link with the structure of the ripresa. Another notable feature of the work is the presence on a number of occasions of notated accidentals—E-flats and A-flats—a practice that is somewhat rare in Florentine sources of this period. Altogether, Pintelli's ballata furnishes a charming example of the kind of music that was much in vogue during Lorenzo's day, and knowledge that its composer was another Italianized Franco-Netherlander serves to underline the international character of Florentine polyphony at the time.

Ser Matteo, ser Felice, ser Virgilio

No music by ser Matteo, whom documentary sources mention as a composer, is known to have survived. One work each is ascribed to ser Felice and ser Virgilio in the previously mentioned Cappella Giulia manuscript. All three musicians were apparently native Florentines.

Matteo di Paolo is first recorded in cathedral archives in a document, dated 26 June 1478, which names him among the choristers who assisted the adult singers of polyphonic music in the chapel.[60] He was ordained and appointed a substitute chaplain in Santa Maria del Fiore shortly after that time.[61] On 1 January 1479 *ser Matteo di Paolo, contralto*, began serving as an adult member of the cathedral chapel and received an official appointment to the position on the fifth of the following month.[62] He was employed in that capacity until 19 January 1485, when the chapel was temporarily suspended.[63] Information about his activities as a composer is found in another document

---

[60] SMDF 2.2.5, *Deliberazioni, 1476-1482*, fol. 38v:
26 junii 1478
Item deliberaverunt quod salarium quatuor florenorum assignatum quatuor clericis cantare debentibus in cappella cori maioris ecclesie Florentine, solvatur Matheo Pauli, clerico sacrestie; et dictum salarium dicto Matheo assignaverunt.
Ibid. fol. 39:
26 junii 1478
Stantiamenta operariorum ... Johanni Laurentii, clerico; Laurentio ser Verdiani, clerico; Matteo Pauli, clerico; Francesco Jacobi, clerico.
[61] As indicated in a document, dated 29 April 1480, given below in n. 64.
[62] SMDF 2.2.5, *Deliberazioni, 1476-1482*, fol. 49v:
1478 [1479]
Die quinta mensis februarii.
Prefati domini operarii ... volentes dare operam efficacem ut cantores deputati ad canendum canto figurato in coro nostre ecclesie sint copiosi et experti ... conduxerunt in cantores ... ser Matheum Pauli pro contro alto, cum salario Fl. octo quolibet anno.
[63] A. Seay (n. 11 above) 52.

VIII

1. Arnolfo Giliardi
Piagneran gli occhi mey

Florence, National Library
US Magliabechi XIX, 176
fols. 127^V - 129^2

VIII

VIII

VIII

2. Arnolfo
O invida fortuna

Florence, National Library
MS Magliabechi XIX, 176
fols. 40V - 42R

VIII

VIII

VIII

3. Pintello·
Questo mostrarsi adirata di fore

Florence, National Library
MS Banco rari 230,
fols. 50V - 51R

VIII

VIII

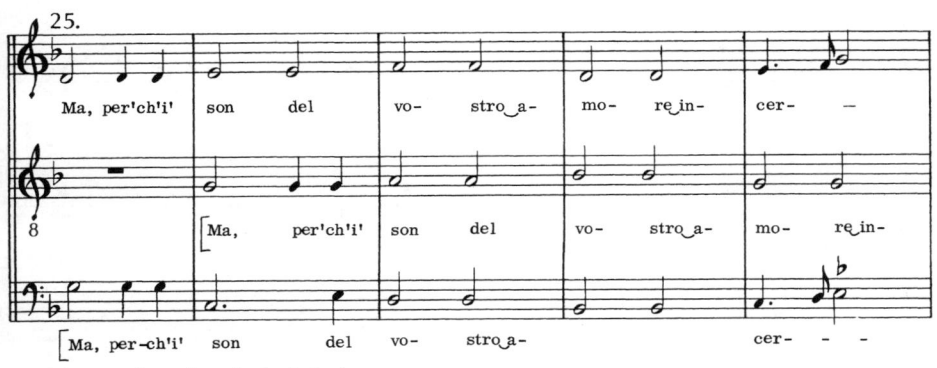

* MS gives a breve here instead of a long.

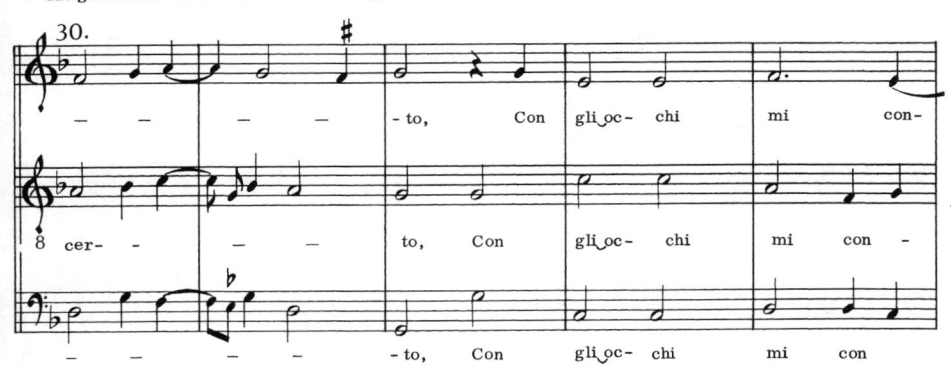

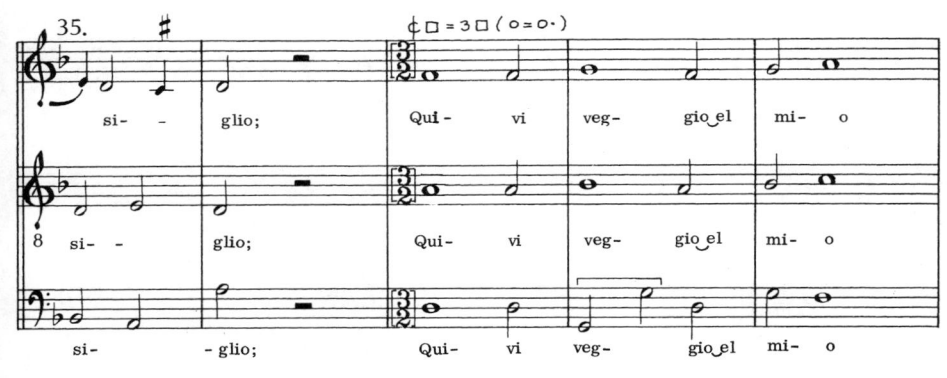

VIII

Se poi vi veggio in acto disdegnosa,
Par che el cor si disfaccia;
Et credo allor di non poter far cose,
Donna, che mai vi piaccia:
Così s' addiaccia el core a tutte l' ore.

Ma, se talhor qualche pietà mostrassi
Negli ochi, o diva stella,
Voi faresti d' amore arder e saxi:
Pietà fa donna bella
Pietà è quella onde amor nasce et more.

from cathedral archives which states that on 29 April 1480 the church's overseers ordered that a payment be made to him

> for settings in figural music of the Lamentations of Jeremiah, the responsories of the same lamentations and of other things which he composed for the said church for the days of Holy Week.[64]

In the following century the performance of polyphony during the last days of Holy Week became a tradition at the cathedral and it is unfortunate that ser Matteo's works do not survive, since they would have furnished us with the oldest recorded Florentine settings of those texts.

Ser Matteo joined the Annunziata's chapel sometime around the end of 1481.[65] His name is listed in the convent's account books until 25 September 1482, when it is reported that he was given two florins, "the remainder of any claim he might have against the convent."[66] A few weeks later he was given another two florins "because the convent felt responsible."[67] He had evidently been discharged abruptly, and with this payment the convent hoped to settle the matter once and for all.

About this same time his name begins to appear in the lists of chaplains associated with the church of San Lorenzo. In one roll from 9 August 1484 he is called ser Matteo, *cantore*, and the inference is that he was also serving as a singer; in another of 1485 his full name, ser Mattheo di Pagholo, is given.[68] On 5 September 1494 it is reported that an agreement, rectifying "certain differences," was reached between the Canons and Chapter of San Lorenzo and ser Matteo di Pagolo, "chaplain of San Lorenzo, titulary of the chapel

---

[64] SMDF 2.2.5, *Deliberazioni, 1476-1482*, fol. 68:
Die XXVIIII aprilis 1480
Prefati operarii deliberaverunt et deliberando stantiaverunt quod camerarius dicte eorum opere det et solvat et dare et solvere possit et debeat ser Matteo Pauli, cappellano substituto dicte eorum ecclesie, libras octo s. quindecim d. X parvorum pro scripturis et intonaturis cantus figurati pro Lamentationibus Hieremie et responsis ipsarum lamentationum et aliarum rerum compositarum [sic] pro diebus ebdomode sancte pro dicta eorum ecclesia.
[65] "Singers" 332.
[66] SSA 246, *Entrata & Uscita, 1479-1482*, fol. 271:
25 settembre 1482
A ser Matteo di Pagolo, piovano chapellano in San Lorenzo, a dì detto Fl. due larghi d'oro in oro per resto d'ogni ragione avesse col convento.
[67] *Ibid.* fol. 274:
5 ottobre 1482
A ser Matteo di Pagolo, chappellano in San Lorenzo, a dì detto Fl. due larghi d'oro in oro i quali si gli danno perchè ... el convento si sentiva gravato s'e' licentiato; e detti danari si gli danno per satisfacimento d'ogni suo danno benchè n'abia auti dua altri fiorini.
[68] Florence, Archivio Capitolare di San Lorenzo 74, *Liber Camerarii A, 1484*, fol. 10; *Ibid.* 75, *Liber Camerarii, 1485*, fol. 9v.

of San Lorenzo."[69] A final document from the church's archives, dated 10 July 1499, states that he was given leave to visit the baths at Monte Catini, probably because he was in poor health.[70] No further mention of him is made in the next few years, so it may be that he settled outside the city after that time.

Ser Felice di Giovanni Martini, contratenore, was appointed to the cathedral chapel on 26 January 1478. He had been associated with Santa Maria del Fiore for several years before, however, and his name figures in lists of the church's chaplains dating from as early as July 1469.[71] A document of 26 June 1478 records the salary paid him for his services as a singer during the previous five months.[72] He died shortly after that, and on 14 August 1478 his position as a chaplain was assigned to ser Antonio di Marco da Montughi.[73]

Ser Felice can probably be identified with the *Felice* who is named in the Cappella Giulia manuscript as the arranger of a five-part version (the original *a tre* with two added parts) of the well-known chanson *Fortuna desperata*.[74] Since one of the added parts (the altus) is found together with the original three-part version in musical sources presumed to be earlier than the Cappella Giulia collection, there is good reason to believe that Felice composed only the fifth part (the second bassus) which, interestingly, is preserved only in that manuscript.[75] If this is so, it appears that Felice was an amateur. Taken

---

[69] *Ibid.* A 2, *Partiti, 1482-1501,* fol. 52:

Ricordo come a dì 5 di septembre 1494 per cagione di certa differentia exorta fra 'l capitolo nostro e ser Matteo di Pagolo cappellano di San Lorenzo al titolo a cappella di San Lorenzo per se come cappellano di dicta e predicta cappella ... d'accordo fecono general compromesso.

[70] *Ibid.* fol. 77v:

10 luglio 1499

Item dicto dì si die licentia a ser Matteo di Pagolo, nostro cappellano, d'andare al bagno Monte Catini lasciando ongni dì la messa in suo luogo.

[71] SMDF 8.1.50, *Quaderno Cassa, com. Luglio, 1469,* fol. 34v; *Ibid.* 8.1.61, *Quaderno Cassa, com. Luglio, 1475,* fol. 4.

[72] Seay (n. 11 above) 49; the record of his appointment to the chapel is also printed here.

[73] ASF, Archivio dell'Arte della Lana 223, *Partiti, 1478,* fol. 76:

MCCCCLXXVIII, die XIIII mensis Augusti

Supradicti domini consules ... audita morte ser Felicis Johannis Martini, olim cappellani ... elegerunt ... in cappellanum dicte cappelle, loco dicti ser Felicis, honestum et religiosum virum ser Antonius Marci de Montuchio, cum prebendis, distributionibus, emolumentis et aliis.

[74] The original version by A. Busnois also served as the basis for Mass compositions by Josquin and Obrecht. See G. Reese, (n. 2 above) 102.

[75] A list of concordances for the four-part version is given by D. Plamenac, "A Reconstruction of the French Chansonnier in the Biblioteca Colombina" 3, *The Musical Quarterly* 38 (1952) 262. Three sources give the same altus part as the Cappella Giulia manuscript; two other sources have an altus part very similar to it. I am grateful to Mr. Allan Atlas of New York University, who is at present preparing a doctoral dissertation on the Cappella Giulia manuscript, for this information.

alone, the added part is rather monotonous because of its frequent repetition of similar rhythmic patterns; within the polyphonic complex it creates several awkward harmonies and on occasion even lapses into ungainly parallel octaves. What reasons prompted the compiler of the Cappella Giulia manuscript to include Felice's added part to the collection can, naturally, only be surmised. It is worth noting, however, that the manuscript, long thought to have belonged to Pope Leo X, contains works by Isaac, Agricola, Arnolfo and Stochem, all of whom were associated with Florence. It may be that the collection represents a group of works that the compiler presumed were familiar to Leo X; or it may be that the collection was planned to contain works by those composers who were known to have been personally connected with the Medici. In any case the inclusion of a chanson with an added part by a sometime composer would probably have appealed to the music-loving Leo X, who himself was the composer of a work based on another well-known chanson of the time.[76]

Ser Virgilio, contralto, is first mentioned in a personnel list of the cathedral chapel dating from 13 August 1507.[77] The cathedral's account books do not mention the exact date of his entrance into the chapel; but since his name is lacking in an earlier list, dating from 25 February 1502, it is obvious that he began serving during that five-year period.[78] Another document shows that on 6 January 1513 twenty-four lire were paid to *prete Vergilio, cantore,* part of his salary for the past six months.[79] Previously, on 22 August 1510, he had been engaged, along with his colleagues in the cathedral chapel, to perform at the baptistry.[80] On 4 July 1515 the cathedral singers, among

---

[76] See G. Reese (n. 2 above) 286.
[77] SMDF 2.2.10, *Deliberazioni, 1507,* fol. 5v:
Die 13 augusti 1507
Prefati operarii desiderantes cappellam cantus figurati eam in aliqua parte corrigere . . . deliberaverunt etc. ser Raffaelem debere in dicta cappella canere et servire, serviendo [?] cum famulis vel fanciullis pro sobranis . . . ser Franciscum Boscherinum et ser Ioangualbertem chericum pro tinoribus; ser Iacobum Bonaiuti et ser Niccolum Pedoni et ser Davit Sandri pro cantori bassi; ser Magdolum de Aretio et ser Ioanfranciscum et Vergilium pro cantori alti; Serraglium vero voluerunt esse magistrum cappelle.
[78] *Ibid.* 2.2.9, *Deliberazioni, 1498-1507,* fol. 41.
[79] *Ibid.* 8.1.128, *Quaderno Cassa, com. Luglio 1512,* fol. 53v:
La chapella del chanto fighurato de' dare . . . a dì 6 di gienayo [1513] L. 24 piccioli per lui a prete Vergilio, chantore, per suo salario.
A subsequent payment to him dates from 1516: *Ibid.* 8.1.135, *Quaderno Cassa, com. Luglio 1516,* fol. 40v:
Cappella e cantori di canto figurato de' dare . . . a dì 25 detto [settembre] Fl. due in oro larghi per loro a ser Vergilio cantore, portò lui detto.
[80] AC 23, *Deliberazioni, 1508-1513,* fol. 78:
Die XXII augusti 1510 . . . pertanto per la presente provisione . . . ordina che in decta chiesa et oratorio di San Giovanni Baptista si possi et debbi fare una cappella di cantori, et che in detta et per detta cappella da ora s'intendino essere et sieno electi tutti gl'in-

them *ser Virgilio di Domenico*, received an increment in salary from the baptistry's overseers.[81]

Subsequent documents from San Giovanni make it appear that he also received a chaplaincy there. Some confusion, however, is evident in the baptistry's records which name a *ser Virgilio d'Antonio, cappellano*, in a document from 22 August 1515; the next list of chaplains, dating from 26 April 1516, merely calls him *ser Virgilio*.[82] It is difficult to determine whether the difference in patronymic was a slip of the pen on the part of the clerk who copied the records or whether there was another Virgilio in the baptistry's service at the time. Later lists of San Giovanni's chaplains, dating from 11 December 1522 to 17 December 1527, do little to clarify the situation, for in these documents there appears yet another Virgilio, *ser Virgilio di Guasparre*.[83] Further information about ser Virgilio the musician is found in a letter, dated 5 August 1518, which begins:

> The present bearer is sent especially to tell you on behalf of the Magnificent [Lorenzo de' Medici, duke of Urbino] that you should send Baccio the organist and ser Virgilio here early tomorrow morning, and tell them to bring a soprano and singing books with them.[84]

Evidently ser Virgilio had been in the duke's personal service even prior to this time, since three payments in his name are recorded in the ducal accounts of 1516.[85]

---

frascripti otto cantori . . . ser Iacopo di Bonaiuto et ser Niccolaio Pedoni per due contribassi; ser Francesco Boscherini et ser Giovanni Serragli et ser Davit per tre tinori; ser Giovanfrancesco d'Antonio et Vergilio per due contrialti; ser Raffaello di Piero per sovrano insieme con sei cherici almeno, o que' più che vi cantassino a electione di decto ser Giovanni Serragli, maestro della vostra scuola de' cherici.

[81] *Ibid.* 26, *Deliberazioni, 1514-1515*, fol. 79.
[82] *Ibid.*, 84v; *ibid.* 24, *Deliberazioni, 1514-1522*, fol. 114.
[83] *Ibid.* 28, *Deliberazioni, 1522-1528*, fol. 11v; fol. 85v; fol. 210.
[84] ASF, Medici avanti il Principato 111 fol. 407; quoted in G. Pieraccini, *La stirpe de' Medici di Cafaggiolo* (Florence 1924) 1.260.
[85] ASF, Medici avanti il Principato 132, *Entrata & Uscita di Lorenzo, Duca d'Urbino*, fol. 32v:

febbraio 1515 [1516]

E a dì detto [28] Du. LXXV per tanti pagati a ser Gherardo e Giovambatista musico e ser Virgilio per vestirsi di paonazo che li dette loro per conto della mancia di natale. Du. 75.

Ibid. fol. 42v:

maggio 1516

Et a dì XXVIII di detto Fl. uno s. XII d'oro pagati per mandato di Pagolo de' Medici a ser Virgilio cappellano per le spese da Firenze in campo. Fl. 1 s .12

Ibid. fol. 44:

luglio 1516

Et a dì detto [8] L. V piccioli per resto di vettura d'uno cavallo per ser Virgilio quando andò a Urbino. S. 14. 4

NEGLECTED COMPOSERS IN FLORENTINE CHAPELS 283

One work, *a tre*, *Nec mihi nec tibi*, is ascribed to *Virgilius* in the Cappella Giulia manuscript. Given the pronounced Florentine character of the collection, it seems reasonable to suggest that the composer named there is the same person as the Florentine musician. Ser Virgilio's connections with Leo X's nephew Lorenzo offer further confirmation of this suggestion. Objections to accepting the ascription, however, can be raised on several grounds. There are both two-and three-part versions of the piece in five other manuscripts, one of which was compiled during the 1490s—at least a decade before we have any record of the Florentine musician's activities.[86] Another of these sources names Obrecht as the composer of the three-part version of the work.[87]

With regard to the first point, it may be noted that ser Virgilio could have been a practicing musician long before he joined the cathedral chapel, even though we lack information about him before that time. In fact, one could assume that he had already had a certain amount of experience before being appointed to the chapel. His authorship, therefore, cannot be discounted on the grounds that on the basis of known documents he was too young to have composed a work that dates, at the latest, from the early 1490s.[88]

The conflicting attribution to Obrecht, on the other hand, does provide sufficient reason for questioning the Cappella Giulia ascription. Since the piece exists also in a two-part version and since no other works by Virgilio are known, one might assume that he, too, was an occasional composer and that in this case the Cappella Giulia collection again contains an arrangement of a preexisting work by a Florentine who was associated with the Medici. An examination of the three-part version offers strong support in favor of this assumption.[89] The bottom part, for example, gives the impression of being an added rather than an integral member of the polyphonic complex, for it leads an existence noticeably independent of the others. It does not contribute to the contrapuntal development of the various motives that

---

[86] The piece is also preserved in Florence (MS Banco rari 229); Hradec Králové (Museum, Codex Speciálník); Segovia (Cathedral, MS without number); and in a two-part version in Perugia (Communal Library, MS 431); and Turin (National Library, MS I 27). The Florence manuscript is believed to date from ca. 1491.

[87] H. Anglès, "Un manuscrit inconnu avec polyphonie du xve siècle conservé à la cathedrale de Ségovie (Espagne)," *Acta musicologica* 8 (1936) 14.

[88] Various other musicians named Virgilio, however, can be discounted on these grounds. These musicians, mentioned among the personal of the Papal and Julian chapels during the 1530s and 1540s, are obviously too late chronologically to be connected with the piece in question. For information on these musicians see F. X. Haberl (n. 33 above) 274, 267, 269; R. Casimiri, "I diarii Sistini," *Note d'archivio* 4 (1927) 258; A. Ducrot, "Histoire de la Cappella Giulia au xvie siècle," *Mélanges d'archéologie et d'histoire* 85 (1963) 195, 199, 209, 514. Yet another Virgilio is recorded in the Julian chapel in 1524, during the Pontificate of the Medici Pope Clement VII (*ibid.* 191). Could this be the Florentine Virgilio? Other Florentine musicians are known to have been employed in Rome by the Medici Popes.

[89] The piece will be published in H. M. Brown's edition of MS Banco rari 229, mentioned above, n. 31.

appear in the upper parts and generally serves merely to complete triadically the harmonies implied there. Moreover, the two-part version, though not a very distinguished work, does stand as a complete piece in its own right. Aside from these considerations, however, the problem remains: it is the three-part version that is attributed to both Obrecht and Virgilio, and until more information becomes available, it is impossible to say with certainty which was the original version of *Nec mihi nec tibi* and who was its composer.

SER GIOVANNI SERRAGLI

Ser Giovanni Serragli was one of the group of Florentine composers active around the turn of the sixteenth century to whom reference has been made above. Although manuscripts containing works of his have been cited often in musicological literature, until recently the composer's name was completely unknown to the history of music. Documents from various Florentine archives disclosed the existence of a singer of this name who was also a music teacher at the cathedral and baptistry schools. A subsequent search through Florentine musical sources revealed that five complete and six incomplete works of his are extant. These sources present his name in such a way, however, that a positive identification of the composer would have been impossible had the name not appeared elsewhere. One manuscript from the cathedral, for example, gives his name as *Johannes Serra*; a second manuscript, also of Florentine origin, shortens it further to *Johannes Ser*; a third Florentine collection, using a common scribal abbreviation of the time, merely records it as & *Jo.* & = ser Jo[hannes] Ser[ragli].[90] Clearly, in his own day the composer was well enough known by both Florentine music copyists and persons for whom these manuscripts were prepared that more precise identification was evidently thought unnecessary.

Serragli was probably a member of the prominent Florentine family of that name. None of the documents relating to the family that I have been able to see, however, makes reference to him.[91] Born perhaps about 1480, he must have been educated at the Cathedral School of Chant and Grammar and ordained at the turn of the new century, for a document of 25 February 1502 gives him the title "ser." The document records his appointment to the cathedral's newly reconstituted chapel and shows that at the time he was already employed as one of the two music teachers in the cathedral school.[92]

---

[90] B. Becherini (n. 3 above) 109, 110, 111, reads the abbreviation as Ser Jo. Francesco.
[91] The sources consulted are listed in nn. 51, 52 above.
[92] SMDF 2.2.9, *Deliberazioni, 1498-1507* fol. 41:
Die 25 februarii 1501 [1502]
Spectabiles viri consules artis lane . . . elegerunt in cantores pro dicta ecclesia . . . magistros qui docent clerichos musicam . . . qui sunt duo videlicet ser Franchus et ser Ioannes de Serraglis.

Payments to him for his services as a singer are listed in cathedral account books over the next several years.[93] One of them, dated 21 February 1508, indicates that he subsequently became master of the chapel.[94] He continued in this capacity until the fall of 1512, when he was replaced by Bernardo Pisano. Serragli continued as a singer in the chapel, however, and later also served under Rampollini and Verdelot.[95]

Some years previously, on 22 August 1510, the cathedral singers, among them *ser Giovanni Serragli, tinore*, had been engaged to perform at the baptistry.[96] The document that records their appointment shows that, even prior to being replaced by Pisano as master of the cathedral chapel, Serragli had begun to be more closely associated with the baptistry. He assumed the position of "master of the boys" at its school, established on 26 August 1508.[97] He also obtained a chaplaincy in San Giovanni around the same time, and later, on 12 December 1512, it is reported that ser Giovanni Serragli, "a chaplain and master of the school," was granted a month's leave of absence by the baptistry's overseers.[98]

A few other documents record his continuing service at San Giovanni during the next several years.[99] The most interesting of these is one dated 1 July 1523, which states that on that day the baptistry's overseers granted "maestro Verdelotto, ser Giovanni Serragli and Brueto, singers in the church of San Giovanni," permission to take a month's leave of absence.[100] Serragli

---

[93] *Ibid.* 8.1.109, *Quaderno Cassa, com. Luglio, 1502*, fol. 52v:
Ser Francho e ser Giovanni Serraglio, chantori di duomo, deono dare a dì 22 d'ottobre L. quindici, portò ser Francho chontanti.
Ibid. 8.1.115, *Quaderno Cassa, com. Luglio, 1505*, fol. 17v:
Chappella del chanto fighurato de' dare ... a dì 13 di settembre L. cinquantatre, portò ser Giovanni di Iacopo Seragli, distribuitore agli altri cantori.

[94] *Ibid.* 8.1.120, *Quaderno Cassa, com. Gennaio 1507/08*, fol. 28v:
La chapella del chanto fighurato de' dare a dì 21 di febbraio 1507 [1508] L. settanta piccioli, portò ser Giovanni Serragli, maestro della chappella.
An earlier document (n. 77 above) suggests that he was already master of the cathedral chapel in August 1507.

[95] Rampollini is mentioned as master of the chapel for the first time in an account book begun July 1520; Verdelot, in one begun January 1523.

[96] See n. 80 above.

[97] G. Baccini, "L'antica cappella dei musici di San Giovanni," *La Cordelia* 14 (1894); offprint (Rocca San Casciano 1895) 23. Baccini apparently drew his information from a volume of the AC that has since disappeared.

[98] AC 24, *Deliberazioni, 1514-1522*, fol. 25v:
Die XII settembris 1512
Prefati domini consules ... concesserunt licentiam ser Johanni [gap] de Serraglis, cappellano et magistro schole, pro uno mense proxime futuro.

[99] *Ibid.* 26, *Deliberazioni, 1514-1515*, fol. 79; ibid. 28, *Deliberazioni, 1522-1528*, fols. 11v, 20v, 28v.

[100] The document is printed in A. Bragard (n. 2 above) 121, where the name of the third musician is given as "Bracio (?)."

had been serving under Verdelot in the cathedral and baptistry chapels since the latter's arrival in Florence, but this is the only evidence extant that shows him to have been on friendly terms with one of the most gifted composers of the age. The details of Verdelot's Florentine period have only recently been uncovered and it now seems quite certain that his stay in Florence contributed immeasurably to the formation of his madrigal style. Whether Serragli was in any way connected with Verdelot's first efforts in the new genre, or whether Verdelot, a master composer in the Franco-Netherlands tradition, had some influence on Serragli's work, are questions that unfortunately can only be asked for the moment.

Although Verdelot resumed service at the baptistry after his month's leave, the absence of Serragli's name in the lists of San Giovanni's chaplains, dating from 22 April 1524 and 16 December 1525, suggests that he did not.[101] He must have returned later, however, for a final document from the baptistry states that on 2 March 1526 ser Giovanni Serragli was relieved of his duties as a singer and appointed instead to the less prestigious job of keeping the chapel's attendance records.[102] The lack of any other information about him in San Giovanni's account books from the following years indicates that he did not accept the position. Perhaps he received an appointment in another city, since no further mention of him is found in Florentine musical archives. The date and place of his death remain unknown.

Serragli's only known sacred work, *O redemptor sume carnem*, exists in two versions, one for two parts, the other for four, in an early sixteenth-century Florentine manuscript now in the cathedral archives.[103] Some of the other polyphonic works in this predominantly monophonic collection may also be his, but only the four-part version of the piece carries his name.

Four complete secular works are found—three anonymously, another with an abbreviated version of his name—in MS Banco rari 230 of the National Library in Florence.[104] The bass parts of these four works, as well as those of six others, are attributed to him in another Florentine collection, MS Banco rari 337.[105] Serragli is the most frequently represented composer in the latter

---

[101] AC 28, *Deliberazioni, 1522-1528* fols. 85, 151.

[102] *Ibid.*, fol. 163v:
2 marzo 1525 [1526]
Item simili modo cassaverunt de officio cantoris dumtaxat ser Iohannem de Seraglis, et eumdem elegerunt in coristam dictorum cantorum, cum auctoritate apuntandi dictos cantores in illis apuntaturis et prout dispositum fuerit per dictos dominos consules et officiales musaici.

[103] His name here is given as *Johannes Serra*. The manuscript is described by F. Ghisi, "Un processionale inedito per la settimana santa nell'Opera del Duomo di Firenze," *Rivista musicale italiana* 55 (1953) 362-369. The work is printed in a modern edition in "Music of the Florentine Renaissance" 2.121-122.

[104] The one ascribed work gives his name as *Johannes Ser*.

[105] By means of the scribal abbreviation mentioned above.

manuscript, which, judging from its format and contents, must have been compiled during the period between 1515 and 1525. For this reason, as well as from what we know of his biography, it appears that his surviving secular works were written sometime around the end of the first decade of the sixteenth century.

Two pieces *a quattro*, *Per non trovare* and *Quel principe*, are typical examples of the Florentine polyphonic carnival song.[106] In duple meter with contrasting sections in triple time, both works are predominantly homophonic in texture, but varied occasionally with short sections in imitation. All parts are vocally conceived and carefully fitted to the text. The formal variety observable in other Florentine settings of this type is also present in these works. *Per non trovare*, poetically a ballata, provides new music for each line of text except for the second pair of piedi, which are repeated to the music of the first pair. The seven-line stanza of *Quel principe* is, on the other hand, through-composed. As was customary, only the first stanza of each poem is set, the remaining stanzas being sung to the music of the first.

With its low vocal ranges and sombre G dorian modality, *Per non trovare* is generally successful in depicting the text of the "Song of the Baptized Jews." Solemn declamatory phrases such as "et battezati siano" and "che tre dì qui da voi fumo accettati" are skillfully contrasted with imitation on the words "l'ebrea lasciata abbiano" and the more joyous, dancelike section in triple time that sets the words "colle donn'e figliuol sanza paura." The piece, however, is the least defined tonally of Serragli's works. The ripresa ends in the dominant instead of the usual tonic, and intermediary cadences on the tonic, subdominant and mediant do little to relieve the meandering structure of the whole.

Quel principe, a *trionfo* whose text celebrates the four temperaments, has a tightly organized tonal structure. It begins and ends in the untransposed mixolydian mode on G, and its intermediary cadences are contrived to stress only the tonic, dominant and subdominant chords. Imitative sections for two and three voices provide variety within the prevailing four-part chordal texture. The well-spaced sonorities, the bright quality of the high tessituras employed in the upper voices and the clear harmonic progressions outlined in the bass also contribute to the general appeal of the setting.

Donna, el pianto is at present the only known example of a frottola set by a Florentine in this period.[107] Traditionally, this type of poetry was set by the North Italian composers, the Florentines generally preferring the more literary ballata or the various forms of the native carnival song. Emulating the North Italians, Serragli furnishes his setting with a sprightly melodic cantus whose phrase structure and rhythms unerringly reproduce those of

---

[106] Both works are printed in a modern edition in "Music of the Florentine Renaissance" 2.44-46.

[107] Printed in a modern edition in "Music of the Florentine Renaissance" 2.39-40.

the octosyllabic verses. In contrast to the North Italian prototypes, however, the lower parts of Serragli's setting are eminently singable, conforming more to the Florentine concept of vocal part writing. The piece is firmly grounded in a bright F major tonality, which is emphasized at the end by the addition of a seven-measure coda outlining the submediant, subdominant and tonic chords.

Grato ognora, the longest of Serragli's works, is also the most ambitiously planned.[108] The text, in ballata form, is set to new music in the ripresa and in the first pair of piedi. The second pair of piedi has the same music as the first pair while the volta, which begins with new material, returns to the final part of the ripresa at its close. In this case the symmetrical musical structure of ripresa and volta mirrors exactly the form of the poetry in which the two final lines of the ripresa text also serve to close the volta. As might be expected, the musical setting closely follows the rhythms and accents of the text. Some attempt at word painting is also present in the juxtaposition of the static, low-voiced phrase on the words "Poi che tu, signora, in terra" with the brighter, more rhythmically active, then finally plaintive setting of the following line "Cagion sei del mio martire."

At the outset all of the voices share in lively imitation before moving into the homophonic texture that characterizes the piece as a whole. The basic homophony, however, is occasionally varied by quicker moving figures in the inner voices as well as by a few passages *a tre* that are more freely contrapuntal in nature. The four parts, each encompassing the range of a ninth, are vocally conceived. Melodic jumps of more than a fifth are rare, larger leaps generally occuring between phrases. At times individual melodic phrases outline the interval of a seventh or of an octave, but these are so constructed that no difficulties arise in vocal execution. Serragli's concern for well-defined tonal organization is also evident here. The piece is in the transposed dorian mode on G, in which the ripresa begins and ends. Intermediary cadences on the subdominant and dominant occur in ripresa and strophe, both of which close with a two-measure coda whose simple plagal cadence effectively echoes the words "del mio martire."

With this discussion of Serragli and his music I close this survey of certain still obscure composers in the Florentine chapels. In fact, it was during Serragli's lifetime that the course of Italian polyphony began to undergo radical changes that, in the hands of composers such as Serragli's colleagues Pisano and Verdelot, were soon to lead to the formation of the madrigal style—and to a new era in the history of Italian secular music.

---

[108] Printed in a modern edition in "Music of the Florentine Renaissance" 3.40-42.

IX

ALESSANDRO COPPINI AND BARTOLOMEO DEGLI ORGANI
TWO FLORENTINE COMPOSERS OF THE RENAISSANCE

Practically nothing is known about Alessandro Coppini and Bartolomeo degli Organi, the two leading Florentine composers from the turn of the 16th century. Most studies devoted to Italian music of the period merely refer to them as contemporaries of Isaac at the court of Lorenzo the Magnificent or mention them in passing along with the North Italian frottolists. Actually, both composers were considerably younger than Isaac, and what little of their music does survive shows marked differences from that of the contemporary frottolists. Significantly, Coppini was one of the first Italians to compose in both the frottola style and the polyphonic style of the Franco-Netherlanders. Bartolomeo's music stands as a link between Isaac's Italian works and those by later Florentine composers such as Bernardo Pisano, Francesco de Layolle and Francesco Corteccia. The works of Alessandro Coppini and Bartolomeo degli Organi may thus be described as heralding the confluence of Italian and Franco-Netherlandish elements that was to be typical of mid-16th century Italian music.

Despite the important positions both composers hold in the history of Italian Renaissance music, only a few of their works have been published in modern editions, and these generally without benefit of adequate musical analysis. Biographical information currently available about both composers is also fragmentary and at times misleading. The object of this study, therefore, is to present hitherto unknown documents concerning their lives and careers and to give a critical survey of their extant works.

Documents regarding A l e s s a n d r o C o p p i n i ' s family and his birth seem not to have come down to us. Later records of payment call him a Florentine, and one of them gives his full name as *Alessandro di* [the son of] *Bartolomeo di Marchione Choppini*[1]. Florentine tax registers of the 15th century do not list his father's or grandfather's names, although the same volumes make it clear that families named Coppini were then residing in

---

[1]) See notes 12 and 21 below. Here, as in all subsequent quotations and documents, the original spelling has been maintained, punctuation added and dates changed to conform to our present system. (The Florentine new year began on March 25, and documents recorded between January 1 — March 24 generally carry the date of the previous year.)

the city[2]. A report, which states that he began studying for the priesthood in 1475[3], gives us good reason to believe that he was born in the mid-1460's. But his name does not figure in the baptismal records of the Florentine Cathedral from those years, or for that matter from the years 1450—1470, the extreme limits of the period in which he must have been born. Perhaps Coppini's forebears, although Florentine citizens, lived in one of the subject cities of the Dominion or in the Florentine countryside. If this were the case, the family would have been enrolled in another set of tax registers and he himself baptized in a church outside the city's walls. Whatever the cause of the lack of corroborating evidence, however, there is no reason to doubt that later records of payment are correct in calling him a Florentine[4].

Coppini presumably entered the Order of the Servi di Maria in 1475, the year he began studying for the priesthood. Three years later, on Sep-

---

The abbreviations used to indicate sources for documents and quotations are as follows:
  ASF   Archivio di Stato, Florence
  MAP   ASF, Medici avanti il Principato
  SMDF   Archivio dell'Opera di Santa Maria del Fiore, Florence
  SL   Archivio Capitolare di San Lorenzo, Florence
  SMN   ASF, Archivio del R. Arcispedale di Santa Maria Nuova
  SMNo   ASF, Corporazioni Religiose Soppresse N° 102, Santa Maria Novella
  SSA   ASF, Corporazioni Religiose Soppresse N° 119, Santissima Annunziata
  Ba   ASF, Corporazioni Religiose Soppresse N° 78, Badia di Firenze

[2]) The tax registers, for example, list a Bartolomeo di Agostino Coppini, of the parish of Santa Felicita, who filed his last will and testament on June 17, 1467. (ASF, Notarile ante-cosimiano, Vol. P 357, fols. 49r—50v.)

[3]) The report is given by L. C e r r a c c h i n i in his *Fasti teologali;* see note 19 below.

[4]) The confusion regarding Coppini's Florentine origins may be traced here briefly. G. C e s a r i, basing his assumption on the fact that some of Coppini's music is preserved in Milan, was the first to state that Coppini was a singer in the Duke of Milan's chapel (*Musica e musicisti alla Corte Sforzesca*, Rivista Musicale Italiana, Vol. XXIX [1922], p. 18). A singer named Alexander was, in fact, employed at the Milanese court, but other documents show that the musician in question was Alexander Agricola. (See E. M o t t a, *Musici alla Corte degli Sforza*, Archivio Storico Lombardo, Serie II, Vol. IV [1887], pp. 323, 532; see also C. S a r t o r i, *Organs, Organ-Builders, and Organists in Milan, 1450—1476: New and Unpublished Documents*, The Musical Quarterly, Vol. XLII [1957], p. 64.) Cesari's assumption was accepted by F. G h i s i (in *I canti carnascialeschi* [Florence 1937], p. 57), and led Ghisi to assert that the Florentine organist Alessandro was not the same person as Coppini and that there were, therefore, two composers (besides Agricola) named Alessandro writing carnival music in Florence at the same time (Ibid., pp. 45, 60). Later A. E i n s t e i n (in *The Italian Madrigal* [Princeton 1949], Vol. I, p. 277) not only accepted Cesari's and Ghisi's assumptions, but further obfuscated the matter by stating that it is doubtful that Coppini was an Italian. The circle was recently completed in the notes accompanying a recorded anthology of Italian music, Coppini being described there as a Flemish musician. The information assembled in the present study should leave no doubt about Coppini's origins. Research in various archives has also shown that he was the only Florentine organist-composer named Alessandro who was active in Florence during the period in question.

tember 18, 1478, his name is found in a list of novitiates who received shoes from the Florentine convent of the Santissima Annunziata, parent house of the Servite Order[5]. Subsequent records from the Annunziata's archives reveal that after completing his initial training there, Coppini was sent to Bologna, apparently to study at the University. A document, dated July 5, 1486, states that he had been in Bologna before that time[6]. Another document, in which he is called *frate Alexandro di Bartolomeo da Firenze, nostro frate e studente a Bologna*, lists expenditures made on his behalf for the period February 14, 1488 — June 20, 1492. (Doc. 1: The documents will be found in the Appendix to this article.) An entry in this account, from March 13, 1491, records the final payment for a horse, „*when he went to Bologna.*" It is obvious, however, that the expense had been carried over from a previous year, for a receipt which Coppini himself signed on June 20, 1489, shows that by that time he had returned to Florence and taken up duties at the Annunziata as assistant organist and music teacher to the novices[7]. Later he was also appointed to the Convent's chapel. He served the Annunziata in these capacities until the end of April, 1493[8].

During this period several musicians of international reputation, among them Isaac and Agricola, were also employed at the Annunziata. It is more than likely that Coppini studied composition with one of them, for his extant sacred music clearly shows that he was well trained in the techniques of northern polyphony[9]. We can also assume with some certainty that Coppini received his keyboard training from one of the several Italian organists who were associated with the Annunziata during his formative years, or even from one of the Squarcialupis, the most eminent Florentine organists of the time[10].

---

[5]) SSA, Vol. 698, *Giornale del Camerlengo, 1477—1479*, fol. 61v. An earlier payment to him for four lire, his allowance from the Convent for 1475, is also recorded in the Annunziata's accounts: SSA, Vol. 693, *Entrata & Uscita, 1475—1478*, fol. 28r.

[6]) SSA, Vol. 198, *Debitori & Creditori, 1486—1493*, fol. 230r: „Frate Alexandro da Firenze de' dare .... per conto di suo vestimento quando era a Bologna a studiare .... L. 4".

[7]) SSA, Vol. 1050, *Ricevute, 1486—1493*, fol. 81v: „Io frate Alexandro da Firenze ho ricevuto a dì 12 di settembre [1492] per pagamento di vestimento di organo e insegnare a cantare per el mese d'aghosto lire octo. . . ." In a later receipt his signature reads „frate Alexandro di Bartolomeo da Firenze." (Ibid., fol. 152r).

[8]) SSA, Vol. 857, *Vestimenti di Frati, 1469—1492*, fol. 137r. See also Doc. 1.

[9]) On Isaac, Agricola and other northern composers in Florence see my *The Singers of San Giovanni in Florence during the 15th century*, Journal of the American Musicological Society, Vol. XIV (1961), pp. 343 ff. One of Coppini's first teachers may have been the mysterious Arnolfo, who is recorded as a teacher of figural music to the Annunziata's novices in 1477 (SSA, Vol. 697, *Entrata & Uscita, 1477—1478*, fols. 54v, 56r).

[10]) Several itinerant Italian organists are recorded at the Annunziata during this period. The Convent's principal organists were frate Bernardo di Luca da Firenze (from 1471—1493) and ser Piero di Giovanni d'Arezzo (from 1481—1484).

After April 30, 1493, Coppini's name disappears from the Annunziata's account books for several years, an indication that he was away from Florence during that period. His reasons for leaving the city are easy to deduce. In the spring of 1493 the chapels at the Santissima Annunziata, the Cathedral and the Baptistry, all of them staffed for the most part with the same singers, were disbanded. This action, without doubt a result of Savonarola's fiery denunciations of polyphonic music, caused most musicians to leave Florence in search of employment elsewhere[11]. The banishment of the Medici little more than a year later further contributed to the decline of opportunities available to professional musicians, for by then musical services in the major Florentine churches had been reduced to the barest essentials, plain-chant and organ music. In view of these facts it is not difficult to imagine that Coppini would also have left the city. His whereabouts during the mid-1490's, however, remain unknown. Perhaps he returned to Bologna for further study at the University. It is also possible that he traveled during those years — to Milan where, for example, some of his sacred music was copied shortly after this time in a volume compiled under the supervision of Franchino Gaffurio.

Coppini was back in Florence by the late summer of 1497, and on the following September 6 he was engaged as organist and chaplain at the hospital of Santa Maria Nuova[12]. His association with that establishment was to continue until the end of October, 1516, although in later years he was assisted in his duties there by another monk of the Servite Order, frate Ambrogio di Gismondo[13]. Shortly after his appointment to Santa Maria Nuova Coppini also resumed his position as organist at the Santissima Annunziata:

1497

I recall how on this day, the 28th of November, our father prior, maestro Giovanfilippo da Pisichatone, engaged our brother, frate Alessandro di Bartolomeo, who is presently living at Santa Maria Nuova of Florence, to play the organ of above and [that of] below for all our needs and for additional Masses [as well, providing] we send for him at a reasonable hour [beforehand.] And we must give him nine gold florins each year for his salary and services at the said organs; and with the stipulation that he will forfeit four grosoni every time he is absent without permission from the prior or from the vicar, unless he becomes sick on the same day or the day before and cannot find a substitute. And I Bernardo Mini have made this record with my own hand on this above-said day. (Doc. 2)

---

[11]) F. D'Accone, Op. cit., pp. 348 ff.
[12]) SMN, Vol. 5880, *Libro mastro rosso D, 1497—1501*, fol. 19r: „*Frate Alessandro di Bartolomeo di Marchionne, frate de' Servi, nostro chapelano e organista . . . ven[ne] a servire questo ispedale 6 di settembre, 1497. . . .*"
[13]) SMN, Vol. 5884, *Libro mastro verde C, 1508—1513*, fol. 375r.

Another document from the Annunziata's archives, dated January 31, 1498, confirms the terms of this contract[14].

On November 30, 1500, Coppini was appointed organist at San Lorenzo, the family church of the Medici[15]. It is reported that he was given quarters there on September 4, 1501[16], and that repairs to the church's organ were later ordered upon his recommendation[17]. No further mention of him is made in San Lorenzo's records until November 12, 1503, when it is stated that

> Our Chapter, assembled in the customary manner, was publicly informed that our organist, maestro Alexandro, a monk of the Servite Order, was not serving us properly, playing in such a way that he was creating great scandal among our Chapter and our parishioners. Therefore, in order that our church be better served and also to remove this big expense for bad service, the Chapter deprived maestro Alexandro of his position as organist and immediately elected in his place ser Mariotto di [gap], a priest who has been trained in the monastery of San Niccolò di Cafaggio[lo] of Florence, with a salary of 60 lire a year .... (Doc. 3)

It is doubtful that the „*great scandal*" was due to a lack of professional competency on Coppini's part. Rather, it must have been caused by his failure to be present at all the required services in San Lorenzo. At the time he was also serving as organist and chaplain at Santa Maria Nuova and as organist, teacher and singer at the Santissima Annunziata[18]. Meanwhile, he had evidently been pursuing his theological studies as well, since he was admitted as a master to the Florentine College of Theologians on November 17, 1502[19]. A payment to him from Santa Maria Nuova for services up to July 1, 1504, accordingly refers to him as *maestro Alessandro di Bartolomeo, maestro in sagra teologia e frate di Santa Maria de' Servi et nostro orghanista*[20].

Another document from Santa Maria Nuova, dated April 17, 1505, shows that on that day Coppini deposited twenty six florins in the hospital's

---

[14]) SSA, Vol. 50, *Ricordanze C, 1494—1504*, fol. 46r.
[15]) SL, *Partiti, A. 2, 1482—1501*, fol. 88v: „. . .eleggiemmo per sonatore del nostro organo . . . maestro Alexandro . . . frate de' Servi. . . ."
[16]) SL, *Partiti, A. 3, 1501—1516*, fol. 6v.
[17]) Ibid., fol. 12v.
[18]) SSA, Vol. 700, *Entrata & Uscita, 1494—1504*, fols. 107v, 115r, 120v.
[19]) L. Cerracchini, *Fasti teologali ovvero notizie istoriche del collegio de' teologi della sacra università fiorentina della sua fondazione fino all'anno 1738* (Florence, 1738), p. 212: „*Alessandro di Bartolomeo Coppini de' Servi li 17 novembre 1502 si incorporò come maestro: e dopo fu creato decano nell'anno 1517. Costui si incorporò già a leggere sul maestro delle sentenze nel 1475, e dopo lunga lettura si addottorò per mezzo del suo generale; non facendosi però far buono per l'anzianità quell'ingresso nel nostro collegio, sono necessitato porlo qui.*"
[20]) SMN, Vol. 5882, *Libro mastro F, 1504—1508*, fol. 125v.

treasury, with the stipulation that were the money not to have been withdrawn at the time of his death, it should be paid to mona Antonia, „*donna di Piero*" — apparently his sister — or to his nephews[21]. From this it would appear that Coppini was planning another trip and wished to settle his financial affairs before his departure. Indeed, but for one payment to him in the Annunziata's accounts for all of June, 1505[22], no mention of him is made in Florentine archives for the next four years, a good indication that he was once again outside the city. Perhaps it was during this period that he visited Milan. As on the previous occasion, however, no information has survived concerning his whereabouts or the purpose of his trip.

On July 1, 1509, Coppini signed a new contract to teach singing at the Santissima Annunziata[23]. Several months later payments to him for playing the organ are resumed in the account books of both the Annunziata and Santa Maria Nuova[24], and over the next few years his services are regularly recorded at the two institutions[25]. The Annunziata's account books also show that during this period he made several trips on the Convent's behalf to Rome and Bologna[26].

A document from October 13, 1514, informs us that Coppini had become provincial vicar of his order by that time[27]. Payments to him from Santa Maria Nuova, however, continue to be recorded until November 5, 1516, after which his name disappears from the hospital's accounts[28]. It may be that he terminated his duties there because of the demands imposed upon him by his new administrative position. Elsewhere it is reported that he was made a deacon of the Florentine College of Theologians in 1517 and that he received his doctorate a few years later[29].

After that time Coppini appears to have traveled throughout Tuscany in his new capacity of provincial vicar of the Servite Order. Later he settled in Rome, where in 1522 he is mentioned among the singers of the Papal

---

[21]) SMN, Vol. 5639, *Depositi, 1500—1516*, fols. 174v—175r: „*Maestro Alessandro di Bartolomeo di Marchione Choppini, maestro in teologia, del ordine de' Servi.* . . ."
[22]) SSA, Vol. 199, *Debitori & Creditori, 1504—1510*, fol. 76r.
[23]) SSA, Vol. 51, *Ricordanze A. 2, 1504—1510*, fol. 208r.
[24]) SSA, Vol. 702, *Entrata & Uscita, 1507—1509*, fols. 137v, 149v; SMN, Vol. 4529, *Uscita, 1508—1510*, fol. 102r.
[25]) SSA, Vol. 704, *Entrata & Uscita, 1509—1511*, fol. 137r; Vol. 705, *Entrata & Uscita, 1512—1516*, fol. 85r; Vol. 199, *Debitori & Creditori, 1504—1519*, fol. 408r; SMN, Vol. 4531, *Uscita, 1511—1513*, fol. 2v; Vol. 5884, *Libro mastro verde C, 1508—1513*, fol. 204v.
[26]) SSA, Vol. 704, *Entrata & Uscita, 1509—1511*, fol. 114v; Vol. 705, *Entrata & Uscita, 1512—1516*, fols. 123v, 148r.
[27]) SSA, Vol. 705, *Entrata & Uscita, 1512—1516*, fol. 147v.
[28]) SMN, Vol. 5887, *Libro mastro giallo F, 1516—1518*, fol. 27r.
[29]) See note 19 above.

Chapel[30]. No other information about him has come to light except for a record in the Annunziata's archives which states that he died in Florence during the summer of 1527, a victim of the plague[31].

If biographical information about Alessandro Coppini is scanty, the opposite is true of B a r t o l o m e o   d e g l i   O r g a n i, whose life is richly documented in various Florentine archives. Bartolomeo, also called Baccio by his contemporaries, was descended from a family of artists and artisans traceable in Florence from around the middle of the 14th century. The family had no surname at the time of Bartolomeo's birth, *degli Organi* having been acquired by the composer during his lifetime in reference to his profession. Later the surname was also given to, or adopted by, his children.

During the 1440's and 1450's Bartolomeo's grandfather, Giuliano di Jacopo di Lorino, a painter by profession, operated in company with two others of his trade a successful *bottega* on the Corso degli Adimari, in the same quarters that had once belonged to the painter-composer Bonaiuto Corsini[32]. In 1444 Giuliano bought the house on the Arno just outside the city gates known as „la Casaccia," a building that remains a well-known Florentine landmark to this day[33]. Bartolomeo eventually inherited the house and in turn bequeathed it to his sons[34].

Toward the end of his life Giuliano's business failed, and when he died in 1460 he left his family in dire financial straits[35]. A tax return filed from

---

[30]) F. X. H a b e r l, *Die römische „schola cantorum' und die päpstlichen Kapellsänger bis zur Mitte des 16. Jahrhunderts*, Vierteljahrsschrift für Musikwissenschaft, Vol. III (1887), p. 259.

[31]) I am indebted to Father Eugenio Casalini, curator of the Convent's private archives, for this information.

[32]) For an exhaustive study on Bartolomeo's grandfather see U. P r o c a c c i, *Di Jacopo di Antonio e delle compagnie di pittori del Corso degli Adimari nel XV secolo*, Rivista d'Arte, Vol. XXXIV (1961), pp. 3—69.

[33]) Ibid., p. 31.

[34]) The house apparently passed first to his son Giovanbattista. In his last will and testament, dated May 31, 1559, Giovanbattista, „*quondam egregi organiste Bartolomeo Michaelisangeli alias Baccio degli Organi*," left the house to his brother Michelagnolo, „*iam per multos annos absentem a dominio florentino et nunc Rome habitator*," on condition that their mother, mona Lionarda, „*filiam quondam Matthei Francisci de Arrighis civis florentini*," be permitted to live there the rest of her days. (ASF, Notarile ante-cosimiano, Vol. G 301, fols. 425v—426r.) Michelagnolo later returned to Florence and took possession of the house. (ASF, Corporazione Religiose Soppresse N° 88, San Pancrazio, Vol. 46, *Debitori & Creditori, 1560—1586*, fols. 17v—18r.) (I am indebted to Mr. Edward Sanchez of Florence for this information.) After Michelagnolo's death, in the absence of direct male heirs, „la Casaccia" was acquired by the Salvini family of Florence, into which Bartolomeo's daughter Cassandra had married. (Ibid., Vol. 70, *Ricordanze, 1528—1598*, fol. 106v; Florence, Biblioteca Marucelliana, Codice A 162, fol. 204r.)

[35]) U. P r o c a c c i, Op. cit., p. 35.

the parish of Santa Maria Nipotecosa in 1480 by his two surviving sons, Michelagnolo and Piero, shows that they had meanwhile been forced to sell their property in town and move to „la Casaccia". (Doc. 4) Michelagnolo, unemployed at the time, was by then head of the family, which included his brother Piero, „*infirm, crippled and mute*"; his wife, mona Lucretia; and their five children, Giuliano, Antonio, Bartolomeo, Lorenzo and Chaterina.

In the tax return Michelagnolo mistakenly reported that his son Bartolomeo was three years old. Actually, the boy was nearer six, for the baptismal records of the Florentine Cathedral show that *Bartolomeo e Stephano di Michelagnolo di Giuliano of the parish of Santa Maria Nipotecosa* was born on December 24, 1474 and baptized two days later[36]. Given the exact name of the son, father and grandfather in the document, as well as the name of the parish in which the family had originally lived and filed taxes from as early as 1427, there is no reason to believe that the Cathedral's baptismal records are mistaken or that the infant named in the document was not Bartolomeo. We need not, however, be too surprised at this discrepancy between the report given by Michelagnolo (who should have known how old his son was) and the baptismal record in Cathedral archives. Possibly it was negligence on Michelagnolo's part, or on the part of the clerk who copied the tax return. Ages, as given in the Florentine tax registers, furthermore, have been shown to be only approximate on other occasions, and indeed, it was not uncommon then — as now — for people to falsify or pretend ignorance of age when filing official documents.

Bartolomeo must have been a musically precocious youngster, for soon after his thirteenth birthday he earned his first professional appointment, as a singer at the Santissima Annunziata:

I recall how on this day, the 24th of March, 1488, with the permission and consent of our father prior, maestro Giovanni Philipo da Pizleoni, we appointed Baccino, the son of Michelagnolo the goldsmith, as a singer of laude and figural music for the four years beginning on March 1, 1488 and ending on the last day of March, 1492, [at a salary] of two lire and ten soldi each month, and shoes. And for clarity's sake this record has been made with these terms and conditions: that he is not to sing in any other place without permission from the Convent and from the prior; nor, in addition, is he to be sent elsewhere without his father's permission etc. And in keeping with this his father will affix his signature below as proof that he approves this appointment.
I the above-mentioned Michelagnolo obligate myself to what is contained above, and in faith of it I have subscribed on this above-said day with my own hand. (Doc. 5)

---

[36]) The record was published by M. F a b b r i in *La vita e l'ignota opera-prima di F. Corteccia,* Chigiana, Nuova Serie 2, Vol. XXII (1965), pp. 194f, n. 31.

Those years at the Annunziata must have been of great value to the young musician. As we have learned, several famous composers were employed by the Convent at the time, and Bartolomeo probably had some opportunity to study and perform their music under their direct guidance. A few of Bartolomeo's surviving works point to a connection with Isaac, who was in Florence throughout most of the younger musician's formative years. Bartolomeo could, of course, have studied with the renowned master any time during that period; but it is possible that he began receiving instruction from Isaac even at this early date. Like Coppini, Bartolomeo was undoubtedly trained at the keyboard by some Italian organist, perhaps Coppini himself. In later years Bartolomeo may also have studied with Francesco Squarcialupi, for upon Squarcialupi's death Bartolomeo was appointed to succeed him as organist at the Cathedral, an indication that he may have been prepared for the position by the older musician.

By the mid-1490's Bartolomeo had entered fully into the city's musical life, and in the course of the next decade he served as organist at several of the major Florentine churches. His name was first recorded in the account books of Santa Maria Novella on February 23, 1495, when he received a payment of six gold florins, his salary for the preceding six months[37]. He was associated with Santa Maria Novella until December 1, 1502[38]. Extant accounts from Santo Spirito indicate that he had been employed there since December 1, 1504, although it is possible that his employment at that church began even earlier[39]. He remained at Santo Spirito until the end of October, 1505[40]. Previously, on May 1 of the same year, Bartolomeo had also become organist at the Badia[41]. He held that position until the time of his appointment to the Cathedral, in December, 1509[42]. Meanwhile, on July 1, 1499, Bartolomeo returned to the Annunziata's service, but this time as an organist. His first payments from the Convent make no mention of his duties there[43]. A later payment, dated January 15, 1500, is more explicit:

To Bacio who plays [i. e., accompanies] laudi . . . one gold florin . . . for having played the organ for two months. L. 7. (Doc. 6)

Bartolomeo was employed at the Annunziata until the end of December,

---

[37]) SMNo, Appendice Vol. 19, *Entrata & Uscita, 1488—1497*, fol. 109r.
[38]) Ibid., fols. 110v, 114r, 117r, 124v; Appendice Vol. 20, *Entrata & Uscita, 1497—1510*, fols. 80v, 97r, 116r.
[39]) ASF, Corporazioni Religiose Soppresse N° 127, Santo Spirito, Vol. 9, *Entrata & Uscita, 1498—1506*, fol. 107r.
[40]) Ibid., fol. 112r.
[41]) Ba, Vol. 262, *Memoriarum II*, fol. 118v.
[42]) Ibid., Vol. 82, *Debitori & Creditori, 1505—1515*, fol. 74r.
[43]) SSA, Vol. 700, *Giornale del Camerlengo, 1499—1504*, fols. 55r, 124r.

1509, when, notwithstanding the terms of his appointment to the Cathedral, he voluntarily discontinued his association with the Convent:

1509
I recall how on this 26th day of November we [the Convent of the Santissima Annunziata] promise to pay Lorenzo di Filipo Strozi 12 gold florins at the rate of 6 gold florins a year, that is, one half florin each month for two years, beginning on December 1, 1509. This promise is made on behalf of Bacino di Michelagnolo, organist in the chapel of the Annunziata. And we are making the said promise to the said Lorenzo on condition that Bacino serve the Convent.
The said promise was not kept because the said Bacino left [our service] after the above-said month of December and did not play the organ any longer; on the contrary, he went to play the organ in Santa Maria del Fiore. (Doc. 7)

The document recording Bartolomeo's appointment to the Cathedral has survived in the archives of the *Arte della Lana*, the guild responsible for the administration of Santa Maria del Fiore:

On the 20th day of the month of December, 1509
The above-said lord consuls ... elected and appointed Bartolomeo di Michelagnolo alias Baccio degl'Organi as organist and player of the organs of Santa Maria del Fiore with the usual salary and other customary benefits, [and] with the condition that he personally serve the said church and that he not perform in churches other than the aforesaid Santa Reparata [Santa Maria del Fiore], the oratorio of Orsanmichele and in the church and oratorio of the Annunziata of the city of Florence. (Doc. 8)

The Cathedral's records show that Bartolomeo began serving there the very next day, December 21, 1509, at a salary of seventy gold florins a year[44]. Bartolomeo was to hold the position until the time of his death, which apparently occurred on December 12, 1539, the day on which payment to him in the Cathedral's accounts ceases[45].

From the document of November 26, 1509, given above, it is quite evident that Bartolomeo had borrowed money from Lorenzo di Filippo Strozzi and that the Annunziata had agreed to pay the debt by subtracting

---

[44]) SMDF, VIII. 3. 11, No. 64, *Entrata & Uscita, com. gennaio 1509/10*, fol. 29v. A letter written to the Grand Duke of Florence many years after Bartolomeo's death states that the canons and Chapter of Santa Maria del Fiore had been moved to give him an extra stipend of two scudi each month because he was „*burdened with family and most poor.*" (See E. Sanesi, *Maestri d'organo in Santa Maria del Fiore, 1436—1600*, Note d'Archivio, Vol. XIV [1937], p. 174.) In 1515 Bartolomeo's salary was raised to one hundred gold florins a year by the Cathedral's overseers. He continued to receive that salary until 1527, when, owing to the straitened financial circumstances of the Republic, the increase was removed. On February 23, 1533, the overseers again decided to raise his salary to one hundred gold florins a year, a sum he continued to receive until the time of his death. (SMDF, Ia. 3. 1, *Agnus Dei*, fol. 127v.)

[45]) SMDF, VIII. 1. 176, *Quaderno cassa com. luglio 1539*, fol. 61r. During his years of service at the Cathedral Bartolomeo was once again employed by the Annunziata, from 1523—1531. (SSA, Vol. 200, *Debitori & Creditori, 1523—1535*, fols. 43r, 436r.)

part of the amount from his monthly earnings. Many other documents, far too numerous to record here, also testify to Bartolomeo's financial difficulties and show that he was continually striving to accomodate his various creditors[46]. Indeed, even the two extant documents written by the composer himself make vivid reference to his habitual indebtedness[47]. In one of them, an undated letter to Giovanni da Poppi, secretary to Lorenzo de' Medici, Duke of Urbino, Bartolomeo implored his friend's assistance in raising the money to pay for the rent of a town house from which he apparently had been evicted. That Bartolomeo was not without a sense of humor, even at that trying time, is well illustrated by a passage in the letter where he described himself as living at „*la Casaccia, with lots of water* [the house is on the right bank of the Arno] *and little wine.*" (Doc. 9)

Around 1500 Bartolomeo married Lionarda Arrighi, daughter of Matteo di Francesco Arrighi of Florence[48]. Documents in the Florentine State Archives reveal that some fifteen years later Lionarda's younger sister, Maddalena, also married a musician, Francesco de Layolle[49]. While still a youth Layolle had been employed as a singer of laudi at the Santissima Annunziata, during Bartolomeo's tenure there as an accompanist to the *laudesi*, and shortly after that time he became a pupil of Bartolomeo[50]. Given these circumstances, it is reasonable to assume that Bartolomeo later arranged, or helped to arrange, for the younger musician's marriage to Lionarda's sister. That Lionarda herself was also a musician is evident from notes appended to a manuscript collection of frottola texts, now in the Florentine National Library[51]. The compiler of the collection, Giovanni Mazzuoli detto Stradino, a poet and man of letters, states that the frottole were sung by Maria, the wife of Bianchino da Pisa, Masina, and Lionarda, the wife of Baccino degli Organi, and that some of the songs were brought from Rome by Maria while others were furnished him by Lionarda, who had received them „from Rome *in sul chanzoniere.*"

---

[46]) SMDF, II. 2. 11, *Deliberazioni, 1507—1515,* fol. 204r; ASF, Orsanmichele, Vol. 28, *Partiti, 1515—1516,* fols. 8v, 15r; ASF, Notarile ante-cosimiano, Vol. C 194, fol. 445r; Ibid., Vol. P 13, I, fol. 72r.

[47]) MAP, filza 68, c. 362; Ibid., filza 115, c. 495. The second is given in partial transcription in the Appendix, Doc. 9, and also reproduced here in full. (See the Illustration.)

[48]) Her full name is given in the document mentioned above, n. 34. Mona Lionarda died on February 8, 1561, and was buried in the Santissima Annunziata. (Florence, Biblioteca Nazionale Centrale: C i r r i , G., *Necrologio Fiorentino,* Vol. XIII, p. 405.)

[49]) ASF, Notarile ante-cosimiano, Vol. I 122, fols. 134r—134v.

[50]) SSA, Vol. 706, *Entrata & Uscita, 1504—1507,* fols. 101r, 137v, 145v; ASF, *Carte Strozziane,* V[a] Serie, Vol. 88, fol. 38v.

[51]) Florence, Biblioteca Nazionale Centrale, Cod. Maglia. VII, 735: quoted in A. E i n s t e i n , Op. cit., p. 78.

IX

Alessandro Coppini and Bartolomeo degli Organi

Autograph letter of Bartolomeo degli Organi to Giovanni da Poppi,
secretary to Lorenzo de' Medici, Duke of Urbino
(ASF, MAP, filza 115, C. 495)

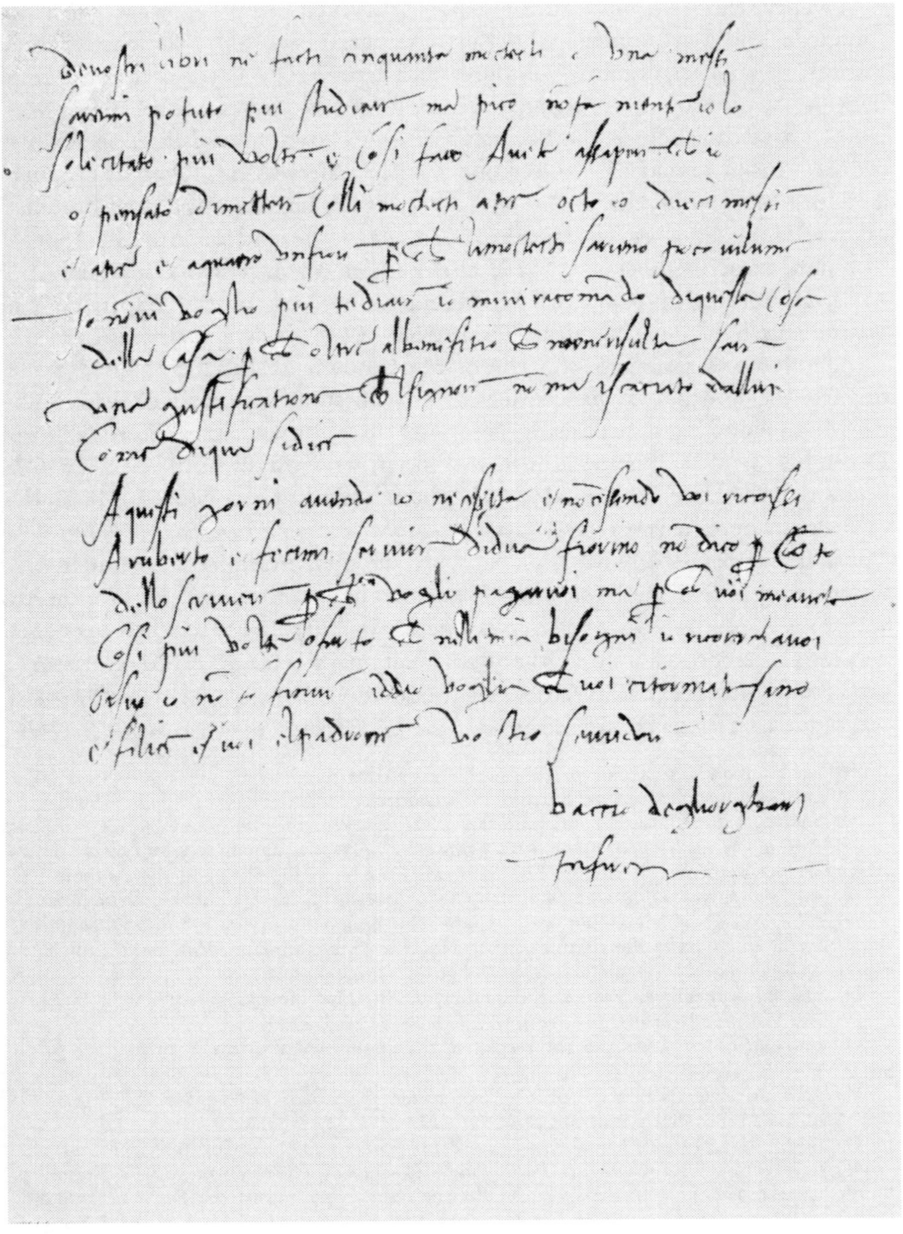
de nostri [illegible] ne facti cinquanta [illegible] e una [illegible]
[illegible] potuto piu studiare ma pero [illegible] io lo
solecitato piu volte e cosi fara [illegible]
o pensato di mettere colli medici [illegible] otto o dieci mesi
[illegible]
se non voglio piu tediare [illegible] mi ricomando di questa cosa
della casa [illegible]
[illegible] giustificatione [illegible] signore [illegible]
Come degno sidire

A questi giorni [illegible]
A ruberto [illegible] fiorino [illegible]
dello servire [illegible] voglio paghare [illegible]
Cosi piu volte [illegible] bisogni [illegible]
[illegible] voi ritornate [illegible]
[illegible] vostro servidore

barto degli organi
in furia

Twenty children, not all of whom survived infancy, were born to Lionarda and Bartolomeo, who thus compares favorably, at least in one respect, to another organist-composer of a later age[52]. Three of the children became professional musicians. Antonio, born March 22, 1504[53], was trained as a choirboy at the Baptistry of San Giovanni and later took holy orders[54]. From January 1 — December 31, 1531, he was employed as organist at Santa Maria Novella[55]. On January 1, 1532, he was appointed organist at the Badia, and served at that church until the end of August, 1536[56]. Lorenzo, born October 17, 1519, also became an organist. On March 17, 1540, he succeeded Francesco Corteccia as organist at the Baptistry[57], a position he held until his death in March, 1544[58].

Bartolomeo's youngest son Piero, also known as Pierino, gained fame toward the middle of the century as the outstanding pupil of Francesco da Milano and as a promising composer in his own right. Pierino, born December 8, 1523[59], is mentioned in Florentine archives until May, 1536[60]. Some months later, in January, 1537, he is found at the court of Paul III in Rome, where he is referred to as „*creato di messer Francesco Milanese*"[61]. Thus, his association with the renowned lutenist must have begun in the intervening period, perhaps when Francesco passed through Florence on his way to Rome. Pierino was still in Rome on January 1, 1538, when his name was again recorded among the Papal retainers who received Christmas gifts from Paul III[62]. In October of the same year the Papal treasurer paid ten scudi to „*Pietrino organista, so that he might return to Siena*"[63]. It is

---

[52] M. Fabbri, Op. cit., p. 197, n. 40, gives this number. In my researches I have found mention of seventeen of Bartolomeo's children.

[53] SMDF, Libro Battesimi, *Maschile dal 1501 al 1511*, fol. 39r.

[54] Antonio is mentioned, along with Francesco Corteccia, among a group of choristers serving at the Baptistry on August 22, 1515. (M. Fabbri, Op. cit., p. 191.) Antonio left the Baptistry's service on August 14, 1519. (ASF, Arte di Calimala, Vol. 24, *Deliberazioni, 1514—1522*, fol. 251r.) It is not known when he became a priest, but later documents show that he did receive the tonsure. (ASF, Notarile ante-cosimiano, Vol. B 222, fol. 82v; Florence, Biblioteca Nazionale Centrale, Poligrafo Gargani, busta 1430, „*degli Organi*".)

[55] SMNo, Appendice, Vol. 2, *Ricordanze, 1527—1555*, fols. 29r—29v.

[56] Ba, Vol. 85, *Debitori & Creditori, 1533—1544*, fol. 123v.

[57] Lorenzo's birth date and the record of his appointment to the Baptistry are given by M. Fabbri, Op. cit., p. 197, n. 40.

[58] ASF, Arte di Calimala, Vol. 60, *Provvisioni & Partiti, 1539—1563*, fol. 91r.

[59] SMDF, Libro Battesimi, *Maschile dal 1522 al 1532*, fol. 16v.

[60] Ibid., VIII. 1. 170, *Quaderno cassa, com. gennaio 1535/36*, fol. 62v.

[61] L. Dorez, *La Cour du Pape Paul III d'après les Registres de la Trésorerie Secrète* (Paris, 1932), Vol. I, p. 99. On Pierino's surviving music, see E. Wienandt, *Perino Fiorentino and His Lute Pieces*, Journal of the American Musicological Society, Vol. VIII (1955), pp. 2—13.

[62] L. Dorez, Op. cit., Vol. II, p. 174.

[63] Ibid., p. 245.

uncertain, however, whether this payment refers to Pierino or to an organist named Pietrino.

No information concerning Pierino's whereabouts during the following years has yet come to light. But an entry in the Papal accounts, dated March 5, 1546, shows that by that time „*maestro Pierino, creato di maestro Francesco da Milano*", had returned to the service of Paul III[64]. Recently discovered documents show that Pierino was associated with the Papal court from that time until May 8, 1548. (Doc. 10) According to Luca Guarico, an associate of Pierino at the Papal court, Pierino later traveled to France, „*where he was received by the Queen*," probably the Florentine Catherine de' Medici[65]. A now destroyed epitaph in the Roman church of Santa Maria in Aracoeli stated that Pierino died in 1552, at the age of twenty nine[66]. In the same year Antonfrancesco Doni wrote that

Our Pierino di Baccio degli Organi, now that he had had a taste of success and had begun to realize the fruits of his talent, has been cut down by death. Oh, what an admirable youth the world has lost! . . .[67]

Equal praise had previously been paid Pierino by another Florentine, Cosimo Bartoli, in his *Ragionamenti accademici*[68], written during the mid-1540's but published only in 1567:

L. I recently heard our Florentine Pierino di Baccio in Rome, and I liked the way he played the lute very much.
P. Certainly he is very talented, and if he lives, he will one day show that he is a true student of Francesco da Milano. Indeed, today there are those who listen to him most willingly, and perhaps even more than they would have listened to his teacher Francesco. And this is truly not a small honor to the blessed memory of his father Baccio, who, as you know, was very gifted.

---

[64]) A. Bertolotti, *Speserie segrete e pubbliche di papa Paolo III*, Atti e memorie delle RR. deputazioni di storia patria per le provincie dell'Emilia, Nuova serie, Vol. III (1878), p. 199; L. Dorez, Op. cit., Vol. I, 232.

[65]) Guarico gave the information in his *Tractatus Astrologicus* (Venice, 1552), fol. 84r, so it must be that Pierino was in France several years before that date.

[66]) The epitaph was erected by the poet Giacomo Marmitta of Parma, a friend of Pierino. Its text is given in I. Affo, *Memorie degli scrittori e letterati parmigiani* (Parma, 1793), Vol. IV, pp. 61ff; P. F. Casimiro, *Memorie istoriche della chiesa e convento di S. Maria in Araceli di Roma* (Rome, 1736), p. 172; V. Forcella, *Iscrizioni delle chiese e d'altri edifici di Roma* (Rome, 1869) Vol. I, p. 253; M. Pocciantio, *Catalogus scriptorum fiorentinorum* (Florence, 1589), p. 144. (The text given by the latter differs slightly from the others.) A letter from Marmitta to Pierino, dated Rome, July 17, 1550, has also come down to us. It is given by F. Turchi (ed.), *Delle lettere facete et piacevoli di diversi grandi huomini . . . Libro secondo* (Venice, 1575) pp. 265ff. I acknowledge my thanks here to Prof. H. Colin Slim of the University of California, Irvine, who kindly put this information at my disposal. [67]) *I Marmi*, part III (Venice, 1552), p. 12f.

[68]) Libro terzo (Venice, 1567), p. 38. The passage is also quoted in G. Benvenuti (ed.), *Andrea e Giovanni Gabrieli e la musica strumentale in San Marco I* (Instituzioni e monumenti dell'arte musicale italiana), Vol. I, p. LV.

Many documents survive attesting to Bartolomeo's friendship with some of the most prominent Florentines of the day. Especially noteworthy is his association with the grandson of Lorenzo the Magnificent, Lorenzo, Duke of Urbino and virtual ruler of Florence from 1516—1519. The letter Bartolomeo wrote to the Duke's secretary, mentioned above, apparently received the Duke's personal attention, for on July 6, 1516, forty florins were drawn from the Medici account „*for Baccino degli Organi, in order to pay for the rent of his house*"[69]. Later in the same year the Duke's steward listed an expenditure of fourteen florins for clothing „*which Baccio wore during the month of December, when he was in Rome*"[70]. Evidently Bartolomeo had performed at the court of Leo X, Lorenzo's uncle. Another entry in the ducal accounts records eleven florins spent „*at Baccio's command*" to have two volumes of music bound[71]. It is possible that these are the volumes copied by Bartolomeo himself, which he referred to in the above-mentioned letter to Giovanni da Poppi. (Doc. 9) Another glimpse of Bartolomeo's duties in the Duke's household is contained in a letter, dated August 5, 1518, which begins:

The present bearer is sent especially to tell you on behalf of the Magnificent [Duke Lorenzo] that you should send Baccio the organist and ser Virgilio [a singer in the Cathedral chapel] here early tomorrow morning, and tell them to bring a soprano with them and singing books. . . .[72]

Somewhat earlier, on April 23, 1518, the Duke had had Bartolomeo appointed as a singer to the Baptistry's chapel[73]. A month later the Duke also arranged for him to receive an honorarium from the Santissima Annunziata, apparently in recognition of his past services there:

I recall how on this day, the 5th of May, 1518, our father prior, maestro Tito, ordered that Bartolomeo di Michelagnolo the organist be given the same provision from our Convent that the singer Arrigho d' Ugo [Isaac] da Fiandra had, that is, twelve gold florins a year[74]. And our father prior said that he had done this at the order and request of the magnificent lord Duke Lorenzo de' Medici, who wished, indeed, that this record be made on this above-said day. (Doc. 11)

Even after the Duke's death Bartolomeo remained in close rapport with the

---

[69]) MAP, filza 132, *Entrata & Uscita di Lorenzo, Duca d'Urbino*, fol. 37r.
[70]) Ibid., fol. 37v.
[71]) Ibid., fol. 47r.
[72]) MAP, filza CXI, c. 497; quoted in G. P i e r a c c i n i, *La Stirpe de' Medici di Cafaggiolo* (Florence, 1924), Vol. I, p. 260.
[73]) ASF, Arte di Calimala, Vol. 24, *Deliberazioni, 1514—1522*, fols. 155v—156r.
[74]) Isaac had been given the honorarium at the command of Leo X. See my *Heinrich Isaac in Florence: New and Unpublished Documents*, The Musical Quarterly, Vol. XLIX (1963), pp. 473f.

Medici family. An entry in the Papal accounts from the reign of Clement VII (Giulio de' Medici) records ten florins paid „*to Baccio*", who had apparently performed at the Papal court, „*so that he might return to Florence*"[75].

Bartolomeo was a friend of the Florentine poet Francesco Cei, whose strambotto, *Pietà, pietà*, he set to music. A report of the wedding of Giovanbattista de' Nobili and Francesca Salviati states that Cei sang the canzona *Non è pietra tanta dura* „*in su la lira, the way Baccio degli Organi had taught him*"[76]. The wedding festivities had been arranged by Lorenzo di Filippo Strozzi, mentioned above as one of Bartolomeo's creditors. Bartolomeo was on close terms with this younger scion of the famous Florentine banking family, and it is reported that he even accompanied Strozzi to Ferrara in February, 1502, for the wedding of Lucrezia Borgia and Alfonso d'Este[77]. Lorenzo Strozzi is the author of three poems, *Questo mostrarsie lieta, Quando e begli occhi* and *Se talor qunesta,* set to music by Bartolomeo. Two of these poems, as well as several others by Strozzi, were later set by Bernardo Pisano, who probably was a pupil of Bartolomeo[78]. Bartolomeo also collaborated with Filippo Strozzi, Lorenzo's younger brother, in a mascherata given during the carnival season of 1507. Filippo gave a detailed description of the event in a letter[79] to Lorenzo, who was in Venice at the time:

. . . We portrayed l a D o v i z i a (Abundance), who was [impersonated] by Antonfrancesco dressed like a woman with a cornucopia in one hand and a basket full of different kinds of fruit on her head. We two [Antonio degli Albizzi and Filippo] were youths who guided her, dressed in costumes of yellow silk trimmed with black velvet . . . . Three singers, ser Raphaello, ser Cecchino and il Giocondo, dressed like us in black and yellow, followed . . . and 13 grooms, 9 in black and yellow livery . . . [and] 4 moors, who kept the crowd back and brought up the

---

[75]) H. W. F r e y, *Regesten zur päpstlichen Kapelle unter Leo X. und zu seiner Privatkapelle,* Die Musikforschung, Vol. IX (1956), p. 145.

[76]) The report is given by Francesco Z e f f i, Lorenzo Strozzi's biographer. See P. S t r o m b o l i (ed.), *Le vite degli uomini illustri della Casa Strozzi, commentario di Lorenzo di Filippo Strozzi ora intieramente pubblicato con un ragionamento inedito di Francesco Zeffi sopra la vita dell'autore* (Florence, 1892), p. XII. The wedding must have occurred before 1505, the year of Cei's death.

[77]) Ibid., p. IX. In this passage Zeffi refers to Bartolomeo as „*principe musico della città nostra*".

[78]) See my *Bernardo Pisano- An Introduction to His Life and Works,* Musica Disciplina, Vol. XVII (1963), pp. 124 ff.

[79]) The letter, given in the Appendix (Doc. 12), is dated March 8, without year. Another letter to Lorenzo Strozzi, in the same source as Filippo's, however, makes reference to the same mascherata, and thus enables us to date the event. That letter, written by Lorenzo Cambi, is dated February 25, 1507: „ . . . *feciono maschere in chassa Prinzivalle, e la finzione fu della Dovitia, chome da Filippo mi stimo sarette raghagliatto.* . . ." (ASF, *Carte Strozziane,* III Serie, 178, N° 46).

rear. ... I am sending you the music, which is by Baccio, and the words, which are by Piero Rucellai....[80]

Because of his association with both the Duke of Urbino and Lorenzo Strozzi one wonders whether Bartolomeo contributed music for the presentation of Strozzi's *Commedia in versi*, first given in the *sala grande* of the Medici Palace, with scenery designed by Franciabigia and Ridolfo Ghirlandaio[81]. A contemporary description of the performance informs us that Strozzi not only produced the play, but also arranged for the music: And then, after having provided various places for the different instruments, he divided them in this manner: before the comedy were heard the loud sounds of the t r o m b e, c o r n a m u s e and p i f f e r i, which aroused the emotions of the listeners; in the second act there appeared three richly dressed moors with three l i u t i, the sound of which, in the silence, sweetly charmed everyone present; in the third act sopranos, raising their voices according to the action on stage, sang to four v i o l o n i; in the noisy scene of the fourth [act] he used the most shrill s t r u m e n t i d i p e n n a; the music for the last [act] was played by four t r o m b o n i, their voices modulating artfully and sweetly. This music has since been imitated many times, but at that time it had never been used [in plays], nor perhaps even considered....[82]

Bartolomeo was also acquainted with other Florentine men of letters, among them Niccolò Machiavelli and Benedetto Varchi. In a letter, dated April 17, 1527, written by Guido Machiavelli to his father, the boy stated that he would resume „*singing, playing and writing counterpoint a 3, as soon as Baccio has recovered from his illness*"[83]. Varchi, who mentions Bartolomeo's house, „la Casaccia", in his *Storia Fiorentina*[84], must have been a particularly close friend, for he commemorated the composer's death in a moving sonnet, which begins:

Baccio, you who full of years and honor ...[85].

Manuscript sources preserve thirteen secular pieces (one incomplete), four motets and a Mass by Coppini, thirteen secular pieces (two incomplete)

---

[80]) The poem may be identified with the *Canzona della dovizia di frutti*, which begins, „*Donne, come vedete*". Its full text is found in C. S i n g l e t o n (ed.), *Canti carnascialeschi del rinascimento* (Bari, 1936), p. 163. Only the bassus part of Bartolomeo's setting has survived.

[81]) The play was for a long time attributed to Machiavelli, and published accordingly in most early editions of his *Opere*. See P. F e r r i e r i, *Studi di storia e critica letteraria* (Milan, 1892), p. 224; I. S a n e s i, *La Commedia* (Milan, 1954), Vol. I, p. 250. Vasari furnishes the information on the painters who collaborated in the production in his *Vite*. See the edition of G. M i l a n e s i (Florence, 1880), Vol. V, p. 195.

[82]) Zeffi's description; see P. S t r o m b o l i (ed.), Op. cit., p. XIII.

[83]) N. M a c h i a v e l l i, *Lettere*, ed. G. L e s c a (Florence, 1929), p. 244.

[84]) B. V a r c h i, *Storia Fiorentina*, ed. G. M i l a n e s i (Florence, 1858), Vol II, p. 56.

[85]) B. V a r c h i, *Opere* (Milan, 1834), Vol. II, p. 495: „*Per la morte di Baccio degli Organi*".

and two laudi (one incomplete) by Bartolomeo. This relatively small number of extant works suggests that only a fraction of both composers' production has come down to us. And indeed, in Bartolomeo's case, we know of at least one other work that has not yet come to light, a motet a 4, *Cantate Dominum*, cited by G. Pitoni in his *Notizie de' contrappuntisti*[86].

As we have learned, Coppini began his career as a professional musician in 1489. His first works must have appeared around that same time. In fact, it seems that all but one of his surviving sacred pieces date from the last decade of the 15th century, for, as will be noted below, they are preserved in a volume that was compiled around the turn of the new century. Some of his extant secular music may also date from the 1490's. Eight of the thirteen works are c a n t i c a r n a s c i a l e s c h i or related types, and it is possible that a few of these were commissioned by Lorenzo the Magnificent (d. 1492), whose efforts in developing that genre are well known. But some of Coppini's carnival songs must also have been composed during the first years of the 16th century, when, after Savonarola's fall and before the Medici restoration, carnival celebrations were resumed with fresh vigor and the production of canti carnascialeschi in Florence entered a second, equally prolific, phase. As one of the few composers living in the city at the time, Coppini would certainly have been called upon to assist in the revived festivities[87].

Bartolomeo's extant secular pieces probably date from the same period rather than from the time of Lorenzo the Magnificent's reign. R. Gandolfi, who had no knowledge of the composer's biography, first suggested the earlier date[88]. Later A. Einstein, noting that two of Bartolomeo's ballate are to poems by Lorenzo and Poliziano — poems also set by Isaac — conjectured that Bartolomeo had composed his works in a kind of artistic competition with Isaac, a competition fostered by Lorenzo the Magnificent himself[89]. But Bartolomeo was only eighteen years old at the time of Lorenzo's death, and it is difficult to imagine that he would have been encouraged, or himself sought, at that youthful age to compete with the older master. Bartolomeo's settings must date, instead, from a decade or so later. Doubtless they were written in emulation of Isaac's works, some of which, as will be noted below, evidently served as models for the younger composer. Other factors, such as the report that Bartolomeo composed

---

[86]) Rome, Biblioteca Apostolica Vaticana, Ms. Cappella Giulia I, 2, (2), p. 47: „*Baccio Fiorentino: si vedono in due libri antichi scritti a mano appresso di me alcune composizioni, cioè un canto a 3. intitolato ‚Meyor d'este non ày' e un mottetto a 4 ‚Cantate Dominum'* . . .“ [87]) A. E i n s t e i n, Op. cit. p. 34, suggests this date.

[88]) R. G a n d o l f i, *Intorno al codice membranaceo . . . N. 2440*, Rivista Musicale Italiana, Vol. XVIII (1911), p. 539. [89]) Op. cit., p. 32.

carnival music in 1507, and his settings of texts by Lorenzo Strozzi and Francesco Cei, poets with whom he was closely associated in the early 1500's, also point to a later date for Bartolomeo's compositions.

The secular music of both composers reaches us in manuscripts of Florentine provenance[90]. This is not surprising, since judging from what we know of their activities, as well as from the poetry they set, it would appear that their secular works were written, for the most part, for specific occasions or directed exclusively at local circles. Coppini's sacred music, on the other hand, with its universal texts, seems to have enjoyed wider currency, for it is preserved in non-Florentine sources.

Secular works of Alessandro Coppini[91]

title, no. of voices	source	poetic type	author of text
1. *Aprite in cortesia*, 4v	F 230, fols. 37v–39r FR, fol. 59r	carnival song	G. F. del Bianco
2. *Bench'i' cerchi*, 4v	F 230, fols. 29v–30r FR, fol. 7v	canzonetta	unidentified
3. *Con teco, sempre*, 3v	F 230, fols. 55v–56r	ballata	Biagio Buonaccorsi
4. *Contrar' i venti*, 4v	F 230, fols. 41v–42r FR, fol. 60v	carnival song	G. F. del Bianco
5. *Dall'infelice grotte*, 4v	F 230, fols. 40v–41r	carnival song	Guglielmo detto il Giuggiola
6. *De' qualche charità*, 4v	F 230, fols. 39v–40r	carnival song	Guglielmo detto il Giuggiola
7. *La città bella*, 4v	F 230, fols. 42v–43r FR, fol. 78v	carnival song	G. B. dell'Ottonaio
8. *Lanzi maine*, 4v	F 230, fols. 112v–113r F 121, fols. 10v–11r	carnival song	Guglielmo detto il Giuggiola
9. *Perch'ogni cosa*, 4v	F 230, fols. 100v–101r	carnival song	G. B. dell'Ottonaio
10. *Queste quatro sorelle*	F 230, fol. 111v (cantus and tenor only)	carnival song	unidentified
11. *Tanto è la donna mia*, 3v	F 230, fols. 47v–48r FR, fol. 91v FB, fols. 26v–27r	canzonetta	unidentified
12. *Teco signora mia*, 4v	F 230, fols. 28v–29r FR, fol. 1v FB, fols. 46v–48r	ballata	unidentified
13. *Troppi, donna, ne vuoi*, 4v	F 230, fols. 56v–57r	ballata	unidentified

---

[90]) In the list of works given below the following abbreviations are used: Florence, Biblioteca Nazionale Centrale: Ms. Banco Rari 230 = F 230; Ms. Banco Rari 337 = FR; Ms. Maglia. XIX, 117 = F 117; Ms. Maglia. XIX, 121 = F 121; Florence, Biblioteca del Conservatorio, Ms. Basevi 2440 = FB; Rome, Biblioteca Apostolica Vaticana, Ms. Cappella Giulia XIII, 27 = CG.

[91]) Works by Coppini in modern editions are found in: P. M a s s o n (ed.), *Chants de Carnaval Florentins* (Paris, 1913), pp. 16, 29, 74, 98; F. G h i s i (ed.), *Feste Musicali della*

Secular works of Bartolomeo degli Organi[92]

1. *Amore, paura et sdegnio*, 3v	F 230, fols. 53v–54r FB, fols. 31v–33r	ballata	unidentified
2. *Donna, s'i' fu'*, 3v	F 230, fols. 54v–55r	ballata	unidentified
3. *Donne, come vedete*	FR, fol. 64v (bassus only)	carnival song	Piero Rucellai
4. *Donne, per electione*, 4v	F 230, fols. 133v–134r FR, fol. 53v F 117, fols. 17v–18r	carnival song	Jacopo da Bientina
5. *Meyor d'este non ày*, 3v	CG, fols. 59v–60r	instrumental	
6. *Piangeran gl'ochi mia*	FR, fol. 9v (bassus only)	incipit only	
7. *Pietà, pietà*, 4v	FB, fols. 1v–2r	strambotto	Francesco Cei
8. *Quando e begli occhi*, 4v	FB, fols. 48v–50r	ballata	Lorenzo Strozzi
9. *Quell'amor che mi legò*, 4v	FB, fols. 3v–5r	ballata	unidentified
10. *Questo mostrarsi adirata*, 4v	F 230, fols. 12v–13r FR, fol. 8v FB, fols. 11v–13r	ballata	Angelo Poliziano
11. *Questo mostrarsi lieta*, 4v	FB, fols. 13v–15r	ballata	Lorenzo Strozzi
12. *Se talor questa*, 3v	FB, fols. 33v–35r	ballata	Lorenzo Strozzi
13. *Un dì lieto già mai*, 3v	F 230, fols. 49v–50r	ballata	Lorenzo de' Medici

All but three of the poems set by Bartolomeo are b a l l a t e. In addition to ballate, Coppini set c a n t i c a r n a s c i a l e s c h i and c a n z o n e t t e[93], poetic types closely closely allied to the formal structure of the ballata. Thus, the typical poem, whether a carnival song, a canzonetta or a ballata proper, consists of a ripresa of from two—four lines and several strophes, each of which contains two pairs of alternating rhyming couplets (the piedi) and a closing section of a variable number of lines (the volta). The ripresa, in theory if not perhaps always in practice, was repeated between each strophe, and certainly always after the final strophe. For every poem, therefore, the

---

Firenze Medicea (1480—1589) (Florence, 1939), p. 14; R. G a n d o l f i, Op. cit., musical supplement, no. 5; A. W. A m b r o s and O. K a d e, *Geschichte der Musik* (Leipzig, 1889), Vol. V, p. 531; H. E n g e l (ed.), *Das mehrstimmige Lied des 16. Jahrhunderts in Italien, Frankreich und England* („Das Musikwerk"; Cologne, n. d.), Vol. IV, p. 16.

[92]) Works by Bartolomeo in modern editions are found in: R. G a n d o l f i, Op. cit., musical supplement, nos. 1 and 6; A. W. A m b r o s and O. K a d e, Op. cit., p. 530; H. E n g e l, Op. cit., p. 13; J. W o l f, *Geschichte der Musik* (Leipzig, 1925), Vol. I, p. 85; W. R u b s a m e n, *From Frottola to Madrigal*, in *Chanson and Madrigal*, ed. J. H a a r (Cambridge, 1964), p. 191. My edition of the collected works of Bartolomeo and Coppini will appear in Vol. II of *Music of the Florentine Renaissance* (Corpus Mensurabilis Musicae, 32, Vol. II).

[93]) A distinction has been made between c a n z o n e t t a and b a l l a t a on the basis of the number of syllables per line. Thus, poems with octosyllabic lines are designated c a n z o n e t t e, while those containing seven- or eleven-syllable lines are called b a l l a t e.

musical setting given the first strophe is to be applied to all subsequent strophes, with the ripresa music recurring as a refrain after each strophe, ad libitum.

A certain variety may, nevertheless, be observed in the settings of these strophic texts. The most frequent scheme is that found in six of Bartolomeo's works, *Amore, paura et sdegnio; Donne, per electione; Quando e begli occhi; Questo mostrarsi lieta; Se talor questa; Un dì lieto già mai,* and in one work by Coppini, *Con teco, sempre.* In these works each line of the ripresa is given a new musical phrase, and the entire section is marked off by bar lines. There follows a shorter section of new music, also marked off by bar lines, which is repeated for both pairs of couplets. A third section, again comprised of new musical material, sets the lines of the volta. Thus, with the exception of the second pair of couplets, each line of the ripresa and of the strophe is set to new musical material. Differing only slightly from these works is Coppini's setting of *La città bella,* where some repetition of material occurs within the music of the ripresa.

Another type of setting is found in three pieces by Coppini, *Bench' i' cerchi; Teco signora mia; Troppi, donna, ne vuoi,* and in one work by Bartolomeo, *Quell'amor che mi legò.* Here, the ripresa is through-composed and the new music for the piedi repeated, as in the works mentioned above. But a partial or total repetition of the ripresa music now occurs in the volta. Coppini's *Contrar' i venti* is similarly treated except for the ripresa, which itself contains some internal repetition of material.

A less frequent scheme is exemplified by Bartolomeo's *Donna, s'i' fu'* and *Questo mostrarsi adirata.* Here, each line of the ripresa and of the strophe, including both pairs of couplets, is given a new musical phrase so that the entire stanza is comprised of new music. This type of setting, in effect one that anticipates the early madrigal, was also adopted by Bernardo Pisano, a Florentine composer of the following generation. Closely allied to these pieces are Coppini's *De' qualche charità* and *Lanzi maine,* in which the music of the two-line ripresa is followed by a through-composed section that sets the four-line strophe. His *Aprite in cortesia* also approximates the form of these works but for its ripresa, which contains some internal repetition of material.

The remaining texts are easily distinguished from these ballata-type works. Among them are Coppini's *Dall'infelice grotte* and *Perch'ogni cosa,* carnival songs that are comprised of a number of seven-line stanzas. In these works each line of text is given a new musical phrase with the result that the setting of the first stanza is through-composed. Subsequent stanzas are then sung to the music of the first. Coppini's *Tanto è la donna mia,* comprised of a number of six-line stanzas, is similarly treated except that a partial repetition of previous material occurs at the end of the stanza. Bartolomeo's *Pietà, pietà* is a typical example of the s t r a m b o t t o. Here only the first two lines of the o t t a v a   r i m a are set to music, which is then repeated for the six remaining lines of the poem.

All these settings are characterized by a chordal-homorhythmic texture that is frequently enlivened by the use of passing notes, suspensions and other non-harmonic tones. Brief imitative passages occur sporadically. Duple meter prevails, although sections in triple meter usually make their appearance toward the end of the volta, in the piedi, or sometimes in both sections. Clear-cut rhythms follow unfailingly the accents of the text. Generally all voices begin and end together, with masculine cadences. Full triads are used as a matter of course, except for the final chords of phrases, where the third is sometimes conspicuously lacking. On the average chord changes occur twice in a measure, though there are frequent passages where the harmonic rhythm moves at a brisker pace. Chords progress logically and certain harmonic schemes are in sufficient evidence as to invite analysis of these pieces by means of the familiar system of Roman numerals. This is, of course, not meant to imply that these Florentine composers were consciously thinking in terms of the harmonic system for which the symbols were devised. But an examination of their music does reveal that they were quite aware of the effectiveness of well defined tonal organization as a means of structural unification.

Bartolomeo's ballate, for example, all have riprese that begin and end in the tonic. Similarly, all of Coppini's riprese end in the tonic, although only five begin on that chord. (The remaining pieces begin on the dominant note in unison or on the dominant chord.) The piedi invariably begin and end on the tonic, dominant or subdominant chords. The volte also begin on one of these chords, and, but for two exceptions (on the supertonic and dominant chords), come to a close on the tonic chord. Of the works that have no division between the piedi and volta, three have strophes ending in the tonic, one in the dominant. (Two begin on the dominant, one each on the tonic and subdominant.) It is obvious, therefore, that the works are planned so that the tonic outlines of the ripresa are buttressed by sections which in turn emphasize the primary degrees of the scale[94].

Harmonic color is provided by the frequent cadences within the larger sections. Since each line of text is usually set to its own phrase, or at times to two phrases, of music, there are many of these subsidiary cadences.

---

[94]) The works not mentioned here, Coppini's settings of three stanzaic texts and Bartolomeo's s t r a m b o t t o, all begin and end on the tonic chord.

IX

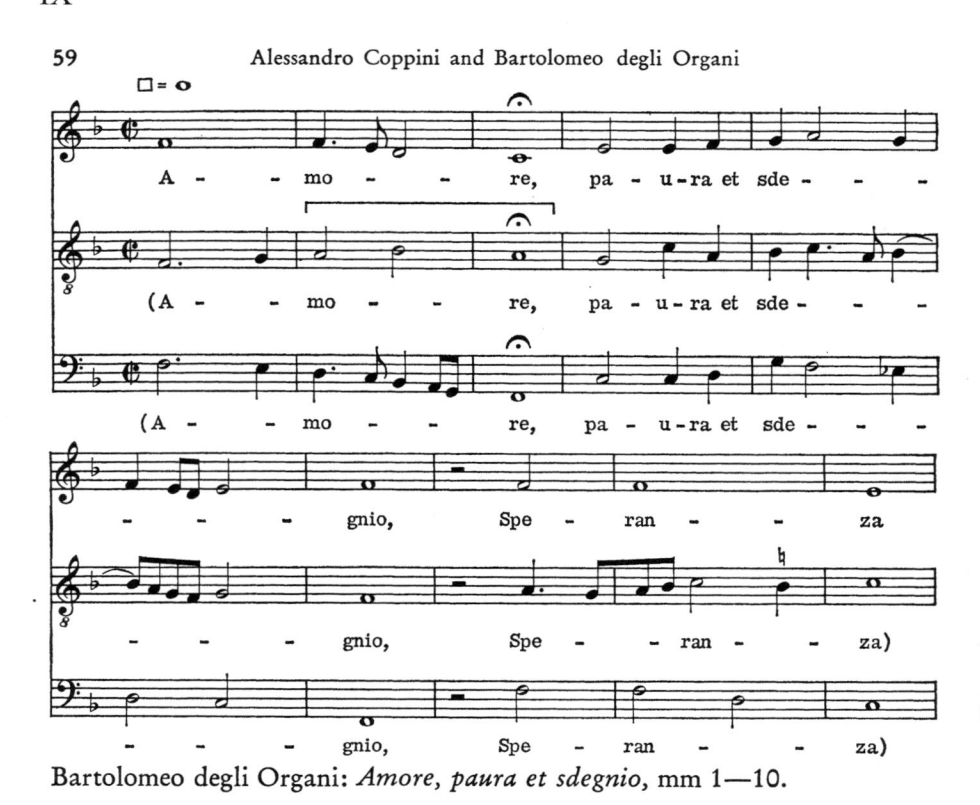

Bartolomeo degli Organi: *Amore, paura et sdegnio,* mm 1—10.

They are, for the most part, authentic, with a 4—3 suspension in one of the upper voices. On occasion, striking use is made also of the deceptive cadence. Use of any one mode does not determine the frequency with which certain degrees of the scale are used at phrase endings[95]. Consequently, these subsidiary cadences are apt to occur as often on the supertonic, mediant, submediant and subtonic triads as they do on the tonic, dominant and subdominant triads. By applying the standard rules of *musica ficta,* secondary dominant chords are introduced at these points of articulation. Far from weakening the basic tonal scheme, the chromatically altered chords have a functional purpose and also provide another important source of harmonic color. A phrase ending on a degree of the scale other than the tonic does not, of course, signify that a modulation has occurred at that point. But there are a few instances in these works, admittedly rare, where

---

[95] Of Coppini's thirteen secular works, six are in the Mixolydian mode, four in the transposed Ionian mode on *F*, two in the transposed Ionian mode on *C*, one in the transposed Dorian mode on *G*; of Bartolomeo's twelve secular works with text, five are in the transposed Dorian mode on *G*, four are in the transposed Ionian mode on *F*, and onen each in the transposed Ionian on *C*, transposed Ionian on *G* and transposed Mixolydian on *C*.

there is every indication that a change of mode has taken place during the course of a phrase. The example below shows the music moving from the tonic chord of G (the piece is in the Mixolydian mode) to a deceptive cadence on the subtonic chord. In the next phrase the music passes briefly into the Dorian mode and a cadence appropriately follows on *D*, the dominant of the original tonic. Subsequently a return to the tonic is made.

Alessandro Coppini: *Contrar'i venti*, mm. 36—45

Coppini's parts generally encompass the range of an octave. Bartolomeo's instead frequently extend to a tenth and more. In both composers' works the cantus is the most important part melodically. Its range seldom exceeds a sixth in a single phrase. The inner voices have wider ranges, even within single phrases, and jumps of an octave are not uncommon in these parts. Since the bassus determines the harmonic progressions, it is necessarily more angular than the other parts. The root progressions in the bassus, the suspensions in the inner voices, the awkward intervals frequently found between the cantus and the tenor, are all factors that serve to show that the parts were conceived simultaneously.

Generally the parts are not furnished with complete text in the manuscript sources preserving these works. For the ballate and canzonette sometimes only the cantus is given text throughout, while at other times all voices are supplied with text through the ripresa, the cantus alone carrying the text of the piedi and volta. When the same work is found in two sources, it may be furnished with text in these two ways. Perhaps the latter method of texting is an indication that the strophes were to be sung by an accompanied solo voice, with the vocal ensemble joining in for the ripresa. But both methods of texting may also represent a short cut devised by copyists in the interest of saving time. Indeed, this is suggested by the fact that often the carnival songs, which are preserved in the same sources as the ballate and canzonette and which were obviously meant to be sung in all parts, are supplied text only in the cantus, until that voice rests, at which point text is given to the lower parts. This procedure clearly shows that the text in the cantus was also to be sung by the untexted lower parts. Surely the same must hold true for the ballate and canzonette, so closely allied in style and concept to the carnival songs.

Further proof that all parts in all sections were meant to be sung may be found in similar works by Bernardo Pisano, who, as mentioned above, was probably a pupil of Bartolomeo. Several of his ballate and canzonette are found in the same sources that preserve Coppini's and Bartolomeo's works, and they are given text in one of the ways described above. Yet some of the same works by Pisano, that are also preserved in printed sources, carry text in all parts throughout the work[96].

Finally, evidence is furnished by the works themselves. All parts generally exhibit independence of melodic line and a thoroughly vocal character, qualities which help distinguish this music from much of the secular music that was being written in Italy at the time. Consequently, it is possible to adapt text to each part with a minimum of effort and with correct accentuation occuring as a matter of course, a good reason for supposing that the parts were conceived as primarily vocal. In the example below, as in the previous examples, only the cantus is supplied with text in the manuscript source.

---

[96]) F. D'Accone, *Bernardo Pisano*, p. 127.

Bartolomeo degli Organi: *Un dì lieto già mai*, mm. 29—42.

 In performance, of course, the works must have been executed by whatever vocal and instrumental forces were available at the time. But the point to be made here is that these Florentine works were conceived vocally and thus furnished yet another impulse toward the development of the madrigal.

 Two of Bartolomeo's works may be singled out for their obvious relationship to similar works by Isaac. In *Questo mostrarsi adirata* the older master's influence on Bartolomeo's work is apparent not only in the phrase structure and common modality of the ripresa, but more particularly in the setting of the strophe, where much of Bartolomeo's cantus, as well as parts of the tenor and bassus, paraphrase Isaac's earlier work[97]. Actually, the two settings also serve to illustrate the differences between the two composers' works, Bartolomeo's being greater in length and more adventuresome harmonically. In his three-part instrumental work, *Meyor d'este non ày*, Bartolomeo uses the initial motive of Isaac's well-known *Benedictus* as an accompanying figure to the opening motive of his piece, which in turn resembles one of Isaac's subsequent motives[98].

Despite Bartolomeo's thirty-year association with the Florentine Cathedral, only a slight trace of his music — two parts of a laude a 4 — has survived in the archives of that church[99]. We can nevertheless imagine, in view of his lifelong association with church music and with the performance of laudi, that his production in those fields must not have been a limited one. Some of his secular music was also adapted by the laudesi, as is evidenced by the travestimento spirituale of his carnival song, *Donne, per electione*. The music of this piece was published by Serafino Razzi in 1563 as a setting of Feo Belcari's poem, *S'i' pensassi a' piacer del paradiso*[100]. Interestingly, Belcari's text, first printed around 1480, was originally sung to the music of another secular work, *Rose, gigli e viole*, of which no trace seems to have survived[101]. Another laude by Bartolomeo, *Signore, soccorr' et aita*, appears in complete form only in Razzi's collection[102]. It may be

---

[97]) Modern edition of Isaac's work in A. Einstein, Op. cit., Vol. III, p. 2; H. Isaac, *Weltliche Werke*, ed. J. Wolf (Denkmäler der Tonkunst in Österreich), Jahrg. XIV/1 — Band 28), p. 42. Bartolomeo's work is found in R. Gandolfi, Op. cit., musical supplement, no. 1.

[98]) Modern edition of Isaac's *Benedictus* in his *Weltliche Werke*, p. 112; H. Hewitt (ed.), *Harmonice Musices Odhecaton* (Cambridge, 1942), p. 379. Isaac's and Bartolomeo's works share common motives with two other instrumental tricinia: Turin, Biblioteca Nazionale, Ms. qm III. 59, fol. 50v *(Benedictus)* and Florence, Biblioteca Nazionale Centrale, Ms. Banco Rari 229, fols. 147v—148r (without title).

[99]) The laude, *Sguardate il Salvatore*, is preserved in SMDF, Musica Vol. 21, fol. 40r. The volume has been described by F. Ghisi in *Un processionale inedito per la Settimana Santa nell'Opera del Duomo di Firenze*, Rivista Musicale Italiana, Vol. LV (1953), pp. 362—369. On p. 365 of that study, as well as in his *Strambotti e laudi nel travestimento spirituale della poesia musicale del Quattrocento* (Collectanea Historiae Musicae, Vol. I [1953], p. 51), Ghisi describes the piece as a laude a 2, although the two parts found in the ms. are clearly designated „altus" and „bassus"; at the top of the page the name „Bartholomeus Florentinus Orghanista" can be easily read, even though it has been erased a bit.

[100]) *Libro primo delle laudi spirituali da diversi eccell. e divoti autori, antichi e moderni composte* . . . (Venice, 1563), fols. 51v—53r, given anonymously.

[101]) G. C. Galletti (ed.), *Laudi spirituali di Feo Belcari* . . . . (Florence, 1863), p. 2. Text also in E. Levi (ed.), *Lirica italiana antica* (Florence, 1908), pp. 278 ff.

[102]) On fols. 18v—19r, given anonymously. Text reprinted by E. Levi, Op. cit., pp. 292 ff., with ascription to Lorenzo Tornabuoni.

that this work is also a contrafactum, for its structure follows the typical form of the ballata. But we cannot know for certain, because only the bassus, without text, survives in the contemporary manuscript source that ascribes the work to Bartolomeo[103].

Coppini's extant sacred music has come down to us in two non-Florentine sources, a set of manuscript part books in the Landesbibliothek at Kassel (one motet a 6)[104] and a choir book in the archives of the Milanese Cathedral that was compiled under the supervision of Franchino Gaffurio (three motets a 4 and a Mass a 5)[105]. How a work of Coppini's found its way into the first source, which carries dates of 1534 and later, is a matter of conjecture. The inclusion, on the other hand, of his music in the second source, a volume copied in Milan around the turn of the 16th century, may be accounted for by his presumed visits to that city, either between 1493—1497 or between 1505—1509, as mentioned above.

These sacred works reveal Coppini's mastery of the standard Franco-Netherlandish techniques of the day and reflect the training he must have received from some northern master. Predictably enough, however, the spontaneity and originality of his musical thought is best revealed in those sections where free counterpoint prevails rather than in those which employ strict imitative devices.

One of the three motets in the Milanese volume survives without text. F. Ghisi imagined that the work was preserved that way because it was fitted on various occasions with different texts honoring the Duke of Milan[106]. While it is perfectly possible that this was the case, it should be pointed out that Coppini does not appear to have been employed at the Milanese court and consequently that it is difficult to associate the piece, or at least the text to which it must have originally been composed, with the Sforza family. In all probability the work appears the way it does in the

---

[103]) FR, fol. 70v.
[104]) 4° Mus. 38 D[ominicali] ex S. S[riptura] et Patr[ibus], no. 1: *Hodie nobis caelorum rex.*
[105]) Liber Capelle F. Gafori, Vol. 30, Librone N° 3, fols. 54v—56r: *In illo tempore;* fols. 56v—57r, 106v—108r: *Fiat pax in virtute tua;* fols. 189v—190r: textless motet; fols. 82v—87r, fols. 147v—154r: various sections of the *Missa Si Dedero.* This volume belongs to a set of four that were copied under the direction of Gaffurio during the last decade of the 15th century and the first years of the following century. One of the four volumes carries the date June 23, 1490. Accordingly, K. J e p p e s e n believed that the volume in which Coppini's works are found was copied „around 1500" (*Die 3 Gafurius-Kodizes der Fabbrica del Duomo, Milano,* Acta Musicologica, Vol. III [1931], p. 15.) Recently, however, C. S a r t o r i has argued for placing the volume after that date, during the first decade or so of the 16th century. (*Il quarto codice di Gaffurio non è del tutto scomparso,* Collectanea Historiae Musicae, Vol. I [1953], pp. 26 f.)
[106]) *I canti carnascialeschi,* p. 57.

volume simply because its text was unavailable at the time the music was copied. The motet is in the transposed Dorian mode on G, with all principal cadences in the tonic, and is comprised of five overlapping phrases, each of which is built on a point of imitation. But even though the principle of pervading imitation is in evidence throughout, repetition and transformation of material play a more vital role in the structure of the work: the subject of the first phrase (mm. 1—12; the breve = a whole note) returns transformed twice, first as the subject of the fourth phrase, which is itself extended to include two new subsidiary imitative passages in alternating duets (mm. 34—48), and then as the subject of the final phrase, which is also extended in free counterpoint (mm. 49—61). Another subject is used to introduce the second phrase (mm. 12—23), the whole of which is immediately repeated (mm. 23—34). The form of the piece may thus be diagrammed as A B B A' (+ x + y) A" (+ z).

In illo tempore, a setting of the Gospel for Easter Sunday (Mark 16, 1—7), is considerably longer (160 mm.) than the work mentioned above. In the transposed Dorian mode on G, the work is comprised of two equal partes, the second of which ends in the tonic. Frequent cadences on B♭ (on which chord the prima pars ends), gives the work a kind of modal ambivalence that can best be described as a fluctuation between the tonic minor and its relative major. The work opens with a freely treated motive that is particularly striking because the initial notes of its successive entries are doubled at the octave:

No one technique obtains throughout. Phrases in pervading imitation alternate with sections in free counterpoint and sections for paired voices.

Contrast is also provided toward the end of the secunda pars through the introduction of a brief section in triple meter. Coppini's concern for unifying both partes of the work, however, is evident from the appearance at the outset of pars II of a motive that was previously used in pars I.

a: mm. 16—18, b: mm 86—91.

Fiat pax in virtute tua, a supplication to St. Sebastian for deliverance from the plague, was doubtless written for performance at the Santissima

Annunziata. Devotion to the Saint was particularly widespread in Florence during the Renaissance, and his mediation was repeatedly invoked in times of pestilence. The city boasted five religious *compagnie* that were placed under his patronage. One of them regularly held services in the chapel dedicated to him at the Annunziata, where special celebrations were also held each year on January 20, the Saint's feast day[107]. Thus, it is more than likely that Coppini's motet was commissioned by the Confraternity of St. Sebastian for performance at the Annunziata during one of the frequent plagues that ravaged Florence in those years.

The motet is divided symmetrically into halves, both of which end on the tonic, the transposed Ionian on *F*. Although the music is generally continuous, with much phrase overlapping, there are also several prominent cadences, on the chords of the tonic, dominant and subdominant. A very simple cantus firmus of five long notes (10 mm.) governs the formal structure of the work. It is stated five times in the tenor of each of the partes, its initial appearance occuring after ten measures rest. Successive entries in pars I, separated by ten measures rest, are made on the descending notes of the scale, from the dominant to the tonic. In pars II the cantus firmus is inverted, and successive entries, also at the interval of ten measures rest, are made on the ascending notes of the scale, from the tonic to the dominant.

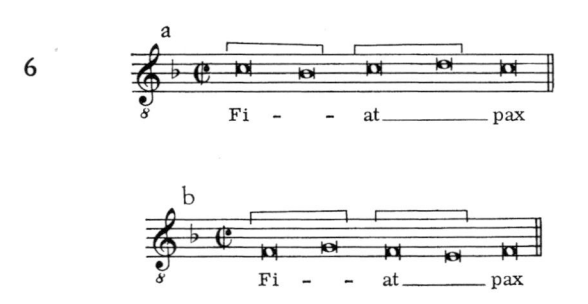

The two forms of the cantus firmus: a = pars I; b = pars II.

The other voices also occasionally draw upon the material of the cantus firmus, either as a motive treated in free counterpoint or as the subject of a point of imitation:

---

[107] I record here my gratitude to Father E. Gori and to Father R. Taucci of the Servite Order, who secured this information for me from volumes in the private archives of the Santissima Annunziata.

mm. 61—66

Sections in pervading imitation and free counterpoint alternate throughout both partes. Several distinct rhythmic patterns, in which the interval of a fourth is always present, appear repeatedly in the course of the work and thus gain structural importance because of their prominence. Indeed, the composer's desire to unify the piece is seen not only in the frequent recurrence of these motives but also in the deliberate recall of the first motive, expanded and varied, at the close of both partes.

Hodie nobis caelorum rex, which draws its text from the first two responsories of Matins for Christmas, is also divided into two partes. Coppini's strong sense of tonal organization is again apparent; each of the partes begins in the tonic (pure Mixolydian), pars I ending in the dominant, pars II in the tonic. A slow harmonic rhythm and frequent repetition of the same progressions give the work a static quality which is only occasionally relieved by a change of modality. As in *Fiat pax in virtute tua*, sections in imitation and free counterpoint alternate, and at times all voices pause for a cadence. Although the motet is composed for six voices, it is obvious that Coppini was more comfortable writing a 4, for generally it is only toward the end of phrases, as the cadence is approached, that all the voices are used together. Coppini contrasts the partes by writing the first in triple meter, the second in duple meter. Toward the end of the latter a section in triple meter is introduced, after which the original mensuration is resumed. The influence of the canti carnascialeschi is apparent here in the chordal-homorhythmic texture and the dance-like rhythms, which contrast strongly with the preceding material.

The five-voice *Missa Si Dedero*, lacking the *Kyrie* in the Milanese volume, is based on Agricola's song-motet a 3 of the same name[108], and may represent one of the direct results of Coppini's studies with that master during the early 1490's. Although the Mass is primarily a cantus firmus type, the parody principle is also in evidence in several sections, revealing Coppini's awareness of one of the more modern practices of his day. The superius and tenor of Agricola's work furnish the material for the cantus firmi, which all voices have a share in presenting. Thus, in *Agnus* I the old superius is stated completely by Coppini's superius. (Segments of the old tenor also appear simultaneously in his tenor I.) In *Agnus* II the old superius, transposed down a fourth, is assigned to the altus, while the other voices make imitative entries with material derived from Agricola's motives. Coppini makes use only of the third phrase of the old superius (mm. 18—25) in the *Pleni*, stating it three times in tenor I. Similarly, in the *Benedictus* the second phrase of the old tenor (mm. 20—35), somewhat shortened, appears four times in the bassus, first on its original pitch, then transposed successively up a major second, up a fourth and up a fifth. The old tenor appears incomplete in tenor I of the *Sanctus*. But here Coppini states the first phrase of the old superius three times in his superius, so that two voices of the model are drawn upon simultaneously at some length.

The parody principle is more fully utilized in the *Gloria* and the *Credo*. In the first section of the *Gloria* (to „*Filius Patris*") Coppini states the first 53 mm. of the old tenor (with some embellishment) in his tenor I. The other four voices occasionally quote a measure or two of the old superius and bassus or make imitative entries with new material, which is, nevertheless, permeated with one or another of Agricola's motives. It is only toward the end of the section that Coppini begins to draw on all three voices of the

---

[108]) Preserved in many sources and reprinted in modern editions several times. (See G. R e e s e, *Music in the Renaissance* [New York, 1954], p. 211.) Reference here is to the edition of H. H e w i t t, Op. cit., p. 339.

model simultaneously. The example given below shows his borrowing at its most extensive:

Gloria, mm. 83—91; the numbers above the staff refer to the corresponding measures in Agricola's work.

Section II of the *Gloria* (to „*suscipe deprecationem nostram*"), for three voices, presents the old superius complete in the bassus as the upper voices provide new material. In section III (to „*Amen*") the five-voice texture of section I is resumed and with it the old tenor (from m. 54) in tenor I. Coppini draws on all three voices of his model at the outset of this section before abandoning them in favor of new material, which is, however, once again inspired by Agricola's motives. The three voices of the model are then quoted simultaneously for some ten measures before the movement is brought to a close. The *Credo,* divided into four sections, displays a similar combination of the cantus-firmus and parody techniques.

In the *Missa Si Dedero,* as in his motets, Coppini ingeniously combines his feeling for chordal sonority and clear tonal progressions with some of the most advanced contrapuntal practices of the day. By doing so he reveals that he had found a solution to one of the principal problems then confronting Italian musicians: the formation of a musical style embodying the technical achievements of the Franco-Netherlanders and the tonal-harmonic precepts of Italian music. The problem was to continue to occupy Italian composers over the next thirty years. Coppini's secular works, like Bartolomeo's, also foreshadow the music of a later generation. There, the tendency to follow clearly the accents of the text and to rely less on repetition in the setting of the stanza, the variety and elegance of the melodic lines and the sensitivity to harmonic color all point in the direction of the early madrigal. Thus, as precursors of a later generation which fully realized these tendencies, Alessandro Coppini and Bartolomeo degli Organi must be deemed significant figures in the development that was to bring Italian music to the fore during the latter half of the 16th century. But in stressing their historical significance, one should not underestimate the music of these two minor Florentine masters. Its charm and spontaneity assuredly merit them a place in the history of Italian Renaissance music.

APPENDIX: DOCUMENTS

Doc. 1 (SSA, Vol. 857, *Vestimenti di frati, 1469—1492,* fols. 87v—88r)
(fol. 87v) [febbraio 1488]

Frate Alexandro di Bartolomeo da Firenze de' dare a dì 14 di detto per uno vestito, avere c. 94, L. 6.
E a dì 9 di novembre L. 12 portò lui detto conto. . . .

[in margin: 1489]
E a dì 20 di gugnio 1489 L. 6 portò e' detto. . . .
E a dì 31 luglio 1489 L. 4. . . .

E a dì 12 di settembre 1489 L. 8. . . .
E a dì 16 d'aprile L. 16. . . .
E de' dare a dì 2 di luglio 1490 L. 18. . . .
E a dì 26 di settembre L. sette s. 11. . . .

[in margin: 1490 (1491)]
E a dì 13 marzo L. due s. dieci, portò Bevilaqua per resto di tutti d'uno chavallo quando andò a Bologna, a usc. G, c. 108. L. 2. 10.
E a dì 17 di luglio Fl. due larghi d'oro. . . .
E a dì 26 settembre Fl. due larghi d'oro. . . .

(fol. 88r)
Frate Alexandro di Bartolomeo da Firenze, nostro frate e studente a Bologna, de' avere per suo vestimento da dì [primo d'ottobre 1487, crossed out] 15 d'aghosto 1489 a dì 30 d'aghosto 1491, sono mesi XX4 + chè dà in di' llà è paghato chome appare a llibro azuro D, c. 230; portò vestimento dare in questo c. 117. L. 49.

E deve avere per mesi otto finiti per tutto aprile 1492 posto vestimento in questo, c. 131. L. 16.

E de' avere L. cinquanta piccioli: sono per avere sonato l'orchano e chantato e insegniato i fanciugli chome disse ser Stefano da Milano. E de' avere L. quattro piccioli: sono per vestimento di maggio e giugno 1492; portò vestimento in questo c. 131. L. 54.

▶

Doc. 2   (SSA, Vol. 50, *Ricordanze C, 1494—1504*, fol. 40v)
1497
Richordo questo dì 28 di novembre el nostro padre priore maestro Giovanfilippo da Pisichatone è tolto per sonare l'orghano di sopra e di sotto per tutti e nostri bisongni e di messe strasordinarie, mandando per lui a otte [sic, ore] ragionevole, frate Alessandro di Bartolomeo nostro frate, al presente abita a Santa Maria Nuova di Firenze. E dobia[m]gli dare ongni anno fiorini nove larghi d'oro in oro per suo mercè e faticha di detti orghani, e chon pato che ongni volta manchassi a sonare sanza licenzia del priore o vichario, che in quel chaso changia in pena di grosoni quatro, se già non fussi amalato chome dire el dì o 'l dì dinanzi per non potere trovare uno che sonassi per lui. E io Bernardo Mini ò fatto questo richordo di mia mano questo dì detto di sopra.

▶

Doc. 3   (SL, *Partiti, A. 3, 1501—1516*, fol. 25r)
         [in margin: privatio & electio organiste]
Die 12 novembris 1503
Congregato el nostro capitolo ut supra et essendo a quello noto publice come maestro Alexandro, frate de' Servi, nostro sonatore dell'organo molto male ci serviva del sonare in modo che al capitolo e a' nostri parrochiani generava grande schandolo; onde per essere meglio servito la nostra chiesa e per levar via la spese grande e essere mal serviti, capitularmente decto maestro Alexandro fu privato della sonatura del nostro organo e in luogo di questo statim fu dal capitolo nostro

IX

73 Alessandro Coppini and Bartolomeo degli Organi

electo ser Mariotto di [gap], prete allenatosi nel monastero di S. Niccolò di Cafaggio di Firenze, con salario ciascun anno di L. 60. . . .

▶

Doc. 4 (ASF, Archivio del Catasto, Vol. 1024, *Campione delle portate dei cittadini, 1480, San Giovanni, Vaio*, fols. 112r—112v)

Michelangnolo et
Piero   di Giuliano d'Iachopo dipintore, quartiere et gonfalone sopradetti danno dinanzi alle vostre signorie la portata delle infrascripte loro substantie et beni, incharichi et boche et beni alienati, et e quali ebbono di catasto nell'anno 1470 insieme con Bartolomeo loro fratello oggi morto, soldi dieci. S. 10.
Et di sesto nell'anno 1474 lire tre soldi nove et danari due.   L. 3 s. 9 d. 2.

Le quali substantie et beni sono questi, cioè:

Substantie

Una chasa con sua habituri et aparte[ne]ntie et con una bottega sotto detta chasa apta all'exercitio del targonaio et per l'adrieto all'exercitio del dipinctore, posta nel popolo di Sancta Maria Nipotecosa . . . la quale e sopradecti solevano tenere per loro uso et habitatione, et oggi alienata come di sotto ne' beni alienati si dirà.

Item una chasa con corte dinanzi et con altri suoi habituri et appartenentie, posta nel popolo di San Salvi, luogho detto alle Casaccie . . . la quale casa tengono e sopradecti per loro uso et habitare.

Beni alienati

Una bottega della quale di sopra si fa mentione, posta sotto la casa di sopra in primo luogo nominata, la quale fu adiudicata per compromessaria conventione et per lodo da quella seguito a maestro Antonio di Lotto, canonico di S. Lorenzo di Firenze, sotto dì [gap] di gennaio 1471, carta di compromesso per ser Agnolo di ser Alexandro notaio. . . .

Item una casa di sopra in primo luogo nominata, posta sopra la sopradecta bottega, la quale fu per lodo adgiudicata per virtù di compromesso per sopradecto ser Angnolo, sotto dì [gap] d'ottobre 1474. . . .

Incharichi

Della sopradecta chosa [sic, casa] nel 2° luogo posta et confinata ne pagano e sopradecti alla Badia di San Salvi in nome di censo overo avillaro overo ficto perpetuo, l'anno, L. 3.

Boche

Michelangnolo decto d'età d'anni . . . . 30 non fa
exercizio alcuno

Piero decto d'età d'anni . . . . 26 ractracto e
mutulo et infermo

Mona Lucretia, donna di decto Michelangnolo, d'età d'anni 22
Giuliano lor figliuolo d'anni 7
Antonio lor figliuolo d'anni 5
Bartolomeo lor figliuolo d'anni 3
Lorenzo lor figliuolo d'anni 2

La Chaterina lor figliuola d'età d'anni 1
Somma la sua sustanza Fl. 371. 8
Abatesi per 5 per cento di Fl. 371. 8, Fl. 18. 11. 5
       resta .... Fl. 352. 16. 7
Rendono a Fl. 7 per cento Fl. 24. 13. 10
Tochagli di graveza per la schala a Fl. 7 per cento ...... Fl. 1. 14. 6
Arbitio soldi cinque di fiorini larghi .... S. 5

▶

Doc. 5 (SSA, Vol. 49, *Ricordanze B, 1477—1494*, fol. 161r)

    Ricordo si fa oggi questo 24 di marzo 1488 come di licentia e volontà del nostro padre priore, maestro Giovanni Philipo da Pizleoni, si conduce a cantare e per cantore di laude e canto figurato Baccino di Michelagnelo battiloro per anni quattro comminciando a dì primo di marzo 1487 [1488] e finendo di marzo 1491 [1492] per lire due e soldi dieci el mese e scarpe. E per chiareza di ciò s'è fatto questa ricordanza con questi patti e conditione che non n'abbia a cantare in nessuno luogo senza licentia del convento e del priore ne anchora non sia di qui mandato altrove senza volontà del suo padre etc.
    Io Michelangnolo detto di sopra m'obbligho a quantto di sopra si chontiene e per fede di ciò mi sono soscritto di mia propria mano questo dì detto di sopra.

▶

Doc. 6 (SSA, Vol. 700, *Giornale del Camerlengo, 1499—1504*, fol. 65v)

gennaio 1499 [1500]
    A Bacio, suona le lauda, a dì 15 Fl. uno largho d'oro in oro . . . per aver sonato 2 mesi l'orghano, a c. 128. L. 7.

▶

Doc. 7 (SSA, Vol. 51, *Ricordanze A 2, 1504—1510*, fol. 208v)

1509
    Richordo questo dì 26 di novembre noi promettiano a Lorenzo di Filipo Strozi Fl. dodici larghi d'oro in questo modo: Fl. sei larghi d'oro ogn' anno, cioè Fl. $^{1}/_{2}$ el mese insino in 2 anni, chominciando a dì primo di dicie[m]bre 1509. La quale promessa si gli fa per Bacino di Michelagnolo che suona l'orghano alla chapella della Nunziata. E detta promessa si gli fa a detto Filipo in chaso che detto Bacino serva el chonvento di sonare.
    La detta promessa non eb[b]e luogho perchè detto Bacino si partì per tutto el mese di dicie[m]bre sopradetto e più non sonò l'orghano; anzi andò a sonare in Santa Maria del Fiore.

▶

Doc. 8 (ASF, Archivio dell'Arte della Lana, Vol. 247, *Partiti, 1509*, fol. 88v)

Die XX mensis decembris 1509
    Prefati domini consules . . . elegerunt et deputaverunt in orghanistam seu sonatorem organorum Sancte Marie del Fiore Bartolomeum Michelangeli alias

Baccino degl' Organi, cum salario et aliis consuetis, cum conditione tamen quod dicte ecclesie contenito serviat personaliter et non possit sonare in alia ecclesia quam Sancte Reparate predicte et in oratorio Orti Sancti Michaellis et in ecclesia seu oratorio Annu[n]tiate civitatis Florentie.

▶

Doc. 9   (MAP, filza 115, c. 495)

Messer Giovanni carissimo:

La causa che io non ve ò più scripto si è perchè mi ricordo a rRoma le lectere che non sono di qualche importanza voi legevi solo chi la mandava; e io nonn avendo bisogno d'alcuna cosa, nonn ò voluto darmi questa bliga [briga]. Hora io vi priego che voi siate contencto leggere tucta la presente perchè a mme importa assai. Voi sapete o ricordavi quanto caldamentte voi isponesti a Giovanni Cappegli la cosa mia della casa, la quale so che ve ne ricorda. Lui non m' à servito, anti me à dileg[i]ato. . . . Di modo che io sono alle Casacce con di molt'aqua e poco vino. Io mi vi racomando, e se vi pare di scrivere a G[i]ovanni Cappegli, credo che faresti grandissima opera perchè me pare che voi abbiate subbiecto . . .

De' vostri libri n' è facti cinquanta moctecti e una messa. Sare' mi potuto più studiare, ma Pico non fa niente. Io l' ò solecitato più volte e così farò. Avete a ssapere che io ò pensato di mettere colli moctecti a tre, octo o dieci messe, e a tre e a quattro un fiore perchè li moctecti sarieno poco vilume.

Io non vi voglio più tediare. Io mi vi racomando di quella cosa della casa, perchè oltre al benefitio che me ne risulta, sarà un g[i]ustificatione che 'l Signore non mi à iscaciato da llui, come di qua si dice.

A questi g[i]orni avendo io necessità e non c'essendo voi, ricorsi a Ruberto e fecimi servire di dua fiorino. . . .

Orsù, io non so finire. Iddio voglia che voi ci torniate sano e felice e voi e 'l padrone.

                                        Vostro servidore

[verso, but in another hand: Baccio degli Orghani in Firenze

        Excell. Viro D. Johanni de Puppio
        Secretario ILL. D. Capitanei generalis suo honorando etc.]

▶

Doc. 10   (Rome, Archivio di Stato, Camerale Primo, Vol. 1293, *Tesoreria Segreta, Entrata & Uscita, 1545—1548*)

fol. 82r

1546

A dì 5 di marzo ▽ tre a maestro Pierino, creato di maestro Francesco da Milano, per la provisione che N[ostro] S[igno]re gli ha ordinato per un suo compagno che sona in terzo con li leuti quando fanno musica a S[ua] B[eatitudi]ne, commenzando il presente mese. ▽ 3

fol. 84v

1546

A dì 5 d'aprile ▽ tre a maestro Pierino degli Organi musico per la provisione del suo compagno per il presente mese. ▽ 3

merits them a place in the history of Italian Renaissance music.

IX

fol. 103r
1546
    A dì 20 di ottobre ▽ tre a maestro Pierino degli Organi, musico, per la provisione del compagno che sona di leuto seco in terzo per il presente mese. ▽ 3

fol. 156r
1547
    A dì 23 di dicembre ▽ tre a maestro Pierino musico per provisione del suo compagno che sona seco per novembre prossimo passato. ▽ 3

fol. 172v
1548
    A dì maggio ▽ tre a maestro Pirino musico per sua provisione del compagno per il presente mese. ▽ 3
    (Similar payments to Pierino are found on fols. 108v, 114v, 134v, 138v, 143v, 150r, 156r, 162r, 163r, 166r and 169v.)

▶

Doc. 11   (SSA, Vol. 52, *Ricordanze B, 1510—1559*, fol. 104v)
[in margin: provisione di Bart° Michelagnolo m° di sonare orghani]
    Richordo chome questo dì 5 di magio 1518 el nostro padre priore, maestro Tito, ordinò e fece che Bartolomeo di Michelagnolo, maestro di sonare orghani, havessi dal nostro convencto la medesima provisione che soleva havere Arrigho d'Ugho di Fiandra, chantore, cioè Fl. dodici larghi di sugello l'anno. Et questo disse detto nostro padre priore faceva per ordine e volontà del Magnifico Signore ducha Lorenzo de' Medici che però volle che si facessi questo richordo questo dì sopradetto.

▶

Doc. 12*   (ASF, *Carte Strozziane*, III serie, 178, N° 46)
    ... Facemo masc[h]ere ... Fingemo la Dovitia, che fu Anton Francesco a uso di donna con un corno in mano et una cesta in capo piena di frutte di varie ragioni. Noi dua eramo come giovani che la menavano, con vestiti di raso giallo stampato di velluto nero. ... Seguivano dipoi tre cantori, ser Raphaello, ser Cecchino e 'l Giocondo, vestiti di panni come noi, nero et giallo ... dipoi 13 staffieri, 9 a livrea neri et gialli ... 4 erono mori per rompere la calca et soste[ne]re di dritto. ... Mandoti el canto, ch'è di Baccio, et le parole, che sono di Piero Rucellai. ... Raptim. Die 8 martii.
[verso: Laurentio Philippi Strozzi   P[hilippus] S[trozzi]
       fratri meo carissimo
       Venetiis]

---

    * I am very much indebted to Prof. Gino Corti of Florence for the transcription of this and Doc. 4, given above.

ADDENDA AND CORRIGENDA

Up-to-date biographical sketches of many of the musicians associated with the Florentine chapels can be found in *The New Grove Dictionary of Music and Musicians*, 2nd edition (London, 2001) and its Online version. In general, references here are limited to studies of musicians not covered in *The New Grove Online* (hereafter, NGOL).

II. Una nuova fonte dell'Ars Nova Italiana: il codice di San Lorenzo, 2211

For additional information on the manuscript's structure and identification of several works see John Nádas, "Manuscript San Lorenzo 2211: Some Further Observations," *L'Ars Nova Italiana del Trecento* 6 (Certaldo, 1992): 145–60.

III. Music and Musicians at Santa Maria del Fiore in the early Quattrocento

p. 103: The suggestion that the musician Dopnus Paulus monacus might be the composer Paolo Tenorista is no longer tenable in view of the copious information about him and his music that has been found in recent years. See the entry on Paolo da Firenze by David Fallows in NGOL.

p. 105: On Curradus, see the entry on Conradus de Pistoria in NGOL by Ursula Günther.

p. 106: A new contribution toward Ugolino's biography is in Osvaldo Gambassi and Luca Bandini, *Vita musicale nella cattedrale di Forlì tra XV e XIX secolo* (Florence, 2003), 11–17.

IV. The singers of San Giovanni in Florence during the fifteenth century

p. 307n: Most of the documentation was subsequently published in essay III of this volume.

p. 309, n. 6: On "the extent and limitations of Cosimo's political power in Florence" and his patronage of the arts, see Dale Kent, *Cosimo de'Medici and the Florentine Renaissance. The Patron's Oeuvre* (New Haven and London, 2000), especially 348–66.

pp. 310–11: Pamela Starr subsequently identified Benotto as the singer-composer Benedictus Sirede, otherwise known as Benoit, who was previously employed in Florence and later served in the Ferrarese and Papal chapels. See her entry on Benoit in NGOL. Iannes de Monte is apparently the Giovanni dal Monte who sang in the Ferrarese chapel from 1443 to 1450, when he left to join the Papal chapel. See Lewis Lockwood, *Music in Reniassance Ferrara 1400–1505* (Cambridge, MA, 1984): 49, n. 15, 95, n. 2, 317. Franciscus (Francesco) Bartoli has recently been identified by Arnaldo Morelli as the father of the well-known Florentine artist Jacopo di San Gallo. See his "Il ritratto di musicista nel Cinquecento: tipologie e significati," forthcoming in *Il ritratto nell'Europa del Cinquecento. Arte, letteratura, società. Atti del convegno (Firenze, Palazzo Strozzi, 7–9 novembre 2002)*, ed. Massimiliano Rossi and Aldo Galli (Florence, Istituto Nazionale di Studi del Rinascimento).

p. 312: Information about singers' salaries in several major Italian chapels at mid century and later is summarized in my *The Civic Muse. Music and Musicians in Siena during the Middle Ages and the Renaissance* (Chicago and London, 1997): 251–52. During the 1480s some, if not all, singers of San Giovanni earned 6 florins per month, a sum mentioned by Filppotto de Dortenche in a letter of 1471, as given below in essay IV, 323. Also see essay VII, 473 for a letter which indicates that Heinrich Isaac earned a combined monthly salary of 8 florins when he, like many of the other singers, served in the chapels of the Cathedral, the Baptistry and the Santissima Annunziata. Some musicians received room and board as well as salary (essay IV, 332, 333). Some supplemented their salaries by performing for the Medici and other noble families, by teaching and by serving as teachers at other churches (essay VI, 322–3).

p. 313: Ser Goro di Maso is the same person as ser Goro di Pavolo, who sang in the Sienese chapel from 1456–1467. The patronymic as given in the Cathedral document is erroneous. See *The Civic Muse, cit.*, 217, 742.

p. 317: The Neapolitan singers' visit and Neapolitan-Florentine musical exchanges are discussed further by Allan W. Atlas, *Music at the Aragonese Court of Naples* (Cambridge, 1985): 34; and in his "Aragonese Naples and Medicean Florence: Musical Interrelatioships and Influence in the Late fifteenth Century," *La musica a Firenze al tempo di Lorenzo il Magnifico*, ed., Piero Gargiulo (Florence, 1993): 15–45. The Neapolitans also performed in Siena at this time (*The Civic Muse, cit.*, 190–191).

p. 321: Details of Jachetto di Marvilla's career in Italy are summarized in *The Civic Muse, cit.*, 208.

p. 325: Filipotto's Neapolitan service is discussed by Allan W. Atlas, *Music at the Aragonese Court of Naples, cit.*, particularly, 39–40.

pp. 331ff.: Several of the musicians hired during the 1480's and early 1490's also served in Naples, Ferrara and Siena. They are listed in the indices of studies by Lockwood, Atlas and D'Accone cited above.

p. 328, n. 55: Some years later I was able to decipher Arnolfo's surname as Gilardi. See essay VIII below and also *The Civic Muse, cit.*, 268–274, for a new edition of his *Sena vetus*, a motet in honor of Siena. For the most recent summary of his Italian years see the note on 264 of essay VIII below.

p. 332: For Rubinetto, see the entry on Robinet by David Fallows in NGOL.

p. 334: For Cornelio di Lorenzo's service in Ferrara see Lockwood, *Music in Renaissance Ferrara, cit.*, particularly, 161–165. This Cornelio is apparently not the Cornelius Heyns discussed in the entry by Allan W. Atlas and Jane Alden in NGOL.

p. 337: More recent studies on the Milanese, Ferrarese and Papal chapels are mentioned in note 5 of the Introduction to this volume and in several notes here. For the Savoy chapel see Marie-Therese Bouquet, "La cappella musicale dei duchi di Savoia dal 1450 al 1500," *Rivista musicale italiana* 3 (1968): 233–85. A reassessment of music at the Burgundian court is in the entry on Burgundy by Craig Wright and David Fallows in NGOL.

p. 339: Giovanni degli Ans, recorded in Florence until June 1492, is possibly the singer (Jo. De Lannis) who joined the Papal chapel in July 1492. See the entry on Hillanis, Johannes by Richard Sherr in NGOL.

p. 344: Carlo di Piero de Launoy is evidently not the composer called Colinet de Lannoy. See the entry on this latter by Fabrice Fitch in NGOL.

p. 345: It is uncertain whether Johannes Petit alias Baltazar is the composer known as Ninot Le Petit. See the entry in NGOL by David Fallows and Jeffrey Dean.

V. Lorenzo the Magnificent and music

p. 260: The most recent study of Lorenzo and his time is F. William Kent's *Lorenzo de' Medici and the Art of Magnificence* (Baltimore, 2004).

p. 272: Barbara Sparti offers a comprehensive study of Guglielmo's art in her *Guglielmo Ebreo of Pesaro: De pratica seu arte tripudii / On the Practice of the Art of Dancing* (Oxford, 1993).

p. 283: As mentioned above in the note to IV, 344, Carlo di Piero de Launoy is evidently not the composer called Colinet de Lannoy. See the entry on this latter by Fabrice Fitch in NGOL.

p. 287: Recent research has established another date and context for Isaac's "Alla Battaglia." See William F. Kent, "Heinrich Isaac's Music in Laurentian

Florence: New Documents," in *Die Lektüre der Welt: zur Theorie, Geschichte und Soziologie kultureller Praxis (Festschrift für Walter Veit)*, ed. Helmut Heinze and Christiane Weller (New York, 2004): 367–71. Isaac's work is treated extensively by Blake Wilson in his "Heinrich Isaac among the Florentines," *Journal of Musicology* 23 (2006): 97–152.

p. 288: New research now places Josquin's sojourn in Milan at a considerably later date. See Paul A. Merkley and Lora L. M. Merkley, *Music and Patronage in the Sforza Court* (Cremona, 1999): especially 197–215, 425–466.

VI. Sacred music in Florence in Savonarola's time

p. 312: A comprehensive study of Savonarola and music is Patrick Macey's *Bonfire Songs: Savonarola's Musical Legacy* (Oxford, 1998); see also William F. Prizer's illuminating essay "The Music Savonarola Burned: The Florentine Carnival Song in the late 15th Century," *Musica e Storia* 9 (2001): 5–33.

p. 331: The earliest surviving inventories of Cathedral music, from 1651, 1657, 1660 and 1661, are reproduced and discussed by Gabriele Giacomelli in "Due granduchi in cent'anni (1621–1723): Continuità e tradizione nel repertorio della cappella musicale di Santa Maria del Fiore," *Cantate Domino: Musica nei secoli per il Duomo di Firenze*, Atti del VII Centenario del Duomo di Firenze 3, ed. Piero Gargiulo, Gabriele Giacomelli, Carolyn Gianturco (Florence, 2001): 195–218.

VII. Heinrich Isaac in Florence: new and unpublished documents

p. 464: A recent review of the documentation regarding Isaac's Florentine years is given by Giovanni Zanovello in his "Heinrich Isaac, the Mass Misericordias Domini, and Music in Late-fifteenth-Century Florence," Ph.D. dissertation, Princeton University, 2005. New light on Isaac's composing in Florence and his commanding musical presence in the Florentine life of his time is given by Blake Wilson in his "Heinrich Isaac among the Florentines," *Journal of Musicology* 23 (2006): 97–152.

p. 476: Giovanni Zanovello, in chapter 2 of his "Heinrich Isaac, the Mass Misericordias Domini, and Music in Late-fifteenth-Century Florence," *cit.*, gives new evidence to show that Isaac was a member of the Flemish confraternity of Santa Barbara in Florence from 1502 until his death in 1517.

VIII. Some neglected composers in the Florentine chapels, ca, 1475-1525

p. 264: Arnolfo's Italian career is summarized in the entry on Arnoul Greban by Darwin Smith in *Die Musik in Geschichte und Gegenwart*, Personenteil 7

(Kassel, 2002): 1544–1546. A more recent paper by Smith, "De la France à l'Italie: la carrière di maitre Arnoul (ca. 1429–apres 1485)" was read at the meetings of the International Congress of the International Musicological Society in Leuven, Belgium, 2002.

p. 286: The latest summary of documents regarding Verdelot's Florentine years is given by Alessandra Amati-Camperi, "A Fresh Look at the Life of Verdelot, Maestro di Cappella at the Duomo of Florence," *Cantate Domino: Musica nei secoli per il Duomo di Firenze, cit.*, 89–105.

p. 286: The processional (MS V–21 of the Archivio dell'Opera di Santa Maria del Fiore, Florence) was subsequently studied by Giulio Cattin in *Un processionale fiorentino per la settimana santa: studio liturgico-musicale sul Ms. 21 dell'Opera de S. Maria del Fiore* (Bologna, 1975).

IX. Alessandro Coppini and Bartolomeo degli Organi: two Florentine composers of the Renaissance

p. 44: Further information on Coppini's Roman years was furnished by Richard Sherr, "Verdelot in Florence, Coppini in Rome and the Singer 'La Fiore,'" in *Journal of the American Musicological Society* 37 (1984): 402–11, reprinted in *Music and Musicians in Renaissance Rome and Other Courts*, XIX (Aldershot, 1999).

p. 56: Three other pieces by Bartlomeo were subsequently identified by Richard Wexler. See his "Newly Identified Works by Bartolomeo degli Organi in the MS Bologna Q 17," *Journal of the American Musicological Society* 23 (1970): 107–13

p. 48: Mazzuoli's miscellany, including the songs sung by Lionarda and Maria, has been treated in depth by William F. Prizer, "Wives and Courtesans: The Frottola in Florence," *Music Observed: Studies in Memory of William C. Holmes*, eds., Colleen Reardon and Susan Parisi (Warren, MI, 2004): 401–15.

p. 52: *La Dovizia* was performed during Carnival in 1506, as William F. Prizer shows in his "Reading Carnival: the Creation of a Florentine Carnival Song," *Early Music History* 23 (2004): 185–252, particularly199, 241; also see Prizer's "Petrucci and the Carnival Song: On the Origins and Dissemination of a Genre," in *Venezia 1501: Petrucci e la stampa musicale* (Venice, 2005): 215–251.

p. 63: See the note above on 286 of essay VIII for Giulio Cattin's study of the manuscript.

INDEX

Except for those better known to posterity by their surnames, musicians are generally listed here, as they are in Florentine sources, by their given names in the vernacular. Alternate names found in those sources, or names as they appear in standard biographical dictionaries, are given in parentheses. In a few cases some names are cross-referenced.

Acciaiuolo, Angelo, bishop: III 104
Adimari family: I 145, 146
Affo, I.: IX 50n
Agostino, trombone: V 282
Agricola, Alessandro (Alexander), singer, composer: IV 344, 345; VI 329; VII 466; VIII 281; IX 39n, 40, 69, 71
    his chanson, *Gentil galans*, model for Pintelli's *Missa Gentilz gallans de France*: VIII 277
    his song-motet, *Si dedero*, model for Coppini's *Missa Si dedero*: IX 69, 70
Agostino da Fivizzano, Frate, organist: VI 323
Alabanti, Antonio, Prior of the convent of Santissima Annunziata: IV 335
    brings polyphonic Masses, motets and laudi from Rome: VI 331
Alamanni, Piero: V 284, 285n
Alberto d'Alesso, singer: IV 336, 337
Alberto de' Boccacci da Cremona, Frate, organist, teacher: VI 323
Alessandro da Bologna, Frate, organist: VI 321, 324
Alessandro di Matteo Bastiani, organist: VI 327
Albizzi, Antonio di Maso, degli: IV 319
Alessandri, Alessandro degli: V 278
Alexander VI (Borgia), pope: IV 350; VIII 273
Alfonso I, king of Naples: IV 317, 318, 321, 337; V 269
Amadeus IX, duke of Savoy: IV 337
Ambros, A.W.: IX 56n
Ambrosio (Ambrogio) di Maestro Gismondo da Cortona, organist: VI 324; IX 41

Ames-Lewis, F.: V 267n
Andrea, Maestro: I 140n
Andrea de' Servi, Fra, composer: II 12n; VI 321
Andrea di Giovanni da Fiandra (Andrea Francioso), Frate, singer: IV 334; VII 475
Andrea di Giovanni da Prato, organist: VI 321, 326
Andrea di Pasquino, Ser: VII 472
Angelo da Firenze, Don, singer: IV 331
Anglès, H.: VIII 283n
Animuccia, Giovanni, composer: VI 317n
Antonio, chiericho: II 16n
Antonio, Maestro, canon of Fiesole, organist: VI 322
Antonio, Magister scholarum, singer: III 112n
Antonio, Messer, singer of the duke of Ferrara: V 283
Antonio, Messer, organist: VI 324
Antonio da Pescia, bass: IV 350
Antonio da Vercelli, Frate, singer: IV 339, 341, 342, 343, 345
Antonio del Bessa of Florence: VII 465
Antonio di Antonio Gabassoli, contrabasso: IV 335, 337, 338, 339
Antonio di Bianciardi, Ser, bass: IV 329, 330
Antonio di Guido (Antonio della Viuola), poet, improvisor: V 263, 264, 272, 278
Antonio di Marco da Montughi, Ser, master of the chapel, teacher of figural music: IV 328, 329, 330, 331; V 280; VI 325; VIII 266, 280n
    as music copyist: VI 331
Antonio di Matteo da Prato, Ser, singer:

IV 313
Ardovino, ser, singer: I 145, 150
Argyropoulo, Isac, organist: VII 465
Armanno de Atrio, singer: IV 343, 345
Arnolfo di Arnolfo Giliardi, Ser (Arnolfo da Francia, Arnolfo d'Arnolfo), singer, composer: IV 325, 326, 328, 329n, 335, 337, 345, 346; V 280; VI 329, 331; VIII 264, 281
  as composer: VI 330; VIII 266
  as teacher of figural music: VIII 265; IX 40n
  Corteccia's assessment of his responsories: VIII 267
  his ballata, *Piagneran gli occhi mey*: VIII 269, 270 and Musical Supplement 1
  his Italian piece, *O invida fortuna*: VIII 270, 271 and Musical Supplement 2
  his Magnificat in the 6th Tone: VIII 267, 268
  his Magnificat in the 8th Tone: VIII 268
  his motet, *Sena vetus*: VIII 268
Arrigo di Bartolomeo, copyist of figural music: VI 331n
Arrigo d'Ugo da Fiandra, *see* Isaac, Heinrich
Arte di Calimala, Florence, consuls: IV 310n, 311n, 314, 316, 320, 327; V 260; VI 318; VII 473, 474
Arte della Lana, Florence, consuls: III 100, 101; IV 309, 314, 327, 338, 340, 349; V 260; VI 318; VIII 280n, 284n; IX 47
Atlas, A.W.: V 267n, 280n, 285n, 287n; VI 312; VIII 380n

Baccini, G.: IV 311, 314, 317, 319, 320, 323; VIII 285n
Bagnesi family: I 147
Baldasseroni, F.: II 19; VI 325n
Baldese, pesciauolo: I 141
Banchino di Sandro: I 147
Bandini, A. M.: V 271n
Barfucci, E.: V 259n, 278n, 282n
Bartholo, nacherino: I 141
Bartholus, composer: III 114
Bartholomeo, bass: I 324
Bartholomeus, singer: III 107
Bartoli, Cosimo: IV 330n; IX 50
Bartoli, Francesco: IV 310, 313;
Bartolino da Padova, composer: II 7, 8, 14
Bartolomea di Piero Bello, *see* Isaac, Heinrich
Bartolomeo d'Arrigo de Castris, contralto:
IV 333, 334, 335, 336, 337, 338, 341, 345; V 284
Bartolomeo da Pavia, organist: VI 321
Bartolomeo degli Organi (Baccio, Bartolomeo Fiorentino, Bartolomeo di Michelangelo, Bartholomeus Florentinus Orghanista), organist, singer, composer: IV 350; V 289; VI 313, 322, 324, 334, 335; VII 468; VIII 275, 282; IX 38, 44, 45, 46, 47, 48, 49, 50, 51, 52, 53, 54, 55, 56, 57, 58, 59, 61, 62, 63, 64, 71
  autograph letter: IX accompanying plate
  family origins: IX 44, 45, 47, 48, 49
  his ballata, *Amore, paura et sdegnio*, excerpt: IX 59
  his ballata, *Questo mostrarsi adirata*, a paraphrase of Isaac's work: IX 62, 63
  his ballata, *Un dì lieto già mai*, excerpt: IX 62
  his carnival song, *Donne per electione*, fitted by Serafino Razzi to a laude text by Feo Belcari, *S'i'pensassi a' piacer del paradiso*: IX 63
  his children: IX 47, 49
  his grandfather, the painter Giuliano di Jacopo di Lorino: IX 44
  his instrumental piece based on Isaac's *Benedictus*: IX 63
  his laude, *Sguardate il Salvator*: IX 63n
  his motet *Cantate Dominum*, now lost, cited by G. Pitoni in *Notizie de' contrapuntisti*: IX 54
  his sister-in-law, Maddalena, wife of Francesco de Layolle: IX 48
  his son Antonio, choirboy, priest: IX 49
  his son Lorenzo, organist: IX 49
  his son Pierino Fiorentino, lutenist: IX 49, 50
  his wife, Lionarda di Matteo di Francesco Arrighi: IX 48; frottole from Rome sung by her, Maria di Bianchino da Pisa and Masina: IX 48
  secular works, list: IX 56
  secular works, poetic forms: IX 56, 57
  secular works, musical characteristics: IX 59, 60, 61, 62
  teacher of counterpoint: V 281; IX 53
Bartolomeo Duccini, Frate, organist: VI 323
Bartolomeo d'Ugo da Fiandra, singer: IV 340
Bartolomeo Trombonicino: V 282
Bartolotto Catalano, actor, acrobat: I 140
Basiron, Philippe (Philippon), composer: VI 330

INDEX

his *Missa L'homme armé*: IV 343n; VI 329
Bastiano di Girolamo, Ser: VI 325
Battista di Biagio of Florence, Frate, singer: IV 335
Becherini, Bianca: II, 3n; III 104; IV 318, 321n, 323n; 328n, 345n; V 264n, 266n, 268n, 271n; VII 465n; VIII 264, 268n, 273n, 284n
Bedyngham (Bedingham), Johannes, composer: V 267n, 281n
  his chanson *Fortune helas* as the *Fortune* sung by Piero de' Medici's daughters: V 270n
Belcari, Feo, poet: V 264
  his laude, *S'i' pensassi a' piacere del paradiso*, once sung to a secular song, *Rose, gigli e viole*, and reset by Razzi to music by Bartolomeo degli Organi: IX 63
Beltramo di Feragut of Avignon, tenorista, composer, *see* Feragut, Bertrand
Beltramo di Giannot (Bertrandus Jannet), singer: IV 341, 342, 344, 345
Benedetto d'Antonio da Bologna, Frate, organist: VI 321
Benedetto da Peretola, organist: VI 323
Benedetto di Bartolomeo, Don, bass: IV 330, 332
Benoit, *see* Benotto di Giovanni
Benotto di Giovanni (Benoit): IV 310, 311, 313, 314, 315;
Bernardino di Messer Iacopo, organist: VI 321
Bernardo, master of the chapel, singer: IV 326
Bernardo di Luca da Firenze, Frate, organist: VI 321, 322, 324; IX 40n
Bernardo Mini: IX 41
Bernardo Pisano, *see* Pisano, Bernardo
Bertolotti, A.: IV 344n; IX 50n
Bertrandus Jannet, *see* Beltramo di Giannot
Besseler, H.: III 116n
Benvenuti, G.: IX 50n
Biagio, Frate, organist: IV 318
Biagio, maestro: I 132
Biagio di Alberto, organist: VI 321
Biagio di Giovanni, Hungarian priest: sells a book of figural music: VI 331
Biaxio de Antonio de Caglie, Frate, singer: III 112n
Binchois, Gilles, composer: V 267n
  his chansons, *Dueil engoisseux* and *Mon cuer chante joyeusement*, sung by Piero de' Medici's daughters: V 270

Bonaiuto, trumpeter: I 141
Bonaventuri, Piero di Angelo de': V 267n
Bonciani, Gaspare: V 284
Boniface VIII, Pope: I 143n
Borghese: I 146n
Borgia, Lucrezia: IX 52
boy singers: IV 328, 329, 331, 349; VI 318, 324, 330; VIII 281n, 282n
Bozzolini, Castoro, di Fiesole: II 6
Bracio, singer, *see* Brueto
Bragard., A. M.: VI 317n, VIII 264n, 285n
Brambilla Ageno, F.: V 277n
Bridgman, N.: VIII 268n
Brown, H.M.: V 284n. 285n, 286; VI 312n; VIII 268n, 272n, 283n
Brueto (Bracio), singer: VIII 285
Bruno, prete: I 147
Büser, B. V 270n, 272n
Burgis, Carlo de, *see* Carlo de Burgis
Busnois, composer, his *Fortuna desperata* arranged by Felice di Giovanni: VIII 280n

Cambi, Lorenzo: IX 52n
cantore: duties at Florence Cathedral: III 112, 113
  comparison with cathedrals in Fano, Padua, Brescia, Vicenza, Siena: III 112n,113
cantori tedeschi: III 115
Cappelli, A: IV 317n, 343n; VII 465n
Capponi, family: III 104
Capponi, Bernardo di Nichola: IV, 326
Carboni, F.: V 274n
Cardiere, il, improvisor, violist: V 279n
Carlo de Burgis, singer, teacher of figural music: VI 322; VIII 276
Carlo di Giovanni, organist: VI 325
Carlo di Jacopo del Maestro Antonio, Ser, organist: VI 325
Carsidone, Giovanni, Ser, notary: VII 471
Casalini, E.: VII 483
Casimiri, R.: III 112n; VIII 283n
Casimiro, P. F.: IX 50n
Castiglione, Baldassare: V 280, 290
Cattin, G.: II 4n; V 262n
Cecchini, G.: V 264n
Cei, Francesco, poet: IX 52
Cellesi, L.: V 262n
Cerrachini, L.: IX 39n; 42n
Cesari, G.: IV 323n, 336n; IX 39
Charles, duke of Burgundy: IV 337n
Charles V, king of France: II 10
Charteris, R.: VI 331n
Chiari, A.: I 148n

Ciarles Premerani, singer: VIII 271
Chimenti Tedesco, Frate, singer: IV 334
Christiano da Fiandra, singer: III 115
Christofano di Niccolò of Florence, Frate, singer: IV 335
Ciconia, Johannes, composer: V 267n
Clement VII, pope (Giulio de' Medici): VIII 283n; IX 52
Colaprico, P.: V 271n
Compare della viola, il, improvisor, violist: V 260, 277, 279n
Compère, Loyset: composer: VIII 274n
Condivi, A.: V 279n
Conradus of Pistoia, see Curradus of Pistoia
Coppini, Alessandro, Frate, organist, composer: IV 346n; V 289; VI 313, 321, 326, 334, 335; VII 468; VIII 275; IX 38, 39, 40, 41, 42, 43, 44, 46, 53, 54, 55, 56, 57, 58, 60, 61, 64, 65, 66, 67, 68, 69, 71
  as music teacher: IX 40
  family: IX 43
  family origins: IX 38, 39
  his carnival song, *Contrar'i venti*, musical excerpt: IX 60
  his *Missa Si dedero*, based on Agricola's chanson: IX 69, 70
  his *Missa Si dedero*, *Gloria*, excerpt: IX 70
  his motet, *Fiat pax in virtute tua*, cantus firmus: IX 67
  his motet, *In illo tempore*, musical excerpts: IX 65, 66
  list of secular works: IX 56
  sacred music: IX 64
  secular works, musical characteristics: IX 59, 60, 61, 62
  secular works, poetic forms: IX 56, 57
Cordier, Johannes, singer: IV 323, 324, 325
Cornelio di Guglielmo (Cornelis Willyelmi de Climbert), singer: IV 343
Cornelio di Lorenzo, singer: IV 334, 337, 341, 342, 343, 287; VI 329; VII 466
Cornelius, singer: IV 316
Corteccia, Francesco, composer: II 5; IV 350; V 287n, 289; VI 313, 331, 333 334, 335; IX 38
  composing and acquiring music for the Cathedral: VI 333
Corti, G.: IV 307; V 277n; VIII 264n, 273n; IX 76
Count of Altavilla: V 270n
Cristoforo Fiorentino called Altissimo, poet, improvisor: V 264n
Cummings, A.: V 265

Currado Tedescho, Frate, singer: IV 335
Currado Tedesco Piccolo, Frate, singer: IV 335
Curradus (Conradus) of Pistoia, singer, composer: III 105, 107, 113

Damiano da Lucca, organist: VI 323
D'Amore, L.: V 279n
D'Ancona, P.: II 19; VI 325n
Davari, S.: V 279
Davidsohn, R.: I 143n
Davit d'Alessandro, bass, tenor: IV 350n; VIII 281n, 282n
Davitte: V 276n
Della Stufa, Ugo: V 268
Della Torre, A.: V 270n, 271n, 273n
Del Lungo, I.: V 261n, 272n, 277n, 278n, 282n
Del Migliore, F.: III 100n, 101
Del Piazzo, M.: IV 327n, 336n; VII 465n; VIII 267n
De Robertis, D.: V 263n, 264
Dempsey, C.: V 277n
Di Cesare, M.: V 273n
Domenico Francioso, singer, teacher: IV 334
Domenico Panichini, Ser, tenor: IV 328
Donatello, sculptor: II 9
Donato da Firenze, composer: II 8, 14
Doni, Antonfrancesco: IX 50
Dorez, L.: IX 49n, 50n
Dovizi, Piero da Bibbiena: V 261n
Dovizio, Agnolo da Bibbiena: V 287
Ducrot, A.: VIII 283n
due Franceschi sonatori: I 141
Dufay (Du Fay), Guillaume, composer: IV 318, 319, 322, 323; V 267n, 270, 271; VI 329; VII 476
  his *Nuper rosarum flores* performed at Florence Cathedral: III 116; V 266
  letter to the Medici: V 266n
Dufour A.: IV 337n
Duke of Milan: I 323n, 324; IX 39n

Eggebrecht, H.H.: II 13n
Egidio, singer: IV 313;
Einstein, A.: IV 323n; IX 39n, 48n, 54, 63n
Engel, H.: IX 56n
Epifani, Gregorio: II 6
Este, d', court: IV 324; V 284
Este, Alfonso d': IX 52
Este, Beatrice d', duchess of Milan: IV 322n
Este, Ercole d', duke of Ferrara: IV 343n; V 282n, 283, 287n; VI 329; VII 471

Este, Isabella d', marchesa: IV 344n; V 279
Eugene IV, pope: III, 116; IV 308, 309; V 280
Eustace de Havresse, singer: VII 466

Fabbri, M.: II 5n; IX 49
Fage, A. de la: IV 327n
Fano, F.: IV 312n;
Felice di Giovanni, Ser, contratenor: IV 328; VIII 278, 280
his arrangement of *Fortuna desperata*: VIII 280, 281
Fenlon, I.: VI 317n
Feo di Giovanni, organist: VII 468
Feragut, Bertrand (Beltramo de Feragut of Avignon, tenorista), singer: III 113n; IV 310, 311, 312n
Ferrante, king of Naples: IV 321, 325, 327; V 270n
Ferrieri, P.: IX 53n
Ficino, Marsilio: V 271n, 273
Filippo, Ser, singer: I 145, 146, 150
Filippo sonator: VI 325
Filippo degli Organi, organist: II 20; VI 325n
Filippo Pichardo, frate, singer: IV 334
Filipotto de Dortenche, singer: IV 325
Fisher, K. von: II 4n, 12, 13n 18n; III 104, 113n, 114n; IV 313; V 262n, 267n
Flamini, F.: V 264
Florentinus, singer: IV 316
Forcella, A.: IX 50n
friars minor: I 145
Franciabigia, as scenery designer: IX 53
Francesco, Don: I 143
Francesco, Ser: V 266n
Francesco da Bologna, Don. singer: IV 332
Francesco da Milano, lutenist: IX 49, 50
Francesco d'Antonio d'Androagli, singer: IV 346
Francesco Boscherini, Ser, tenor: IV 328, 329, 330, 340, 341, 342, 344, 345, 350n; VIII 281n, 282n
Francesco di Bartolomeo, organist: I 137
Francesco di Giovanni, Frate, singer: IV 330
Francesco di Lorenzo, Ser, contralto: IV 329
Francesco di Martino Migliotti (Miletti, Millet), singer: IV 323n, 335, 336n, 337, 338, 339, 342, 343
Franciesco ciecho, *see* Landini, Francesco
Franciesco, Ser: I 132
Franciscus, notary: IV 316
Francesco d'Andrea (Franco), Ser, teacher of figural music, singer: IV 350n;

VIII 285n
Franco, Matteo: V 261n
Frey, H.-W.: V 265n; IX 52n

Gabriello Gabbasoli, singer: IV 336, 337, 338, 339, 342, 344, 345
Gaffurius, Franchinus (Franchino Gaffurio, Gafori): IX 41, 64n
Galletti, G.C.: III 114n; IX 63n
Gallo, F.A.: II 20n, 21n; VI 325n
Gallucci, J.: V 276n, 282n
Gandolfi, R.: IX 54, 56n, 63n
Garfagnini, G.C.: VI 312n
Gargani: VIII 275n
Gagliano, Marco da: VI 317n
Gargiulo, P.: VI 312
Gaspare, Frater, singer: III 112n
Gaudenti, M.: VII 471, 472
Gaye, G.: V 266n; 267n
Gherardello, Ser (Niccolò di Francesco): I 142, 143, 144, 145, 146, 147, 148, 149, 150; II 11, 14, 21n; III 99n
Gherardo, Ser: VIII 282n
Gherardo di Giovanni, organist: VI 320
Ghirlandaio, Ridolfo, as scenery designer: IX 53
Ghiselin, Johannes alias Verbonnet (Verbonetto di Giovanni), singer, composer: IV 345, 346; VI 329; VII 466
Ghisi, F.: I 131, 139; II 14; IV 323n; V 262n; VI, 311n, 312n; VII 466n, 467n; VIII 286n; IX 39, 55n, 63n, 64
Ghottifredo di Thilman de Liegio, singer: IV 332
Ghuasparre Siciliano, Messer, singer: IV 346
Giacomelli, G.: VI 317n, 320n
Gianfigliazzi, Symone de', Dom: I 135
Giannes (Iannes Piccardo?, Japart?), singer, *see* Johannes Piccardo
Giannes d'Angio, singer: IV 338, 339, 341, 342, 344, 346
Giliardi, Arnolfo, *see* Arnolfo di Arnolfo Giliardi
Giazotto, R.: V 273n
Gill, J.: IV 308n
Giorgio de Alamania, Ser, organist: VI 322
Giorgio di Giovanni d'Allemagna, tenorista: IV 340, 341
Giorgio di Niccolò d'Austria, discantista: IV 339, 341
Giorgius Christofani of Durazzo, singer: III 108
Giovambatista, musico: VIII 282n
Giovan Ambrosio da Pesaro, *see* Guglielmo Ebreo

Giovanfilippo da Pisichatone, Maestro, prior of the convent of Santissima Annunziata: IX 41
Giovanfrancesco d'Antonio, contralto: IV 350n; VIII 281n, 282n
Giovangualberto, tenor: VIII 281n
Giovanni da Cascia (Johannes de Florentia), composer: I 133; II 7, 14
Giovanni d'Agnolo da Fiandra, singer: IV 340
Giovanni da Poppi: IX 48, 51
Giovanni d'Antonio, linaiuolo: II 16n
Giovanni d'Arrigo, singer: IV 344
Giovanni degli Ans (Hillanis), singer: IV 338, 339, 341, 342, 344, 345
Giovanni degli Organi: I 132, 133, 134, 140, 150
Giovanni di Giovanni Pintelli, contralto: IV 336, 337, 341, 342, 345, 346; VIII 274, 275
  as teacher of figural music: VI, 322, 323;
  composer: VI 329; VIII 278, 278
Giovanni, Maestro, singer: II 20, 21n
Giovanni, monk, organist: VI 320
Giovanni di Pastore da Picchardia, singer: IV 341
Giovanni Serragli, *see* Serragli, Giovanni
Girolamo d'Andrea d'Arrigo, organist: VI 320, 324, 325
Girolamo d'Antonio, organist: VI 321
Girolamo di Ser Antonio da Firenze, Piovano, Frate, singer: IV 335, 337, 338, 339, 341, 342, 344, 346
Gismondo di Iacopo di Maestro Antonio, organist: VI 320
Giuliano del Zacheria: IV 321, 322
Giuliano sopradetto Castellaccio, viola teacher: V 277
Gori, E.: IX 67n
Goro di Maso, tenorista: I 313
Gottwald, C.: VIII 264n
Grace, M.D.: VI 325n
Grout, D.: III 116n
Grunzweig, A.: IV 316n, 317, 318n, 319n
Guarico: IX 50n
Guasti, C.: III 99n; IV 309n
Günther, U.: II 10, 12; III 104, 105n; V 262n
Guerrini, P.: III 112n
Guglielmo, singer: IV 313;
Guglilelmo (Guglielmus) d'Arnoldo de Steynsel d'Olanda, singer: IV 323n, 335, 336n, 337, 338, 339, 342, 343, 344, 346

Guglielmo Ebreo (Giovan Ambrosio da Pesaro), choreographer, dancer: V 272
Guglielmus, Magister, singer: III 112n
Guglielmus de Ver..., singer: IV 316
Guido di Ser Nicolao, ser, organist: VI 322, 323

Haar, J.: IX 56n
Haberl, F. X.: III 107n, 116n; IV 312n, 323n, 324n, 337n; VIII 272n, 283n
Harrison, F. L.: II 9
Hewitt, H.: VIII 274n; IX 63n, 69n
Hothby, John, theorist: VIII 264
Hubertus (Ymbertus) de Salinas, composer: II 9, 18, 21

Iacopo di Bonaiuto, Ser, bass: IV 350n; VIII 281n, 282n
Iacopo di Giunta di Prato: II 17n
Iannes de Monte of Ferrara, singer: IV 310
Iannes Piccardo, *see* Johannes Piccardo
Isaac, Heinrich (Arrigo da Fiandra, Arrigo d'Ugo da Fiandra, Henricus Yzac de Flandria), singer, composer:
  IV 338, 339, 341, 342, 343, 345;
  V 275, 279n, 280, 283, 284, 285, 288, 289; VI 329, 332, 334, 335;
  VII 464, 465, 466, 467, 468, 469, 470, 471, 472, 473, 474, 475, 476;
  VIII 272n, 277, 281; IX 38, 40, 46, 51, 54, 62, 63
  his *Benedictus a 3*, model for *Meyor d'este non ày* by Bartolomeo degli Organi: IX 63
  his chanson style: V 286
  his sister-in-law, Antonia, and his niece, Maria: VII 476n
  his wife, Bartolomea di Piero Bello: VII 468, 469, 470, 471, 472, 475, 476n
  proposto alla cappella, presidente della cappella: VII 474
  works composed in Florence: V 286, 287
Iurini, Bartolomeo da Pescia, *see* Turini, Bartolomeo da Pescia

Jachetto di (da) Marvilla, singer: IV 321, 323
  his letter to Lorenzo de' Medici recommending 5 voices for the chapel: IX 324
Jachopo Ser, brother of Ser Gherardello, singer: I 142, 143, 144, 146, 150
Jacobus of Arezzo, singer: III 107

INDEX

Jacobus of Forlì, singer: III 106
Jacopo da Bologna, composer: II 7, 8, 9, 14, 18
Jacopo di Bartolomeo Francioso, singer: IV 334
Japart, Jean (Johannes) (*see also* Johannes Piccardo): V 274
Jean II, king of France: II 10
Jeppesen, K.: V 273n, 282n; IX 64
Johannes, singer: III 107
Johannes Aldobrandini of Perugia, singer: III 108
Johannes Piccardo (Giovanni Picchardi, Iannes Piccardo, Johannes Comitus) (Japart?), singer: IV 333, 334, 338, 339; V 284
Johannes Franciosus alias the Abbot, singer: IV 322, 323
Johannes Herrigi of Rieti, singer: III 108
Johannes Hurtault (Ianesi Francioso), singer: IV 332
Johannes Martini, composer: IV 339n
Johannes Vitine [?], composer, singer: IV 333
    bringing Masses from Rome and composing: IV 334
Josquin Des Prez: V 288; VIII 280n

Kade, O.: IX 56n
Kent, W.F.: V 277n
kings of Naples: IV 317, 318, 325; V 267n; VI 319
Kuhner, H.: IV 318n, 319n;

Lambino, Maestro, Papal singer: IV 321
Landini, Francesco, composer, organist: I 133, 134, 135, 136, 137, 138, 139, 146, 150; II 7, 8, 11, 12, 15, 16, 17, 18, 19, 20, 21; VI 325
    guest organist at Santa Trinità: I 134
Landini, Nuccio, brother of Francesco, organist: I 150
    guest organist at Santa Trinità: I 134, 135
Lando, ser: I 132
Lanfredini, Giovanni: V 281, 284
Langhe, Pierre de, master of the choirboys, Tournai Cathedral: IV 317
Lasca, Il: VII 467
laudesi companies: V 261; VI 326, 327;
    continuity of tradition of laudi singing: VI 327
Launoy, Carlo di Piero Francioso, de (Karolus de Launoy), contralto: IV 344, 345. 350n; V 279n, 283;

VII 466, 469, 471
    as brother-in-law of Heinrich Isaac:
    his daughter: Maria: VII 471, 476n
    his wife: Margherita di Piero Bello: VII 469, 471
Layolle, Francesco de, composer: V 289; VI 313, 325, 334, 335; VIII 275; IX 38
    as brother-in-law of Bartolomeo degli Organi: IX 48
Leo X, pope (Giovanni di Lorenzo de' Medici): V 265, 279, 280, 281, 287, 290; VI 332; VII 466, 469, 472, 473, 474, 475; VIII 281; IX 51
Leonardo, piffero: V 281n
Leone, Ser, soprano: IV 350n;
Leopardi, Ioannis: IV 316;
Le Petit, m^e at Lyon, singer: IV 327
Lerner, E.: VIII 264n
Levi, E.: IX 63n
Li Gotti, E.: I 134n. 139n, 145n; III 114n
Lionardo di Bartolomeo called il Besso, organist: VII 465n
Lippi, Raphaelis Brandolini: IV 327
Llorens, J.M.: VIII 277n
Lockwood, L.: V 276n, 282n, 287n
Lorenzo di Donato, organist: VI 325
Lorenzo di Ghottifredo, singer: V 340, 341
Lorenzo di Giorgio, singer: IV 339, 341, 342
Lorenzo di Giovanni, singer: IV 341
Lorenzo di Lansone, singer: IV 342
Lo Spagnolo, sonator di liuto: V 272n, 277n
Louis of France, king, saint: IV 9
Louis of Toulouse, saint: II 9
Luca, Dom: I 144
Lucas of Orvieto, singer: III 102, 103, 105, 109
Luciani, S. A.: VIII 268n
Luisi, F.: V 262n, 276n
Lütlolf, M.: II 4n, 13n

Macey, P.: VI 314n, 315n, 316n, 317n
Machiavelli, Guido: V 280; IX 53
Machiavelli, Niccolò: V 280; VII 472; IX 53
Magdolo d'Arezzo, alto: VIII 281n
Magister Johannes Florentinus Organista, *see* Mazzuoli degli Organi, Giovanni
Manetti, Giannozzo: I 318; III 116; V 279
Manfredi, Manfredo de': V 279n
Mantese, G.: III 112n
Marco di Domenico of Florence, Frate, singer: IV 335
Marcus, Ser, singer: III 103

Mariano di Paolo Tucci, Ser, organist: VI 322
Marianus de Pistorio: IV 323
Mariotto, Ser, organist: IX 42
Marix, J.: IV 337
Marmitta, Giacomo of Parma, poet: IX 50n
Marrocco, T.: II 12n
Martelli, Bartholomeus Niccolai, de: IV 316
Martelli, Braccio: IV 325, 326, 327; V 272n, 277n; VIII 285
Martelli, Golino: I 321, 324
Martelli, M.: V 278n
Martelli, Niccolò: IV 324
Martin V, pope: III 107, 115, 116n
Martini, Johannes, singer, composer: IV 339n, 344n
Martini, Lorenzo di Guidotto, monk: I 132
Martini, Piero, singer: IV 339, 340; VII 466
Martino, singer: IV 336
Martino, Frate, singer: VI 323
Masini, Lorenzo, Ser, composer: II 21
Maso, trumpeter: I 141
Masson, P.: IX 55
Matteo da Perugia, singer, composer: III 113; IV 311n
Matteo da Prato, organ builder: IV 313; VI 324, 325, 326
Matteo da Siena, Ser, organist: I 134, 138, 150;
Matteo di Paolo (Mattia) (Pagolo), Ser, contralto, composer: IV 329, 330, 332; VI 326; VIII 278, 279, 280
  as composer: VI 330; VIII 279
  his Lamentations of Jeremiah and responsories: VIII 279
Matteo di Piero, Ser, organist: IV 346n
Matteo Tedesco, singer: brings polyphonic Masses from Rome: VI 331
Mattis, tenorista: I 315
Maximillian, archduke of Austria, emperor: IV 323; VII 470
Mazzuoli detto Stradino, Giovanni, poet and man of letters: IX 48
Mazzuoli degli Organi, Giovanni, organist, composer: I 139, 150n; II 8, 11, 14, 15, 18, 21
Mazzuoli degli Organi, Niccolò, organist: I 138, 139, 141, 146, 150;
Mazzuoli, Piero di Giovanni, organist, composer II 10, 11, 15, 16, 17, 18, 20n, 21; VI 325
McGee, T.J.: V 272n, 287n
Medici de', family: II 3; IV 308, 312, 314, 317, 320, 348, 350; V 260, 265, 266, 267, 270, 278, 280, 281, 282, 283, 289; VI 312, 316, 319, 329, 332; VII 466, 469, 472, 473; VIII 266, 281; IX 40, 42, 52, 54
Medici patronage of music: IV 308, 309, 312, 314, 320, 326, 327; V 282, 283, 284
Medici, Alfonsina Orsini de': VII 475
Medici, Antonio de': V 281; VII 470
Medici, Bianca and Nannina daughters of Piero di Cosimo de' Medici:
  sing and dance for Pope Pius II: V 269, 270
Medici, Carlo di Cosimo de': V 266n
Medici, Catherine de', queen of France: IX 50
Medici, Clarice Orsini de': IV 323n; V 271, 272, 278, 284n
Medici, Cosimo de': IV 309, 310, 312, 314, 320, 326, 350; V 265, 266, 267, 269n; VIII 265
Medici, Cosimo de', duke, later Grand Duke of Tuscany: IV 350; VI 333
Medici, Giovanni di Cosimo de': IV 315, 318; V 266, 267, 268, 269, 280
Medici, Giovanni di Lorenzo, see Leo X, pope
Medici, Giuliano di Lorenzo de': V 279, 280n, 290n; VII 472, 473, 474
Medici, Giulio de', see Clement VII, pope
Medici, Lorenzo di Giovanni di Bicci de': IV 309, 310, 312
Medici, Lorenzo de', "The Magnificent": IV 321, 322, 323, 324, 325, 329n, 335, 336, 343n, 344, 347; V 259, 260, 261, 263, 265, 269, 270, 271, 273, 274, 278, 279, 280, 281, 282, 283, 284, 285, 286, 287, 288, 289, 290; VI 318, 319; VII 466, 467, 469, 473, 474; VIII 265, 266; IX 38, 51, 54
  as choreographer, dancer: V 272
  as performer: V 276, 277
  his ballata, *Un dì lieto giammai*, set by Isaac: VII 467
  his sacred play, *La Rappresentazione di San Giovanni e Paolo*: VII 466, 467
  lessons on the viola: V 277
  Masses sent to him and Masses furnished by him: V 283; VI 330, 332
  unnamed household musicians in his service: V 262, 264
Medici, Lorenzo di Piero de', Duke of Urbino: VII 472; VIII 282; IX 48, 51
Medici, Lucrezia Tornabuoni de': V 268, 269, 275, 276n

INDEX

Medici, Pagolo de': VIII 282n
Medici, Piera de', Donna: II 16n
Medici, Piero di Cosimo de': IV 315, 316,
  318, 320, 321, 322, 323, 324, 326;
  V 266, 269n, 280; VI 316
  his assessment of Dufay: V 267
  letter to him and his brother Giovanni
    from Dufay: IV 322; V 266
  music books in his library: V 267n
Medici, Piero di Lorenzo de': IV 344, 346,
  349; V 261; VII 466, 469, 475;
  as improvisor: V 278
  musicians in his private service: V 279;
    VIII 273
  sends polyphonic Masses to Isabella
    d'Este: V 279
Michele d'Alemagna, shawmist: V 281
Michele di Bartolo Chricci, singer: IV 342,
  343, 344, 346
Michele di Bartolomeo Mazzi, organist:
  VI 322
Michele di Guglielmo da Ludicha di Brabante, singer: IV 332
Michele Federigi, copyist: II 5
Michelozzi, Niccolò: V 277, 278
Milanesi, G.: VII 468, 472n, 475n; IX 53n
Millen, R. F.: II 3. 4
Millet (Miletti, Migliotti), Francesco, *see*
  Francesco Migliotti
Minerbetti, Tommaso, Frate, organist:
  VI 325
Moreni, D.: II 5n; VI 326n
Motta, E.: IV 323n, 324n, 337n, 339n,
  344n; V 272n
Murray, B.: IV 343n
music copyists: VI 333
musical improvisation in Florence: V 272,
  273, 274, 275, 276, 277
music manuscripts and printed sources:
  Bologna, Civico Museo Bibliografico-
    Musicale, MS Q 18: V 285n;
    VIII 272n
  Buxheim organ book (Munich, Bayerische Staatsbibliothek, Cim. 325b
    (olim Mus. 3725): V 270n
  Canti C (Venice, Petrucci,1504/R):
    VIII 277n
  Choralis Constantinus (Nuremberg,
    1550, 1555: VII 476
  Florence, Biblioteca Nazionale Centrale:
    MS Magliabechi XIX, 117: IX 53n
    MS Magliabechi XIX, 121: IX 55n
    MS Magliabechi XIX, 164–167:
      VIII 277n
    MS Magliabechi XIX, 178: V 285n

MS Banco rari 229: V 285n, 286;
  VIII 272n, 274n, 277n, 283n;
  IX 63n
MS Banco Rari 230: VIII 277n, 286;
  IX 55n
MS Banco Rari 337: VIII 286;
  IX 55n
Florence, Biblioteca Riccardiana:
  MS 2356: V 285n
  MS 2794: VIII 273
Florence, Biblioteca del Conservatorio
  "L. Cherubini": MS Basevei 2440:
    IX 55n
Florence, Archivio dell'Opera di Santa
  Maria del Fiore: MS Serie V–21:
    VIII 286n
Florence, Biblioteca Medicea Laurenziana, San Lorenzo, MS 2211:
  II *passim*
Glogauer Liederbuch (Kraków, Biblioteka Jagiellonska, Mus. Ms. 40098):
  VIII 271, 272
Harmonice musices odhecaton (Petrucci, 1501, 1503, 1504R):
  VIII 274; IX 63n
Hradec Králové, Muzeum Vychodnich
  Cech, II a 6. 367 (Codex Speciálnik)
  M2. 2. M6: VIII 283n
Milan, Archivio della Fabbrica del
  Duomo:
  MS Liber Capelle Franchini Gafori,
    vol. 1 (MS 2269, Librone 1):
    VIII 268
  MS Vol. 30, Librone 3 (MS 2267):
    IX 64n
Paris, Bibliothèque Nationale de France:
  MS fonds fr. 15123 ("Pixérécourt"):
    V 285n
  MS Rés. Vm.[7] 676: VIII 268
Perugia, Biblioteca Comunale Augusta,
  MS 431: VIII 283n
Segovia, Catedral, Archivo Capitular.
  MS without number: VIII 272n,
    283n
Seville, Biblioteca Colombina, MS
  5–1–43 (chansonnier): VIII 280n
Sicher's Orgelbuch (St. Gall, Stiftsbibliothek, Cod. 530): VII 471
Turin, Biblioteca Nazionale Universitaria:
  MS I. 27 (olim MS qm. III, 59:
    VIII 283n
Vatican City, Biblioteca Apostolica
  Vaticana:
  MS Urb. Lat. 1411: V 267n

Capella Giulia, Cod. XIII, 27:
  V 285n; VIII 272n, 280, 283
Cappella Sistina, Cod. 41: VIII 277
Washington, Library of Congress, M2.
  1. M6 Case (Wolffheim): VIII 272n

Neapolitan singers: I 318
Niccolò Cieco, improvisor: V 263
Niccola, tenorista: III 107
Niccolaus Zaccherie, singer: III 106, 107, 113
Niccolò del Proposto, composer: I 145, 146, 148; II 14, 21n
Niccolò di Lore, Ser, bass: IV 329, 330, 331, 336, 337, 338, 339, 341, 345, 346; VII 466
Niccolò di Simone da Empoli, organist: VI 323
Niccolò Pedoni, bass: VIII 281n, 282n
Nicholaus Ihoannis, singer: IV 335
Nicolao di Matteo della Colomba da Pisa, Ser, organist: VI 322
Nobili, Giovanbattista de': IX 52
Nobili, Mario de': V 281n

Obrecht, Jacob, composer: VI 330; VIII 280n, 283, 284
  Mass by: IV 343n; VI 329
Opera di Santa Maria del Fiore, overseers: III 100, 102, 108, 109; IV 310, 328, 330, 331; VII 473; VIII 279, 281n
organ playing in Florentine churches: continuity of the tradition: VI 327
Organi degli, Bartolomeo, *see* Bartolomeo degli Organi
Orsini, Clarice, *see* Clarice Orsini de' Medici
Orsini, Niccolò: V 287
Orvieto, P.: V 277n

Paatz, W.: I 132
Pallavicino, Gaspare: V 290n
Palmarocchi, R.: IV 348n; VI 312n
Panzano, Fruosino da: IV 315
Paolo Tenorista da Firenze, Don (Abbas Paulus), composer: II 9, 12, 13, 15, 17; III 103, 104, 113
Paolucci, R.: III 112n
papal singers: II 20n; III 116; VI 319
Parigi, L.: IV 347n; V 259n, 279n
Pasquale, singer: III 105, 106, 109
Passino di Eustachio, organist: VII 465
patronage of music in Florence: V 260, 261, 262, 263; VI 318
Paul III, pope: IX 49, 50

Paulus of Aquila, singer: III 102, 103. 109
Paulus, Dopnus, Monacus, singer: III 103, 113
Pazzi, family: IV 326; V 283
Pellegrino da Prato, Ser, organist: VI 322
performing forces in Florence:
  comparison with performing forces in Naples, Savoy, Milan, Ferrara: IV 339
  at Orsanmichele: VI 327
  at San Lorenzo: II 20; VI 326
  at Santa Trinità: I 141
  at Santissima Annunziata: IV 337; VI 381
  at Santo Spirito: VI 323
  at the Baptistry: IV 315; VI 318, 319; VI 318, 334; VIII 281n
  at the Cathedral: III 102, 107, 109, 114; IV 310, 313, 328, 329, 330, 339, 340, 341, 346; VI 318, 319, 334, 349; VIII 281n
  of the Company of San Zanobi: VI 326
Perrens, F.T.: V 270n
Petit, Johannes alias Baltazar, singer: IV 345
Petri, Petrus, singer: IV 316
Petrucci, O.: VIII 277n
Philip the Good, duke of Burgundy: IV 337n
Philippon, *see* Basiron, Philippe
Piattoli, R.: III 100n
Pico della Mirandola: V 279n
Pieraccini, G. : V 266n, 268n, 269n, 270n; VIII 282n
Pierino Fiorentino (Pierino di Baccio degli Organi), lutenist, *see* Bartolomeo degli Organi
Piero, Frate, singer: VI 323
Piero Bello, butcher, father-in-law of Heinrich Isaac: VII 468, 469, 470, 471
Piero d'Andrea Vaiaio, organist: VI 321n
Piero d'Andrea Mazzi, organist: VI 322
Piero del Bambo, barber: II 17n
Piero del Marrone, Don, organist: II 16
Piero del Pace, organist: VI 323
Piero di Domenico d'Arezzo, Frate, organist: VI 321
Piero di Francesco da Poggibonzi, organist: VI 322
Piero di Giovanni, Frate, tenore alto: IV 329
Piero di Giovanni da Colonia (Piero Bianco), Fra, organist: VI 323, 324
Piero di Giovanni d'Arezzo, Ser, organist: VI 321; IX 40n
Piero di Matteo, organist: VI 325

INDEX

Piero Loba (overo Pietrachione), tenorista: IV 343, 344, 346
Pierre de la Rue, composer: IV 343n
Pietrequin (Petrus Bonnel de Piccardia, etc.), singer, composer: IV 342, 343, 346; V 279n, 283; VII 466; VIII 272, 273
Pietrichino Bonegli da Piccardia (Pietriquinus de Piccardia, Petrus Bonnel de Piccardia), *see* Pietrequin
Pietrobono, lutenist: V 276
pifferi: V 260
Pignatella, Marino: IV 321
Pintello (Pintelli), composer, see also Giovanni di Giovanni Pintelli, Thomaso Pintelli
  his ballata, *Questo mostrarsi adirata*: VIII 274, 277, 278, Musical Supplement 3
  his *Missa Gentilz gallans de France*: VIII 274, 277
Pirro, A.: IV 312n; V 265
Pirrotta, N.: I 133n, 139n, 145n, 149n, 150n; II 12, 13, 14; III 104, 105n, 114n, 115n; IV 307; V 272, 273n, 276n, 278n, 279n; VIII 275n
Pisano, Bernardo, singer, master of the chapel, composer: IV 350; V 289; VI 313, 332, 334, 335; VII 474; VIII 264, 275, 288; IX 38, 52, 61
  as copyist or composer: VI 331
  Corteccia's remarks about his responsories: VI 333
Pitratto, singer: IV 315
Pitti, Niccolò: V 284; VI 319; VII 466n, 474
Pittoni, G.: IX 54
Pius II, pope: V 269
plainchant choir at Florence Cathedral: III 100, 101, 102
Plamenac, D.: VIII 268n, 273n, 280n
Pocciantio, M.: IX 50n
Poggi, G.: III 100n
Poliziano, Angelo: V 271, 272n, 273, 276, 278, 286; IX 54
  his ballata *Questo mostrarsi adirata*, set by Isaac: V 286; by Pintello: VII, 277 and Musical supplement 3
  his threnody on Lorenzo de' Medici's death *Quis dabit capiti meo aquam*: V 287
Polk, K.: V 262n
Pontieri, E.: V 270n
Portinari, Tommaso: IV 322; V 284n
Prioris, Johannes, composer:
  his chanson, *Gentil galans de Franza*, model for Pintelli's *Missa Gentilz gallans de France*: VIII 277
Prizer, W.F.: V 269n, 270n

Rabut, F.: IV 337
Raffaello di Piero, Ser, soprano: VIII 281n, 282n
Rampollini, Mattia, composer: V 289; VI 335; VIII 264, 285
  as teacher of figural music: VI 326
Razzi, Serafino, compiler of laudi, editor: V 275; VI 317; IX 63
  Ben venga maggio, musical excerpt from his *Primo libro delle laudi spirituali*: V 276
Reaney, G.: II 4n, 9; III 107n
Redditi: V 271n
Reese, G.: VIII 264n, 272n, 280n, 281n; IX 69n
repertories of polyphonic music: loss of: VI 329, 332, 333;
  at San Lorenzo: II: 19
  at Santo Spirito: VI 333;
  at the Cathedral: VI 330, 331;
  at the Cathedral, the Baptistry and the Santissima Annunziata: VI 329;
  at the Santissima Annunziata: VI 330n, 331, 332
Repetti, E.: I 132, 135, 143
Ricci, Piero de': V 266n
Riccio, C.M.: IV 337
Richa, G.: I 147
Ridolfi, R.: IV 347; VI 315n
Rinaldo Francioso, Don, singer: IV 334
Rochon, A.: V 259n, 277n, 282n
Ronga, L.: II 9
Roselli, Rosello: V 266n; 268n, 269n
Rossi, V.: V 266n, 268n, 269n
Royllart, Philippus, composer: II 10
Rozo, cantorum prepositus: III 100
Rubinetto Francioso, Frate (F. Rubinet), singer: IV 332; VIII 271, 272n
  his chanson, *Adieu Florence la iolye*: VIII 273
  his chanson, *Mais que ce fut secretement*: VIII 273n
Rubsamen, W.: V 270n, 282n, 285n; IX 56n
Rucellai, famiy: V 260
Rucellai, Costanza: V 277n

Sabbatini, A.: VI 323n
Sacchetti, Franco: I 145n, 146, 148
Salviati, Francesca: IX 52

Salvini, Salvino: III 101
Sanesi, E.: VII 468n; IX 47n, 53n
Sano di Giovanni, tenorista: VI 327n
Sartori, C.: III 113; IV 311n, 312n, 324n, 337n, 344n; VII 464, 465n; VIII, 264n, 268n; IX 39n, 64n
Savonarola, Girolamo, Fra: IV 331, 346, 347, 348, 349, 350; VI 311, 312n, 313, 314 315, 316, 317, 319 327, 328, 329, 332, 334, 335; IX 54
   abolition of polyphonic singing chapels during his time: IV 348, 349; VI 316
   laude performance during his time: IV 349; VI 314, 316, 327
   retention of organ playing in Florentine churches during his time: IV 327, 328
   sermons regarding music and dance: IV 312n, 313n, 314n, 315n, 316n
Scufeleere, Robijn, singer: IV 317;
Seay, A.: III 101n, 106n, 110n; IV 328n, 329n, 330n, 331n; V 280n; VIII 265n, 266, 272n, 278n
Serragli, family: VIII 275n
Serragli, Giovanni, teacher of figural music, singer, composer: IV 350n; VIII 282n, 284, 285, 286, 288
   his ballata, *Grato ognora*: VIII 287
   his carnival songs, *Per non trovar, Quel principe*: VIII 287
   his frottola, *Donna el pianto*: VIII 287
   his *O redemptor sume carnem*: VIII 286
Settesoldi, E.: IV 307; VI 320n
Sforza, court, dukes: V 284; VI 319
Sforza, family: IX 64n
Sforza, Galeazzo Maria, duke of Milan: IV 337, 344n; VII 465
Sforza, Gian Galeazzo, duke of Milan: V 270n
Sforza, Lodovico, duke of Milan: IV 323n, 336n; V 276n;
   sends Masses to Lorenzo de' Medici: V 283; VI 330
singers' duties: at the Cathedral: III 109, 110, 111,112; IV, 311
   at the Baptistry: IV 311
   at the Santissima Annunziata: IV 333
singers' platform:
   at Santa Trinità in 1360: I 140
   at San Lorenzo in 1352, 1360: II 20
singers' salaries: IV 312, 314; VI 319; VII 474; IX 51
Singleton, C.: V 282n, 290n; IX 53n
Simone, singer: IV 322
Slim, H.C.: IX 50n

Smijers, A.: VIII 268
Spinelli, Lorenzo: III 108
Squarcialupi, Antonio, organist: I 137n; II 17; IV 318, 319, 324; V 260, 266n, 268, 269n, 270, 271, 276n; VI 319, 320, 327; VII 465, 468;
   letter to Dufay: IV 322; V 267
Squarcialupi, Francesco, organist: VI 320; VII 468; IX 40, 46
Stappen, composer: VIII 277n
Stefano, Ser, organist: VI 325
Stefano da Napoli, Maestro, singer: IV 334
Stefano di Niccolò of Florence, Frate, singer: IV 335
Steynsel, Guglielmo d'Arnoldo d'Olanda, singer, see Guglielmo de Steynsel
Stochem, Johannes, composer: VI 329; VII 466; VIII 272, 281
Stromboli, P.: IX 52n
Strozzi, family: V 260
Strozzi, Filippo: IV 317;
Strozzi, Filippo di Lorenzo: IX 52
Strozzi, Lorenzo di Filippo: IX 47, 52, 53
   instrumental ensembles for a production of his *Commedia in Versi*: IX 53
Strozzi, Niccolò: IV 317

Tani, Angelo: IV 315;
Tassino d'Anversa, singer: IV 341, 342
Taucci, R.: IX 67n
Terry, C.S.: VII 466, 470
Tesi, M.: II 3n; IV 307;
Thibault, G.: II 18
Thomaso da Venegia, singer: IV 334
Thomaso di Giovanni Pintelli, singer: IV 336n, 341, 342, 344; VII 466; VIII 274, 275
Tornabuoni, Giovanni: V 284
Tornabuoni, Lorenzo: IX 63n
Tornabuoni, Nofri: V 284
Trexler, R.C.: V 263n
trombetti: V 260
Turchi, D.: IX 50n
Turini, Bartolomeo da Pescia: VII 473

Ugo di Parisetto di Champagnia de Reams, singer: IV 339, 341, 343
Ugolini, Baccio, improvisor, poet, singer: V 273, 278
   music to his *La morte tu mi dai*, excerpt: IV 274
Ugolino of Orvieto (Ugolinus Francisci de Urbeveteri), theorist, singer, composer: II 9, 10, 18, 21; III 106, 107, 108, 109, 113

Valdrigi, L.F: IV 319, 324n, 338n
Valori, Niccolò: V 271n
Van, G. de: III 116n
Van Dijk, S.J.P.: II 19n
Van Doorslaer, G.: IV 337n
Varchi, Benedetto, historian, poet: IX 53
Vasari, Giorgio: IX 53n
Verbonetto di Giovanni, *see* Ghiselin, Johannes
Verdelot, Philippe, composer: V 289; VI 317n; VII 475; VIII 285, 286, 288
Villani, Filippo: III 114
Villani, Giovanni: IV 309n;
Villari, P.: IV 347n
Vincenzo da Rimini, composer: II 11, 14
Virgilio (Virgilius), Ser, singer, composer: VIII 282, 28; IX 51
  his *Nec mihi nec tibi*: VIII 283, 284
Vitry, Philippe de, theorist, composer: II 11, 18

Viviani, Tommaso: II 17n
Volpi, G.: V 278n

Walker, D.P.: V 273n
Warburg, M.: V 279n
Warden, J.: V 273n
Weinstein, D.: VI 315n
Wienandt, E.: IX 49n
Wilkens, N.: II 13n
Wilson, B.: V 261n; 262n, 282n
Wolf, J.: V 275n; VIII 277n; IX 63n
Wuttke, D.: V 279n

Zanobi da Ameria: V 278
Zanobi di Giovanni Lenzi, organist: VI 324
Zanobi Ghuidetti, organist: VII 468
Zeffi, Francesco: IX 53n
Zenobi di Felice, tenor: IV 350n;
Ziino, A.: V 274n
Zippel, G.: V 262n